Date Due

42.80

04-18-02

Charting a New Course

The Politics of Globalization and Social Transformation

Fernando Henrique Cardoso

Edited and Introduced by Mauricio A. Font

ROWMAN & LITTLEFIELD PUBLISHERS, INC.
Lanham · Boulder · New York · Oxford

ROWMAN & LITTLEFIELD PUBLISHERS, INC.

Published in the United States of America
by Rowman & Littlefield Publishers, Inc.
4720 Boston Way, Lanham, Maryland 20706
www.rowmanlittlefield.com

12 Hid's Copse Road, Cumnor Hill, Oxford OX2 9JJ, England

British Cataloguing in Publication Information Available

Library of Congress Cataloging-in-Publication Data

Cardoso, Fernando Henrique.
   Charting a new course : the politics of globalization and social transformation / by
Fernando Cardoso ; edited and introduced by Mauricio A. Font.
      p. cm.
   Includes bibliographical references and index.
   ISBN 0-7425-0892-7 (alk. paper)—ISBN 0-7425-0893-5 (pbk. : alk. paper)
      1. Brazil—Economic policy. 2. Latin America—Economic policy. 3. Brazil—Politics and
government. 4. Latin America—Politics and government. 5. Dependency. I. Font,
Mauricio A. (Mauricio Augusto) II. Title.

HC187 .C219 2001
338.98—dc21
                                                                               00-066468

Printed in the United States of America

♾™ The paper used in this publication meets the minimum requirements of American
National Standard for Information Sciences—Permanence of Paper for Printed Library
Materials, ANSI/NISO Z39.48-1992.

Contents

Acknowledgments

A volume tracing Fernando Henrique Cardoso's intellectual trajectory is surely long overdue. One of the very top social scientists and thinkers from Latin America, his ideas about development and social change, dependency and globalization, Western Hemisphere dynamics, democracy, and reform have received worldwide attention since his early works in the 1960s. Cardoso emerged as an early leader in the prodemocracy movement that eventually succeeded in returning the Brazilian military to their barracks in 1985, after two decades of authoritarian rule. In 1994 this top intellectual-turned-politician was elected president of Brazil, with a mandate to reform its economic and political system. His ideas about reform and the politics of change are of major significance in understanding political and economic developments in the contemporary world. Cardoso himself needs to be thanked for providing access to his private collection and for taking time from his busy schedule to discuss his role as intellectual, politician, and statesman.

Dean Birkenkamp, senior editor at Rowman and Littlefield, deserves special credit for being an early believer in this project—as well as for his unflappable patience throughout its evolution. Albert and Sarah Hirschman, Juarez Rubens Brandão Lopes, Enzo Faletto, Maria Hermínia Tavares de Almeida, Francisco Weffort, Luiz Carlos Bresser Pereira, and Eduardo Graeff stand out in providing advice. They are part of the international network of scholars, colleagues, collaborators, and friends familiar with Cardoso's intellectual evolution. Others in this circle, too many to list individually, provided useful comments, information, and assessments.

Still, culling writings representing Cardoso's long and rich intellectual evolution proved to be a challenging task. Cardoso's thought appears in many books and articles, but also in countless shorter pieces and interviews published in newspapers and magazines. This oeuvre originally appeared in diverse publications in different countries, historical contexts, and languages. Fortunately, the collection maintained by

Danielle Ardaillon, a close Cardoso associate since the 1970s, made it considerably easier to take full measure of this vast body of writings. Ardaillon's profound knowledge of Cardoso's intellectual evolution is reflected in the authoritative bibliography accompanying this volume.

In preparing this volume, we have benefited from the assistance and advice of many other individuals. Gary Aguayo and Cristina Bordin at the Bildner Center (The Graduate Center, City University of New York) and Claudia Carvalho helped process and edit the texts. J. Tyler Dickovic translated several of the original Portuguese, Spanish, and French texts. Danielle Ardaillon provided access to photographs. Jehanne Schweitzer took charge of coordinating the last stages in the production of the book. Library collections consulted include those at CEPAL (United Nations Economic Commission for Latin America and the Caribbean), CEBRAP, and Princeton University. The Bildner Center for Western Hemisphere Studies and the department of sociology at Queens College, both at the City University of New York, need to be thanked for the institutional support shaping the preparation of this volume.

⤙ Introduction ⤚

To Craft a New Era: The Intellectual Trajectory of Fernando Henrique Cardoso

Mauricio A. Font

The appointment of Fernando Henrique Cardoso as finance minister in May 1993 is one of those moments when biography and history intersect to shape each other in intriguing ways. A world-class intellectual, Cardoso was known particularly for his critical, historical-structuralist approach to Latin American development. But success in stabilizing the Brazilian economy propelled Cardoso to the role of statesman, the first sociologist to become president of a large country. His presidency (1995–2002) sought to open a new chapter in Brazilian political and economic history, liberalizing and opening the economy while reforming the state. Observers mused about a change of heart, perceiving such policies to be at odds with the dependency theory he authored in the 1960s and 1970s. The character of the societal and personal transformations, the balance between continuity and rupture, the mix and reciprocal effects between structural change and personal dynamics—these are and will remain grist for the mill of intellectuals and scholars for time to come. This introduction seeks to contribute to that effort by sketching key aspects of that remarkable trajectory.[1]

Cardoso's intellectual trajectory is an important aspect of the political and economic transformations in contemporary Brazil. But it is also a fascinating subject in its own right. At issue is the legacy of an intellectual movement that first received world acclaim in the 1960s. How it evolved since then, how it changed in response to the demands of political life, and how this intellectual tradition shaped Brazil's transformation are important questions in need of clarification.

Becoming finance minister and its outcome were proverbially ironic. Cardoso's criticism of Brazil's traditional economic and political regimes cost him a period of exile in the 1960s as well as "mandatory retirement" from his teaching position at the University of São Paulo (USP). Thirty years later, this left-leaning intellectual, Latin America's best-known sociologist, found himself with the task of saving the economy from one of its deepest crises in the twentieth century. Hyperinflation posed the most pressing problem. There was growing consensus that the state-centered development model—dirigisme, heavy state spending, and high tariffs—pursued for decades needed to be overhauled; to many, the country needed a new economic model.

Some Brazilians wondered if an intellectual was the right person for the job. But Cardoso's stabilization plan brought inflation down to 25 percent shortly after implementation and gradually lower after that. The success of the Real Plan—named after the *real,* the new currency it introduced—made Cardoso a presidential contender and may have been the main factor in his victory.

Cardoso's presidential inauguration in January 1995 was a turning point in Brazilian politics. Not since 1930 had a political movement centered in São Paulo held national political leadership. The success of the stabilization plan and Cardoso's election rekindled hope that Brazil could overcome its economic and political woes. The new government promised reforms that would profoundly alter the role of the state and the economic model. The task was nothing less than to usher in a new era in Brazilian political and economic history.

Cardoso's first term (1995–1998) consolidated the stabilization plan and initiated some other reforms. Though Brazilians gave overwhelming support to his reelection in October 1998, considerable suspense built up shortly after. For a few months stretching into 1999, the winds of an international financial crisis battered the Brazilian currency and imposed a perilous devaluation. The very achievements of the stabilization and reform process through 1998 seemed endangered. Cardoso's popularity plummeted. New political dynamics were set in motion. All of a sudden, the very fate of his presidency seemed in question. But the Brazilian economy recovered faster than economists and the media expected. As the Cardoso government refocused on the reform drive, it faced the additional challenge of regaining its political footing and lost momentum. The old political and economic model was coming to an end. Whether Brazilians as a whole were as certain about the direction as when they reelected Cardoso was less clear.

A WORLDLY INTELLECTUAL

But what, in the first place, had made Cardoso a prince of hope in the gloomy context of the early 1990s? How can one explain that the best-known critic of the Brazilian development model was entrusted with the mission of saving it?

Political and civic engagement were part of his upbringing. Cardoso's father, uncles, and grandparents had begun military or political careers early in their lives. His father had reached the rank of general in an era when the armed forces were highly involved in politics and became a national deputy after retirement from military service.[2] As a result, public concerns ran in the family. Politics was a matter of daily discussion in Cardoso's home as he grew up. But Cardoso decided to make his mark as a sociologist, rather than follow in their footsteps. His adult intellectual trajectory since the late 1950s was one of engagement with the key events of Brazilian history. This intellectual and professional trajectory more than anything else governed the path that would lead to the presidency.[3]

MAKING OF AN ACADEMIC

Early in the 1960s, a small group of recent graduates from the University of São Paulo invited French philosophers Jean-Paul Sartre and Simone de Beauvoir to visit their state. Sartre, then at the peak of his career, gave talks in the city of São Paulo and in the coffee town of Araraquara. Cardoso was one of the organizers of the event and translated several of Sartre's talks. This episode was yet one more indication of the claim to the intellectual limelight by the state's young intellectuals—a group that also included Cardoso's wife, the anthropologist Ruth Corrêa Leite Cardoso. (These intellectuals had also founded the city's fabled Marx Seminar in the late 1950s.[4]) Meeting for several years, this group explored in depth substantive and methodological issues in the main works by this founding figure in sociology. It played a role in the development of the social sciences in Brazil, as several of its members went on to experience highly successful academic careers. A leader in this group, Cardoso earned an early and enduring reputation as a Marxist.

These were key moments in the rise of modern social science in Brazil. But Cardoso's generation was not working in a vacuum. The broader context was the coming of age of the University of São Paulo.[5] Organized in 1934, the original impetus behind this institution had been to enhance the intellectual capacity of the state of São Paulo, one whose elite often found itself at odds with the centralizing national government of the Getúlio Vargas era. Already by the 1920s, São Paulo had become the main locus of Brazilian industrialization, economic development, and modernization. But the revolution of 1930 and internal political splits put in question that state's preeminence not only in national political life, but also in organizing its own political process.[6] The new, modern university would prepare a new intellectual elite to help face this challenge. A contingent of French social scientists helped launch the advanced social science program. Roger Bastide was the key figure in the sociology program. Anthropologist Claude Lévi-Strauss, geographer Pierre Monbeig, economist Paul Hugon, philosopher Martial Guéroult, historians Charles Morazé and Fernand Braudel taught at the USP and helped develop its program. Of humble origins and hailing from the interior of the state, Florestan Fernandes was the pioneer in Paulista sociology and the main sociologist of the small first cohort of Ph.D.s taught at the USP. The key founding figure in what would be known as the Paulista school of sociology, Fernandes influenced Cardoso as much as the European faculty.[7] Under his leadership, this group turned to the empirical study of race and race relations, class formation, and social change in Brazil. Cardoso also enjoyed a noteworthy presence in the internal politics at the University of São Paulo early in his career.[8] Above all, he was the rising star of the Paulista school of sociology and his generation of social scientists.[9]

Cardoso's doctoral thesis, *Capitalism and Slavery in Southern Brazil*, provided an analysis of the rise and demise of the slavery system in nineteenth-century Rio Grande do Sul, the southernmost state in Brazil. His thesis approached the subject using a dense dialectical approach inspired by Karl Marx.[10] Reflecting the empirical orientation of the Paulista sociologists, this major work marshaled diverse bodies of evidence that included provincial newspapers and government reports in archives, surveys and censuses, and field work in Rio Grande do Sul. Its ten-section bibliography included general works by Paul Baran, Ernest Bloch, Fernandes, Lévi-Strauss, Robert Merton, Talcott Parsons, Sartre, and Max Weber, as well as international classics in the literature on slavery and race. This piece of scholarship was Cardoso's second work on race; he had earlier collaborated with Octávio Ianni in writing a book on race relations in the state of Santa Catarina.[11]

Impressing his mentors and academic authorities at the USP with his research and writing efforts, Cardoso was asked to join the faculty.[12] The young professor immersed himself in academic pursuits. Academia occupied center stage against the background of intensifying political polarization and conflict in the 1950s and early 1960s, as Brazil's populist democracy evolved toward crisis and eventual demise. In 1962, the promising sociologist was named the director of the Center for Industrial and Labor Sociology (CESIT).[13] Founded with the collaboration of French sociologist Alain Touraine, the research agenda of this new center at the USP concentrated on class formation and labor mobilization, regional disparities in development, São Paulo's industrial sector, and training levels and needs in the labor force, as well as the role of the state in economic development. This overlapped with the orientation of the sociology program at the university. Cardoso's own long-term research agenda became inseparable from both.

With an academic career firmly in mind, Cardoso set out to write a major empirical study on industrialists, hoping to thereby earn promotion to associate professor. *Industrialists and Economic Development in Brazil* was presented in 1963 as "tesis de livre docência."[14] Based on interviews and surveys of industrialists,[15] this pioneering empirically grounded study challenged the basic premise of an important group of would-be reformers: the idea that a populist-developmental coalition ensuring an effective national project of industrialization was jelling in Brazil.[16] Instead, his book argued that the industrial bourgeoisie lacked the capacity to play the leading role specified in the national-populist model. This social class was too fragmented and timid to be a hegemonic political and systemic force. To Cardoso, this group had in fact abdicated a hegemonic role in Brazilian development, virtually acquiescing to a lesser role in the framework of "subcapitalism," a development model in which transnational capital played a leading role.

The 1964 coup d'état tended to confirm the key argument in the book and put the author in the intellectual spotlight. Cardoso had doubted the viability of the form of populist democracy that had been in place since 1945, and the military takeover supported that conclusion. The overthrow of the populist democracy came shortly after the thesis was presented and made the Paulista professor an international star. Most other works had predicted the further development of democracy in Brazil, while yet others had posited the onset of a revolutionary situation. His book emphasized the inconsistencies of populist democracy, came close to predicting its demise, and intimated the authoritarian form of the emergent model less than a year before the March 1964 coup. Cardoso had gained recognition earlier as a leader in university politics, and as an elected member of the university council representing assistants. He now had a reputation as an astute analyst of Brazilian political and economic dynamics. But the 1964 coup also disrupted career plans. The authoritarian regime persecuted opponents and soon ordered the arrest of the rising, left-leaning professor. Cardoso fled the country. A four-year saga took him to Chile for more than three years as well as a shorter stay in France.[17] It was during this period that he consolidated an international reputation as a world-class social scientist and public intellectual.

THE FOCUS ON DEVELOPMENT

Exile turned out to be a godsend. In the social sciences and in economic thought, Santiago may have been the intellectual capital of Latin America at the time. In size and urban sophistication, Santiago was provincial compared to São Paulo, Buenos Aires, or Mexico City. But Latin American structuralism was experiencing intense elaboration amidst critique from right and left in an atmosphere of vigorous debate and general optimism about the imminence of social transformation. Santiago provided access to a rich theoretical and comparative Latin American context and framework in which to probe ideas about development. The UN Economic Commission for Latin America (CEPAL) was the main source of structuralism in Latin America. Cardoso's appointment at CEPAL meant status, material comfort, and the opportunity for in-depth research on key development issues. Santiago's universities and fledgling research centers provided additional opportunities for the study of Latin American development as well as engagement in major currents of social democratic and socialist thought. Latin America became a durable focus and frame of reference.[18]

While in Chile, Cardoso recast and renamed "subcapitalism," the concept earlier developed in São Paulo, as the "dependent development" model. He elaborated the latter in what became his best-known book, *Dependency and Development in Latin America*.[19] Written in collaboration with Chilean social historian Enzo Faletto, this volume was published in Spanish in 1969. The University of California Press published a somewhat revised English edition almost ten years later. This book advanced one of the most influential interpretations of twentieth-century Latin American dynamics. Rough drafts circulated in Santiago in 1967, while the authors discussed its contents with colleagues and students at the University of Chile and the Facultad Latinoamericana de Ciencias Sociales (FLACSO). Visits to other Latin American countries, the United States, and Europe cemented Cardoso's reputation as the leading figure in Latin American dependency theory. It was at this time that Cardoso met Albert Hirschman, who would become a close colleague and perhaps his main influence in the United States.[20]

Auspicious as it was, the stay in Santiago ended in October 1967. Cardoso went to the University of Paris at Nanterre to teach and write up findings from the comparative study of Latin American industrialists.[21] The French student mobilizations of May 1968 made a lasting impression. The decision was made to return to Brazil later that year. Brazil was still ruled by the military, but the homecoming was supposed to be accompanied by the reactivation of his professorship at the University of São Paulo. However, a wave of repression in 1969 led to the mandatory retirement of Cardoso and other professors. This fateful second denial of his academic career by the military brought Cardoso closer to the path that would eventually lead him to the presidency.[22]

The response to this setback was to launch the Centro Brasileiro de Análise e Planejamento (CEBRAP; Brazilian Center for Analysis and Planning) in 1969. This independent research center was able to draw support from international foundations as well as from national sources.[23] Cardoso's leadership was decisive in making CEBRAP a beacon for social scientists challenging the stifling intellectual climate the military had instituted in Brazil.[24]

Cardoso's writing in the 1970s revolved around his role as a major analyst of development. Dependency theory peaked during those years. It emerged as a main social science approach in the United States, where major universities had become sites of considerable dissatisfaction with preexisting paradigms. Debate about the Vietnam War fueled the perception of modernization theory—the approach dominating mainstream discussion of development—as simplistic, conservative, and even ethnocentric. The very resistance to the war and the rising wave of mobilization over civil rights and other issues led to a Marxist revival and intensified calls for an alternative paradigm in comparative studies of social change and development. Dependency theory seemed a good choice.

But rapid success came at a cost. The rush to a coherent counterparadigm tended to fuse rather different dependency perspectives into one. Dependency theory came to be associated with the strand popularized by Andre Gunder Frank, whose *Development and Underdevelopment in Latin America*[25] argued forcefully in favor of the radical position that contemporary Latin American underdevelopment was historically rooted in economic contact with the West and its capitalist system. This "development of underdevelopment" thesis simplified the analysis of underdevelopment and pointed to a radical solution: cutting off contact with Western capitalism and pursuing revolutionary socialism. In the context of the Latin American political ferment of the 1960s and early 1970s, this was close to a blank endorsement of guerrilla action and revolutionary movements associated with the Cuban revolution. The ideological force of radicalism received support from Western fascination with Latin American revolutionaries, with French journalist Regis Debray's *Revolution within the Revolution* leading this movement. Inevitably, dependency theory came to be identified with the radical approach of Frank, who wrote in English and published early in the United States.

Cardoso's dependent development model differed in major ways from these versions of dependency theory and its author found himself increasingly misunderstood. The attempt to clarify the distinctiveness of his approach and answer took considerable time for his not infrequently misguided critics. But passion was now shifting toward diagnosing Brazil's authoritarianism and political system, and— later—toward advancing models of democratization.

With diverse personal interests vying for his attention, Cardoso's academic writing increasingly through the 1970s took the form of shorter essays, papers, and articles presented at international professional meetings or written for Brazilian periodicals. These works addressed criticisms and analytical challenges posed by political debate. They were later published in collections of essays such as *The Brazilian Political Model and Other Essays* (1972), *Authoritarianism and Democracy* (1975), and *Ideas and Their Place* (1980).[26]

Many of these essays seek to clarify the character of Cardoso and Faletto's historical-structural approach and gain distance from other formulations of dependency theory.[27] Some texts challenge what Cardoso saw as analytical distortions and erroneous theses linking "dependent development" to permanent stagnation and underdevelopment. "The Brazilian Development Model: Data and Perspectives" (1973)[28] maintains that Brazil was actually industrializing, even if this process excluded large sectors of rural and urban workers. Another study explores the possibility of bourgeois revolutions in dependent societies.

These works plead for historically and structurally contextualized accounts of development trajectories and models. "Dependency Theory or Concrete Analyses of Dependency" (1970)[29] denies that his version of dependency theory aimed at generalizing propositions or theory. It was written in response to criticism by Francisco Weffort, a former student and fellow exile in Chile in the 1960s. The essays stake out a position against excessive formalization, schematic conceptualizations, and simplistic or reductionistic accounts. The case is made for a historical-structuralism brand of dependency theory guided by a broadly dialectical approach at odds with economic determinism.

These works situate development in the context of class structure and political dynamics. Cardoso offers his own empirically grounded work on the Brazilian state as an example of the research required to clarify the roles of social class and politics in development. Rather than the simple instrument of class or external rule, the Brazilian state is seen as an arena of conflict in which institutional and social interests defined coalitions and lines of cleavage. In Brazil's traditional political system, "bureaucratic rings" partly buttressed by clientelism solidify myriad coalitions advancing particular interests of three key sectors: state elites (including the military), foreign capital, and national capital. The analysis of Brazilian authoritarianism and the possibilities for democracy needs to take such dynamics into full account.

Cardoso's qualifications generally fell on deaf ears. The international debate about dependency theory gravitated toward the simplification he feared and against which he had warned. In the United States, dependency theory continued to be understood as one approach and as a mere extension of radical Marxism.

How can one account for the post-1980s' difficulties of historical structuralism and Cardoso's dependency approach to consolidate and retain its position as a leading paradigm in international social science? As noted, the military regime's decision to cancel Cardoso's professorship prevented this leading figure in this movement from pursuing a normal academic life.[30] If much of his time went to running CE-BRAP and addressing the intellectual problematic of democratization, after 1973 Cardoso became progressively drawn to an active role in the prodemocracy movement itself. Brazil's continental dimensions and distinctive identity encouraged an inward orientation among social scientists. Second, the other Latin American dependency scholars in Santiago, the original headquarters of this intellectual movement, had their academic and personal lives disrupted by the Chilean September 1973 coup. Santiago went into a veritable eclipse in intellectual matters.[31] Third, the rise of the world systems approach as a paradigm in the social sciences contributed to the inability of Latin American dependency theory à la Cardoso to gain ground in the United States as the world systems approach preempted much of the available space.[32]

The 1979 English translation of *Dependency and Development in Latin America* helped return Latin American dependency theory to the limelight. A new postscript written in 1977–1978 updated the approach.[33] This book was frequently found in the reading lists of graduate courses at universities in the United States. The historical structuralism in that volume inspired significant studies. But it came relatively late and was not fully able to redirect the debate. The discussion about dependency theory in the United States continued to center on testing hypotheses derived from the "development of underdevelopment" approach. Cardoso fought one of the last major battles against this trend in "The Consumption of Dependency Theory in the United States."[34]

As the 1970s closed, the tide turned against dependency theory. Studies of newly industrializing Asian countries denied the notion of a causal relationship between dependency and stagnation. By the early 1980s, the very denotation of dependency theory began to acquire negative associations, as criticism discredited key premises of the "development of underdevelopment" thesis. Progressively after that, few new monographs pursued the Latin American version of dependency theory.

When, in the 1980s, Latin American universities and scholars returned to democratic or democratizing contexts, Cardoso himself and fellow Brazilian scientists were increasingly concerned with new themes and foci that claimed the academic agenda in the region. Ironically, globalization, a trend and problematic that the Latin American dependency theory was arguably well suited to elucidate, would shortly claim the limelight.

AUTHORITARIANISM AND DEMOCRACY

Cardoso and associates emerged as significant players in the gradual process of political reopening that began in 1973.[35] The Brazilian Democratic Movement (MDB) was the main political organization demanding the return of democracy in the 1970s. A CEBRAP task force played a distinguished supportive role in MDB's struggle. Its very success in creating a space to study alternative views about Brazilian society turned that research center and its leaders into actors in the democratic movement. Supporters of authoritarianism shared this perception and in 1976 even threw a bomb at its premises.[36]

The struggle for democracy would soon bring out Cardoso's vocation as a politician, but even in the early 1980s many still saw him primarily as a public intellectual. Being elected as the president of the International Sociological Association (1982–1986) crowned his intellectual reputation at home and abroad. He had extended visits to Paris's École des Hautes Études and Collège de France, as well as to Cambridge. Frequent invitations brought him to lecture and research at leading U.S. universities and research centers, including the Institute for Advanced Study,[37] Yale, Berkeley, Stanford, and others.

The timing of the shift in intellectual focus from authoritarianism to democratization emerges as a pivotal question, since Cardoso's writings of the 1960s had posited a causal relationship between dependence and authoritarianism. The post-1969 writings accompany closely the evolution of the authoritarian system. They do that with an eye toward not just further exploring its relationship to the Brazilian model of dependent development, but also detecting possibilities for change. The best known essay from those years is "The Brazilian Political Model." Written in 1970, it provided an influential account of Brazilian authoritarianism. A revised version of this essay was presented at an April 1971 conference on Brazilian authoritarianism at Yale and later published as "Associated-Dependent Development: Theoretical and Practical Implications" in the reader *Authoritarian Brazil: Origins, Policies, and Future*.[38] Cardoso's earlier approach to associated-dependent development had argued that the participation of multinational corporations in domestic processes of industrialization aided a realignment of forces favoring authoritarianism. This essay begins to sketch a more subtle and complex position. The interplay between local social classes and the state and the limits of the nationalist development strategies based on import-substituting industrialization continue at the center of attention. But the historically and comparatively grounded argument denies a reductionistic approach to the politics of development, claiming that overly general or schematic formulations will not greatly advance the understanding of political dynamics.

"The Brazilian Political Model" opens with a critical evaluation of other approaches to Brazilian political dynamics.[39] Philippe Schmitter and Thomas Skidmore had emphasized the extent of continuity with the Vargas era, particularly the authoritarian Estado Novo (1937–1945), hinting that the democratic period of 1945–1964 might have been a deviation from an authoritarian system more than a durable trend toward democracy. In contrast, Cardoso viewed the 1964 regime as a "political rearticulation based on changes from the previous model of social and economic development" (52–53). As a result, the coup represented a major form of political change. It affirmed a new pattern of industrialization and development, as labor now found itself excluded from the political system.[40] If the emergent regime had new social and economic bases, it exercised power in a differentiated manner. However, that the military-bureaucratic political model was embedded in economic dynamics did not imply a necessary causal relationship between economic development and authoritarianism. In fact, and this is the key conclusion, the economic model of dependent development is compatible with democracy. Democratization can take place within the framework of the dependent model of development.[41] New combinations of political actors can likewise articulate alternative strategies for development. The 1972 volume containing this article confirms and deepens the open-ended historical-structural focus.[42] The preface is forceful. The task is to characterize and explain the "fusion" or mutual effects between political and economic processes in dependent societies, even if their relationship to industrialization needs to be at the center of the analysis. The author acknowledges that political analysis is still somewhat "subjacent," but argues that politics is relatively autonomous from structural conditions. A focus on political junctures and the choices made in the selection of public policies is essential. This amounts to an explicit defense of an approach centered on the joint analysis of political dynamics and social structure. This entails "shunning either the static separation centered on one or the other . . . without dissolving one into the other" (2). The preface highlights the need to focus on political liberty, the free flow of information, political organization, civil rights, and participation—that is, democracy (3).

It is important to grasp here that, just before the pivotal year of 1973, Cardoso had settled on a model of Brazilian politics and authoritarianism in which democracy is seen as both possible and desirable. Once again, timing could not have been better. Late that year, General Ernesto Geisel's government began to take the first gradual steps toward political liberalization. Even if Brazilian authoritarianism may have been linked to the new form of dependence and the internationalization of the economy, to Cardoso evolving conditions made democracy possible. The keen sense for detecting the new or emergent trends was at work again. The onset of processes of liberalization and democratization in Greece, Spain, and Portugal in the mid-1970s helped create a firmer comparative context to explore prospects for democracy in Brazil, even if the turns toward authoritarianism in Chile, Argentina, and Uruguay pointed in a different direction.

Cardoso's analysis of authoritarianism has considerable kinship with Guillermo O'Donnell's 1973 account of bureaucratic-authoritarianism,[43] but differs in emphasis. O'Donnell's model incorporates elements of dependency theory into an approach initially tailored to Argentina and broadened to include Brazil, Uruguay, and Chile. It directly linked the new authoritarianism in South America to the crisis of the protectionist model (ISI) previously pursued in the region. By the end of the decade, O'Donnell's ideas had drawn so much attention that a collection of commissioned essays published in 1979 was devoted to its assessment.[44] Cardoso's contribution in that volume brings out the distinctiveness of his own line of analysis. While agreeing that bureaucratic-authoritarianism was a differentiated form of authoritarianism, separate from traditional *caudillismo* or one-party systems such as Mexico's, the author further distances himself from any tendency to treat it as a direct result of economic conditions. The analysis introduces a formal distinction between the character of the state and regime type. If the state in Latin America is necessarily a "dependent capitalist" state, such a state can take different forms, ranging from varieties of authoritarianism to equally diverse democracies. There is no necessary correlation between new forms of dependency and regime type. Moreover, inconsistencies within bureaucratic-authoritarianism make possible turns toward democracy. The study of junctures is critical in this regard. Emphasizing the ambiguous character of historical situations, the author pins his hopes for democratic change in the political capacity of opposition groups to propose creative political mechanisms and policies to address challenges of development and accumulation. The design of better solutions makes a major difference in the success of a democratizing transition.

The deepening shift toward democratization is even more decisive in the 1983 essay "Associated-Dependent Development and Democratic Theory" published in English in Alfred Stepan's 1989 reader on democratizing Brazil[45] and in *A construção da democracia* (1993), a collection of papers written through the 1970s and early 1980s.[46] Published in the 1990s, *In Praise of the Arts of Politics*[47] shows Cardoso fully focused on a *possibilistic* approach to democratization. By now, democracy is not only possible but highly desirable. Positive action by reformers is needed to enhance its likelihood. Cardoso spices the analysis with tactical-strategic reasoning inspired by Niccolò Machiavelli and ethical considerations from Weber's classical essay on politics as a vocation.

Cardoso's writings of the 1980s and 1990s reflect a deepening involvement in the struggle for democracy. The public intellectual had developed a passion for helping understand and shape the processes of political and structural reform in Brazil. For the politician, that passion would be to craft a new democracy.[48]

This involvement further pushed Cardoso to explore the universalistic context of his political thought. Though the works on politics often lack the comparative depth of the previous studies of dependency and development, they are well informed of the international debate on democratic transitions. According to Paul Cammack, Cardoso's approach to politics since the 1960s represented a principled social democratic alternative. The political project in this trajectory calls for "independent activity within the institutions of the existing system to promote, through slow and patient organization, the democratization of the state, the political regime, and society." It is a project for "the . . . democratization of the associated-dependent model of capitalist development."[49] By the early 1990s, this social democratic project "had come to terms with globalization and had four main components: a porous state open to creative partnerships with civil society and non-governmental organizations to enhance the public space, an active economic policy, a commitment to social policy (particularly education and health), and a broadly progressive stance reflecting a broad coalition and oriented to universalistic rather than narrowly sectoral goals."[50]

EMBEDDEDNESS IN THE SOCIAL SCIENCES

Throughout, Cardoso's oeuvre has as enduring themes the growth of sociology as a discipline and of a distinctive Latin American social science.[51] At virtually all stages of this trajectory, he adopts a self-conscious stance to contribute to the development of the social sciences and claims scientific grounding for his evolving ideas about development, authoritarianism, and democracy. There is continuity between Cardoso's leadership in the development of the agenda of the advanced sociology program at the University of São Paulo and his role in developing Latin American social science research while in Chile. The stay at the CEPAL was critical in this regard. Cardoso held a senior position at the Latin American Institute for Economic and Social Planning (ILPES), the research and training center organized by Raúl Prebisch himself in 1963. The director of its social science division was José Medina Echevarría, a Spanish social scientist trained in Germany and who had studied with José Ortega y Gasset.[52] A disciplined scholar with a strong Weberian orientation, Medina Echevarría found in Cardoso a strong kinship and offered him the position as adjunct director. This relationship furthered Cardoso's academic career as well as his own Weberian orientation.[53]

Cardoso and other exiled Brazilians took full advantage of the social science programs and centers mushrooming in Santiago and contributed to their development. ILPES conducted research and trained government and international functionaries. The University of Chile's Escolatina attracted students from the Americas. FLACSO, then in its infancy, recruited several promising young academics from the region.[54] The Christian Democratic think tank Instituto Latinoamericano de Doctrina y Estudios Sociales (ILADES) was also available. The Brazilian Theotônio dos Santos was affiliated with the Center for Socioeconomic Studies, University of Chile (CESO). The list of Brazilian exiles in these and other facilities as students, researchers, or faculty included José Serra, Francisco Weffort, Vilmar Faria, Leôncio Martins, and several others. Cardoso had an active intellectual and social life with fellow Brazilian exiles as well as with noted Chilean intellectuals Aníbal Pinto, Enzo Faletto, Osvaldo Sunkel, and others.[55]

Involvement in programmatic development in Chile and Brazil provided the basis for publications oriented to teaching and research.[56] Cardoso's frequent trips to Latin American universities maintained this focus and partly compensated for the denial of his right to teach Brazilian graduate students after 1964.[57]

The Cardosian approach to the social sciences builds on the historical structuralism rooted in Latin America's intellectual history. Its main features include the focus on social change and development, a comparative framework centered on the region, emphasis on internationalized social relations as well as domestic social structure and the state, a strong historical orientation, and a dual focus on conjunctures and contingencies as well as on long-term structural trends.[58] In the 1950s and 1960s, it concentrated considerable attention on agency provided by social actors. Cardoso's own study of the industrial bourgeoisie in the 1960s was linked to a larger comparative study at CEPAL.[59]

A 1995 lecture at Venezuela's national university reaffirms the concern with disciplinary development and updates Cardoso's views about the evolution of Latin American social sciences and his own place in it.[60] That overview of the history of the modern social sciences in the region highlights the role of Raúl Prebisch and the generation of the 1940s and 1950s, who placed social change and development at the center of the research agenda. Cardoso's own generation built on this legacy. In Cardoso's view, this was the first large cohort of professionally trained social scientists that embraced a self-conscious foundational role.[61] Often trained in French and European schools of thought and traditions, the members of this generation adapted those ideas critically and with an eye toward creating a distinctive approach oriented to the region's problems and identity. According to this lecture, a few hundred Latin American social scientists had been part of this intellectual movement since the late 1950s, with a considerable number of them receiving their education in the United States in the 1970s. These authors are said to share an emphasis on scientific rigor, a critical stance toward the classics, an interdisciplinary (and hence nonreductionistic) joint focus on economic and social analysis, as well as the incorporation of the international dimension and the attention to policy relevance and the role of the state. Latin American social thought emphasizes processes of incorporation into the world economy under conditions of dependency and then globalization, the role of the state, democratic governance, integration, and a regional comparative framework focused on development. Cardoso acknowledges the influence of Albert Hirschman in reinforcing in him and some colleagues a passion for a "possibilistic" approach to development and reform.[62] That is, conjunctures and historical contingency are placed side by side large-scale structures and their dynamics.

In spite of exile and the compelled retirement from his professorship at the University of São Paulo in 1969, Cardoso was not estranged from Brazilian as well as international academic life. During the years spent as the leader of the CEBRAP and those that followed, Cardoso was actively involved in diverse intellectual projects with major academic implications. He appeared in several editorial boards,[63] wrote essays celebrating important academic and intellectual figures,[64] reviewed publications,[65] participated in debates,[66] and freely gave lectures and talks as well as research advice to graduate students and colleagues. And he held fellowships at several universities in the United States and Europe.

Though Cardoso's main contribution to sociology emanates primarily from the foundational efforts in the study of development and political change in Latin America, several essays on social structure and proletarianization,[67] urbanization,[68] globalization, and other subjects reveal a broader, universalistic orientation. These, too, often seek to provide disciplinary direction.

Critics of dependency theory emphasize such themes as insufficient empirical support for the theory as well as the unwillingness or inability of dependency theorists to cast arguments in ways that can be assessed empirically. Though the strongest of these criticisms may have been directed at other strands of dependency theory, Cardoso has not been spared. In fact, the main criticisms of his work have come in this context. Joseph A. Kahl's mid-1970s assessment reflected the previously mentioned concerns.[69] Political scientist Robert Packenham maintained and enhanced this line of attack through the 1980s and early 1990s.[70] Arguing that various findings falsified Cardoso's dependency approach, the latter takes Cardoso to task for failing to acknowledge those results and for being influenced by Marxist ideology.[71] Cardoso has argued since the late 1960s that his dependency approach was not meant as a formal theory and that his work shunned generalizing theory in favor of historically specific "situations of dependency." He maintained that position in Latin America, where Weffort and others argued that the approach relied on nationalism rather than Marxist class analysis. [72]

Critics have hence converged on Cardoso's relationship to Marxism, though with little agreement. Some attacked him for being too Marxist, while to others his work as insufficiently so. Any hard version of either position is probably misguided. Marx's dialectical thought does provide a durable axis in Cardoso's intellectual trajectory. However, enduring interest in academic Marxism and its methodological implications were tempered since the 1960s with the preeminence given to social scientific rigor. Cardoso dismissed hard or "vulgar" Marxism on the basis of its determinism, the inaccuracy of its empirical observations and interpretations, and its inability to deal with new realities. [73]

Dialectics remained a hallmark in the Cardosian perspective. A systematic analysis of the history and dynamics of capitalism, including systems of stratification and trends in the international or global economy, is necessary to understand modern social life. But Cardoso aims at a dialectics that does justice to structural and historical diversity, the role of ideas and historical interaction, and opportunities for change. History and conjuncture need to be combined with structural analysis. Cardoso's dialectics is, above all, an action-enabling one, with a resolute emphasis on emergent trends and possibilities for change. [74]

Cardoso's brand of historical and comparative macrosociology and the focus on bureaucracy owe much to Weber's influence. That founding figure of sociology can be said to have shaped Cardoso's thought as much as any other, including Marx. Weber would also help navigate the transition from scholar to politician.

POLITICS AS A VOCATION

A new phase in Cardoso's life opened in the late 1970s. The middle years of that decade had brought growing political involvement as a public intellectual engaged in the prodemocracy movement. But the first step toward a political career as such came in 1978, when he agreed to run for the Senate at the urging of Ulysses Guimarães, a respected Paulista democrat. Cardoso was elected as an alternate senator to Andre Franco Montoro, another widely admired democratic leader. In 1979 Cardoso became a leader of the MDB of São Paulo and, shortly after, vice president of the Party of the Brazilian Democratic Movement (PMDB), the political party that grew out of the prodemocracy movement. It was a foregone conclusion that he would become senator in 1983, as the prestige of the PMDB at the time made it all but certain that Montoro would be elected governor of the state of São Paulo in that year's elections.

Becoming a senator represented a decisive turn toward a political career, even if expected. But academia still beckoned. In 1982, Cardoso left Brazil for a semester at Berkeley, a point at which the PMDB was making important decisions. [75] From

1982–1986 he was president of the International Sociological Association and a member of several international committees and organizations. The personal transition did not leave intellectual reflection behind: Weber's classic essay *Politics As a Vocation* provided the inspiration for his inaugural speech as senator. But from this point on political stars shone too brightly to interrupt the full transition to a new career. Sociology remained an enduring passion. The two identities continued to coexist. But purely intellectual matters began to recede into the background after that year.

Suspense returned briefly in 1985. Loosing the race for mayor of São Paulo almost killed the budding political career. However, the professor learned his lesson and won a landslide victory in the 1986 senatorial elections. The *New York Times* reported the reversal of political fortune in terms of Cardoso's passage to practical politician. "No longer drawn to the cloistered life of academia, Cardoso has learned to play politics among politicians," Alan Riding wrote.[76] The article puzzled over a career transition. Cardoso himself expressed confidence in his ability to mix the two vocations and continued to write for intellectual and even academic audiences.

But, the notion of a personal transition at this time should not be construed as evidence of sharp discontinuity. Cardoso had been part of the key political events in Brazil since early in the 1980s, including the organization of the PMDB and helping shape the Montoro government in São Paulo. He was deeply involved in the critical moments of the democratic transition in 1984–1985, the mass movement for direct elections, and the election of the first democratic president in 1985. The death of President-elect Tancredo Neves before taking office created a difficult context to initiate the new democratic era. Political alliances and strategies had to be redesigned as Vice President José Sarney assumed the presidency. Cardoso was involved in the selection of the first democratic cabinet. Brazil experienced massive mobilization and lobbying efforts when the elected congress became a new Constituent Assembly in late 1986. As leader in the Brazilian Senate, Cardoso found himself at the vortex of the political process to write a new charter for the nation.

Cardoso and associates founded the Brazilian Social Democratic Party (PSDB) in 1988, in the context of the still effervescent democratic transition. The new party resulted from an implosion of the PMDB, the prodemocracy party that had served as an umbrella to diverse factions, including those that earlier had launched the Workers Party (PT). In São Paulo, Cardoso and a group of political figures lost considerable influence to another political group led by Orestes Quércia, another emergent politician from the interior of that state.[77] A new splinter became inevitable as the *quercistas* gained ascendancy in that state's PMDB. The PSDB was meant as a more cohesive and manageable political organization. Its founders forged a social democratic platform based on what they saw as a realistic and socially responsible program, including an approach to economic policy that sought to balance state action with an expanded role for the market. Opposition to clientelism (*fisiologismo*) was a main banner. The PSDB's call for moderation, realism, reform, and responsibility could only hope to grow slowly. Its small size—its core group was a minority party in São Paulo—raised doubts about prospects. Nevertheless, the party's reputation as a centrist, pragmatic, and reliable political organization gradually took hold.

The last decade of the twentieth century would prove auspicious to Cardoso and the PSDB. The presidential elections of 1990 favored them in unintended but major ways. Fernando Collor de Mello, the telegenic young governor of Alagoas, defeated the PT's Luiz Inácio Lula da Silva, as well as the PSDB candidate. But charges of corruption led to Collor's impeachment right after initiating liberalizing reforms. As Vice President Itamar Franco became president, he appointed Cardoso as minister of foreign relations in 1992 and finance minister in 1993. These appointments reflected a high level of recognition for Cardoso and the PSDB. Success derived from their role in the long and difficult struggle for democracy. Their stars would continue to rise in the months and years that followed, taking them to the seat of power.[78]

Brazil's process of democratization faced a veritable crisis when Cardoso became finance minister. The nine years of democratization after 1985 had witnessed a series of woefully ineffectual economic policies. Three civilian presidents had enacted eight stabilization programs that failed to stop inflation, much less steer Brazil in a new direction. By 1993, the country faced record inflation at a monthly rate of 25 percent to 30 percent as well as economic stagnation. Brazilians felt greatly frustrated. They began to dwell on invidious comparisons with the military era.

Becoming the finance minister was really more an opportunity than a great risk. Failure to slay the dragon of inflation would have been attributed to President Franco or chalked off to his own inexperience in this policy area. However, success in stemming the deepening crisis and averting economic chaos would surely turn him into a top contender in the October 1994 presidential elections. The job provided a decisive test of policymaking and political skills. It was a proverbial Gordian knot whose severance would open the gates to the Brazilian presidency. Boldly and self-confidently, Cardoso availed himself of the opportunity.[79] The intellectual turned politician was now on course to become a statesman.

The victory in the 1994 presidential elections was decisive. A big part of the left, including some old associates, would be unforgiving for the defeat of the PT candidate. The new government claimed a mandate for major reform. The Cardoso presidency aimed at nothing short of crafting a new political and economic era.

STATESMAN: AGENDA AND DILEMMA

With *virtù* and *fortuna* on his side, hopes were high at Cardoso's presidential inauguration in January 1995. Stabilization made victory possible and remained the top priority. Its continued success was a big achievement in subsequent months. By the end of 1996, inflation reached single-digit levels. Many Brazilians thought it was time to focus on the broader reform agenda and to lead Brazil in a new direction and to a new role in the globalizing economy. In order to achieve these objectives, Brazil needed to find a new development model and redefine the economic role of the state. The Cardoso government had to choose from a mix of policy measures that included fiscal reform, privatization, trade liberalization, deregulation, and similar "orthodox" prescriptions.[80]

Reforms worked very well through mid-1996.[81] However, aspects of the stabilization plan itself began to pose new dilemmas later that year. While the *Plano Real* worked splendidly well in the short run, the original winning formula rested on an overvalued exchange rate and high interest rates. Fast growth would be unlikely under these two conditions. By mid-1996, Brazil went from a regime of trade surplus to one of trade deficits. The economic team, unable to reduce the high interest rates under those conditions, feared further capital flight. Under this situation, the Cardoso government recognized the need for structural reforms, but it decided to postpone a hard drive for fiscal adjustment until after the 1998 elections. In addition, the Brazilian government had to deal with the relative political capital needed to pass the reforms as well as a reelection amendment. The fiscal areas needing reforms were specifically protected in the constitution adopted in 1988. Constitutional amendments were required to make changes. From a political standpoint, this was very costly in the presence of a powerful coalition of state governments and public employees opposed to the reforms. It was deemed too much of a political risk to seek both the reelection and the structural adjustment bills.[82]

It became clearer through 1997 that the stabilization strategy would not work much longer as it had in the recent past. Trade and budget deficits implied an incompatibility between aspects of the stabilization plan and growth. But economic growth was essential to put a dent on unemployment, poverty, and inequality—Brazil's main problem. The poor demanded a growth policy, so did the elite and the middle class. Cardoso himself abhorred the idea of at best a stop-and-go plan rather than a sustained pattern of development. The key practical challenge was to extricate economic policymaking from a quagmire. How to do that while making substantial progress in a process of reform of the state and the adoption of a new development model remained a formidable political challenge.

RETHINKING THE STATE

But what, in the first place, are the broader justifications for Cardoso's reforms? Critics often characterize them as "neoliberal," a designation repeatedly rejected by Cardoso. Indeed, several distinctive logics or frameworks had converged in the early 1990s to justify the kind of state and political reform proposed by Cardoso. Whether these coalesce into a coherent or principled policy approach is an important issue.

First, the assessment of Brazil's traditional political system of the 1960s through the 1980s led Brazilian social scientists of diverse persuasions to a strong critique of its clientelism, corporatism, and corruption. Cardoso himself wrote extensively on the shortcomings of the Brazilian authoritarian state as well as on the populist democracy of the 1960s. By the early 1990s, he had joined other social scientists in accepting the argument that these were historically rooted in the Vargas era. There was considerable institutional continuity across the three subregimes since the 1930s: the rise of a centralizing-interventionist regime in the 1930s, the populist democracy working under the constitution of 1946, and the bureaucratic-authoritarian regime of 1964–1985.[83] Corruption, inefficiency as well as inefficacy, patrimonialism, and the lack of accountability and citizen control were the main ills of the system. In important ways, the workings of the Brazilian state as an institution had become even more mired in ineffectual practices in the first phase of the post-1985 democratic era. The constitution of 1988 codified corporatist practices into law, reinforcing them, while making change very difficult to achieve. Corruption and inefficiency did not abate.

Cardoso's 1995 inaugural speech used strong language to announce plans for state reform and the reorganization of the machinery of state: "[Public administration] is very deteriorated, after years of overspending and financial deficits. Clientelism, corporatism and corruption consume taxpayers' monies before they reach the intended legitimate beneficiaries of state action, mainly in the social area. . . . A shake-up will be necessary to clean up and to make the structural reforms needed to give efficiency to public service."[84] Another essay, published in *Novos Estudos* (CEBRAP) toward the end of his first term, confirms the centrality of this reasoning in his policy agenda.[85]

The large and diverse literature on the "exhaustion" of the state-centered development model known as import substitution industrialization provided a second rationale for state reform. Cardoso's own theories of Brazilian development implied that the protectionist model implemented in Brazil after the 1930s was coming to its final phase as a development model. The internationalization of the productive system after the 1960s was accompanied by growing problems, including exclusion and marginalization. Later studies of globalization deepened that line of reasoning, as will be discussed. If the big challenge before Brazilian society was to find a new approach to development, the process called for overhauling the state apparatus. The international literature on the fiscal crisis of the state provides a third rationale for massive state reform. This perspective highlights growing imbalance between taxes and expenditures and constraints on the former.[86] The requirements for successful reinsertion into the globalized economy provided a fourth broad coherent framework. This strand of thought subsumed some of the previously mentioned arguments and will be discussed.

Neoliberal ideology was not the main logic on which Cardoso grounded his approach to state reform and a new development strategy. Alone or in combination, the previous arguments and frameworks provided compelling grounds for massive reform. Moreover, additional justifications for reform came from the literatures on governance and governability and the policy paradigms of recent social democratic governments in Europe and North America.[87] Britain's "New Labour" politics and the Third Way as well as comparable movements in France, Germany, and the United States provided important reference points. Cardoso developed particularly good working relationships with Tony Blair in England, Gerhard Schroeder in Germany, Leonel Jospin in France, and Bill Clinton in the United States. The new social democracy centered on the state's ability to address issues about welfare and solidarity in the context of fiscal responsibility. Cardoso shared this view of the limitations on the state with regard to economic policy, but this is rather different from the principled neoliberal call for minimizing the state.

It should also be noted that political change as such also figured prominently in the Cardosian perspective. As a social scientist, his critical theory of the Brazilian state had diagnosed early weaknesses in the political party system and the overall system of representation. As a statesman, he advocated specific reforms that aimed at increasing party fidelity and the adoption of the mixed district vote.[88]

GLOBALIZATION AND REFORM

Cardoso framed his goals as a statesman in terms of his own intellectual understanding of trends in the international economy. The stints as minister of foreign affairs and finance minister, as well as his preparation for the presidency, led to a serious and noteworthy intellectual effort to analyze prospects for Brazilian development in the changing international economy. This analysis and their policy implications are sketched in several articles.[89]

In 1995, a talk at the Center for Strategic and International Studies in Washington gave the opportunity to compare the approaches to development of the 1990s with those of the 1960s. The comparison of two periods highlights the evolution of his own ideas. The main conclusion is to find in globalization additional reasons for the prominence of politics and the urgency of state reform. The title of this speech refers to development as "the most political of economic themes."[90]

After noting that the 1990s international discussion on development focused on noneconomic dimensions (to include the environment, equity, human development, and the like), Cardoso argues that globalization had deepened and broadened the patterns of dependency observed in the 1960s. Furthermore, industrial production had internationalized and changed. Global financial flows were now a prominent feature of the internationalized economy, as exemplified by the Mexican crisis of 1995. Recognizing the dangers posed by these flows of "hot money," Cardoso calls for international mechanisms to deal with their potentially adverse effects. Globalization is driven by a third industrial revolution entailing the use of more sophisticated science and technology. This is likely to aggravate unemployment in countries with large but untrained labor forces. But the main point is that new forms of dependency do not homogenize the periphery, as many had thought in the 1960s. The right choice of public policies can lead to considerable success, as shown by the "Asian tigers." In general, globalization provides opportunities for development as well as risks. In the 1990s, stewardship and a long-term perspective were necessary to steer away from globalization's pitfalls. Cardoso explicitly confirms here that he had long discarded whatever economic determinism he may have still had in the 1960s.

The biggest change between the 1960s and the 1990s was in the role of the state. Adherents of dependency theory and many others had believed that a strong state was needed to promote development. The developmental centrality of the state ended in the 1990s, following the collapse of grand schemes and illusions about its role in Eastern Europe and elsewhere. The main reason for state reform is not neoliberal ideology, but rather a profound general crisis of the state. The state remains an important actor in development. But from the perspective of the 1990s, the priority is to restructure the state to redefine its mission, refocus, and increase its effectiveness.

If the development approaches of the 1960s often shared "a psychology of distrust" of the international economy and international relations, the 1990s recognize the need to compete successfully in the global economy. That ability hinges on internal reforms to enhance the process of international insertion. The new state needs to be able to stabilize the economy, enforce fiscal equilibrium, and redefine its mission. Privatization, deregulation, and trade liberalization are unavoidable. The state has to sharpen its role with respect to health, education, and other basic services; infrastructure; modernizing the financial system; promoting the spread of entrepreneurial skills; and related areas. Progress in these areas will determine success in international competition for investment and markets.

Development remains a highly political process. The new state is called upon to be democratic in a manner that differs from the forms of democracy of earlier decades. In the 1960s, it was widely believed that a dominant social class or grand coalition would guide the development process in the context of populist democratic practices. Cardoso sees the 1990s as marked by a much more complex civil and political society (parties, nongovernmental organizations, media, trade unions, business associations, and other associations and communities) pressing on the state and monitoring its actions, often with a focus on specific policy domains. Balancing the diverse interests in the broad and diffuse patterns of social participation calls for a more open, complex, and flexible political system and culture.

Cardoso elaborates his views on global trends and the role of Brazil in the international economy in other lectures, often during visits to other countries. These statements dwell on the concept and dimensions of globalization, their impact on emerging societies such as Brazil, and the range of appropriate responses.[91] Globalization encompasses increasing trade and trade liberalization as well as a trend toward institutional convergence, besides the increasingly internationalized production processes and the expansion of financial flows. As a result, globalization and dependence differ in substantial ways. The larger role of the global economy entails an even more constrained role for states and local actors. As trade expands and increases its role in national economies, economic models based on protectionism lose strength. As such, the international economy of the 1990s differs from the dependency of the 1960s and 1970s, when multinational corporations focused on national markets and elaborate projects of national development were meaningful. Much of the recent trade expansion is within global firms and represents flows within internationalized production systems. Some of the new issues pertain to international trade regulation and emerging multilateral bodies such as the World Trade Organization. In essence, though the globalization unfolding in the 1990s intensifies trends explored in the earlier analysis of dependency, it stands for a qualitatively different international economy and society.

In Cardoso's view, international differentiation across nations increases with globalization. The Asian tigers and some large countries such as Brazil and India are able to compete in the manufacturing international economy. Smaller and postcommunist societies face more uncertain prospects and possibly other forms of insertion. Global competition calls for a profound restructuring of the economy. As some sectors and firms find themselves unable to compete, structural unemployment, inequality, and social exclusion may increase within sectors and countries, which may dissolve solidarity and threaten the very idea of national identity. Knowledge becomes more important than labor or natural resource endowments in redefining comparative advantages. Intellectuals and policymakers are called upon to articulate appropriate responses to these challenges.

States find their roles circumscribed by more than the global character of production and trade liberalization. The space for political experimentation in domestic policy agendas is reshaped and reduced in such key national policy domains as macroeconomic policy, labor, and the like. Monitoring of national level information by international actors makes states less able to act on the basis of protected information.

But globalization also brings opportunities. In fact, for some sectors, firms, and states, it may represent a veritable new Renaissance in which advanced technology greatly enhances creativity and productivity. States can enhance the competitiveness of these sectors and firms. The net impact of globalization depends on the national response. Here the reasoning seeks to bring together structural analysis and a prescriptive stance. A strong case is made for international cooperation and regional integration (such as the Mercado Comum do Sul [Mercosul]), together with an ethic of solidarity to enhance the ability to generate alternatives. It is essential to rediscover community values and revive the sense of social responsibility by the elite.

In Cardoso's view, globalization accelerates the dissolution of the capacity of the national bourgeoisie or other domestic entrepreneurs to act as a hegemonic class able to shape the rest of society—a theme present in his earlier writings. This enhances the centrality of democratic or democratizing processes. Democracy is the only way of fashioning a durable national purpose out of an increasingly complex civil society and even fragmented social structure. Polities that are democratic and have "soft power"—that is, the capacity to obtain, process, and apply new knowledge—are able to gain maneuvering space in this new environment.

In a nutshell, globalization is not a demigod enforcing conformity and rationality. It is a diffuse process that is shaped and given meaning by political processes taking place within the nation-state. Globalization not only generates pressures for convergence, but also creates niches for innovation and expansion. Inherently, it is neither panacea nor evil. Only a democratic polity can effectively generate a national purpose via the successful articulation of diverse interests. The challenge for Brazil and Latin America in this regard is to enhance the development of civil society and its rearticulation with policymaking.

A VIABLE UTOPIA

Cardoso's *weltanschauung* provided the basic inspiration and policy guidelines governing his role as statesman. This worldview places realism as well as values in the pursuit of political and development goals. Cardoso embraced the seemingly contradictory notion of "viable utopia" to capture the essentially dialectical and universalistic vision that guided his actions as president.[92] In turn, accomplishments and frustrations while at the helm of the Brazilian ship of state sharpened this orientation. His administration's well defined sense of purpose in the face of challenges and setbacks, which some Brazilians took as headstrong or arrogant, derives from the deep convictions of the intellectual president.

Embedded in his academic and intellectual trajectory, the Cardosian worldview accepts the leading economic role of the market, while maintaining that it does not address all needs, creates problems of its own, and tends to dissolve human solidarity. Twentieth-century experiments with dirigisme show that state action can often be flawed or inadequate. But the state does play a fundamental role in reducing inequalities, poverty, and other social problems. The state and market, however, are not the only choices. Community, noneconomic civil society, and the nonstate public sector can and should play important roles in organizing social life.

This approach has considerable kinship with the "modern reformism" and the search for new partnerships associated with other social democratic governments. Cardoso's contribution to this international debate centers not so much on Brazil's importance as on his own intellectual achievements. Few world leaders match him in that regard. The mature conclusions of his trajectory, the insistence on linking realism and utopia, and the emphasis on the characteristics peculiar to each country are noteworthy additions to the discussion.[93]

In this light, Brazil and Latin America as a whole need to embrace deep reforms oriented to the consolidation and expansion of democracy and economic liberalization. Justified on diverse grounds, these reforms are essential for the region's successful reincorporation into world society. These societies need to reach a new balance in the respective roles of state, market, and civil society.

Early in his presidency, Cardoso called for enhanced world governance and a world constitution to deal with emergent realities created by globalization.[94] This is one instance where more, rather than less, government is required. Cardoso's writings plead for negotiation, coalition-building, and partnerships in constructing superior forms of international cooperation. Regional integration is of major importance in this perspective. There is considerable continuity in this regard with the mid-twentieth-century ideas about Latin American integration in the structuralist thought that so inspired him in earlier decades.

A NEW DEVELOPMENT MODEL?

Cardoso's sophisticated vision and awareness of globalization could not ensure his government's ability to prevent damage from the international financial crisis of 1998–1999. Just as his second term began, financial turmoil threatened great damage. Rapid capital flight and mounting pressure on the exchange rate, linked to financial liberalization, brought great turbulence to the Brazilian economy and polity. The stabilization plan itself was in peril. Under siege, the government let the *real* float freely. The government was reluctant to float the *real* because the overvalued exchange rate had been seen as the key anchor of the anti-inflation program and there was great fear that this move would renew the inflationary spiral.

The episode provided a major test of the stabilization plan. At the worst moment, the exchange plunged to half of its value and interest rates skyrocketed to more than 50 percent. The media and the opposition made dire statements and predictions about the collapse of production, dramatic increases in unemployment, a profound recession, and the return of inflation. Public anxiety peaked. The president's approval ratings plummeted to unprecedented and dangerous lows. The crisis was a reminder of the dangers of globalization even in a country led by an astute analyst of international trends. It was also a sign that the reform process had to deepen to calm the international financial community. Cardoso had warned against this kind of crisis, but he could not prevent it. Ironically, the crisis vindicated Cardoso as an intellectual, as it taxed his skills and reputation as a statesman.

As the crisis unfolded, perplexity and doubts about the reform drive mounted. But the economic authorities maintained the stabilization goals through the depths of the crisis in early 1999 and beyond. The approach worked. By late April, the worst was over and a gradual recovery began. By mid-2000, economic recovery was a firm trend. Production, exports, and employment were increasing. Inflation had actually decreased. The new macroeconomic environment created more policy options. The economic team deserved a great deal of credit, but the country was still in no mood for praise.

This might have been a good time to recast the reform agenda in terms of an active development strategy. But the Cardoso administration felt that stability of purpose and discourse was still essential. The course would be maintained. Decision makers focused on managing the situation created by the free-floating exchange rate. Interest rates had to be brought down to single-digit levels. The fiscal restructuring and reform agenda had to be sustained. The economic shock left in its wake a political crisis that further complicated congressional adoption of reforms. The new political dynamics included the threat of disarray within the ruling political alliance of the PSDB, the Party of the Liberal Front (PFL), the PMDB, and other smaller parties. Itamar Franco (PMDB), the newly elected governor of the state of Minas Gerais, had rebelled against the Cardoso administration, declaring a unilateral moratorium on its substantial foreign debt. In fact, this had been one of the factors precipitating the financial crisis. Throughout 1999 and early 2000, party and factional rivalries contributed to scandals involving illegal wiretappings, charges of corruption, highly visible congressional inquiries, and a climate of turmoil. The opposition intensified its attacks, sensing a moment of high vulnerability for the president. It fostered a new wave of mass demonstrations. Sharp attacks in the congress and the media demanded a roll back of austerity policies and even the president's resignation or impeachment. The precipitous fall in the approval ratings of the president put in doubt the very legacy of the Cardoso government.

As it maintained the course, the Cardoso team had correctly insisted that the crisis was temporary. There were reasons for optimism. The stabilization plan and the reforms had led to significant poverty reduction and conditions for economic growth before the crisis. Above all, the stronger currency had improved the standard of living of the poor; between 1993 and 1995, thirteen million Brazilians experienced an improvement that took them out of dire poverty. Consumption increased by about 30 percent. Levels of employment had increased. Cardoso's social policies targeted basic education and health. Brazil's public health system had been notoriously deficient, with high mortality often associated with the spread of contagious diseases. Entrenched mismanagement and graft were notorious features of the public health system. The educational system posed comparable problems. The Cardoso administration increased allocations and adopted new approaches. Two of Cardoso's star ministers, José Serra and Paulo Renato Souza, directed health and education policy, respectively.[95] The Cardoso team had continued to make incremental but key changes with major long-term implications.

The government also implemented an agrarian reform. Between 1994 and 1998, approximately 280,000 families acquired land through the agrarian reform program—a number somewhat higher than the land distributed in the preceding thirty years. The federal government authorized funds to continue the agrarian reform program, with the goal for the second term to settle an average of eighty-five thousand families annually. Land-related social movements gained political space and continued to make the agrarian reform a major issue in the national agenda.

The consolidation of democracy meant that the poor and other concerned groups could demand measures to address poverty and inequality. Trade unions, trade associations, and even members of the president's own party, as well as the opposition, demanded an economic policy oriented to growth and employment.

As the crisis receded, the Brazilian government was keenly aware that it had a lot more to do to bring dramatic improvement in social conditions. At the dawn of the twenty-first century, Brazil remained a country of high poverty and inequality, with the poor making up at least 40 percent of the population. Inequality was still one of the most pronounced in the world. The post-1993 acceleration in economic restructuring itself fueled the rise in unemployment.

As the crisis faded through 2000, the federal government reconfirmed its focus on the modernizing agenda and laying the ground for future growth. Trade policy was tied more closely to the promotion of exports and key economic sectors. Officials explored opportunities for industrial promotion via import substitution, following the great expansion of imports accompanying stabilization. The Banco Nacional de Desenvolvimento Econômico e Social (BNDES; National Bank for Economic and Social Development) expanded credits to further the restructuring and modernization of key industrial sectors such as steel, paper and cellulose, and petrochemicals. Though some Brazilians demanded a more traditional industrial policy, the government continued to view trade liberalization as a key element of Brazil's economic model and as essential to fight inflation, increase efficiency and competitiveness, and promote trade and foreign investment.

A new development model was being put in place stone by stone. Debate would continue about the precise contours of the new approach. The precise depth and breadth of government activism would need to be defined in the future. Besides laying foundations, the Cardoso administration saw its role as setting the tone of the debate about development policy. Growth and antipoverty policies still tended to work at cross-purposes with anti-inflation and fiscal adjustment drives. But the success in letting the *real* float freely had expanded the space for other policies and political options.

CONCLUSION

Cardoso had studied sociology to change the world. It was remarkable that he achieved the position where he could. Has the intellectual managed to do so? Though this introduction is hardly the place to draw a balance sheet of the Cardoso presidency, there is evidence of substantial accomplishment. The first part of his presidency leaned more toward preserving than changing. The most visible and durable accomplishment was stabilizing the economy. Perhaps more importantly, it also stabilized the polity. To prevent the collapse of the Brazilian economy and polity were hardly revolutionary, but they added up to a major achievement. Enough to justify pride in any politician.[96]

But Cardoso is no ordinary politician. He would insist on having his performance judged on its ability to set Brazil on a new course. Midway through his second term, there was clear evidence of change in the Brazilian state and its relationship to the economy and society. Some—like the construction of a new legal and regulatory framework—may not have been very visible. But together with privatization, deregulation, liberalization, and a new activism on the BNDES, as well as long-term reforms in education and health, they did indeed mark the end of an era and the beginning of a new one. Brazil would not be the same at the end of Cardoso's presidency.[97]

The Cardoso government succeeded in opening and liberalizing the economy, orienting it to integration efforts in South America and negotiations with the rest of the Americas and Europe. Fiscal adjustment and enhanced tax collection helped redefine the role of the state. This amounted to a breakthrough. Dirigisme and corporatism were unlikely to return. In fact, Brazil had begun a fundamental transformation.

This transformation will take time to complete. It is up to future governments to further define the precise contours of the new Brazilian approach to development. Cardoso had looked at the developmental administration of Juscelino Kubitschek as an inspiration, but his government would not, or could not, resemble it in tone or style. It will take a long perspective to establish how close it came to defining a new era in Brazilian development. What seems clear at the dawn of the twenty-first century is that its character and the overall legacy of the reform drive will depend on a durable process of political realignment and the resolution of complex tension points of the polity.

In the end, how should Cardoso's approach and reforms be characterized? Because his policies liberalized the economy and tended toward a redefinition of the state, and the underlying theoretical or ideological framework has been called neoliberal. This is certainly debatable. The main rationales Cardoso used to justify the reform process had little to do with neoclassical or neoliberal economic doctrine. In fact, Cardoso remains a sharp critic of the failures and inadequacies of the market. A more apt view may be to recognize the underlying ideas as a variant of the social democratic reformism of the late 1990s. But Cardoso's closeness to the world of social science suggests that the hypothesis of a non- or postideological framework may need to be considered. In any case, what is essential here is that the role of the state will differ sharply from the interventionist one assigned in the corporatist regimes that had ruled Brazil since Vargas.[98]

Cardoso's contributions in the social sciences have been substantial, particularly in the development of Latin American historical structuralism and the understanding of processes of democratization. Intellectual historians will wonder about the relative neglect of this approach beyond the borders of Latin America. They will also dwell on Cardoso's role in enriching it. Hopefully, this book may help them in that assessment.

The perspective of time is needed to judge historical events and apparent discontinuities. With regard to Cardoso's own intellectual trajectory, there is remarkable continuity between the academically oriented historical structuralism of the 1960s and the equally moderate policy-oriented social democracy of the 1990s. Cardoso's ideas at the start of the twenty-first century remained loyal to the traditional Latin American focus on the international context and regional integration, though it has done so in the spirit of openness about new and emergent trends.

One of the hallmarks of Cardoso's presidency has been its open and reflexive character. Various branches of government have sponsored national and international seminars on reform and change. The president himself has been prone to extensive analytical commentary. Politics imposes limits on what is said and the intention of communication. We look forward to a postpresidential period when one of Latin America's top social thinkers may reflect openly on the enduring lessons from his experience as president of one of the largest countries on earth, and on what to make, ultimately, of the marriage between an impressive intellectual trajectory and the affairs of the state.

NOTES

1. This introduction concentrates on Cardoso's writings during four decades after the late 1950s. Interviews with President Cardoso and intellectuals close to his trajectory provided information and insights. I am particularly grateful to Danielle Ardaillon, Enzo Faletto, Albert Hirschman, Juarez Rubens Brandão Lopes, Luiz Carlos Bresser Pereira, and Francisco Weffort as well as Cardoso himself. Parts of this introduction were initially presented at the seminar, "From Dependency to Development: Challenge and Response in the Intellectual Trajectory of Fernando Henrique Cardoso," *New Americas* Colloquium, Graduate School and Queens College, City University of New York, May 13, 1999.

2. Prior to the 1889 birth of the republic, Cardoso's great grandfather had been the military governor of Goiás and the head of the regional branch of the Conservative Party. His father and several uncles and cousins served in high office during the middecades of the twentieth century, having been part of the reformist *tenente* movement of the 1920s and 1930s. Most supported the movements led by Getúlio Dor-

nelles Vargas. See Brigitte Hersant Leoni, *Fernando Henrique Cardoso: O Brasil do possível* (Rio de Janeiro: Nova Fronteira, 1997); and Roberto Pompeu de Toledo, *O Presidente segundo o sociólogo* (São Paulo: Companhia das Letras, 1998, 340–343).

3. Limitations of space make it impossible to provide a full account of the large secondary literature commenting Cardoso's trajectory and intellectual contributions. The list includes Ted G. Goertzel, *Fernando Henrique Cardoso: Reinventing Democracy in Brazil* (Boulder, Colo.: Lynne Rienner, 1999); Robert Packenham, *The Dependency Movement: Scholarship and Politics in Development Studies* (Cambridge: Harvard University Press, 1992); and Joseph A. Kahl, *Modernization, Exploitation, and Dependency: Germani, González, Casanova, and Cardoso* (New Brunswick, N.J.: Transaction Books, 1976).

4. Besides Cardoso, the Marx Seminar included anthropologist Ruth Corrêa Leite Cardoso, philosopher José Arthur Giannotti, sociologists Octávio Ianni and Juarez Brandão Lopes, historian Fernando Novaes, literary critic Roberto Schwarz, economist Paul Singer, political scientist Francisco Weffort, and others. It started in 1958 and met roughly every two weeks for seven years, with four of them spent on studying *Capital*. See Roberto Schwarz, "Um seminário de Marx," *Folha de S. Paulo*, October 5, 1995 (reprinted in Roberto Schwarz, *Ensaios* [São Paulo: Companhia das Letras, 1999, 86–105], as well as in *Novos Estudos* [CEBRAP] 50 [March 1998]: 99–114) (see also Goertzel, *Fernando Henrique Cardoso*, 17–21). Paul Singer, "Nos arredores da Maria Antônia," in M. C. Loschiano dos Santos, ed., *Maria Antônia: Uma rua na contramão* (São Paulo: Nobel, 1988), also discusses the Marx Seminar.

5. *Maria Antônia: Uma rua na contramão* contains short essays reminiscing on student life at the USP from the very late 1940s through the 1964 military coup, when the social science division and the Faculty of Philosophy, Science, and Letters as a whole was housed in a building on Maria Antônia Street. Starting in 1966, a vigorous student movement there contributed to radical protest in 1968; the military regime confronted it in part by reforming the university and moving the Faculty of Philosophy, Science, and Letters to the current campus of the University of São Paulo. After the transfer was made in 1969, "Maria Antônia" became a memory of mythical proportions in the minds of most of the students and faculty associated with it. Cardoso's "Memórias da Maria Antônia" provides biographical information about his role during those years, his exile, and his frustrated return to the University of São Paulo in 1968. The now cosmopolitan Cardoso found that widespread populism and vulgar Marxism blocked the contributions he could have made at this time; and, in any case, the military forced him and other professors to retire in 1969. Azis Simão, Antonio Candido, José Arthur Giannotti, Paul Singer, and twenty-seven other authors are represented in *Maria Antônia*, a collective portrait of a key chapter in the history of the social sciences in Brazil.

6. For the importance of regional dynamics and Paulista political groups in national political life in Brazil, I draw from my own research, particularly M. A. Font, *Coffee, Contention, and Change* (Oxford: Basil Blackwell, 1990), and M. A. Font, "Failed Redemocratization: Region, Class, and Political Change in Brazil, 1930–37," in F. J. Devoto and T. S. Di Tella, eds., *Political Culture, Social Movements, and Democratic Transitions in South America in the Twentieth Century* (Milano: Fondazione Giangiacomo Feltrinelli, 1997). Rubem Barbosa Filho, "FHC: Os paulistas no poder," in Roberto Amaral, ed., *FHC: Os paulistas no poder* (Rio de Janeiro: Casa Jorge Editorial, 1995), mirrors the public debate from at least the early 1930s about the role of São Paulo in the Brazilian federation.

7. See, for example, Cardoso's "A paixão pelo saber," in M. A. D'Incao, ed., *O saber militante: ensaios sobre Florestan Fernandes* (São Paulo: Paz e Terra/UNESP, 1987), 23–30. In this essay, which is based on a talk at a conference on Florestan Fernandes, Cardoso discusses their relationship from its beginnings in 1949.

8. In a personal exchange, Juarez R. Brandão Lopes calls attention to the importance of this aspect of Cardoso's trajectory. To the extent that prominence in university politics was one of the paths to an eventual political career, there is indeed considerable continuity in Cardoso's professional life.

9. The early evolution of the University of São Paulo was marked by the Vargas era and the authoritarian Estado Novo. Vargas's 1937 coup preempted the possibility that the founder of this university, the state governor Armando Salles Oliveira, would be elected the president of Brazil in 1937. As control of São Paulo passed to the centralizing elites of the Estado Novo, the original mission of the university became contested terrain, but the social science program continued to develop with great rigor. Because of the role of the French academics, who often lectured in their native language, Cardoso learned much of his sociology in French (see "A paixão pelo saber"). The social science program at the USP began to bear fruit in

the late 1940s and 1950s, during the years at Rua Maria Antônia. Besides Cardoso and Ruth Corrêa Leite Cardoso, the list of prominent scholars from the first and second cohorts includes Antonio Candido, Florestan Fernandes, Fernando Azevedo, Roberto Schwarz, Juarez Rubens Brandão Lopes, and Octávio Ianni. Font, *Coffee, Contention, and Change,* and Font, "Failed Redemocratization," provide background on the political and economic problems faced by the elites of the state of São Paulo in the 1920s and 1930s.

10. *Capitalismo e escravidão no Brasil meridional: O negro na sociedade escravocrata do Rio Grande do Sul* (São Paulo: Difusão Européia do Livro, 1962), has not been translated into English. It is discussed in Goertzel, *Fernando Henrique Cardoso,* 25–28.

11. Race relations was a major item in the empirical agenda of the sociology program at the University of São Paulo in part due to the research interests of Roger Bastide.

12. Cardoso had been a teaching assistant in sociology since the 1950s, working under the supervision of Florestan Fernandes and Roger Bastide.

13. Centro de Sociologia Industrial e do Trabalho. See *Sociologie du Travail,* 4 (1961), edited by Alain Touraine. At the time, Touraine was the assistant to Georges Friedmann, who preceded him in São Paulo and who prepared conditions for the CESIT in a faculty seminar attended by Cardoso, Azis Simão, Octávio Ianni, and Juarez Brandão Lopes.

14. *Empresário industrial e desenvolvimento econômico no Brasil* (São Paulo: Difusão Européia do Livro, 1964), has not been translated into English. The first two chapters of the book sketch one of the earliest systematic critiques of various approaches to the sociology of development subsumed under the label of modernization theory. An extensive account of this volume is found in Kahl, *Modernization, Exploitation, and Development in Latin America,* 140–153.

15. The diverse empirical methods used in the research study included ethnography, interviews, and questionnaire surveys applied to a sample of industrialists from five cities—São Paulo, Belo Horizonte, Recife, Salvador, and Blumenau. This study was supported by the CEPAL, the University of São Paulo, Fundação de Amparo à Pesquisa de São Paulo (FAPESP), and the Coordenação de Aperfeiçoamento do Pessoal de Ensino Superior (CAPES). See *Empresário industrial e desenvolvimento econômico no Brasil,* "Nota Introdutória," 5. As part of this study, in November 1962 Cardoso began a four-month internship at the Laboratoire de Sociologie Industrielle of the University of Paris (with Alain Touraine). This study was linked to the CEPAL's multinational project on industrialists. The research agenda of Paulista sociology can also be found in Florestan Fernandes, *A Sociologia numa era de revolução social* (São Paulo: Editora Nacional, 1963).

16. Key advocates of this thesis included Rio de Janeiro's Instituto Superior de Estudos Brasileiros (ISEB) led by Harvard-trained sociologist Hélio Jaguaribe, the economist Celso Furtado, and the Brazilian Communist Party.

17. Cardoso left Brazil on April 19, 1964. During a stop in Buenos Aires, Argentine sociologists José Nún, Gino Germani, and Torcuato Di Tella offered advice and support. Cardoso left Buenos Aires for Santiago on May 1, immediately after receiving an invitation to work with José Medina Echevarría at the CEPAL.

18. The presence of a large group of exiled Brazilian intellectuals and students helped make Santiago a capital of ideas in the mid-1960s. This group included Celso Furtado, Paulo Freire, José Serra, Paulo Renato Souza, Francisco Weffort, Theotônio dos Santos, Rui Mauro Marini, Eduardo Kugelmas, Vilmar Faria, and many others. Serra, Souza, Weffort, Faria, and others would play major roles in Cardoso's presidency. Celso Furtado, *Os ares do mundo* (São Paulo: Paz e Terra, 1991), discusses the experience of Brazilians in Santiago during this period.

19. However, this concept first appeared in *El proceso de desarrollo en América Latina: Hipótesis para una interpretación sociológica* (Santiago: ILPES report, Nov 1965).

20. Hirschman and Cardoso met during a brief trip Cardoso made to New York in 1964. The relationship blossomed during Hirschman's 1967 stay at the UN Economic Commission on Latin America in Santiago de Chile. In 1975–1976, Hirschman invited Cardoso to the Institute for Advanced Study in Princeton, New Jersey, a stay that shaped the English edition of *Dependency and Development.*

21. Much of *Política e desenvolvimento em sociedades dependentes* (Rio de Janeiro: Zahar, 1971), was written during this stay in France. This book is a comparative analysis of industrialists' ideology in Argentina and Brazil. Research was done in 1965 and 1966. Part of the analysis and the integrative writing were carried out in Paris, between October 1967 and March 1968. It was completed in São Paulo in early 1969. This work earned Cardoso a new appointment at the USP as a professor of politics. Colleagues

elected Cardoso to be the director of the sociology program. Cardoso taught for less than one term before the forced retirement ("cassação") in April 1969.

22. Institutional Act # 5 (AI 5, as it is known to Brazilians) provided the legal context for the forced or political "retirement" of professors. Considering that the lists came from Minister of Justice Luís Antonio da Gama e Silva, who had been "rector" at the University of São Paulo and resented Cardoso's growing role there, there are grounds to suspect that the motivation may have had to do with university politics to a large extent (personal communication from Juarez Brandão Lopes). Several professors from the USP experienced Cardoso's fate.

23. Brigitte Hersant Leoni, *Fernando Henrique Cardoso: O Brasil do possível* (Rio de Janeiro: Nova Fronteira, 1997, 154–156), mentions an interview with Peter Bell, the Ford Foundation representative in Rio de Janeiro who approved the first grant to the CEBRAP, reporting that he rejected arguments from the U.S. Central Intelligence Agency to the effect that Cardoso was a subversive who should not receive financial support. Peter Bell confirmed this story in a personal interview.

24. The list of the CEBRAP founders also included José Arthur Giannotti, Cândido Procópio Ferreira de Camargo, Juarez Rubens Brandão Lopes, Elsa Berquó, and Paul Singer (see also Goertzel, *Fernando Henrique Cardoso*, 51–55). The CEBRAP began publishing *Estudos CEBRAP* in 1971. This publication became *Novos Cadernos* (CEBRAP) in 1981. The CEBRAP also published *Cadernos*, a less important series. Several members of this center, including its president, collaborated extensively in *Opinião* and *Movimento*, two key prodemocracy publications of the 1970s. Cardoso was involved in most major events in the long and tense struggle for democracy in São Paulo, the most important metropolis in Brazil.

25. New York: Monthly Review Press, 1967. Before going to Chile, Frank had been a visiting professor at the University of Brasília, where he wrote an essay about feudalism in Brazil (in the journal *America Latina*).

26. *O modelo político brasileiro e outros ensaios* (São Paulo: Difusão Européia do Livro, 1972), *Autoritarismo e democracia* (Rio de Janeiro: Paz e Terra, 1975), and *As idéias e seu lugar: ensaios sobre as teorias do desenvolvimento* (Petrópolis: Vozes, 1980), have not been translated into English, but some of the essays in these collections have. Perhaps the best known outside Brazil is "Associated-Dependent Development: Theoretical and Practical Implications," in Alfred Stepan, ed., *Authoritarian Brazil: Origins, Policies, and Future* (New Haven, Conn.: Yale University Press, 1973, 142–176). This essay is a version of "O modelo político brasileiro," a text widely discussed within the CEBRAP in early 1970.

27. The historical-structural approach of Cardoso and Faletto sought to differentiate itself not only from the "development of underdevelopment" perspective developed by Andre Gunder Frank, but also from comparable strands of thought by the Brazilians Theotônio dos Santos and Rui Mauro Marini, who were also in Chile in the mid-1960s.

28. "O modelo brasileiro de desenvolvimento: Dados e perspectivas."

29. "Teoria da dependência ou análises concretas de situações de dependência."

30. Sociologist Enzo Faletto, the coauthor of *Dependency and Development in Latin America*, was removed from his academic position at the University of Chile soon after the 1973 coup, when the military closed down, albeit temporarily, the university's sociology department. Faletto had been affiliated with FLACSO since 1972 and was able to teach there until 1983, when he joined CEPAL. In the democratizing context of the 1990s, he was "reincorporated" into the sociology department at the University of Chile.

31. Military rule in Chile lasted seventeen years. With academic life in Brazil and much of South America disrupted by rightist military dictatorships, many Latin American social scientists faced precarious conditions to pursue their interests in the politically sensitive field of development. Because of its size and institutional conditions, Mexico was probably the only other Latin American country able to host the further development of Latin American dependency theory. Some Brazilian exiles flourished there after the demise of Santiago as the intellectual haven. Vânia Bambirra and Theotônio dos Santos produced influential works in Mexico that contributed to the radical or "development of underdevelopment" version of dependency theory. With Marxism, anti-Americanism, and nationalism dominating Mexican university life, the milder version of dependency theory did not take hold.

32. Immanuel Wallerstein's *The World System I: Capitalist Agriculture and the Origins of the European World-economy in the 16th Century* (New York: Academic Press), appeared in 1974. After that, Wallerstein published extensively and his approach gained a substantial number of adherents. In the 1970s, members and sympathizers of this approach formed the World Systems Section within the American Sociological

Association. This school of thought focused on exploring the systematic dynamics of world history. National development trajectories or histories are subsumed as components of global structures that are conceptualized as world systems.

33. This postscript was largely written during Cardoso's 1975–1976 visit to the Institute for Advanced Study in Princeton, in the context of discussions with Albert Hirschman. José Serra, another of Cardoso's long-term associates since the days of exile in Chile, was also a fellow at the institute at that time.

34. *Latin American Research Review*, 12 (1977): 7–24.

35. One of the first initiatives was a 1973–1974 lecture series at Rio Grande do Sul's Legislative Assembly (presided by Pedro Simon) by Cardoso, Francisco de Oliveira, Juarez Brandão Lopes, Paulo Singer, and other CEBRAP personnel.

36. The CEBRAP was then located in Rua Bahia, one of its temporary addresses before it moved to its permanent quarters at Rua Morgado de Mateus. Several members of the CEBRAP (including Paulo Singer, Francisco de Oliveira, Fred Mazzuchelli, and others) were briefly detained or imprisoned at various points during the 1970s. Apparently, those forms of repression of intellectuals were part of a reaction by hardliners to the gradual liberalization policies pursued by the Ernesto Geisel government after 1973.

37. Founded in 1930, the Institute for Advanced Study in Princeton, where Albert Einstein had conducted much of his research in earlier years, is separate from Princeton University, a distinction frequently glossed over in reference to Cardoso's stays in Princeton. Princeton is the name of the Ivy-League university named after the small city where it is located. Though the institute sometimes collaborates with programs at the university, they are totally independent institutions. Cardoso was not affiliated with the university as such during his two consecutive, six-month stays at the institute in the 1970s.

38. New Haven, Conn.: Yale University Press, 1973. Versions of "O modelo político brasileiro" were published in 1972 in several Latin American journals, including *Aportes, Desarrollo Económico* (Buenos Aires), and *Estudos CEBRAP* (Brazil). Cardoso's 1972 collection of essays with the same title includes this article and others focused on Brazilian authoritarianism and its evolution. Later, this essay appeared in F. H. Cardoso, ed., *A Construção da democracia* (São Paulo: Siciliano, 1993), and in S. Haggard, ed., *The International Political Economy and the Developing Countries* (Hants, UK: Edward Elgar Publishing Ltd., 1995).

39. In this essay, Cardoso provides critiques of major approaches by non-Brazilians Philippe Schmitter and Thomas Skidmore as well as Brazilians Celso Furtado, Hélio Jaguaribe, and Cândido Mendes.

40. The original thesis about the "underlying" structural process conditioning the 1964 coup appears in "Raízes estruturais da crise política brasileira," published in the volume *Mudanças sociais na América Latina* (São Paulo: Difusão Européia do Livro, 1969), as well as in *Les Temps Modernes* (Paris) (October 1967).

41. By the same token, the still quasi-democratic state of 1969–1970 could also take a turn toward stronger forms of authoritarianism or even totalitarianism. But in this early statement, Cardoso viewed the forces of repression and armed conflict as probably at odds with the times, possibly unnecessary and useless.

42. *O modelo político brasileiro e outros ensaios* contains nine chapters and a preface. The first chapter provides an overview of political processes in Latin America. Others deal with industrialization, dependency and concrete situations of dependency, planning, the concept of social classes in Poulantzas, marginality, and imperialism.

43. Guillermo O'Donnell, *Modernization and Bureaucratic-authoritarianism: Studies in South American Politics* (Berkeley: University of California's Institute of International Studies, 1973.)

44. David Collier, ed., *The New Authoritarianism in Latin America* (Princeton, N.J.: Princeton University Press, 1979).

45. Alfred Stepan, ed., *Democratizing Brazil: Problems of Transition and Consolidation* (New York and Oxford: Oxford University Press, 1989). Cardoso acknowledges in this essay that in 1971, when he wrote the paper for the Yale conference, he "did not see any possibility of the Brazilian regime's metamorphosis" (299). The 1983 essay then proceeds to explore a reconciliation of democratic theory and dependency theory, focusing on "new political contradictions and possibilities that emerge within this late twentieth-century structural-historical novelty—associated-dependent development" (299). Paul Cammack, "Cardoso's Political Project in Brazil: the Limits of Social Democracy," in Leo Panitch, ed., *The Socialist Register 1997: Ruthless Criticism of All That Exists* (London: Merlin Press, and, Atlantic Highlands, N.J.: Humanities Press, 1997), reviews these texts and concludes that from the early 1970s Cardoso espoused a social democratic project for the democratization of state and society in Brazil (231).

46. While the first six of the eleven essays of *A construção da democracia*, written before 1974, still focus on the nature and dynamics of the authoritarian regime, the last five articles, presented or published in the period 1979–1983, concentrate on democratization.

47. *Journal of Democracy*, 7 (3) (1996): 8–19.

48. *A democracia necessária* documents the new focus in breadth. This and other books from the 1980s and 1990s often contain relatively short essays, many written for a weekly column in the newspaper *Folha de São Paulo* or comparable purposes.

49. Cammack, "Cardoso's Political Project in Brazil," 231.

50. Ibid., 237–238.

51. For a general reflection on large-scale social change, see "Problems of Social Change, Again?" *International Sociology*, 2 (2, June) (1997): 177–187. This was Cardoso's presidential address at the International Sociological Association's Eleventh World Congress of Sociology, New Delhi, August 1986.

52. Medina Echevarría served the Spanish republic in the 1930s and went into exile after Francisco Franco's victory, arriving at the CEPAL in Chile after some years in Puerto Rico and Mexico.

53. Cardoso knew some German and had developed an early liking for Karl Mannheim and other German social scientists—interests he shared with Medina Echevarria.

54. For example, Edelberto Torres Rivas from Costa Rica and José Luis Reyna from Mexico were at FLACSO. Brazilian Paulo de Tarso was at the ILADES.

55. Coordinated by Kalman Silvert, the Ford Foundation regional program had a significant role in supporting the growth of think tanks and research facilities throughout Latin America. U.S. influence in this regard waned somewhat after the scandal surrounding Project Camelot.

56. F. H. Cardoso and O. Ianni, eds., *Homem e sociedade: Leituras básicas de sociologia geral* (São Paulo: Companhia Editora Nacional, 1961), was used extensively as a text in Brazil. Cardoso's "O método dialético na análise sociológica" (*Revista Brasileira de Ciências Sociais*, 2 [1, Mar] [1962]), also had a pedagogical and methodological intention. Several collections of papers published as books in Chile had a similar orientation: *Cuestiones de sociologia del desarrollo* (Santiago: Editorial Universitaria, 1968); *Mudanças sociais na América Latina* (São Paulo: Difusão Européia do Livro, 1969); and Cardoso and F. Weffort, eds., *América Latina: ensayos de interpretación sociológico-política* (Santiago: Editorial Universitaria, 1970).

57. Many intellectual and policy leaders of late twentieth-century Chile studied with Cardoso, including Genaro Arriagada, Chile's ambassador to the United States in the late 1990s.

58. The self-conscious foundational effort to build the social sciences in Brazil and Latin America is a durable interest in Cardoso's trajectory. The early work on slavery and entrepreneurs shows theoretical and methodological sophistication in the empirical study of historical processes of social stratification and the application of a dialectical approach. These works resulted from large empirical studies funded by diverse national and foreign institutions. They were close to the agenda of the social sciences division at the University of São Paulo. Several essays of the early 1960s probed the origins of industrialization in Brazil and are still useful perspectives in that regard. In the first part of his career, through 1968, Cardoso conducted research and published empirically grounded works on such other themes as education, nationalism and ideology, working-class formation, the relationship between coffee and industrialization, urbanization, marginalization, planning, and research methods (see the bibliography and the bibliographic essay by Danielle Ardaillon).

59. In a personal exchange, Enzo Faletto reminded the author that the CEPAL held an important conference on social actors in Mar del Plata, Argentina, in 1962. *El desarrollo social de América Latina en la pos-guerra* (Santiago: n.p., 1962), is an expression of that effort. As noted earlier, Cardoso has repeatedly acknowledged the significance of the CEPAL and his three years in Santiago in his own professional development.

60. "A nova agenda sociológica da América Latina," in F. H. Cardoso et al., *A utopia viável* (Brasília: Gabinete Pessoal do Presidente da República, 1995). This is a lecture at a ceremony granting him an honorary degree at the Universidad Central de Venezuela, July 6, 1995.

61. But professional social science had begun at least a decade earlier. In São Paulo, the University of São Paulo and the School of Sociology and Politics had trained or hosted professional scholars such as Fernando de Azevedo, Antonio Candido de Melo e Souza, Lucila Hermann, Ruy Coelho, Egon Schaden, Mario Wagner Vieira da Cunha, Oracy Nogueira, Mauro Brandão Lopes, Octavio da Costa Eduardo, Emílio Willems, Herbert Baldus, and others—several of whom were trained in the United States or Europe. See, for example, the journal *Sociologia*, published by the Escola de Sociologia e Política.

62. Preface to *Dependency and Development in Latin America* (Los Angeles and Berkeley: University of California Press, 1979, xi). See also footnote 2 (xi), where Cardoso quotes "a passion for the possible" from Hirschman's *A Bias for Hope* (New Haven, Conn.: Yale University Press, 1971, 27). Hirschman had also pleaded with Latin American intellectuals to give up the focus on failure and crisis, which he dubbed "failure mania" (*fracassomania*). That message, too, found a receptive ear in Cardoso.

63. Such as *Novos Estudos* and various publications at the CEBRAP as well as many other journals and book series (see the bibliography).

64. For example, "L'utopie et le politique: du professeur au président," in S. Parrais and K. Vinaver, eds., *Pour aborder le XXIème siècle avec le développement durable* (Paris: Centre International de Recherche sur l'Environnement et le Développement, 1998); "Las clases sociales y la crisis de Latinoamerica," in Aldo Solari et al., *Poder y desarrollo en América Latina: Estudios sociológicos en homenaje a José Medina Echevarría* (México: Fondo de Cultura Económica, 1977); "La persistencia democrática (Resumen de la conferencia sobre el tema de la democracia en la obra de José Medina Echevarría)," in *Medina Echevarría y la sociología latinoamericana* (Madrid: Ediciones Cultura Hispánica e Instituto de Cooperación Iberoamericana, 1982); "A paixão pelo saber," in M. A. D'Incao, ed., *O saber militante: Ensaios sobre Florestan Fernandes* (São Paulo: Paz e Terra and UNESP, 1987); "Memórias da Maria Antônia," in M. C. Loschiano dos Santos, ed., *Maria Antônia: Uma rua na contramão* (São Paulo: Nobel, 1988); and "Um ex-aluno," in M. A. D'Incão and E. F. Scarabôtolo, eds., *Dentro do texto, dentro da vida: Ensaios sobre Antonio Candido* (São Paulo: Companhia das Letras and Instituto Moreira Salles, 1992). The list of tributes also includes the Chilean Aníbal Pinto and the Argentines Raúl Prebish and Amilcar Herrera.

65. For example, "Livros que inventaram o Brasil," *Novos Estudos* (CEBRAP), 37 (November 1993); several 1978 reviews in *Senhor Vogue* (on major books by Sérgio Buarque de Holanda, Euclydes da Cunha, Gilberto Freyre, Roberto Simonsen, Celso Furtado, Caio Prado Jr., and Paulo Prado); and "A fome e a crença (sobre *Os parceiros do Rio Bonito*)," in *Esboço de figura: Homenagem a Antonio Candido* (São Paulo: Duas Cidades, 1979).

66. Examples include "A cidade e a cultura," in *Abertura Oficial do Centro Cultural de São Paulo, Primeiro Fórum de Debates "A cidade e a cultura,"* vol. 1 (São Paulo: Prefeitura Municipal de São Paulo, 1983); "O brasil no mundo: participação, reformas e modernização," *Revista Brasileira de Comércio Exterior*, 5 (25, Sep–Oct) (1989); "A construção da democracia no Brasil," in *Documentos Cedec*, vol. 1, *Visões da transição* (São Paulo) (1989).

67. For example, "Classes sociais e história: considerações metodológicas," in *Autoritarismo e democratização* (Rio de Janeiro: Paz e Terra, 1975), discusses systems of stratification and modes of production in the export economies of Latin America and the Caribbean. Cardoso's approach to social structure was influenced by Weber and Mannheim.

68. For example, "A cidade e a política: do compromisso ao inconformismo," in *Autoritarismo e democratização* (Rio de Janeiro: Paz e Terra, 1975).

69. Kahl, *Modernization, Exploitation, and Dependency*, 184–188.

70. Packenham, *Dependency Movement*.

71. For a bitter attack along these lines, see Gabriel A. Almond, "The Development of Political Development," in M. Weiner and S. P. Huntington, eds., *Understanding Political Development* (Glenview, Ill.: Scott, Foresman, and London: Little, Brown, 1987, especially "The Dependency Movement"). Almond had been a major figure in the modernization approach dominant in the field of comparative politics in the late 1950s and early 1960s and was at least reacting to the sharply criticized dependency theory directed at that perspective in the 1960s and 1970s.

72. That debate appears in Francisco C. Weffort, "Notas sobre la 'Teoría de la dependencia': Teoría de clase o ideología nacional?" *Revista Latinoamericana de Ciencia Política*, 1 (3, Dec) (1970): 389–401, and Fernando Henrique Cardoso, " 'Teoria de la dependencia' o análisis de situaciones concretas de dependencia?" *Revista Latinoamericana de Ciencia Política*, 1 (3, Dec) (1970): 402–414. These papers were discussed in a seminar of the FLACSO in Santiago de Chile, November 1970. FLACSO (Santiago) had just begun publishing that journal. For relatively early commentary on Cardoso's methods, see Kahl, *Modernization, Exploitation, and Dependency*.

73. Close associates maintain that discussions of Marx's *Grundrisse* at the Marx Seminar and later at the CEBRAP contributed to a strong, early rejection of hard or "vulgar" Marxism.

74. For Cardoso's importance as a social scientist and his relationship to Marx, see also Goertzel, *Fernando Henrique Cardoso*, chapter 7.

75. Cardoso was approached by Professor Robert Bellah for a permanent position at Berkeley, a possibility he declined in favor of returning to Brazil.

76. Alan Riding, "Brazil's Professor-politician: He Stoops to Kisses," *New York Times* 14 March 1988, 4.

77. The *quercistas* managed to place their leader as vice governor in the Montoro campaign in 1983, after which Quércia was elected governor.

78. Itamar Franco, a mercurial politician from Minas Gerais, would eventually become a bitter enemy, claiming that it was he who gave the big opportunity to an ungrateful Cardoso.

79. As finance minister, Cardoso coordinated the work of the team of economists who developed the plan. Members included Pérsio Arida, Edmar Bacha, Gustavo Franco, Pedro Malan, and André Lara Resende. Several of these were members of the economics faculty at the Catholic University of Rio de Janeiro. Most were affiliated with the PSDB, though Malan was not. The key team had also been involved with the ill-fated *Plano Cruzado* of the 1980s, whose failure they had studied carefully. Pompeu de Toledo, *O Presidente segundo o sociólogo*, chapter 5, contains a candid account of the *Plano Real*, including its relationship to debt negotiations with the International Monetary Fund and the absence of a formal endorsement from that body.

80. For a preliminary assessment of the reforms, see David Fleischer, "The Cardoso Government's Reform Agenda: A View from the National Congress, 1995–1998," *Journal of Interamerican Studies and World Affairs*, 40 (4, Winter) (1998): 118–138.

81. The Cardoso government only speeded up a process of restructuring the private sector begun in the early 1990s (see "Reestructuração produtiva e novos padrões nas negociações capital-trabalho," *Cadernos de Pesquisa* [CEBRAP], 1 [June 1994] [which is based on the CEBRAP–DESEP/CUT Seminar, May 4–5, 1993]). Trade liberalization began with the Collor government and continued during Ciro Gomes's brief tenure as finance minister at the end of 1994.

82. The public bureaucracy presented grave problems. The wage bill of the federal government absorbed 45 percent of the huge budget. The federal government had a pension plan under which workers could retire as young as forty-five years of age or even less, with pensions 20 percent higher than their last wage. The situation was worse at the state level. Overreliance on political patronage had led to highly inflated payrolls at all levels of government. State administrations used state banks liberally and for political purposes.

83. See Pompeu de Toledo, *O Presidente segundo o sociólogo*, 288–289. Historically, Cardoso had shared perspectives on the Brazilian state with some of its strongest critics, including Bolivar Lamounier, Luciano Martins, and Hélio Jaguaribe.

84. *Discurso de Posse* (Brasília: Presidência da República Federativa do Brasil, Secretaria de Comunicação Social, January 1, 1995). Pompeu de Toledo, *O Presidente segundo o sociólogo*, chapter 21, discusses state reform, with particular emphasis on privatization, the new regulatory framework, the banking system, industrial policy, and related themes. Chapter 22 touches on educational and agrarian reforms. Cardoso says in this interview, "what took place in Brazil [from the Vargas era through the military regime] was private appropriation [which Cardoso also calls 'privatization' of the state]. I began to write about this since Geisel times. Our problem is that the private sector grafted itself into the state apparatus. The 'bureaucratic rings' and related phenomena I studied were forms of fortification ('acastelamento') between the public and the private, without control by society. What we have then is a state deformed by clientelism, by private interests and by the state's inadequacy in looking after the general interests of the population" (288).

85. "Notas sobre reforma do Estado," *Novos Estudos* (CEBRAP), 50 (March 1998). In this essay, state reforms are justified in order to increase government effectiveness, participation, the workings of the market, sustained economic growth, and the state's capacity to provide basic services and address demands about social needs.

86. Luiz Carlos Bresser Pereira, the minister of state reform during Cardoso's first term, wrote extensively on the fiscal crisis of the state and applied that perspective to the understanding and reform of the Brazilian state. See, for example, *Reform of the State Apparatus* (Brasília: Presidency of the Republic, State Reform Committee White Paper, 1995).

87. Brazilian policymakers had become sensitive to the conceptual contexts. See Fernando Henrique Cardoso, "Notas sobre a reforma do Estado," *Novos Estudos* (CEBRAP), 50 (March 1998): 5–6, and Luciano Martins, *Crise do poder, governabilidade e governança* (Rio de Janeiro: Jose Olimpio, 1995).

88. See "La contrucción de la democracia: desafíos y dificultades," in J. Cotler, ed., *Estrategias para el desarrollo de la democracia en Perú y América Latina* (Lima: Instituto de Estudios Peruanos, 1990); and Pompeu de Toledo, *O Presidente segundo o sociólogo*, chapter 17.

89. One of the most important essays from his days as foreign minister is "North-South Relations in the Present Context: A New Dependency?" in M. Cornoy, M. Castells, S. S. Cohen, and F. H. Cardoso, eds., *The New Global Economy in the Information Age: Reflections on Our Changing World* (University Park: Pennsylvania State University Press, 1993). *Discursos sobre a ordem mundial* (Brasília: Senado Federal, 1991), "Desenvolvimento" is a series of substantive lectures given during his first year as foreign minister.

90. "Desenvolvimento: o mais político dos temas econômicos," *Revista de Economia Política*, 15 (4, Oct–Dec) (1995). First delivered as a lecture upon receiving an honorary degree at Portugal's University of Porto on July 22, 1995, "A utopia viável" is another noteworthy essay from the mid-1990s dealing with development issues. Its title was used later that year in a small volume containing this and other essays (Cardoso et al., *A utopia viável*). This volume contains interesting assessments of Cardoso's work by other authors, including Francisco Weffort, Heinz R. Sonntag, Boaventura de Souza Santos, and José Madureira.

91. "Conseqüências sociais da globalização," presented at Indian International Center, New Delhi, January 27, 1996; "The Impact of Globalization on Developing Countries: Risks and Opportunities," Colégio de México, Mexico City, February 20, 1996 (a somewhat different version of this essay, apparently based on the transcripts of the actual presentation, appears as "La globalización y el nuevo orden mundial," *Estudios Sociológicos*, 15 [43, Jan–Abril] [1997]); and "Globalização e outros temas contemporâneos," University of Witwatersrand, November 27, 1996. (During Cardoso's presidency, these texts were available at: <www.planalto.gov.br/secom/colecao> [last accessed: December 2000].) For a light, journalistic version of Cardoso's position on globalization, see chapter 6 in Pompeu de Toledo's interviews with Cardoso published as *O Presidente segundo o sociólogo*.

92. Cardoso introduced the term "middle-range utopia" in "North-South Relations in the Present Context." He changed the term to "viable utopia" (or "possible utopia") in "A utopia viável."

93. Reali Júnior, "Jospin opõe-se à tese da 'terceira via,' " *O Estado de São Paulo*, 27 April 1999. Available at: <www.estado.com.br/edicao/pano/99/04/26/int829.html>. Last accessed: December 2000.

94. See Pompeu de Toledo, *O Presidente segundo o sociólogo*; and Oscar Pilagallo "Neoliberalismo: Tese defende controle para globalização," *Folha de São Paulo*, 12 July 1999.

95. For education and health policy, see Pompeu de Toledo, *O Presidente segundo o sociólogo*, chapters 20 and 22.

96. Criticisms of Cardoso's presidency tend to come from the left and cluster on the following arguments: (1) that it has embraced the goals of neoliberalism; (2) that the alliance with the center-right PMDB and the PFL has strengthened the right; (3) that Cardoso's political style has reinforced rather than diminished clientelism; and (4) that the stabilization and fiscal adjustment policies have failed to bring economic development (e.g., Cammack, "Cardoso's Political Project in Brazil"). A full discussion of the arguments by Cardoso's critics and commentators is beyond the purposes of this introduction.

97. For example, Timothy Power, "Brazilian Politicians and Neoliberalism: Mapping Support for the Cardoso Reforms," *Journal of Interamerican Studies and World Affairs*, 40 (4, Winter 1998): 51–73, documents an ideological shift away from statism toward the market among legislators. This change at the level of ideology confirms the view that the Brazilian polity as a whole has moved toward a more market-friendly or economically liberal stance. However, conceptualizing this change as neoliberal is debatable, since social democrats have also embraced this movement on grounds other than neoliberal ideology.

98. See also Cammack "Cardoso's Political Project in Brazil." Cammack, a left-leaning critic of Cardoso's program, believes that it correctly maintains its "social democratic" character and disagrees with the view of Cardoso as being a neoliberal.

→ 1 ←

Slavery and Race Relations in Southern Brazil

While the historical research undertaken in the present study has been limited to Rio Grande do Sul, certain interpretations and findings will serve to characterize the structure of slavocratic and post-slavocratic society in other regions of Brazil.

RISE AND DEMISE OF SLAVERY IN RIO GRANDE DO SUL

The economy of Rio Grande do Sul was of secondary importance to Brazil's colonial tropical agroexport economy. In general, slavery did not develop in this state with the same intensity as in those regions where production, being more lucrative, could provide adequate returns to a greater capital investment in the purchase of slaves. Nor did the slavocratic society of Rio Grande do Sul benefit from the same favorable confluence of conditions that characterized the Brazilian export economy. There never existed in Rio Grande do Sul the tropical and colonial products that were capable of generating great profits or quasi-monopolistic rents. However, these peculiarities of Rio Grande do Sul meant that certain essential characteristics of Brazilian slavery were most clearly manifested here, making it a useful case for a dialectical analysis of the relations between the particular and the general.

In their singular configuration, some of the particular characteristics of organization of the Rio Grande do Sul slavocratic system reveal the general patterns of Brazilian slavery. The inability of the servile system of production to maintain itself when faced with the development of capitalism, for example, can be evidenced in an analysis of the slavocratic economy of Rio Grande do Sul. The principal factors that permit

---

Adapted with permission from Fernando Henrique Cardoso, *Capitalismo e escravidão no Brasil meridional: o negro na sociedade escravocrata do Rio Grande do Sul* (São Paulo: Difusão Européia do Livro, 1962), "Conclusion," 307–316.

this understanding are found exactly in the peculiarities of the Rio Grande do Sul economy. First, the dried meats economy produced in preindustrial, and not agrarian, conditions. Second, dried meats and leather suffered direct competition from industrial capitalist production and were never dominant products in international markets. They were therefore unable to benefit from the favorable terms capable of generating large profits independent of the social, economic, and technical conditions of production. Given these unique conditions, capitalist production, which permitted earnings from relative surplus value, needed to be implanted in Rio Grande do Sul in order for its products to compete. At the same time, it could not be implanted, due to slavery. In this tension, a characteristic of the servile regime is revealed that, while operating in other circumstances and other regions, remained obscured by the functioning of the slavocratic regime in the export sectors of the economy.

Slave hands were used regularly in Rio Grande do Sul starting from the development of mercantilist export production. From that moment forward, the functional balance of the economic system was dependent on a steady stream of imported Africans. Plantation society, which was formed through the complex juxtaposition of pastoral family groups during the era of territorial conquest, thus had its pattern of structural integration redefined. The superposition of the stratum of masters over that of slaves progressively constituted the basic structural nexus of Rio Grande do Sul society.

The material and moral conditions of existence favored, in the colonial period, the formation of a precarious economy, based on mercantilist rent-seeking from the livestock existing in the region. The continuation of this economy depended on the spatial mobility and the coercive capacity of small groups of freemen, led by chiefs who held the power and personal traits necessary for regular predatory activity. When the conditions of struggle between Spaniards and Portuguese permitted the stabilization of dominant groups, plantations (*estâncias*) were organized and the exploitation of slaves began. However, the functions performed by the slaves were ancillary to the activities of the productive economy. The possession of slaves was neither decisive in guaranteeing economic success, nor in assuring positions of prestige for family group leaders. The structure of colonial society in this phase was upheld by the position that the family leaders occupied as landowners and was independent of slave ownership. The domination of the patrimonial functionaries of the Portuguese state, also imposed by violence, compounded the domination exercised by the "family bosses." The major significance of the link between the state and individual producers was that, in the initial appropriation of land, the good favor, the support, and the interest of civil and military functionaries of the crown were essential for the legitimate and effective possession of the means of production.

After the intensification of the flow of trade between the Rio Grande do Sul region and the consumer market linked to the export sectors of the Brazilian economy, new conditions were created for the economic activity of Rio Grande do Sul. Production was reorganized to respond to the large-scale demand for rice, dried meats, and leather. Historically, this process was manifested by the strengthening of the power and the wealth of those families that had appropriated land and livestock. Simultaneously, the regular use of slaves as a basic part of the labor force was applied to the production of merchandise for export. The solution was imposed when landowners were faced with labor shortages and the lack social conditions for the employment of salaried labor.

The new conditions of production led to the reintegration of the social order. The progressive accumulation of wealth of families and the possession of a means of production, such as the slave, which was independent of the direct and immediate competition of the crown, brought about a redefinition of the structure of power in Rio Grande do Sul. State patrimonialism was substituted for a form of patrimonialism closer to patriarchalism: the autonomous power of group chiefs; the pater famílias (whose power came from his status as head of groups of freemen and owner of land and labor of his family) was transformed into a slave owner; and the royal functionaries, for their part, used the power they disposed of to transform themselves into economic producers and lords, mingling their interests with those of the master stratum, for whom they became a political expression. They threw themselves, in this way, into slavocratic domination: the possession of slaves became an essential condition for the production of merchandise and for the exercise of power, and this in turn depended directly on the capacity of each lord to produce these.

From this perspective, it is possible to understand that a slavocratic society was constituted as an attempt to intensify production in order to realize profits in the market. The only form historically capable of reaching this objective was through the intensification of slavery. With this, the specificity of "modern slavery" in Rio Grande do Sul was determined. Simultaneously, it became possible to establish rules for the functioning of the slavocratic-capitalist society as well as the limits that the society itself imposed.

Thus, the slavocratic enterprise in Rio Grande do Sul can be seen as an attempt to respond to the need to intensify production, which was created by the expansion of the country's domestic market. In other words, the expansion of the national consumer market (meats and, to some degree, leather), fed by the development of the export economy (of sugar and coffee), reached and affected premercantilist production in the economically marginal parts of the country. While the integration of the emerging exchange economy of Rio Grande do Sul to the larger market revolutionized the techniques and organization of the economic enterprise in the area, it did it on the basis of slave labor, which was the only resource available to obtain the desired end, due to the sociohistorical conditions of the Brazilian economy. With this, a fundamental contradiction was introduced into the social economic system. The relations of production from which it was planned to intensify mercantile capitalist production impeded the full development of the capitalist regime, to the extent that this required the commodification of the labor force and slavery constituted the commodification of the laborer himself.

As long as slavocratic mercantilist production functioned in economic conditions that permitted high profits, and as long as the supply of slave labor was steady and cheap, the fragility inherent in the system due to the basic contradiction that defined it did not become apparent. It was not impressed upon the social conscience of the producers, nor did it seriously affect the resources that they disposed of to promote structural and functional integration. When the supply of hands stopped and competition altered the favorable terms of trade in the market, the contradiction in the system as a whole was exposed. This in turn permitted criticism of the servile order by those groups that were not direct beneficiaries of slavery.

That point coincided with and was intensified by the decline of slavery in Brazil that occurred with the cessation of the slave trade, and from then on the desegregation of the slavocratic regime in Rio Grande do Sul was continual and accelerating. The efforts made to save the slavocratic enterprise only served to reaffirm the unfeasibility of the system when faced with the new state of the economy, and its new economic ventures in the region, organized on the basis of free labor. Only the incapacity of some groups of slave owners to adjust to the emerging situation led them to insist on continuing slavery in an attempt to save their businesses.

The decline of slavery provoked a readjustment of social groups and social strata. On the one hand, the dichotomy between the caste of slaves and the caste of lords, which expressed the basic relations of production, slowly unraveled against the emerging class-based social order. The new mode of production benefited those groups of property owners and capitalists not directly linked to the slavocratic past (such as immigrants and urban merchants), and worked to the detriment of the former slave lords. Increasingly, positioning in the market came to define the possibilities for obtaining social prestige, for political control of the province, and for new economic ventures. These possibilities occurred independent of whether one belonged to the lords' stratum.

On the other hand, the reintegration of the order occurred in a way as to impede the more general consequences that could have followed from abolition. Former slave owners were at a relative disadvantage and were unable to redefine immediately the forms of economic activity. Despite this, an analysis of the process of abolition and of the desegregation of the servile order shows that the reintegrated society favored groups that had been dominant under the slavocratic order. Immigration was promoted and conditions created for reevaluating the wage labor necessary for the success of the capitalist system. There was no movement, however, that revealed any conscience or social responsibility on the part of Whites for the degraded social situation of Blacks, nor was there any redefinition of attitudes or expectations favorable to Blacks.

The immediate result of the direction assumed by the process of social reintegration was the type of adjustment that Blacks had to develop in order to participate in the forming class society. They did not have the economic opportunities to assume fully the status of a citizen that abolition had formally provided them, nor could they even critically define the position that Whites imposed upon them in the class society, as we will emphasize in the next section.

THE NEGRO IN A CASTE SOCIETY AND IN A CLASS SOCIETY

The conditions of existence for the slave confirm and expand upon known sociological findings on the situation of the Black in Brazilian caste society. In all systems of social intercourse in which slaves participated in Rio Grande do Sul, the basic condition was alienation from the qualities of the human person. The definition of a slave as an object, and the incapacity of the slave to realize his own social designs, or to even conceive of them, marked his social condition. The violent manner by which the lords imposed their interests on the slaves, thereby completing the transformation of the slave into an instrument, expresses the specific form that seigniorial domination took in slavocratic society. Slavery is a system of domination in which one can see in its purest form a relation obscured in any other social system based on the superposition of strata with antagonistic interests. The system was perpetuated by the exercise of violence. The image of the slave as object came from the compliance with the action that the masters of the slavocratic regime imposed through continuous and open coercion, and by the socialization of the slave to violence in the tasks to be completed for the masters. Beyond this, in situations in which the slavocratic regime developed slaves more fully, they were socialized only for the tasks of slave-based production. In this way, the system protected itself from possible reactions on the part of the captives, destroying possibilities for coordinated action against the system. The slave became a partial being, only capable of the most menial forms of labor. For this, partial socialization, inadequate as it was for the development of the human personality, and constant violence constituted the basic mechanisms of the perpetuation of the slavocratic order.

In these situations in which the principal needs of the slavocratic order could be developed in Rio Grande do Sul, the alienation of the slave tended to be complete. The lords represented the slaves as instruments of production and slaves represented themselves as incapable of behaving as free men. Partial socialization and institutionalized violence worked to obtain this result. However, the alienation of the slave in the plan of representations hardly reflected the real situation of the Negro in slavocratic mercantile society. If, in every slavist system, the master-slave relationship is based on social asymmetry and the compliance of the latter assured by violence that leads to reification, in servile society organized as a resource for capitalist mercantile production the slave became merchandise, de facto. Thus, if in the plantations the reification of the slave was relative, in the preparation of meats, the slave effectively performed the functions of an object, and was represented as objective capital.

The relations between masters and slaves, however, were not analyzed in this book from the perspective mentioned earlier. This volume also sought to confront dynamically and concretely the situation of slaves. It considered the inherent contradictions in the general determinations of the master-slave relationship, as well as the differences and contradictions that historically were being constructed at the particular situations of social existence that were configured in Rio Grande do Sul. In effect, the reification of the slave only appeared complete. In truth, the slave subjectively negated the condition imposed upon him and sought to transform, within existing social boundaries, the social situation in which he was placed. Through violent reactions against institutionalized slave owner violence and constant flight, the slave expressed the fundamental quality of man, negating in practice the representation that was being made of him as a being only capable of realizing the will and interests of those who were his social opposites. Thus, slavery was the fire on which society was forged, and it became a fount of violence for both master and slave.

The lords ultimately became another expression of the same alienation. Creators and products of a system designed to provide profits that wound up impeding growth in profits, they too ultimately became socially alienated beings. Whatever desiderata they may have had depended on their enemies, the slaves. Finally, they became victims of their own creation: they clung to the slavocratic system even when it was no longer able to produce the desired profits.

Moreover, due in part to the peculiar situation of the slave in the mercantile capitalist slavocracy, the dialectic between masters and slaves did not express the determinant movement in the social process, and the reaction of the slave was destined to manifest itself as revolt and not as action capable of reconstructing the social order on the basis of its own interests. The essential relations that guided the course of events was based on the contradiction between the need imposed by the capitalist mode of production to intensify relative surplus value production and the unfeasibility of this process in a society whose production was based on slave labor.

Thus, in the same way that in the capitalist regime the operator constituted the true limit, in the slavocratic-capitalist regime, the slave was himself the limit of the system. But insofar as in the first case the contradiction between the operator and the capitalist system may be resolved dialectically, in the second case the contradiction cannot be superseded by any action of the slave. On the contrary, the meaning of this disaggregation of the servile order is given by the groups that historically have been capable of overcoming the dominant contradiction between capitalist expansion and the barrier imposed upon it by slavery. Suppressing the slave while preserving the operator was the conscious expression of the movement of disintegration of the slavocratic order in benefit of the groups involved in the generalization of wage labor.

Historically, however, the slaves varied in their forms of social existence. The differences may be irrelevant in the characterization of the slavocratic domination and in defining the possibilities of alteration of the social order in a way as to attend to the social interests of the slaves; they did not fail, however, to influence the social consciences of the captives or the possibilities of adjustment of the former slaves to the new order created with the disintegration of the servile regime.

Effectively, the analysis realized in this monograph has showed (and this was one of the principal results) the forms of consciousness possible in the situation and the effective forms of consciousness that limited the action of the slaves. The modes of insertion of slaves into productive activity circumscribed the universe of ends and objectives that would polarize their interests and their social behavior. The essential determinants of the condition of the slave in the capitalist-slavocratic society limited the possibilities of altering the order so as to conform to his social interests and circumscribed as a lateral question the presumed "point of view" of the slaves. However, the particular forms by which the slaves integrated themselves into the productive process (in the slaughterhouse, in the urban market, in the family, or on the plantation) opened to them the various possibilities of reaction to Whites and of social readjustment in the phase of the formation of class society.

In Rio Grande do Sul, it is possible to distinguish two basic types of adjustment of Blacks into the new order of classes created after abolition. The large number of slaves that were socially and culturally unprepared for the exercise of the possibilities of social action inherent in the quality of citizen that Blacks had acquired, adjusted passively, conforming to the interests of the ancient master stratum and of the Whites in general. With these, Whites sought to redefine the representations that they maintained regarding slaves, metamorphosing them in a way as to rationalize the social denigration of free Blacks, and compelling them to accept the sense that they wanted to give to the new forms of social participation of the former captives. Thus, for Whites, the Black, from social inferior in the caste society, became the biological inferior in class society. The "prejudice" appeared in the new context as a technique of adjustment between the ethnic groups, necessarily beginning with the previous recognition of the existence of social inequalities, expressed as a form of natural inequalities. Many Blacks effectively facilitated this situation by accepting the idea of the "ideal of whitening" and by the stimulus to an "ideology of compromise" that legitimated the prejudice and accepted the social differentiations that the Whites wanted to impose on Blacks for being black.

The second form of adjustment was the attempt at critical reaction against the social denigration imposed by Whites on Blacks. This reaction began with former slaves, or their descendants, linked to urban artisanship or domestic slavery. Slaves of this type could, benefiting from better material and moral conditions, attempt to construct a new consciousness of the situation of alienation and social deprivation that had been reduced. The attempt at formulation of a new "ideology of negritude" and the struggle against prejudice were the resources utilized for the resocialization of Blacks, for the attempt to reeducate Whites, and for the transformation of moral and material conditions of the Black community. These efforts constituted the most important attempts that Rio Grande do Sul Blacks could undertake in their struggle against social alienation.

The global conditions of the formation of the society of classes and the effective sense of the process of disaggregation of the servile order, already indicated, did not favor, however, in this phase, that Blacks might obtain their insertion into the social order in a quality equal to that of Whites, as they (formally) became after abolition. The lack of success of these attempts puts in evidence, also, the precariousness of the new democratic order that was supposed to have been implanted in the country, and the persistence of accentuated traces of the ancient régime in the class society, which was being formed.

⇥ 2 ⇤

Industrialists and Brazilian Development: The Early 1960s

Economic development cannot be understood if one ignores the political and social conditions of development, and it is not sufficient to refer to these as if they were simply "complementary factors." Insofar as development is a social process, social shifts are junctures that reveal the nature and direction of the development process. For this reason, abstract models of development are as insufficient in explaining the structural changes that enable development, as they are in explaining the transfer of the growth of capitalism from the countries where it originated to underdeveloped countries. The alternative is to relate underdeveloped countries with industrialized nations and to determine how "economic development" is the result of a social shift that affects the structure of international domination.

Viewed from this angle, the "march toward development" goes beyond efforts to expand the formation of a national bourgeoisie. If the industrial entrepreneur is not the demiurge of the crown, then the bourgeoisie as a class is not necessarily, in underdeveloped countries, the springboard of development. In Brazil, the passage from an agroexport economy to an industrializing economy can be seen in two key moments. In the first moment, developmentalist pressures emerged outside the private sector of the economy, as a political aspiration for economic emancipation. In the second, the industrial bourgeoisie, in association with foreign economic interests, attempted to direct the development process to the benefit of the productive private sector. The conditions of insertion of these strata into the social structure, which initially propelled development, limited the possibilities of controlling the direction that it was going to take on. In the same manner, the particular conditions of the national bourgeoisie—linked to international capital and blocked by the traditional

---

Adapted with permission from Fernando Henrique Cardoso, *Empresário industrial e desenvolvimento econômico no Brasil* (São Paulo: Difusão Européia do Livro, 1972), "Conclusion," 192–198.

structure of local domination that it never succeeded in breaking—meant the process of development came to be choked off at certain points, and the political domination of the industrial bourgeoisie was incomplete and contradictory. In the same way, in the analysis of the mentality of businessmen, we circumscribe the types of industrialists to the conditions of the market and of production. Heads of industry, "captains" of industry, and businessmen were the typical categories that, connected with the categories that express "imperfect competition" and "monopolistic competition," and the duality typical between these two types of markets, will permit us to learn the various mentalities and modes of business action. The particular attributes of the behavior of the industrialists, as for example the valuation of hard labor or the taste for risk, had their functions redefined in every moment of the creation of the capitalist market. That which was a positive factor in economic development in one phase became negative in the subsequent phase. For which it may be said that it was not the particular attributes of a type of mentality that, in and of itself, gave rise to entrepreneurial success and gave it direction. On the contrary, they became favorable or unfavorable depending on the situation in which they found themselves, and this "situation" transcended the level of the enterprise. Even so, the capacity for "redefinition" of the orientation of the businessmen, after which a given conjuncture was altered, became essential for the success of every enterprise. For this, it is not appropriate to treat the concrete attributes of the entrepreneurs as "mere epiphenomena." The problem is showing how they were linked to a larger situation that gave them direction, without at the same time relegating them to the level of "mere appearances." The creation of "new market conditions," a process that transcended business action, was fundamental in explaining the transformation of the entrepreneurial mentality, but the analysis was complemented by the discussion of the concrete characteristics of the entrepreneurial mentality that enabled the integration of innovations into effective industrial practice. The "business mentality" sometimes appeared in Brazil as a response to situations created by other social groups that were not businessmen, sometimes as a condition for the creation of new situations based on the interests of the national bourgeoisie. The relative weight of the "entrepreneurial mentality" in the development process varied with the industrial bourgeoisie, which as a class reacted to the pressures emanating from other social groups or tried, as in the present, to develop a policy capable of imposing a social development path compatible with its interests.

Stuck between the traditional motivations and interests that bind it on the one hand to the landed élites (*latifúndio*) and traditional existence, and on the other hand to international capital to which it was associated in order to create economic growth, the industrial bourgeoisie sees itself in the position of realizing a policy on the cliff's edge. At times, it reacts to the immobility that traditional groups hoped to maintain as a limit on the politics and economy of the country, and at other times, it reacts against urban and popular pressures that tended to break the routine. It hesitates not because it recognizes its real interests, but because these interests are contradictory. To affirm itself as the politically dominant class and in order to expand economically, the industrial bourgeoisie is forced to support reforms and measures that oppose the interests of traditionally dominant groups. However, following this, in this same movement of modernization, it contradicts itself by opposing the only allies it can count on in its delicate situation: the urban and popular forces. To assure economic expansion and to try to gain political control of the moment, the risk is losing hegemony in the future. For this reason, it turns itself against its own interests immediately after any step forward, retreating a little in the present in order not to lose the whole future. This juggling act could not be maintained indefinitely. The range of possible compromises gets narrower with each day. The fundamental decisions will not only depend on the industrial bourgeoisie that appears to have opted for "order," that is, for abdicating once and for all the complete hegemony of society, already satisfied to be the minority shareholder of Western capitalism and the vanguard (*guarda avançada*) of the slowly capitalizing agriculture. It remains to be seen what the reaction of the urban masses and the popular groups will be, and what capacity for organization and decision they will be capable of to advance political modernization and the national economic development process. In the end, the question will be this: Subcapitalism or socialism?

⇥ 3 ⇤

Dependency and Development in Latin America: Summary

This book attempts to reconsider the problems of economic development through an interpretation emphasizing the political character of the processes of economic transformation. At the same time, we try to demonstrate that the historical situation in which the economic transformations occur must be taken into account if these changes as well as their structural limitations are to be understood.

This formulation of the relation between economic process, structural conditions, and historical situations makes clear that theoretical schemes concerning the formation of capitalist society in present-day developed countries are of little use in understanding the situation in Latin American countries. Not only the historical moment but also the structural conditions of development and society are different. Recognizing these differences, we go on to criticize the concepts of underdevelopment and economic periphery and to stress both the economic aspects of underdevelopment and the political process by which some countries dominate others. We stress the specificity of installations of capitalist production in dependent societies.

We return to the tradition of political thought that there is no metaphysical relation of dependence between one nation and another, between one state and another. These relations are made possible through a network of interests and coercions that bind some social groups to others, some classes to others. This being the case, it is necessary to determine the way in which state, class, and production are related in each basic situation of dependence.

To characterize these relations, we show that Latin American class relations can be defined both in terms of the relationship between the production system and the international market and in terms of the form of control of production. Defining class

Adapted from Fernando Henrique Cardoso and Enzo Faletto, *Dependency and Development in Latin America*, trans. and ed. Marjory Urquidi (Los Angeles: University of California Press, 1979), "Conclusions," 172–176. Used by permission of the publisher. © 1979 The Regents of the University of California.

relations in these ways reveals two basic historical situations. In one case, we point to the specificity of the enclave economies; in the other, to national control of the export system.

We go on to indicate how these historical transformations occur in particular social formations, and we avoid the two fallacies frequently found in similar interpretations: a belief that the internal or national, socio-political situation is molded by external dominance; and the mechanically conditioned opposite idea that all is due to historical contingency. In fact, even the relation of dependence does not mean that national history in dependent nations will simply reflect changes in the external hegemonic center, although these changes are relevant to the possible autonomy of national history. There are structural limits to possible action, beginning with the available material base of production and the degree of development of the forces of production, and including the way in which these are combined with political and juridical relations within the country and its link with the hegemonic countries. Through the actions of groups, classes, organizations, and social movements in the dependent countries, these links are perpetuated, modified, or broken. Therefore, there is an internal dynamic that explains the course of events and thereby makes possible a political analysis.

We show how the different structural possibilities of an enclave situation and of a situation in which the export system is nationally controlled affect the social, political, and economic changes that take place in the countries under consideration.

In the final chapters we return to the general topic of the structural conditionalist development in dependent countries. We characterize the contradictions between the pattern of dependent industrialization and the interests of the nation, as well as the conflicts in the relations among classes and social groups and between the latter and the state.

We also try to show the relative autonomy, the conflict, and the possibilities of convergence between the economic system and the political process. We point out that for an understanding of the present situation of the industrialized and dependent countries of Latin America, an analysis is required of the increasing control over the economic system of nations by large multinational corporations.

The originality of the hypothesis is not in its recognition of the existence of external domination—an obvious process. It is in its description of the form and the effects of this type of dependence on classes and state with reference to past situations. The present situation of dependent development goes beyond the traditional dichotomy between the terms "development" and "dependence," because it permits an increase in development while maintaining and redefining the links of dependency. The present situation is supported politically by a system of alliances that are different from those that previously assured external hegemony. It is no longer the exporting interests that subordinate the interests associated with the domestic market, nor rural interests that oppose urban ones as an expression of economic domination. The specificity of the present situation of dependence is in part that internal interests are rooted more and more in the sector producing for the domestic market and thus that they are united in political alliances that are supported by urban populations. The formation of an industrial economy in the periphery of the capitalist system minimizes the effects of the typically colonial exploitation; this economy incorporates not only the dominant classes but also social groups tied to modern capitalist production, such as wage earners, technicians, entrepreneurs, and bureaucrats. The great political movements that try to form and strengthen the domestic market and the national economy populism and nationalism lose meaning in the new situation of dependence.

We speculate how far dependence can be maintained within the transformation described, or whether it will have to be replaced by interdependence. In this connection, we analyze the specificity of the structural situation together with the political situation. It is shown that the power interests and the alliances to guarantee the hegemony of internal and external groups and class factions have to be considered if the situation of diversification of the economic system is to be explained.

The basic economic conditions of development are an open market, the exclusion of the dependent economies from the markets of the most developed countries, and the continuous transfer of new units of external capital in the form of advanced technology, which are more appropriate to the intrinsic needs of the mature economies than to those of the relatively backward economies. The combination of these conditions with the ideologies and legal relations among social groups makes possible "industrial economics in dependent societies." Whether the structural barriers to development remain or are overcome will be determined by how these economic conditions are used in the power game rather than by the particular economic conditions themselves. In this sense, we suggest that present or potential opposition may vitalize the industrialized and dependent countries of Latin America. There are structural possibilities for various types of social and political movements.

The course of history depends largely on the daring of those who propose to act in terms of historically viable goals. We do not try to place theoretical limits on the probable course of future events. These will depend, not on academic predictions, but on collective action guided by political wills that make work what is structurally barely possible.

⇢ 4 ⇠

Dependency and Development
in Latin America: Post Scriptum

Although ten years have elapsed since this book was written, we have maintained its original structure and interpretations, for any attempt to bring it up to date would be futile. We have not dealt with all the historically significant situations that occurred in Latin America, nor have we emphasized the description of specific events or circumstances. Rather, we only wished to delineate the main tendencies of the historical-structural development. Moreover, the last ten years have been too rich in significant events for us to have the illusion that we could summarize them in a few additional pages.

The main theme of our essay is the relationship that exists between political struggles of groups and classes, on the one hand, and the history of economic-political structures of domination, both internal and external, on the other. Thus, it is of less interest to us to catalogue events than to seek in them the meaning of basic structural relationships and the stages of their development in their double determination: on the level of local systems of domination and on the level of their relationship with the international order. Political and economic processes appear in the latter as if they were the expression of a struggle between nation-states, but they also involve conflicts between social groups and classes.

In order to explain the historical process from the theoretical perspective of dependence, we must make explicit how international conflicts between states are linked with internal political struggles as well as with the basic ways whereby, both domestically and internationally, the social organization of economic production takes place.

Adapted from Fernando Henrique Cardoso and Enzo Faletto, *Dependency and Development in Latin America*, trans. and ed. Marjory Urquidi (Los Angeles: University of California Press, 1979), "Post Scriptum," 177–215. Used by permission of the publisher. © 1979 The Regents of the University of California. This essay appeared for the first time in the 1979 English version of *Dependencia y desarrollo en América Latina*.

It should be enough to mention some of the important events in Latin American history to suggest that certain fundamental transformations took place in the world during the last ten years, and that those changes were not merely episodic but rather reflect a change in the structural relationships between the two great contemporary socioeconomic systems, capitalism and socialism, as well as within each of them:

- the stabilization and progress of the Cuban socialist regime;
- the "capitalist road" of development, such as manifested itself in the Brazilian "economic miracle," accompanied by a military regime;
- the experiment of the "electoral road" to socialism in Chile and the "destabilization" practices to destroy it;
- Peruvian military reformism and the attempts at autonomy, under military regimes, in Panama (and, more episodically, in Bolivia and Ecuador between 1972 and 1975);
- the arduous road of guerrilla efforts which, although begun before the last ten years, were militarily and politically defeated only recently in Peru, Venezuela, Guatemala, Bolivia, Santo Domingo, Brazil, and Uruguay;
- the persistence of an embryonic state of popular guerrilla insurrections in Argentina before and after the second Peronist government, and of guerrilla nuclei of lesser importance in Colombia and Nicaragua, as well as the emergence of unexpected forms of protest against the dominant order in Mexico since the student movement that led to the tragic episode of Tlalteloco;
- the emergence of Caribbean countries in the Latin American political scene, with Guyana's popular-autonomist strategies, the repressive-enlightened traditionalism of Trinidad-Tobago, and the attempts at articulation between these countries and Jamaica;
- Honduras's populist militarism, its war with El Salvador, and the "stability" of the rest of the area, including Guatemala and Nicaragua;
- the same "stabilization" in the Caribbean, both in the Dominican Republic and in Haiti, after the family succession;
- the persistence of caudillo-style militarism in Paraguay, reinforced by alliances with Brazil (a process anticipating the direction Bolivia would take, after General Banzer's coup);
- finally, almost like an archeological find, the survival of traditional bipartisan elitist democracy in Colombia, and the shakier experimentation with partisan and democratic practices in Venezuela, which, because of oil, has presented the most spectacular rate of economic growth in the area;
- and one might mention the political movements in colonial areas such as Puerto Rico, the Guianas, and several islands and enclaves in the Caribbean, including the Panama Canal Zone.

This bird's-eye view of recent history should suffice to indicate that one or even several new books would be necessary to replace the facile adjectives used above with an analysis of the historical processes involved.

Even so it seems necessary to refer in this post scriptum to the basic tendencies underlying those processes. We shall limit ourselves to a discussion of three general topics: the great changes in the capitalist system and in the international order; the implications for international politics of Latin American participation in world affairs; and the reorganization of the internal political order, especially of the state, in Latin America, together with the reaction of popular movements.

THE REORGANIZATION OF WORLD ECONOMIC ORDER AND MULTINATIONAL CORPORATIONS

In chapter six we considered the effects of the penetration of multinational corporations into Latin American countries. What was but a trend ten years ago is today a marked fact, not only in Latin America but also throughout the fringes of the capitalist world. However, we believe that this phenomenon—the preeminence of multinational corporations—should be analyzed in a global perspective that gives due value to the role of politics in the reorganization of the international economic order. It would be an error, according to the approach proposed in this book, to analyze those political transformations independently from the dynamics of the capitalist system as a whole. The system, in turn, evolves on an international level, and thus it is continuously faced with the presence and the challenge created by the existence of socialist economies and countries. It is therefore necessary to make an effort to understand the predominance and the limitations of international corporations within this wider context. We shall attempt to clarify only three points in this topic: the significance of the reorganization of world capitalism for central economies; the effects of this process on peripheral economies; and finally the relationships between this process and the national state.

The first question is essential to an understanding of some of the difficulties in the contemporary international economy. After World War II, this economy expanded under the uncontested hegemony of the American economy. This process of expansion was rooted in the impact of the American military victory, in the instability of the national states in postwar Europe, as well as in the drain caused by the war effort on the Soviet economy. It was also based on the intrinsic dynamism typical of an oligopolistic economy of large enterprises, and was supported by important technological achievements that were accelerated by the war. The relative advantages of the American economy were undeniable: the political and military predominance of the United States was made manifest by atomic supremacy; and the technological capacity and the increased introduction on the market of new products that could hardly be rivaled reinforced the initial advantage and assured the United States unmistakable leadership in the capitalist world. The value of the dollar and its adoption as reserve currency reflected that reality. Control of international economy by the United States was insured by postwar financial agreements, particularly by the Bretton Woods Agreement, as well as by American control of world trade, which was codified by tariff agreements established by an international conference on the matter (GATT), and also by the establishment of an international mechanism of monetary control (the International Monetary Fund), both under the political domination of the United States. The price paid for this position—especially in the Cold War climate—was the militarization of the American economy and the related notion that the United States should assume a protective role in the "free world." Despite the economic effort imposed by such a policy, control of the international market rewarded the United States Treasury with profit. Because of the surplus in the balance of trade, it was possible both to keep armies abroad and to invest outside the United States. The dollar continued to function as a compass to guide the health of the world economy.

It was under such circumstances that American corporations increased their action in the periphery of the capitalist system, as well as in European countries, by means of increased investments and expansion of their control over local economies. To this end, they invested funds and used their domestic savings primarily to purchase assets belonging to nationals. Later, the profits created by the "foreign sector" of the American economy forced it to expand continually abroad. If we add to all this the reconstruction policy carried out in Europe, we shall have an idea of the power of the American economy. In short, the United States assumed the role of bankers and stockholders in industrial and service companies, and of world policeman. In return, it offered the Western world defense against the Soviets, an industrial-technological civilization, and preservation of "basic values" (among which was the type of economy which assured the United States international predominance).

However, the end of the Cold War and several socialist successes, as well as the renewed strength of the capitalist economies in Europe and Japan (stemming in part from their refusal to defray the costs of defense against the Soviets), began to unbalance the international capitalist order. More and more was required from the Treasury, and United States administrations were led to pressure the allies for a "more responsive" and less competitive attitude. Several factors contributed to this situation. One was the very economic progress brought about by the United States through its investments; another was the more or less permanent technological revolution of the postwar decades and its dissemination and marketing, particularly by Japan and Germany (e.g., the coming of the jet, the space race, transistorization, computerization—in a word, the "communications revolution" with all of its economic consequences—as well as the growing use of synthetic materials and electronic products, etc.). There were also the increased responsibilities of the United States vis-à-vis competition from the Soviet Union, which challenged it first with Gagarin's flight and then by showing itself capable of competing in the atomic race and perhaps of surpassing the United States in conventional armaments.

The allies' response was varied. There was the Gaullist insubordination, which resulted in France's nuclear policy and in its leaving NATO, in addition to more direct consequences on an economic level, such as limitations on American penetration into the French economy, disputes concerning aircraft (the Mirage and the Concorde), and systematic attacks against the supremacy of the dollar. Since the 1960s the French have proposed that gold be substituted for the dollar as the international reserve currency. There was, on the other hand, the growing acquiescence to American pressures on the part of the British economy. Somewhere between the two, the Germans and Japanese took advantage of their strategic position in international confrontation and made concessions in political and military matters, but not in commercial ones.

Even more important, however, the very success of American companies abroad— that is, the multinationals—paradoxically caused difficulties for the American economy. Those corporations accumulated financial assets abroad, thus putting pressure on the United States Treasury, since the growth rate of the investments abroad went up faster than the export rate. By early 1970, it was becoming apparent that American expansion abroad had stimulated the other developed capitalist economies faster than it had the American national economy itself, and that the productivity and technological development of the foreign economies, paradoxically fostered by American penetration, had made them competitive.

None of this means that the American economy "has reached its limits," a static idea which helps little in an understanding of history. It does mean, however, that intercapitalist contradictions have sharpened, and that the threat both to the dollar and to the institutions set up at the end of the war to control the international economy was no longer based, during the 1970s, exclusively on General De Gaulle's policies (which preached the devaluation of the dollar and the need to reorganize the capitalist economic order). In addition, the threat was supported by the behavior of multinational corporations, many of which had their headquarters in the United States. The deficits of the Treasury were matched by the financial solvency of the multinationals, converted into "foreign" currencies: marks, yens, Swiss francs, and French francs. Several runs on the dollar, sometimes stimulated by speculation on the part of the multinationals, but actually based on the imbalance of trade and military expenditures, began to show that serious problems were brewing.

Added to these structural pressures against American economic hegemony were the growing costs of the inglorious Vietnam war and the 1973 oil crisis, brought about not only by OPEC but also by the fact that the oil multinationals adjusted themselves to OPEC policies and benefited from them more than was proportionate. As a result, the dollar crisis became evident, and a domestic inflationary process took hold in the United States. Important measures would have to be taken to set things straight again.

American reaction did not take long. In 1974, Project Independence was initiated to increase oil production and technology; the International Energy Agency was created as a response to OPEC, and the 1974 Trade Reform Act, with its protectionist policies, aimed at safeguarding the position of the United States in the world market. Unemployment, the fight against inflation, and credit control compounded Nixon's and Ford's measures. Thus, at the cost of restrictions on the Third World, of pressures on the Japanese and European allies (who, with the exception of France, joined the "autonomist" efforts of the United States), and at the expense of the American people, who paid the cost of "stagflation" and unemployment, the bases were set for

American Big Business to regain international economic control. In this process the multinational corporations and the United States government complemented rather than fought each other. If results are not so brilliant in the future as in the past, this will be because, in spite of everything, America has lost some of its capacity to control the international political order, and a price will have to be paid for this. The defeats in Vietnam and Southeast Asia, recognition of China, the impossibility of intervening in Africa, side by side with a more appeasing policy toward the Arab countries, have all been the direct expression of a rebalancing of international order. Political facts like these establish the limits for reorganization of the international capitalist economy, but at the same time they are themselves conditioned by it. This picture explains the viability of the moderate and marginally autonomist policies of some peripheral countries: the international political equilibrium has been disrupted, and as a result, more room to maneuver is open to new political situations in the Third World.

It was in the context we have briefly summarized above that multinational corporations expanded in Latin America and in the rest of the world. This expansion has contributed to speculation concerning the future of capitalist economy and the role that the state plays in it. In accord with a recently proposed characterization,[1] three fundamental ways of considering the relationship between the state and the multinationals may be mentioned:

- The liberal theory, followed by those who accept the "sovereignty at bay" model proposed by Raymond Vernon. This model sees in the multinationals the nucleus of future progress and the rationalizing principle of a New World market integrated under their control, and in which the state will play a marginal role.
- The "dependence" model, which denies the balancing effect of multinationals in the redistribution of wealth and benefits on a world scale. This model emphasizes that technical progress and financial control of the results of international expansion are concentrated in a few capitalist centers, which will go on exploiting and preserving the dependence and underdevelopment of the periphery. Despite the critical view of this model, the multinationals remain privileged actors in the world scene.[2]
- The mercantile model, which underlines the importance of the nation-state as a reorienting principle of world order, and which believes that the question of the future is not so much the disappearance of states and the preeminence of a kind of "world corporation" organized on the basis of the multinationals, but rather that it is precisely one of defining limits, conflicts, and compromises between states and multinationals, by means of the formation of regional blocks in the world market.

We believe that an approach combining the last two models offers a more adequate explanation of the role of multinational corporations in Latin America, both as to the countries where they have their headquarters and as to the host countries. We think that to consider the multinationals independently from these countries as if they were demiurges of history leads to a double reductionism: that is, it subordinates local reaction to the "logic of accumulation of multinational corporations" and therefore to "external factors," and it minimizes the importance of political factors in the development of contemporary capitalist economy, both internationally and in individual countries.

It should also be made clear that the type of linkage between industrial multinationals and national economies varies for economic reasons. The backward and forward effects that can be expected vary according to the type of goods produced (industrial, mineral, or agricultural) and according to the production techniques and the stage of consumption aimed at (industrial input, product parts for export, durable goods).[3] In order to evaluate the effects of incorporating peripheral economies into world production, it is further necessary to distinguish at least four situations that can create a linkage between dependent economics and market internationalization:

- "Industrial platforms" for the exportation of industrial products. Products may be established in countries where the multinational corporations primarily seek comparative advantages, such as the use of cheap labor, and where the final product is not consumed (as in the case of Singapore or Hong Kong).
- Former enclaves of colonial production may be transformed into enclaves controlled no longer by colonialist states, but rather by (multinational) corporations, as in the case of mining in Africa and the production of tropical foods.
- Parts for complex industrial products may be produced which, although not necessarily consumed in the local market, presuppose more specialized labor and relatively advanced technology in the local economy.
- Consumer or capital industrial goods may be produced under the control of multinational corporations, but aimed primarily at local markets.

There have been cases of enclave economies in Latin America that have been redefined to the extent that the world economy has become "multinationalized"—for example, bauxite production in Jamaica, oil drilling in Ecuador, or banana production in Guatemala. However, the last two forms of linkage are more significant because their effects are more complex and usually occur together. The region offers few relevant examples of "industrial export platforms" controlled by multinational corporations. Exportable industrial consumer goods, such as shoes and textiles, are controlled essentially by local companies, except in the special case of the cosmetics industry in Mexico. Consumer goods (automobiles, refrigerators, television sets, etc.) produced by multinationals may be exported, but in general this is due to pressures exerted by local governments wishing to solve incidental problems in their balance of payments. Even so, the bulk of durable consumer goods produced is destined for local markets.

This is why, particularly in the industrially more developed countries (Argentina, Brazil, Chile, Colombia, Peru, Venezuela, and Mexico), the issues of historical significance do not have to do with the relationship between a "consuming" bourgeoisie (such as is found in Asia or Africa) and the multinational corporations. Instead, they have to do with the relationships between local bourgeoisie, the state, and the multinationals, together with the various possible reactions to the alliances that these participants may define.

It is for this reason that in the case of the capitalistically more developed countries in the region, one must consider the form that dependence assumes when there is room for some kind of associated capitalistic development. Here the role of the state is fundamental, and it will be treated in a separate section. However, before we develop this theme, we should point out the immediate political effects brought about by the current way in which the internationalizing process of markets and production continues. It should be emphasized that if this line of analysis were followed, it would be too general (abstract) and therefore incorrect to insist solely on economic conditioning (that is, on the "logic of accumulation of multinationals") as if such conditioning (which is a point of departure for the explanation) did not depend on class struggle and, internationally, on conflicts between states. Let us consider, then, in decreasing order of abstraction, how the action of the states appears on the international stage.

DEPENDENCE AND INTERNATIONAL POLITICS

After the failure in April 1961 of the invasion of the Bay of Pigs by Cubans armed and supported by the United States administration, and after the subsequent and consequence of the Cuban missile crisis in October 1962, which ended with the formal agreement between Khrushchev and the Kennedy administration that there would be no new invasions on the island, certain trends in United States–Latin American relations began to take on a clearer outline.

These trends can only be interpreted in the context of the end of the Cold War and the emergence of the Soviet policy of "peaceful coexistence," the consequences of which have led to the policy of détente still in force. This policy, in turn, is linked to developments and imbalances in the technological and military race between the United States and the Soviet Union, which have had widespread repercussions on the international economy and the balance of power as a whole. It is also linked, in a special way, to the dispute between the United States and the European Common Market (France in particular) on the one hand, and between the Soviet Union and China on the other hand. At the same time, as was mentioned in the previous section, the international capitalist economy was entering a phase of competition and new polarization around dynamic centers that previously had been considered mere extensions of the American economy: Japan and Western Europe, and in the latter, France and Germany in particular. In this context, the turning point may have been the signing of the Test Ban Treaty in August 1963 by the Soviet Union, the United States, and England, and the clear refusal of China and France to support it. The French opposition was based on a strategy aimed at guaranteeing its ability to strike "in all directions." From that point, the concept of a policy of unconditional allies lost force in the Western bloc. So as not to leave it to the Russians and Americans to decide whether French territory would be the object of their bargaining or agreements, De Gaulle created an independent military industrial system. By doing so he was able not only to bring down the domestic costs of decolonization—by replacing the old colonial economic interests with a financial industrial economy organized around the creation of an advanced technology and war industry—but also to endow France with an atomic "force de frappe" capable of launching attacks—and therefore of retaliating—independently of Soviet-American will.

The consequences of Chinese opposition were far greater. From 1963 on it became apparent that the world political chessboard was no longer divided into two blocs, but into at least three, and that there were important divisions among the allies in each of the rival blocs. Such divisions led to the dismissal of any notion that the world might be divided in half between the Soviets and the Americans by a new Treaty of Tordesillas, as it were.[4]

Despite these difficulties, the military, economic, and technological superiority of the United States and the Soviet Union is such that in their areas of direct influence, especially after détente and the SALT negotiations, the Kissinger-Brezhnev policy seeks to freeze the developments and rebelliousness which "peaceful coexistence" might encourage in the peripheral countries. The presence of China, added to the economic recession and the American defeat in Vietnam (which are intrinsically linked to successive crises of the dollar, caused by the war costs and the changes in world structure already mentioned, as well as by the struggles against American hegemony), has made it difficult, however, to reach that goal. United States recognition of China in 1972, the growing difficulties of reaching an agreement between the Soviets and the Chinese, and China's public demonstration of atomic capability, all have been highly unsettling factors for the dream of a Soviet-American peace.

The still unsolved problem of redefining the world political order in such a way as to replace the bipolarization of the Cold War period has been made difficult by Kissinger's desire for an "enlightened bipolarization." The Soviet Union might, however reticently, support this game, and show that it also has an enlightened face by granting emigration visas and by a relative tolerance of non-aligned friends in its periphery. However, China's presence and the reopening of several diplomatic missions in Western Europe, as well as the anti-colonial struggle and Third World struggles in general, complicate things and make it difficult for the world order to depend steadily on the Washington-Moscow red telephone connection.

The consequences of the end of the Cold War and the crisis in the world political order, added to the more recent consequences of recession and especially the OPEC reaction, were felt somewhat late in Latin America. Beginning in the 1970s, however, they began to weigh heavily on the foreign policy of the area as well as on the behavior of the great powers.

In the first place, after the Soviet-American agreement on Cuba (and here it should be emphasized that, at first sight, the military victory in the Bay of Pigs invasion was Cuban, not Soviet), it took the ministries of foreign affairs on the continent a decade to recognize that Cuban socialism will not be removed through external pressures. The policy of blockade and sabotage against Cuba began to give way to another, which had always been that of Mexico: a policy of distant tolerance on the part of the majority of the countries that have recognized Cuba diplomatically, and in the case of some governments, such as Peru, one of discreetly supporting the Cubans.

The policy of détente has led the United States to maintain a position of disdainful covert interference with respect to Latin America. Two qualifications, however, are necessary. First, the tolerance which the State Department shows publicly in cases of deviance from the canons of unconditional submission to American interests is counterbalanced by the veiled but always effective support which American special forces lend to local rightist groups organized to "destabilize" governments that might take steps toward more radical forms of nationalism or socialism. Second, the State Department and the military branches of the United States administration show much more rigidity with regard to changes in Central America and particularly in the Caribbean. In this area, United States policy is susceptible to geo-political considerations because of interests that are perceived and defined as strategic for American military defense and that are supported by the existence of colonial enclaves, such as the Panama Canal, Puerto Rico, and Guantanamo. Even though such considerations are anachronistic from a strictly military viewpoint, they find political and economic support among reactionary circles in the United States. Even purely national reformist tendencies (such as those which took shape in Santo Domingo in 1965) are perceived as an intolerable challenge. An exception to this rigidity has been the relative tolerance shown by the United States to the renegotiation of the status of the Panama Canal, where it faces a nationalist and moderately reformist military government. Even in this case, however, the reaction of domestic political interests has been very strong in the United States.

The counterpart of this increased flexibility on the part of the United States has been the discreet withdrawal of Cuba from the politics of the region. This is not so much a consequence of any objective conclusion drawn from the Soviet-American agreements (for guerrilla action and Cuban support to it did not stop after 1962, and even increased until at least 1970); it is rather the result of the failure, which will be mentioned below, of guerrilla tactics and of Cuban support to revolutionary movements in Venezuela, Guatemala, and Bolivia.

Under such circumstances, certain nationalist-reformist experiments of some scope, such as those in Peru, have been assimilated by American policy without major resistance. Peru's decision to resist external intervention, the logistic difficulties of a military expedition outside the Caribbean, added to the hard lesson of Vietnam, were probably sufficient to discourage greater rigidity on the part of the United States in the negotiations. The Peruvian leaders carried out some important changes, but these were limited, in general, to 25 percent of the less impoverished population; this, plus the fact that they have implemented investment agreements considered practicable for the multinational corporations, has probably helped to weaken the temptation of applying to Peru measures based on the Hickenlooper amendment as well as to discourage a more consistent boycott against that country by the international financing centers. However, we should not minimize the Peruvian regime's performance, aimed at implementing measures in terms of a program and certain proposed goals which, although inescapable, had not been worked out or effected by previous regimes. The lack of viable political alternatives that might have been implemented by the internal opposition and the moderate nature of Peruvian policies would have reduced the effectiveness of foreign intervention had it been attempted. As is well known, external action was very different in the Chilean experiment. In this case, the internal conditions existed for "foreign aid" to destabilizing groups to be effective, and the international economic siege was implemented quickly and efficiently.

There is no need for detailed comment on the official American aid to repressive regimes in the region and for the training of anti-guerrilla groups. However, it would be inadequate to limit the analysis of United States action in Latin America to its power of veto and coercion. Equally important is the support given by the United States to certain policies. The most recent American administrations have considered Latin America an area of marginal interest and have carried on a policy that has replaced the more active goals of the Alliance for Progress in the Kennedy period with the restrictive policies mentioned above. The active encouragement given to those repressive military regimes capable of blocking structural changes, and the unrestricted support of economic policies designed to make capitalist growth viable in underdeveloped countries (especially in the case of Brazil), constitute the other constant in the relations between the United States and Latin America.

We do not believe that processes such as the recent growth of an associate-dependent-capitalist economy in Brazil, or the continuing growth of the Mexican economy, can be explained through "foreign aid." This would be to ignore specific local conditions, for other countries, such as Chile and Uruguay, have received foreign aid without reaping the desired fruits of economic growth. But it is undeniable that, as a matter of policy, administrations in the United States have given unrestricted support during the last ten years to any government, military, repressive, or authoritarian as it might be, that showed an interest in fostering the alliance between the local states and the interests of the multinational corporations. In this respect, in spite of speculation about the growing autonomy of those corporations from the United States, there has been, in Latin America at least, a concurrence of interests and policies between Big Business and American administrations. It may be argued that the interests of some companies were not sufficiently defended at crucial moments by the American government in Peru or in Chile. It is true that the American state has not equated the interests of the United States as a nation with those of one corporation or another, and it is also true that given the political goals of the United States in Latin America, as well as the current world situation, it would be unrealistic to expect an invasion in response to each expropriation; however, as a matter of general policy, the United States administrations have tried to guarantee the maximal success of market internationalization with a minimum of political friction.

It must be recognized that, considering its goals and without passing judgment on the means employed ("destabilization," "dirty conspiracy," support of repressive governments, etc.), the main objectives of American policy in the region have been attained. The cost of this success may be measured by the fact that there were few situations in Latin America in which regimes guaranteeing some public freedom survived, and even fewer regimes that constantly tried to support development policies beneficial to the welfare of the majority. In general, distant goals for the welfare of all are proposed, and in the meantime, not only the freedom but also the material well-being of the national majority is sacrificed, in spite of economic performances that are impressive for those who benefit from them in Latin America.

To conclude this section, several policies of reaction against the international order that have been attempted in Latin America should be mentioned. In this regard, it might be useful to point out that there have been four basic forms of reaction to the international order in Latin America:

1. A number of countries have not only kept a low profile but have also remained close to the norms of a submissive acceptance of American goals (sometimes because of an absence of any real alternatives) in the reorganization of the international order.

2. The voting record of countries like Paraguay, Nicaragua, or Haiti at the United Nations offers concrete examples of the extent to which national states can be limited by a situation of pervasive dependence. Even in a rebellious U.N., many Latin American countries have failed to take part in the movement labeled "the dictatorship of the majority" by the United States representative when it began to oppose American goals.

3. Socialist countries like Cuba, or those which at certain moments had governments with socialist aspirations, like Chile, or nationalist-reformist aspirations, like Peru or Guyana, have tried to strengthen their policies of solidarity with the Third World and of support to the reorganization of the economic order by the formation of cartels such as OPEC, OCIPEC (copper), bauxite, and so forth.[6] Their capacity to implement such policies was obviously restricted, given the precariousness of local governments and the lack of a real base of economic interests in some of the proposed experiments (with the exception of oil).

4. Attempts to eliminate or decrease dependence were made by the countries that formed the Andean Pact and by those that proposed the creation of an Economic Office for Latin America (SELA), without United States participation and with the objective of self-reliance. In the case of the Andean Pact, Bolivia, Chile, Peru, Ecuador, Colombia, and Venezuela, following Peru's initiative, negotiated a treaty on foreign investments, which gives the national states some power to control the multinationals, and which tries to develop the concept of subregional integrated markets as a response to the limitations of local markets. In the case of SELA, Mexico and Venezuela (the latter motivated by the availability of exchange currency as a result of the oil boom) led in an articulation of embassies, with the unenthusiastic support of Brazil, to encourage the proposal of policies of Latin American interest and scope. The Venezuelan government opened credit lines for several Caribbean and Central American countries to compensate for difficulties in the balance of

payments and to create assistance funds. In an effort to dispel apprehensions about the possibility of a "preimperialist" type of action, the countries leading SELA have negotiated agreements generally favorable to the countries that participate in them.

5. Finally, some Latin American countries besides Cuba, particularly Mexico and Venezuela, seem to concentrate their efforts on developing a foreign policy on a world level. Venezuela, stimulated by OPEC, has become active not only in SELA but also in international meetings, where it has defined itself within a political range that goes beyond the relationship of economic subordination of a country that depends upon its oil exports to the United States. Mexico has tried to implement Third World policies, keeping up a strong autonomist rhetoric, even though it has maintained, if not expanded, its structural economic dependence upon the United States. Its international position in Latin America has been marked by its strong diplomatic support for the Chilean socialist experiment as well as by the continuation of its traditional policy of limited but permanent contact with Cuba.

In this context, Brazil shows some less-expected facets, given its current economic model and its explicit policy of support for the United States since 1964. The consequences of the breakdown of world bipolarity and of the fact that military confrontation between the United States and the Soviet Union is not expected, as well as of the presence of China on the world scene, have led the Brazilian governments since 1968 to define an international policy that keeps its distance from American foreign policy on some important points: Brazil did not sign the Atomic Agreement and later established its own agreement with Germany for the building of atomic reactors and the transfer of nuclear technology; like other Latin American countries, it unilaterally declared its sovereignty over territorial waters up to two hundred miles; pressured by the need to import oil, it has signed agreements with the Arab countries, and more recently, in 1974, it recognized the MPLA government in Angola, a country with which Brazilian governments have been trying for years to negotiate economic agreements.

It should be emphasized that the more significant changes in the foreign policy of Latin America would be unthinkable but for the prevailing conditions in the world scene, which have disrupted the previous balance and opened opportunities for new national policies. These, of course, can only have strength and credibility abroad when the domestic political order is relatively stable; for this reason Argentina, the Latin American country that in the past was most active internationally, has had a lessened role in recent years.

It is also evident that the emergence of Latin American countries trying to exercise power at the international level poses questions with regard to the areas of regional influence. Without going into the details of this controversial question, we should clarify the fact that neither Mexico nor Venezuela nor Brazil—three of the most active countries in international politics—has limited its action to Latin America. They seem to aim at establishing a place for themselves in the international political order, particularly in the case of Brazil, which has intensified not only its political but basically its economic relations with Germany, Japan, and Africa. This observation does not diminish the impact that the more active presence of economic and political interests of these countries may have upon neighboring nations. The expressed concern of Trinidad or the Guianas about Venezuela, or of Central American countries about Mexico, or the action of Brazil in Paraguay, in Bolivia, and even in Uruguay have shown this. However, it seems premature to speak of sub-imperialism, as if the multinationals were behind the foreign policy of these countries in a direct way, or as if their international political action were the expression of some supposed need to export capital or consumer goods caused by limitations of its domestic market. There are indeed relationships between economic interests and foreign policies, and there is interference by some Latin American states in other countries in the area; however, the role of the state in the economy and in the articulation of economic and political interests in those countries must be analyzed more carefully, as we shall see below, before we can qualify those interventions as the result of sub-imperialism. Not always and not necessarily do Latin American embassies respond only to the interests and pressures of the United States or the multinationals. There are other interests—and other passions—that lead some states in the periphery to act in search of a place among the powerful nations. Some of these interests and these passions (or ideologies), as well as their limitations, will be pointed out below in the discussion of the relationships between the local states and the economic order.

The more developed countries of Latin America are attempting to define foreign policy objectives that take advantage of contradictions in the international order and allow these countries some independent policy-making. But these countries remain dependent and assure an internal social order favorable to capitalist interests and consequently fall to challenge one of the basic objectives of American foreign policy. Multinational enterprises continue to receive support from the foreign policies of their countries of origin, as well as from local states.

How can these contradictory forces act together? It is through contradictions that the historical process unfolds. Dependent development occurs through frictions, accords, and alliances between the state and business enterprises. But this type of development also occurs because both the state and business enterprises pursue policies that form markets based on the concentration of incomes and on the social exclusion of majorities. These processes demand a basic unity between these two historical actors as they confront popular opposition, which may be activated when nationalist of socialist movements question the existing social order. So, the conflicts between the state and Big Business are not as antagonistic as the contradictions between dominant classes and people.

Within the last ten years, the strengthening of the state and the penetration of multinational corporations occurred within the context of a new set of class relations. On one hand, attempts were made to break (sometimes radically) with the global situation of dependency, with the aim of transforming society in the direction of socialism. On the other hand, dominant classes were reordered, with emphasis placed on the repressive role of the state and on the simultaneous transformation of the state into a tool for the fortification of the capitalist economic order.

The exhaustion of the prior populism and the aggravation of class tensions gave rise to various political attempts to break with the prevailing style of development. In one form or another, during the past decade, the politics of Latin American popular forces were profoundly marked by the presence of the Cuban revolution. The shadow of Guevara's deeds and the quasi-substitution of the process of mass politics by the military actions of guerrilla groups (though this was not implicit in their theory) considerably polarized Latin American revolutionary movements. These attempts failed nearly everywhere, the only exception of consequence being the case of Argentina, where the two principal guerrilla currents were not completely dissociated from the remaining socio-political movements. Though not constituting a real political power alternative, the guerrillas of Argentina exert a certain veto capacity, conditioning other political movements and attempts at reformulating class alliances.

Attempts at radical rupture with the capitalist-developmentalist path were not limited to the politics of the guerrilla. The Chilean popular unity of the Allende period, as one case, and the Peruvian military reformism, as another, were reactions based on broader popular forces to development that is tied to international capitalist-oligopolistic expansion. In both cases, the state was viewed not as a "bourgeois institution" to be destroyed, but as the lever for a possible total transformation of society, on condition that its control remain in the hands of popular forces.

Both the battle between classes and the basic dependency relationship find in the state a natural crossroads. The contradiction of a state that constitutes a nation without being sovereign is the nucleus of the subject matter of dependency. Our rereading the history has proceeded throughout the book toward specifying the fundamental historical actors: classes and groups defined within specific forms of production. Now, after ten years of reasonable rates of economic growth, the expansion of global commerce, the industrialization of important segments of the periphery of the capitalist world, and the strengthening of the state productive sector, the problem unfolds in a more complex manner. *Strictu sensu,* the capacity for action of various Latin American states has increased. In this sense, one might consider that they are "less dependent." Our concern is not, however, to measure degrees of dependency in these terms—that fail to ask, "less for whom? For which classes and groups?" Which classes have become more sovereign? Which alliances and class interests within each country and at the international level lead the historical process of economic development?

If the state has expanded and fortified itself, it has done so as the expression of a class situation which has incorporated both threats of rupture with the predominant pattern of capitalist development, as we have said, and policies of the dominant classes favorable to the rapid growth of the corporate system, to alliances between the state and business enterprises, and to the establishment of interconnections, at the level of the state productive system, between "public" and multinational enterprises. To accomplish this, the state has assumed an increasingly repressive character, and dominant classes in a majority of countries have proposed policies increasingly removed from popular interest. They have rendered viable a "peripheral" capitalist development—adopting a growth model based on the replication almost in caricature—of the consumption styles and industrialization patterns of the central capitalist countries. The tendencies indicated in chapter six developed with increasing velocity, achieving successes for that style of development (the "Brazilian miracle" and the type of growth that occurred in Mexico until 1970 are notable examples of the trend). Given conditions in Latin America, this process, while producing economic growth, urbanization, and wealth, has redefined without discriminating, or else in certain cases has aggravated, the existential, social, and economic problems of a majority of the population upon a resource. This majority has come to be looked upon as a resource for the accumulation of capital more than as the effective potential for the creation of a society modeled on its own interests.

Under these conditions, the state and the nation have become separated: all that is authentically popular, even if lacking the character of specific class demands, has come under suspicion, is considered subversive, and encounters a repressive response. In this vein, even problems which Western capitalist democracies confront and absorb, like the discussion of income distribution, minority movements (blacks, Indians, migrants, etc.), feminist or youth demands (not to mention the freedom of syndical and political organization), appear threatening to the existing order. From the perspective of the dominant classes, the nation has become increasingly confused with the state, and the latter in turn has identified its interests, with theirs, resulting in the confusion of the public interest with the defense of the business enterprise system.

Local dominant groups in Latin America responded to the external influences on economic growth and to the need to guard against attempts to transform the prevailing order, with an amalgam between a repressive state (often under corporate military control) and an entrepreneurial state. What lends dynamism to this form of state, and what characterizes its movement is not the bureaucratic aspect it may have assumed in some countries (Peru, Mexico, Brazil, Chile, among the most characteristic cases), but rather its entrepreneurial aspect, which leads it to ally itself, in production, with the multinational corporation. Somehow, the state has become a strategic element, functioning as a hinge that permits the opening of the portals through which capitalism passes into industrializing peripheral economics.

The generalization of this model, in Brazil, Mexico, Peru, and Venezuela, for example, transferred the conflicts among associates to a more directly political sphere. In addition, it married foreign interests with the local bourgeoisie, and in certain countries, with the interests of local states insofar as they were direct agents of production, as occurred in Brazil, in Mexico, and to a lesser extent in Venezuela. The consequences of this process are enormous and are far from having been exhausted by historical practice or by analysis. The character of this state-as-entrepreneur and of the state associated economically with imperialist forces without being politically associated state has lent to the contemporary form of the state a significance different from that which it had until mid-1950.

What is novel is the expansion of the state's direct productive investment in capitalistically profitable sectors. While state investments in these sectors originally came about with resources obtained through taxes and duties, they subsequently reproduced and expanded through the profits generated by the state enterprises (petrochemicals, mining, direct consumer goods, etc.). In countries like Brazil, Chile, Colombia, Peru, Mexico, and Venezuela, the public sector contributes more than 50 percent to the annual formation of capital, with the remainder contributed by private national and foreign enterprises. Of this total, in a majority of these countries, the state enterprises (as an individual portion of public expenditure) constitute more than half of the investment of the public sector. In Brazil, in 1975, this figure exceeded 30 percent of the total investment (public and private). Also in Brazil, the only two local enterprises which, by the scope of their action, could hope to qualify as multinationals (aside from the Itaipu hydroelectric corporation) are state enterprises: the Vale do Rio Doce and Petrobrás. Counted among the largest enterprises operating in Brazil, in terms of assets and the value of production or trade (and leaving foreign enterprises aside), are not the enterprises controlled by local private capital, but rather those of the state. In 1975, fifty-six of the one hundred largest Brazilian enterprises were state owned.[7]

The role of bureaucracies and of technocrats is considerable in practically all of the industrialized countries of Latin America. In a penetrating essay on this subject,[8] Guillermo O'Donnell attempts to show the nature of this form of regime and the conditions under which it emerges. He points out that regimes of this type established themselves in the region as the response of local dominant classes to the challenge presented by the mobilization and popular pressure generated by the collapse of previous political orders (either populist or traditionally authoritarian). He adduces further that this collapse occurred when economic difficulties that followed the import-substitution stage of industrialization created an inflationary situation and led the economy into an impasse. The solution required, aside from stability to ensure economic predictability, additional capital flows and greater entrepreneurial centralization in order to proceed along an oligopolistic route toward the continuation of the process of accumulation and toward the development of productive forces. O'Donnell concludes that, for all of these reasons, there exists a relationship of "mutual indispensability" between bureaucratic-authoritarian states and international capital (which needs to penetrate local economies and which possesses the technological and financial requisites to undertake the "deepening of development").

The lack of local private investment potential, the political need to prevent multinational corporations from single-handedly appropriating the most strategic sectors of the economy and their most dynamic branches, and even, at times, the nonexistence of international capital flows to attend to the investment needs of peripheral countries during any given period (since multinationals act on a global scale, aiming at maximizing results and not toward the continuity of local development), has led local states, despite the capitalist ideology they defend, to expand their functions and thereby to create a national basis from which to bargain with the multinationals. In this process, neither the decisions of the state nor the pressure from multinationals excludes local enterprises from the game. But in practice these local enterprises continue to lag behind the principal agents of transformation: the multinationals and the state. By the very force of expansion, new investment prospects do at times open up for segments of the local bourgeois sectors. Some of these return to the political-economic offensive, often allying themselves with the multinational enterprises in the "anti-statist" struggle.

This summary of contemporary development lies within what we perceived as possible ten years ago. The role of the state and how it supports itself in industrialized-peripheral countries has become clearer, however. If it seems necessary for the state in a dependent-capitalist country to become bureaucratic if expansion is to be viable, then the risk is run of relying on economic reductionism, which cannot take account of historical processes.[9] For example, it may be true that Argentina's General Onganía made a vivid effort to demonstrate that the "mutual indispensability" between oligopolistic accumulation and bureaucratic-authoritarian regimes passes through the sieve of class struggles and through the accidents of history had a corporativist political plan, which tended to bureaucratize the state apparatus and implement repressive policies. Nonetheless, the Cordobazo—a mass rebellion—together with the force of the labor movement, Peronism, and the enunciations of guerrilleros and revolutionaries, prevented Onganía's plan from working. President Lanusse later proposed a pact with Peronism, which aimed at preventing an alliance between revolutionary movements and the Peronist masses, which would have been dangerous to the capitalist order. After Peron's death, the inability of a government controlled by a mass bureaucratic party to thwart the revolutionary challenge led to the coup of General Videla. Was this coup an implementation of a bureaucratic-authoritarian regime based on the dynamism of public enterprise? Not necessarily. In the Argentinean case, social classes and the private economy constitute a force which until now has escaped the political-corporativist control of the state (though the labor movement and labor unions contain corporativist ties). Corporativist projects expire under syndical pressures and under the economic pressures of export sectors when these demand free market prices (one of General Videla's first acts was to remove the commercialization of meat from state control). In the Argentinean case, in moments of advancing revolutionary pressures, the state has assumed a repressive-military form, without having produced until now a stable bureaucratic-authoritarian regime.[10]

In Venezuela and Colombia, especially in the former, the state is promoting ties between multinational enterprises and the public sector to strengthen the public sector, but without a bureaucratic-authoritarian regime. To be sure, enterprises now challenge "outlaws," as does every dominant order. But it does not exclude party politics, the representation of interests, and some public freedoms. These are examples of a pact of domination favorable to big business in a situation of class conflict in which a formally democratic regime does not give way to the emergence of more repressive forms of political organization.

The Argentinean example demonstrates the "open process" of history. A simple "structural" analysis, demonstrating the contradictions between social forces and the drawbacks of the process of accumulation with its cycles and crises, is insufficient to explain the concrete course of political events. Nor does it suffice to point out the affinities and battles among dominant classes and the plans for political institution-alization which they support. It is even insufficient to view the political behavior of ruling classes in terms of reaction to a popular challenge. Popular reaction, under the guerrilla form, as we saw in Argentina, was capable of conditioning and of vetoing but not of transforming the political structure. There have been no viable alliances capable of imposing a form of state which could recover not only the aspiration to sovereignty but the primacy of the popular interest. The incapacity for hegemony of popular groups adds to the repressive capacity of dominant classes the fatal ingredi-ent that leads to a policy of advance and retreat within the iron circle of prevailing structures.

In Brazil and in Peru, the fortification of a formally bureaucratic-authoritarian order can be seen more clearly. The state in Brazil does not adopt, as an ideology, the authoritarianism which it practices. Thus the regime is guided by a duality of prin-ciples: the constitutional order that anticipates, for example, elections; and the insti-tutional acts that transform the military president into de facto dictator, as long as the political order is perceived to be threatened, according to criteria determined by the organs of military security. Despite these instruments of discretion, the failure to explicitly recognize the validity of an authoritarian order leads the regime into the exercise of electoral practices which at times jeopardize authoritarianism. The government dismantles the very "legal" order it created, by impeding the rotation in power of the two parties, by eliminating elected deputies, by going against the "democratic ideal."

In Peru, where the regime is clearly non-participatory, the qualifying phrase "bu-reaucratic authoritarian" is more immediately applicable: public enterprise and the state as a bureaucratic organization both expand while remaining under the control of the military corporation. Meanwhile, social and economic policy in Peru, while not revolutionary, is not income-concentrating, in comparison with what occurs when the multinationals and the private sector of the local economy direct the process of accumulation. In addition, political control does not assume traits that are abusive of human rights, as occurs in Chile and in Brazil or Argentina.

The contradiction between the state as the agent of capitalist enterprise, and the nation as something that is essentially popular, follows a movement that is not only different but opposite, in the recent history of Peru and Brazil. Though the Peruvian state may be bureaucratic-authoritarian, its policies are oriented toward the incor-poration of the masses, or at least toward the partial consideration of peasant and popular interests. These objectives may have been frustrated and difficult to secure within a policy that stifled the spontaneity of popular reaction, congealed political parties, and harbored seeds of military-bureaucratism. However, its ideology and what it has done to reorganize the socioeconomic order distinguish the Peruvian state from that of the bureaucratic-authoritarian state of Brazil.

Political regimes vary, as does the relation of bureaucratic-authoritarianism to the social bases of the state (viewed as a pact of domination). Nevertheless, the current form of dependency and the crucial role performed in it by multinational enterprises and by the state productive sector are no accident. It is necessary to draw a distinction between the state as a basic part of domination (and not as the expression of a "social contract"), which unites dominant classes in the exercise of domination over the rest of society, and the variable forms assumed by political regimes. The state expresses a situation of domination, reflects the interests of dominant classes, and expresses their capacity to impose themselves on subordinate classes. At the same time this discriminatory relationship (the domination of one part over the rest) must appear to the national consciousness to be the expression of a general interest. Consequently, the state constitutes a relationship of domination incorporating an ideology that masks that partiality. This process is not a simple distortion: it must also mirror, in some way, the generality it wishes to represent. Hence, even the most openly classist and repressive states use a language and propose policies (generally nonviable) that purport to reflect the "General Interest."

So, the state expresses the imposition of one class or alliance of classes over others. But while it serves those interests on that it bases itself, the state proposes measures that lend verisimilitude to the "generality of interests" which it must assume to exist (people, equality, nation). In addition to expressing a relationship like this at this level, the state is also a bureaucratic-regulative organization and, in the case of modern states, becomes even a productive economic organization.

To summarize, any state, through bureaucratic and productive organizations, expresses a relationship of class domination (and consequently has social bases), assumes an ideology as if in the common interest, develops and implements policies that respond to the fundamental pact of domination, but also claims to attend to the aspirations of dominated groups. Officials of the state (notably in the judicial sector) have to adopt both an ideology of equality and generality ("all citizens are equal before the law") and a practice in which dominant interests impose themselves.

In the industrialized countries of Latin America, which we are considering, the state embodies an alliance between the interests of the internationalized sector of the bourgeoisie and those of public and entrepreneurial bureaucracies. The local bourgeoisie links itself to these sectors. In part, the state in dependent capitalism generates its own social base, since its productive function is to assure capital accumulation, and since in performing this function, it creates a sector of public entrepreneurs. At times this stratum is called the "state bourgeoisie," to emphasize that these social agents are not simple bureaucrats nor do they simply implement the "public good." They function, sociologically, as the "officeholders of capital." For they support the accumulation of capital in the state enterprises. Both the accumulation of capital by public enterprises and the placing of all of the national wealth (mineral ore, impounded taxes, lands, roadways, etc.) at the disposal of private capital are fundamental requirements for the advancement of associated-dependent capitalism.

The state extends a bureaucracy and bases itself on a civil and military technocracy. The latter carries out the interests that are expressed by the state. Certainly, an inversion of this relationship can occur. The actors may occupy prominent positions on the political scene. The military bureaucracy may predominate in the control of the state. But in the end, long-term policies must be compatible with the social bases of the state. In the realization of policies of accumulation and development, though

the bureaucratic framework may be in the hands of a technocratic-bureaucracy or a corporative military (together or separately), the nature of the dominant state relationship develops through the strengthening of the alliance between the local entrepreneurial sector, associated with the multinational foreign enterprises, and the state productive sector.

The same fundamental alliance, which constitutes a dependent industrial capitalist state, may organize itself institutionally within a context of authoritarianism, restricted democracy, or totalitarianism. There is little credibility in its structural compatibility with substantive forms of mass democracy, populism, or even traditional caudillo (bossist) authoritarianism, since in these regimes the requisite policies leading to the expansion of industrial dependent capitalism become difficult to implement, because of the masses' interests in economic redistribution and political participation.

Not that Venezuela, Colombia, and Argentina will necessarily have to adapt themselves to the Brazilian or Peruvian military-bureaucratic-authoritarian model. These last two regimes are themselves quite different, both in the nature of their policies and in the nature of their respective social bases. The bureaucratic-authoritarian form of a regime like that of Brazil is not the only one capable of adapting to the "present stage" of capital accumulation. Economic reductionism in this case would fail to consider the changes that might occur from government to government (with, we repeat, the basic state pact maintained). There are many factors that function as sources of dynamism in history: (1) circumstantial factors such as explosions of collective protest (the 1974 Brazilian elections provide an example different from the Cordobazo, because the correlation of forces differs in the two countries); (2) struggles within dominant sectors; (3) the emergence of objective economic challenges (recessions, soaring inflation, a "new stage" of import substitution in the capital goods sector, for example); (4) the ability of the governing group to resolve problems and the opposition's ability to debate them, and so forth. Not all changes are always possible, to be sure, nor do political forces capable of taking advantage of opportunities for transformation always exist. But even in bureaucratic-authoritarian regimes, and even with the persistence of the alliance that underlies the state, there is room for regime-types to vary historically. What is at issue is not just a "mere change in form." The differences between a torturing autocratic regime and a "restricted democracy" arise out of the very possibilities for struggles among classes, and they in turn influence the historical opportunities of the dependent capitalist-industrial state.

A basic problem exists, posed by the present moment and by Latin American situations of dependency: the very penetration of multinationals requires a state that is capable of furnishing the multinationals with the resources for accumulation. So national wealth is necessary for foreign private accumulation. But this process is contradictory: for this to work, the state must fortify itself and expand its functions at both the administrative and the economic levels, in this way increasing its prospects for sovereignty. Faced with the political challenges of dominated classes to radically reorder society, this entrepreneurial-regulative state militarizes itself, becoming even stronger and more autocratic. At this point the relative loosening of ties between the state and its social base may occur, which the economically ruling classes may perceive as a risk of "Bonapartization" of the state. The spectrum of this perceived risk ranges from the emergency of a new Peron to a "mythical Peruvianism" that would lead the armed forces to ally with the people. In the process of exercising sovereignty and equipping the state with entrepreneurial skills, which allow both international and local accumulation, the entrepreneurial-repressive state dissociates itself from the nation. This is the specific political contradiction in the current form of Latin American dependent development.

There may have been a redefinition of the "forms of dependency," in certain Latin American countries there may be "less dependency," and the state in these countries may be capable of exercising a greater degree of sovereignty. But for us, what is at issue is the nature of class conflicts and alliances that the dependency situation encompasses.

As we stated previously, the political struggle revolving around the state shows what is essential in this form of dependency: the style of development of the possibility of alternatives depends upon the resolution of this question of the state. In the Chilean Popular Unity, in Peru, and in the Popular Assembly of the Torres period in Bolivia, popular forces or forces with popular intentions momentarily assumed control of the state. We find, in these cases, ambiguity about what constitutes the "popular" and unanimity regarding national demands. The fundamental challenge of the present moment in Latin American social development consists in linking these two aspects of radical political movements, the popular and the national, and in getting to the bottom of the opposition between the popular and the proletarian. What is specific to the Latin American situation of dependency is the difficulty in conceiving of a political passage to socialism by a strictly proletarian route, given the structural conditions of industrial capitalism in the periphery. So, alliances between popular movements, national-popular demands, and properly working-class struggles are required to enforce new paths in society.

These questions, however, are not posed today as they were during the populist period. The advance of mass industrial society, urbanization, the revolution in communication, even the situations of dependent-development themselves, pose the political question of popular participation in such a way as to exclude manipulative links with dominant classes through the state as an option. Such links were the basis of populism's policy. The internationalization of production and of the market have advanced, and the state productive sector has expressed itself in capitalist form. For the ruling groups, the nation is embodied in the state as the stimulus for an enterprise economy. But, at the same time, for dominated classes, the paternalism of the traditional Latin American State (in both the oligarchical and populist versions) has been broken. Although politically frustrated, the guerrilla movements did serve the function of disrupting this paternalism and putting an end to manipulative types of alliance, which once tied the people to the state in the name of the nation.

The practical issues that will permit development of an alternative type of state involve: first, knowing which course "substantive democratization" must take to affirm what is essential in the national and the popular and free from the rancidity of bureaucratization and authoritarianism, and second, knowing how to balance the need for organization and the vitality of spontaneous mass behavior. As in any case of social transformation, such questions go beyond analysis and anchor themselves in values: they are projected into the future to assist in the practical escape from a situation that reinforces the prevailing exploitative order. It is not within the boundaries of this book to pursue these questions. It is barely within those boundaries to point out, as we have, that social practice in Latin America has already begun to deal with these questions (even if in experiences that failed).

Researchers have directed their attention to ideology and corporativist forms in Latin America.[11] It appears to us that the fusion between enterprise and the state, both of them based on bureaucracies, and the role of armies in Latin American regimes, underscore the corporativist ties between the state and society.[12] During certain periods of political life, the relationship between civil society and the state seems to dispense with the mediation of parties: classes just appropriate segments of the state apparatus to defend their interests. Sometimes connections are formed through "bureaucratic rings," which are organized around high officials (cabinet ministers, generals, etc.) and which articulate the immediate interests of enterprises, government bureaus, the press, sometimes unions, repressive groups, and so forth around some specific policy or issue. In bureaucratic-authoritarian politics these semiformal structures substitute for an organization that is more stable and representative of class interests, namely parties. Particularly when regimes are centralized and positions at the top are decisive in the articulation of interests (Mexico, Chile, Brazil, and Peru), bureaucratic rings seem to constitute the form of political linkage that establishes connections between civil society and the state. The linkage is not very stable, since the key official can be dismissed and the ring thereby broken.[13]

These formal aspects of the juncture between the state and civil society should not obscure the characteristics of the state in contemporary Latin America that we have already pointed out. The state is the expression of the dynamism of business enterprises and of the classes that control them as they operate in a context in which bureaucracies and the regulative and organizational capacities of the state are expanding. The basic ideology of the state is fundamentally "developmentalism." In view of the explicit ends of economic growth and national grandeur, the exploitation of workers, if not openly defended by the state, is justified by the argument that the tightening of belts is necessary "at the moment" so that "in the future" the results of this economy may be redistributed. We do not endorse studies of Latin American corporativism that see in it a "profound cultural trend," consonant with that society's patrimonialist structures. These structures were real in another and bygone situation, but in the current period of industrial-financial capitalist development, an insistence on the "necessity" of the corporative form in Latin American political relations seems to us an anachronistic and conservative point of view. When corporativist forms exist, and there are circumstances in which they do, they express the pact of dominion among classes trying to implant capitalist development, and the opposition which these attempts encounter in the political movements of subordinate classes.

Instead of insisting on the immutability of the "cultural dimension" and historical roots of corporativism, it seems to us that what is important is an understanding of the essence of contradiction between interests of people and current style of development, between the state and the nation. In these relationships of opposition, if any cultural dimension exists and carries significance, it is what Gramsci called a relationship of hegemony: the capacity to rule. The effective battle is not between corporativism and the democratic tradition. It is between technocratic elitism and a vision of the formative process of a mass industrial society which can offer what is popular as specifically national and which succeeds in transforming the demand for a more developed economy and for a democratic society into a state that expresses the vitality of truly popular forces, capable of seeking socialist forms for the social organization of the future.

NOTES

1. See Robert Gilpin, *U.S. Power and the Multinational Corporation: The Political Economy of Foreign Direct Investment* (New York: Basic Books, 1975).

2. It should be clear from reading this essay that the authors do not accept this formulation of the dependence thesis. Nevertheless, they recognize that this was the version generally disseminated in the United States.

3. On this point see Albert Hirschman, "A Generalized Linkage Approach to Development with Special Reference to Stapely" (Institute for Advanced Study, mimeo, 1976).

4. Reference is to the fifteenth-century treaty whereby Portugal and Spain divided the territories to be discovered.

5. On the Peruvian situation and the themes mentioned here in particular, see Abraham F. Lowenthal, "Peru's Ambiguous Revolution," especially p. 13, in A. Lowenthal, ed., *The Peruvian Experiment* (Princeton, N.J.: Princeton University Press, 1975).

6. Obviously, we cannot go into details here. For an examination of advances in the attempts at economic defense on the part of producers of raw materials, see Constantine V. Vaitsos, "Power, Knowledge and Development Policy: Relations between Transnationals Enterprises and Developing Countries," in G. K. Hellenir, ed., *A World Divided: The Less Developed Countries in the International Economy* (Cambridge: Cambridge University Press, 1973).

7. It should be made clear that despite the importance of the role of the state productive sector in the Brazilian economy, foreign enterprises control between 40 and 50 percent of the large groups, according to measures of fixed assets, liquid assets, employment, and invoicing.

8. Guillermo O'Donnell, "Reflexiones sobre las tendencias generales de cambio en el Estado burocrático autoritario" (Buenos Aires: CEDES, 1975).

9. We are not referring here to O'Donnell's analyses. There exists in these (especially in "Notas para uma explicação histórico-comparativa," mimeo) a vivid effort to demonstrate that the "mutual indispensibility" between oligopolistic accumulation and bureaucratic-authoritarian regimes passes through the sieve of class struggles and through the accidents of history.

10. On the contradictions in the recent evolution of the economy and politics of Argentina, consult O'Donnell, "Reflexiones sobre las tendencias generales de cambio en el Estado burocrático autoritario." The alliance between part of the local bourgeoisie and the popular-worker movement constitutes, for that author, a defensive alliance whose limits emerge clearly when the cyclical oscillations of the economy lead agro-exporting sectors to demand corrections in the economic policies proposed by this alliance.

11. See Philippe Schmitter, "Still the Century of Corporativism?" *World Politics*, 25 (January 1973), and his important book *Interest Conflict and Political Change in Brazil* (Stanford: Stanford University Press,

1971); also Alfred Stephan, *The State and Society: Peru in Comparative Perspective* (Princeton, N.J.: Princeton University Press, 1978). See especially chapters 1 and 2.

12. See Stephan, *State and Society*, where corporativism is not inappropriately generalized to describe all authoritarian regimes. See also, in Schmitter, *Interest Conflict and Political Change in Brazil*, the specifications made in describing corporative relations between the state and civil society and among parts of the latter.

13. See especially, F. H. Cardoso, "A questão do Estado no Brasil," in *Autoritarismo e Democratização* (Rio de Janeiro: Paz e Terra, 1975).

5

The Consumption
of Dependency Theory

If an observer from outer space had landed his UFO at any meeting of Latin Americanists during the last few years, he would have had to agree with the structural anthropologists. He would have said that at these meetings, versions of the same myth are constantly repeated: dependency and development, exploitation and wealth, backwardness and sophisticated technology, unemployment and extreme concentration of income. Somewhat wearily, our creature from space would have commented: "The brains of these beings appear to limit their images and thoughts to binary opposites." Returning to the debate on the meaning of analyses of dependency gives one the sensation of entering a discussing in which imagination is bound by preestablished models. Nevertheless, as though I were one of the "founding fathers" of dependency, I endorse the ceremonial consumption of the theme. How to escape from this uncomfortable position?

A little while ago, in Princeton, I was present at a talk by an English anthropologist, recently knighted by the Queen. With his characteristic irony, Sir Edmund Leach told how he tried to stifle his own amusement at the ceremonial rite to which he had to submit, by comparing his consecration at the Court of St. James to sacrificial ceremonies on the high plains of Burma. His talk was entitled, "Once a Knight Is Enough." Nevertheless, the irony, mingled with erudition and with pious respect for the ritualized reenactment of a moment of passage from the condition of "commoner" to that of member of a noble order (which, even if it is not sacred, has something of the distinction that is reserved for the upper ranks of the hierarchy), could not conceal the fact that the ritual and the symbolic renaming to which he was submitted did hold some kind of meaning for him. The scientific consumption of the rite of passage did not eliminate its force. The game of comparative-formal analysis

From Fernando Henrique Cardoso, "The Consumption of Dependency Theory in the United States," *Latin American Research Review*, 12 (3) (1977): 7–24.

did not expose the political and social interests that underlay these ritual ceremonies but simply reaffirmed the universal value of them.

By using the title "Consumption of Dependency," and at the same time participating in this critico-commemorative celebration (which is, naturally, a more plebeian ceremony than the English knighting ritual), do I not run the same risk? There is no way to deny it. I hope, nevertheless, to maintain a sufficiently critical (and self-critical) position to avoid merely consenting to the ritual consumption of the theme.

The risk of ceremonial celebration becomes greater as studies of dependency arouse a certain movement of conversion among social scientists. Susanne Bodenheimer, grasping the critical power that these studies contained, gave wider currency to some of these formulations (since she wrote in English, which is the Latin of our times) and presented them as a new paradigm.[1] From that point on (although it was not her fault), what had been an endeavor to be critical and to maintain the continuity of previous historical, economic, sociological, and political studies in Latin America was transformed into an article for consumption in various versions that include references to the original myth but in large measure constitute the expression of a quite distinct intellectual universe from that which gave it birth.

Every myth requires a simple structure and a moment of revelation. The first, drastic simplification carried out by some popularizers of these studies was to treat them as a sort of mental thunderclap that occurred at a given time and place. Now the discussion revolves around the question of in whose head the thunderclap was produced; with that kind of beginning, the celebratory aspect is inevitable. Each interpreter seeks to locate his prophet. However, anyone who is aware of the social nature of thought knows that every new paradigm results from a complex discussion among persons, institutions, and groups, which in the modern world are located in different countries. With time, the discussion is enriched and provokes internal controversies.[2]

However, after establishing the immediate origins of the "dependency paradigm," popularizers who are not aware of the process of intellectual production attempt to describe its prehistory. Here, two principal currents are generally cited: ECLA and the Marxian and neo-Marxian North American ideas current (Baran, Sweezy, and Gunder Frank). At times, some spice is added to the debate by saying that the *dependentistas* (a term that makes me shudder) are of distinct ideological hues: there are those who are closer to ECLA (and to the "petty-bourgeois nationalism" that is supposed to have been derived from ECLA's research work), and there are those who adopt a position of more authentic opposition to capitalism and are thus more influenced by the abovementioned Marxian economists prior to the dependentistas. These assertions are plausible—indeed, perhaps they are typologically correct—but they do not correspond to the intellectual history of these ideas as it really happened.

The analyses of dependency situations in Latin America done in the second half of the sixties did not represent new methodological propositions. What happened was that a current which was already old in Latin American thought managed to make itself heard in the discussions that were taking place in institutions normally closed to it: ECLA, the universities, some government planning agencies, and—last but not least—the North American academic community.

As for the renovating influence of the North American neo-Marxian current, if it was real (principally the contribution of Baran), it was certainly not greater than that of Marx himself, and it did not "reveal" anything not already present in the perspective of critical Latin American thought before 1960. In practically all the principal Latin American intellectual centers, a critique of the critics was also developed which paralleled the development of a current of analysis and interpretation based on Prebisch and Furtado (and, along with or before them, Ragner Nurske, Hans Singer, Myrdal, and Hirschman—to cite just a few of the authors who opposed "orthodox" theories justifying the non-industrialization of the region in view of the comparative advantages that might be obtained with agricultural production for export). It arose within ECLA itself, at times explicitly, as in the studies by Jorge Ahumada and Aníbal Pinto dealing with Chile and the concentration of benefits from technological progress, or in the essays of José Medina Echevarria on the social conditions of development and on the "instrumental rationality" of the developmentalist approach. At other times the critique of the critics was implicit in the work of intellectuals who, in the universities or in political movements, emphasized not only the "obstacles" and the "distortions" of capitalist development (often inspired by structural-functionalist analysis), but also the inequality of opportunities and wealth that was inherent in forms of development derived from the expansion of capitalism and the strengthening of imperialism.

Historians Sergio Bagú and Caio Prado, Jr.; sociologists Florestan Fernandes, Pablo González Casanova, and Jorge Graciarena; and economists Armando Córdoba, Antonio García, and Alonso Aguilar are examples of efforts to present alternatives both to orthodox analyses and to what we might call the ECLA–Keynesian analyses. A rereading of the *Revista Brasiliense*, published in Brazil in the 1950s—and there were journals of the same sort published in almost all the cultural centers of the area— shows that criticism of structural-functionalism and Keynesianism occurred in Latin America at the same time as the criticism of "orthodoxy" was being elaborated. In an effort to develop a double edged critique, a few groups of intellectuals in Santiago in the mid-1960s took up the ECLA problematic and tried to redefine it radically, while seeking to avoid "vulgar Marxism." To compare what ECLA predicted as the outcome of industrialization with what was in fact happening was easy. It was more difficult to propose an alternative that could not be limited to a methodological-formal critique; one that, starting from the analysis of historical-social processes, would be able to define an alternative problematic and break with both the prevailing "economicism" of analyses of development and the "apoliticism" of sociological analyses. How was that to be accomplished?

A study of the history of ideas in the twentieth century would show that each generation of critical intellectuals seeks to revive Marxism with a new breath of life. The crust of so-called "vulgar Marxism"—"economic determinism," "mechanistic" analysis, the difficulty of capturing social movement due to conceptions that give a deterministic weight to the structures, etc.—is so recurring that it must have something to do with Marxism itself. From time to time things are shaken up by rereading the classics, by some new interpretation, or by the support that some author outside the tradition of dialectical thought lends to Marxian analysis. In the 1950s and the beginning of the 1960s, this bridge was made by Sartre and by the publication in French of *History and Class Consciousness* by Lukacs. It took years to emerge from the impasse between dialectics and the notions of "project" and "possible consciousness."[3] For those like myself who had undergone prior training in Dilthey, Weber, and Mannheim, the preoccupation with ideology and its incorporation in analysis came to be constant and was frequently equivocal. In the following generation, Althusser reread Marx in another way and structuralism nearly killed the movement of dialectics. Late (and in a few countries, like Argentina, even as early as the sixties, Gramsci appeared as a life raft for those who wanted to understand the political processes, ideology, the will in history, etc., and avoid drowning in the abovementioned "deviations" of mechanistic Marxism.

Studies of dependency, then, constitute part of this constantly renewed effort to reestablish a tradition of analysis of economic structures and structures of domination; one that would not suffocate the historical process by removing from it the movement which results from the permanent struggle among groups and classes. Instead of accepting the existence of a determined course in history, there is a return to conceiving of it as an open-ended process. Thus, if structures delimit the range of oscillation, the actions of humans, as well as their imagination, revive and transfigure these structures and may even replace them with others that are not predetermined. These studies also had a peculiarity within this tradition of criticism: instead of limiting themselves to the theoretical-abstract plane, they sought to utilize the historical-structural, "nonvulgar" method to analyze concrete situations. And instead of limiting their studies to the analysis of circumscribed problems, they sought (returning to the theme of development) to define questions relevant to national politics and to the relations between the central capitalist economies and the dependent and non-industrialized periphery, following in this respect the tradition of the ECLA perspective. It did not interest them merely to describe abstractly the consequences of the accumulation of capital and of its expansion at the global level; they also posed questions arising from the historically determined point of view of dependent societies: What are the forces that operate in them, and what are their objectives? How and under what conditions is it possible to overcome a given situation of dependency?

Thus, an initial reevaluation of the manner in which the consumption of dependency theories occurs in the U.S. must reconsider the point of view from which the "new paradigm" was established, through the work of a group of intellectuals at ILPES (Latin American Institute for Economic and Social Planning, at ECLA) and CESO (Center for Socioeconomic Studies, University of Chile). Some intellectuals in these organizations played a certain role in the proposal of a set of themes and in the critique of Keynesianism and of structural-functionalism—a role to be discussed further on—but they did not propose any new methodology.[4]

Once the methodological contribution of the dependentistas has been limited and the possible influence of North American Marxism on proposing studies of dependency has been redefined, it is necessary to look at the contribution of André Gunder

Frank to the themes of dependency. Some of his studies in *Capitalism and Development in Latin America* had great critical impact and were contemporary with the elaboration of what is called here the "theory of dependency." Earlier works, such as his paper criticizing the thesis about Brazilian agrarian dualism, may have been stimulating, but frequently missed the point as far as proposing new themes is concerned.

The central question in Brazilian discussions concerning the past nature of social relations in rural areas and their specific weight in determining a certain type of socio-historical formation was not a debate between the partisans of the existence of a feudal structure and those who believed that "since colonial times" the concept of capitalism best described the existing social relations and forms of production. Nor was it a debate between precapitalism and capitalism tout court (although this discussion was more common). These propositions lost their force when confronted with the concern of those who tried to characterize the mode of production that prevailed in the past by taking colonial slaveholding into account. Except for the crudest of the evolutionist Marxists who really did see "feudalism" as an important characteristic of Brazilian society, the discussion had for a long while centered on slaveholding colonial production and on the specific nature of a social formation which, although created by the expansion of mercantile capitalism was based on slave-labor relations and reserved the most dynamic part of it output for the international market.[5] (This outlook is already noticeable in the works of Gilberto Freyre, dating from the 1930s, despite their commemorative quality.) Gunder Frank simplified the debate, disdained the specificity of the situation (a procedure contrary to that of the dependentistas), and failed to attempt any sort of theoretical scheme of a dialectical type that might draw together the general and the particular in a specific whole. With the masterful polemics that are his special skill, he mortally wounded the dualists and blamed the confusion, sometimes correctly and sometimes not, on Marxists and ECLA theorists.

Nevertheless, the paradigm of dependency is consumed in the U.S. as though its contribution to the historical debate had been centered on a critique of Latin American feudalism. That is, some of Gunder Frank's works are taken to mark the beginning of a "new" perspective in Latin America. Bagú, Caio Prado, Simonsen, Celso Furtado, Florestan Fernandes, Alonso Aguilar, and many others had already written on the colonial period or on the structure of agricultural production for export, basing their analyses on considerably more complex themes than the simple duality between feudalism and capitalism.

The second distortion produced in the consumption of dependency theories concerns the relationship between the social, economic and political structures of the dependent countries and the international capitalist system. Dependency analyses in the years 1965–68 were preoccupied much less with the external conditioning of the Latin American economies, which was taken for granted, than with the development of a type of analysis that could grasp the political alliances, the ideologies, and the movement of structures within the dependent countries. How was this to be done? The "vulgar" current was predominant in analyses that regarded imperialism and external economic conditioning as the substantive and omnipresent explanation of every social or ideological process that occurred. Certain political forces endorsed that formulation for tactical reasons. Clearly the target of the struggle was evident—North American imperialism—and the allied camp was also clearly defined—everyone, except the agro-exporting latifundists linked to imperialism.

The dependentistas put the question the other way around: social movement cannot be theoretically represented by means of a "mechanical" opposition between the internal and the external, in which the latter cancels out the existence of the former. The approach ought to be historical, and it therefore starts from the emergence of social formations. Underdevelopment then comes to be seen not merely as a process that is a concomitant of the expansion of mercantile capitalism under industrial capitalism, but as one that is actually generated. The approach ought also to emphasize the specificity of dependency as against societies in countries of the economic center. In other words, although the social formation underlying situations of dependency is the product of the expansion of capitalism, it is distinguishable from the classical pattern to the extent that "slaveholding colonialism," or some other form of colonial exploitation, is present as the basis of the articulation between dependent and dominant societies. On the other hand, after the passage from the colonial situation to situations of dependency of national states, it is observed that: (a) the passage implies the creation of states in answer to the interests of local property-owning classes; (b) these, however, have their structural situation defined within the larger framework of the international capitalist system and are thus connected and subordinated to the conquering bourgeoisies of the western world and to those classes which succeed them; in this way alliances are established *within the country*, even though in contradictory form, to unify external interests with those of the local dominant groups; and (c) as a consequence, the local dominated classes suffer a kind of double exploitation.

The "movement" that had to be understood, then, was that deriving from the contradictions between the external and the internal viewed in this complex fashion and summed up in the expression "structural dependency." If imperialism was embodied in the penetration of foreign capital (invasions by Americans in the Caribbean, by the English in South America, etc.), it also implied a structural pattern of relations that "internalized" the external and created a state which was formally sovereign and ready to be an answer to the interests of the "nation," but which was simultaneously and contradictorily the instrument of international economic domination. Certainly, the phases and forms of capitalist expansion (colonial-mercantile, mercantile-financial and industrial-financial capitalism, oligopolist forms of "multinationalized" capitalism, etc.) are constituent parts of dependency situations, but the latter are explicable only when those forms cease to be taken as an entelechy or as an abstract and general conditioning factor, and reappear concretely in the analysis of their articulation in each local economy at different moments of time. This process was to be explained not as the "abstract" unreeling of forms of accumulation, but as historico-social process through which certain classes impose their domination over others, certain factions of classes ally or oppose themselves to others in political struggles. In this struggle, what appears at first as inevitable because of the "logic of capitalism" is revealed without disguise: one side wins or loses, one form or another of dependency is maintained or makes way for another, the general conditions for capitalist development are sustained or reach their limits, and other forms of social organization are foreseen as a historical possibility. Thus, right from the initial propositions,[6] dialectical analysis was the point of departure. What was significant was the "movement," the class struggles, the redefinitions of interest, the political alliances that maintained the structures while at the same time opening the possibility of their transformation. The structures were regarded as relations of contradiction, and therefore dynamic.[7]

This aspect of the relations between the internal and the external was quickly accepted and was put forward, with slight variations, in various works.[8] The most competent North American commentators took note of these propositions and saw in them something new.[9] New it certainly was, but within the spirit of efforts that, every ten or fifteen years, in different countries, attempt to recall that dialectical analysis should above all be analysis of contradictions, of the reproduction of forms of domination, and, at the same time, of the transformation and expansion of a given economic form or type of society.

In the process of disseminating these studies in the U.S., however, the characterization of dependency acquired local color. There was a preoccupation with the denunciation of forms of "foreign aid"—the intervention of the CIA in foreign policy, the invisible and Machiavellian hand of the multinationals, etc.—a politically legitimate preoccupation that emphasized real aspects of the contemporary historical process. Little by little, however, this ended by reestablishing the priority of the *external* over the internal (which may be well-founded), and it led in the end to the elimination of the dynamic proper to dependent societies as a relevant explanatory factor (which is not acceptable). Once again, in metaphysical fashion, the two terms of the opposition external and internal were separated, and the opposition passed from dialectical to structural-mechanical, when it was not conceived of in terms of antecedent causes and inert consequences.

The most general and formal of Gunder Frank's works are taken as though they were his best, the formal definition of dependency furnished by Theotônio dos Santos is appended, the problematic of "sub-imperialism" and "marginality" is sometimes inserted, one or another of my works or Sunkel's is footnoted, and the result is a "theory of dependency"—a straw man easy to destroy.

Therefore, instead of demanding an empirico-analytical effort of reconstructing a "concrete whole" with the abovementioned characteristics, dependency came to be consumed as a "theory," implying a corpus of formal and testable propositions. I was always reluctant to use the expression "theory of dependency" because I was afraid of formalizing the approach. Nevertheless, Latin Americans and North Americans began to make the effort to create a "theory." The Latin American authors who moved in that direction were nearly all of Marxist inspiration although they yielded to the glorious temptation to construct a theory (a temptation that led them to formulate abstract formal definitions and elaborate typologies),[10] they nevertheless held on to the concern for establishing "laws of movement" of "dependent capitalism."[11]

In my opinion, they did not always succeed in their difficult undertaking, since there was even a difficulty in logic to be overcome: how to establish a legitimacy that, by definition, is contained in a separate and distinct situation? On the other hand, some North American specialists began clamoring for "internal consistency" in the theory of dependency and established a body of hypotheses deduced from the principle of dependency in order to test them empirically. In this type of reformulation of dependency, the concepts must be one-dimensional and precise and must refer to clearly established variables. With their help it ought to be possible to measure the continuum that goes from "dependency" to "independence" and to characterize variable degrees of dependency.[12]

However, this kind of definition of the notion of dependency also modifies the "theoretical field" of its study: instead of making a dialectical analysis of historical processes, conceiving of them as the result of struggles between classes and groups that define their interests and values in the process of the expansion of a mode of production, history is formalized; the specific contribution that these analyses of dependency might make from a methodological point of view (that is, the idea of contradiction) is withdrawn. The ambiguity, the contradictions, and the more or less abrupt "breaks" in reality are reduced to "operational dimensions" which, by definition, are univocal but static. The result is somewhat like a dialogue between two deaf people, in which one group says: give me precise concepts, with clear dimensions, and I will tell you, after testing them, if the relationships among the variables defined within their theoretical framework conform to the hypotheses which you propose. The other group says: I am not interested in defining univocal concepts; what interests me is pointing out contradictions and formulating relationships in which *the same* thing is transformed *other* by means of a process which takes place in time and which certain classes or fragments of classes into relation with others through struggle and opposes them to rival blocs—for example, how one and the same "national" bourgeoisie is internationalized into *something else*, or how "public servants" are transformed into the "state bourgeoisie" redefining the allied and enemy camps. In this analytical perspective, processes involve changes in quality and not merely in degree.

The divergence is not merely methodological-formal; it is, rather, at the very heart of studies of dependency. If these studies do in fact have any power of attraction at all, it is not merely because they propose a methodology to substitute for a previously existing paradigm or be cause they open up a new set of themes. It is principally because they do this from a radically critical viewpoint.

Indeed, by admitting that structures have movement and that changes cannot be explained through factors conceived of only as external (which act as conditioning of and interfering in the social process), the dependentistas affirm the existence of domination and struggle. The question, "How does the *transition* from one situation of dependency to another occur?" or "How can situations of dependency be eliminated?" ought to be asked in terms of "Who are the classes and groups which, in the struggle for control or for the reformulation of the existing order (through parties, movements, ideologies, the state, etc.), are making a given structure of domination historically viable or are transforming it?" In these analyses, therefore, there is no presumption of scientific "neutrality." They are to be considered more "true" because they assume that, by discerning which are the historical agents capable of propelling a process of transformation and by providing those agents with theoretical and methodological tools for their struggles, these analyses thus grasp the meaning of historical movement and help to negate a given order of domination.

They are therefore *explanatory because they are critical.* In any case, there is no intention to put "arbitrary" in place of "objective" knowledge. What is intended is an approach that accepts and starts from the idea that history is movement and that structures are the result of impositions; even though these impositions may become crystallized, they contain tensions among classes and groups that always make them, at least potentially, dynamic.

In the struggle that takes place among the components of a structure there are no "dimensions" of "variables" at stake, but tensions between interests, values, appropriations of nature and society, all of which are unequal and in opposition. Therefore, when speaking of "dependent capitalist development," one speaks necessarily and simultaneously of socioeconomic exploitation, unequal distribution of income, the private appropriation of the means of production, and the *subordination* of some economies to others. On the other hand, one also necessarily inquires into the conditions under which this order of affairs is negated.

To sum up, then, studies of dependency continue a live tradition in Latin American thought, reinvigorated in the 1960s by the proposition of themes and problems defined in a theoretical-methodological field not only distinct from what inspired Keynesian and structural functionalist analyses (the theory of modernization, and of the stages of development that would repeat the history of the industrialized countries), but radically distinct with respect to its inherent critical component. If this kind of study acquired force and penetrated the contemporary world, it was because it explained more accurately certain erring in Latin America, while certain changes in the countries of the center itself (above all the U.S.), beginning in the 1960s, brought out clearly the inadequacy of the assumptions of structural-functionalism. The protest of American blacks, the war in Vietnam and the movement in opposition to it, the counterculture, the student movement, the feminist movement, etc., all demanded paradigms that were more sensitive to the historical process, to social struggles, and to the transformation of systems of domination. In such a perspective, analyses of dependency correspond better to this search for new models of explanation, not only in order to comprehend what is happening in Latin America, but also what is happening in the U.S.

Up to this point, I have somewhat inelegantly been putting the blame for all the misunderstandings on the consumers of dependency theory, as though the reestablishment of the original myth would resolve all the problems. An ill-disposed critic might quickly respond that I not only content myself with the ritualization of the theme, with more indulgence than Sir Edmund Leach, but I even aspire if not to "true prophet-hood" at least to being one of the most zealous of apostles.

However, if there have been so many distortions in the consumption, it is because the original production was not clear regarding several of these points, and may even have included, in latent form, much that later appeared as simplification and inconsistency. I shall not repeat here what I have already said in previous works. I want merely to emphasize that, if it is to be judged on the basis of its own assumptions, the point of view of dependency ought to be confronted with at least three types of questions:

1. Have dependency studies been able to whet the imagination so that discussion is opened on themes and forms of comprehending reality that are compatible with the contemporary historical process?
2. Does the theoretical representation of the dynamic of this process proposed by dependency studies permit us to comprehend the forms of capitalist expansion on the periphery and realistically to make out the alternatives to it?
3. Do the studies enable us to define the classes and groups that give life to dependent structures through their political struggles? Do they make it possible to go beyond the structural frame of reference in order to clarify the relations between ideologies and social and political movements in specific political conjunctures, so as to assist action to transform reality?

As for the first question, if the initial studies of dependency possessed any novelty, it certainly was not the affirmation that dependency exists, but it was rather the characterization and the search for an explanation of *emerging forms of dependency*. The studies sought to show the meaning of the industrialization of the periphery (and thus the formation of an internal market, since in Latin America this process did not involve the construction of mere export-manufacturing enclaves), under the control of what later came to be called "multinational corporations." The recognition of the effects of this process—the "new dependency"[13]—was the point of departure for reflection on this theme. Today, this appears to constitute another banality. Nevertheless, in Latin America up to the end of the decade of the 1950s there was a deeply rooted conception that the international economic trusts were not interested in the industrialization of the periphery, since they exported finished goods there; their fundamental interest was the control and exploitation of primary agricultural and mineral products. The theory of imperialism reinforced this point of view, which was moreover consistent, at least in part, with what happened up to that point. The anti-imperialist struggles were at the same time struggles for industrialization. The local states and national bourgeoisie seemed to be the potential historical agents for capitalist economic development, which in turn was looked upon as a "necessary stage" by a considerable part of critical opinion.

The dependentistas showed that a kind of industrialization was occurring under the control of the multinationals, and they drew certain conclusions from it. There was even an attempt to propose a more general model of the process, to characterize a "transnational capitalism" and to estimate its effects, not only on the periphery, but also on the very center of the capitalist economies.[14]

The revision proposed on the basis of these perspectives—that of the industrialization of the periphery and the internationalization of internal markets—made it possible to generalize the criticisms of the theory that the national bourgeoisies could repeat the function they served in the center as the leaders of the capitalist process in underdeveloped countries. It also displayed the insufficiencies of the theory of modernization and the expectation that there would be stages of development identical to and in the same sequence as those in Europe. From that point on, the question of the state came to be reformulated, and the role of the bureaucracy (and what later on I called the "state bourgeoisies") came to be discussed in greater depth.[15] On the other hand, thanks to the characterization of the specific form of capitalist industrial development on the periphery—where what dominated was oligopolistic-corporative production oriented toward consumption by the high income classes—numerous hypotheses were advanced and some studies were made on the theme of marginality and of the formation and behavior of the working class.[16]

On balance, the effect of dependency theories on the sociological imagination seems to me to have been positive. Thanks to these theories (but not, exclusively so, since the ECLA group had already pointed in that direction), attention was called to a thematic frame that ceased to see capitalist development on the periphery as a mere "consequence" of accumulation of capital in the center, and began dealing with the historical form that this process acquired in dependent societies.

I have more reservations concerning the explanations proposed in many of these studies to account for the historical process. I shall limit myself to one question that has served to divide the dependentistas; that is, the question of the form of analysis of the movement provoked by the expansion of capitalism on the periphery. Here there are two polar modalities (although I simplify somewhat) to conceive of the process of capitalist development:

1. There are those who believe that "dependent capitalism" is based on the hyper-exploitation of labor, that it is incapable of broadening the internal market, that it generates constant unemployment and marginality, and that it presents a tendency to stagnation and a kind of constant reproduction of underdevelopment (thus Gunder Frank, Marini, and to a certain extent, dos Santos).

2. There are those who think that, at least in some countries of the periphery, the penetration of industrial-financial capital accelerates the production of relative surplus-value; intensifies the productive forces; and, if it generates unemployment in the phases of economic contraction, absorbs labor-power in the expansive cycles, producing, in this aspect, an effect similar to capitalism in the advanced countries, where unemployment and absorption, wealth and misery coexist.

Personally I believe the second is more consistent, although the "dependent-associated development" model is not generalizeable to the entire periphery. At times the "theory of dependency" is thought to be impugned, or contradictions are seen in it, when it is pointed out that there can be *development* and *dependence* and that there exist more dynamic forms of dependence than those characterizing enclave or quasi-colonial situations (even allowing greater degrees of maneuver to the national states and to the bourgeoisies locally associated to the state and to the multinationals). The argument most commonly used is that in this case a relationship of "interdependence" comes into being. Nevertheless, when one examines the relationship between the economies of "dependent-associated development" and the central economies, it is not hard to perceive that the international division of labor persists, based on very unequal degrees of wealth, on unequal forms of appropriation of the international surplus, and on the monopolization of the dynamic capitalist sectors by the central countries. All of which leaves no doubt about the distinction between central and dependent economies. The sectors of production of capital goods and the generation of new technologies, which are the most revolutionary sectors at the level of productive forces and are decisive in the scheme of extended reproduction of capital, remain in the central nuclei of the multinational firms. And the external debt is oscillating but continuous in the dependent countries.

Finally, in this very summary balance, I also find very debatable the analyses produced up to now to categorize the "historical agents" of social transformations. Both the "stagnationist" or "underconsumptionist" authors—who believe that the internal market is insufficient to make way for the capitalist-dependent expansion—as well as those favorable to the possibility of capitalist development in certain countries of the periphery, have generated up to now a relatively impoverished political analysis. Either they emphasize the "structural possibility" of revolution and go on to discuss the overcoming of dependency in terms of a historical horizon in which socialism appears as the result of growing crises peculiar to a stagnating capitalism, or they foresee a "new barbarism" and display an inclination for repeating clichés that explain little. Those who do not share either idyllic or catastrophic vision (and I am one of them) are reticent concerning the political alternatives. At any rate, the "catastrophists" make a "mechanico-formal" analysis, and the latter either reveal a good will toward an "autonomous capitalism" (although it is not clear how it can be brought about), or they sketch out their hopes of a socialism whose historical persona is not described in their analysis, nor perhaps in reality.

Both the mechanico-formal style of those who believe in the ultimate aims of history, guaranteed by the *necessary* structural incapacity of dependent capitalism to expand and reproduce itself, and the elliptical style of those who wish to escape this Frankenstein politics, lead the critics of dependency to the conviction that a catastrophic vision of history or permanence in definition must be inherent outcomes of this kind of analysis. To avoid this, they ask that better dimensions be defined, so that degrees of dependency may be measured. With these, they think it is possible to demonstrate that as long as the local states increase their capacity to regulate the economy and counterbalance the multinationals, the area of independence will enlarge.

I do not agree with the idea that to improve the quality of analysis, the theory of dependency should be formalized so that, after testing hypotheses derived from this formalization, one could venture out into the world waving the banner of the percentage of variance explained by each factor within the situation of dependence. Instead of asking for analyses within the mold of empiricist structural-functionalism, it would be better to ask for an improvement in the analyses.

In saying this, however, I do not want to endorse the ingenuous expectation that theories about dependency explain *everything* or that, if they do not yet explain everything, it is because the method has been badly applied. It is necessary to have a sense—I will not say of proportion—but of the ridiculous, and to avoid the simplistic reductionism so common among the present-day butterfly collectors who abound in the social sciences and who stroll through history classifying types of dependency, modes of production, and laws of development, with the blissful illusion that their findings can remove from history all its ambiguities, conjectures, and surprises. It is necessary, on the contrary, to have the patience for research disciplined by a dialectic that is neither listless nor complacently constructing abstract and general formulations that seek to be taken for syntheses. Luckily, as much as social scientists strive to enclose the structural possibilities of history in their own constructs, history continually makes us *dupes de nous-mêmes*, and astonishes us with revelations.

NOTES

1. Susanne J. Bodenheimer, *The Ideology of Developmentalism: The American Paradigm-surrogate for Latin American Studies* (Beverly Hills, Calif.: Sage Publications, 1971), especially "Toward a New Conceptual Framework: The Dependency Model," 34–40.

2. Some original formulations of dependency studies try to avoid the simplistic presentation of the subject. The same is true for some commentators. Several books and papers are available in English about "dependency theory." See, for a historical view on Latin American sociology, Joseph A. Kahl, *Modernization, Exploitation, and Dependency in Latin America* (New Brunswick, N.J.: Transaction Books, 1976). For an extensive review of Latin American literature on dependency, Ronald Chilcote and Joel Edelstein, *Latin America: The Struggle with Dependency and Beyond* (New York: John Wiley and Sons, 1974), "Introduction," 1–87. For some criticism and an alternative but not incompatible perspective, see Albert Hirschman, "A Generalized Linkage Approach to Development with Special Reference to Staples," mimeographed, 1975. For a critique and a summary assuming another paradigm, Robert Packenham, "Latin American Dependency Theories: Strengths and Weaknesses," mimeographed. For brief, but consistent summaries, Philip O'Brien, "A Critique of Latin American Theories of Dependency," mimeographed, Institute of Latin American Studies (Glasgow); and Juan E. Corradi, "Cultural Dependency and the Sociology of, Knowledge: The Latin American Case," in June Nash and Juan Corradi, eds., *Ideology and Social Change in Latin America* (New York: Gordon and Breach, 1977). For an overview and bibliography, see Frank Bonilla and Robert Girling, *Structures of Dependency* (Stanford, Calif.: Stanford University Press, 1973).

3. The debate between the "humanistic" and the "ontological" approaches in the interpretation of Marxist dialectics has influenced most of the attempts to use this methodology by Brazilian social scientists. The methodological introduction to my Ph.D. dissertation, "Capitalismo e escravidão no Brasil meridional" (São Paulo: Difusão Européia do Livro, 1962), for instance, expresses this mood. On the other hand, the concept of "project," with all its metaphysical implications, was also behind most of the publications of the influential Brazilian Institute for High Studies (ISEB) since the fifties.

4. The methodology of the book *Dependência e Desenvolvimento* (whose first version was an ILPES document) is quite close to the methodology that I used in previous studies on slavery and capitalism, as well as in research on problems of development and entrepreneurship in Brazil (see, for instance, *Empresário industrial e desenvolvimento econômico no Brasil* [São Paulo: Difusão Européia do Livro, 1964]). Several other Latin American authors have published since the early fifties attempting to revitalize the dialectical approach.

5. Brazilian literature on this topic is considerable. The classic studies are the well-known books by Roberto Simonsen, Caio Prado, and Celso Furtado on the colonial economy. From the sociological viewpoint, Florestan Fernandes's analysis of slave society and the "ancien régime" provides insightful interpretations. All those books (as well as Octavio Ianni, *As metamorfoses do escravo* [São Paulo: Difusão Européia Do Livro, 1962], and my own book on slave society in southern Brazil) were already published when Gunder Frank discussed his thesis on "feudalism" and "capitalism."

6. This is the perspective of interpretations proposed in F. H. Cardoso and Enzo Faletto, *Dependência e Desenvolvimento* (Santiago: ILPES, 1967). The draft version was distributed in Santiago in 1965.

7. In spite of that, the usual conception of a static analysis of structures leads to misinterpretations of some of my writings. In criticism I have been considered a structuralist in the Levi-Strauss tradition, or even a defender of a non-class-struggle style of analysis. See, for this kind of naive understanding of the methodology that I propose, John Myer, "A Crown of Thorns: Cardoso and the Counter-revolution," *Latin American Perspectives*, 2 (1) (Spring 1975).

8. Theotônio dos Santos, for instance, presents a similar view in the study he wrote after the discussion in Santiago of the essay written by Faletto and myself (*Dependência e Desenvolvimento*). See dos Santos, *El nuevo carácter de la dependencia* (Santiago: Cuadernos de Estudios Socio-Económicos 10, Centro de Estudios Socio-Económicos [CESO], Universidad de Chile, 1968). In other essays that dos Santos published after his first comprehensive writing about "la nueva dependencia," the same pattern of dialectical and nonmechanical connection between external and internal interests is described in a simple and clear way. See especially, "La crisis de la teoría del desarrollo y las relaciones de dependencia en América Latina," in Hélio Jaguaribe et al., *La dependencia político-económica de América Latina* (México: Siglo Veintiuno Editores, 1970), 147–187.

9. See, apart from Kahl's book that is more comprehensive in historical terms and is not limited to the discussion on dependency, Bodenheimer, *The Ideology of Developmentalism*, and Chilcote and Edelstein, *Latin America*. See also, Packenham, "Latin American Dependency Theories," 4–5.

10. Even dos Santos proposes a formal (and thus static and nonhistorical) definition of dependency in his well known article "The Structure of Dependency" (*American Economic Review*, 60 [2] [1970]: 231–236). Vania Bambirra also succumbed to the temptation of helping dos Santos to develop a "theory of dependency" or of dependent capitalism, as the latter suggested in his essay "La crisis de la teoría." The result of that attempt was a new typology of forms of dependency and some formal possibilities of structural changes. See Vania Bambirra, *El capitalismo dependiente latinoamericano* (México: Siglo Veintiuno Editores, 1974). Bambirra misinterprets the analysis of situations of dependency suggested by Faletto and me when she refers to them as if we were proposing "types" of dependency.

11. The preoccupation with "laws of transformation"—in the Marxist tradition—is quite dear in dos Santos, as well as in Bambirra's book. Rui Mauro Marini, in "Brazilian Sub-imperialism" (*Monthly Review*, 9 [February 1972]: 14–24), and *Subdesarrollo y revolución* (México: Siglo Veintiuno Editores, 1969), refers also to some kind of historical laws. But Marini's views are more analogical-formal than historical-structural and his presentation of dependent capitalism's characteristics (in terms of overexploitation of the labor force and permanent crisis of capital realization) does not fit with the real historical process.

12. Examples of this are Packenham's criticism of dependency studies and, correspondingly, his contributions towards evaluating the performance of states and economies in terms of degrees of independence. See, especially, his article "Trends in Brazilian Dependency since 1964," unpublished. Others, in spite of more adequate understanding about the theoretical meaning of dependency studies, have committed methodological fallacies. One example is the quite provocative paper by Chris Chase-Dunn, "The Effects of International Economic Dependency on Development and Inequalities: A Cross-National Study," unpublished. The author makes comparisons between different situations of dependency as if they form part of the same continuum of dependency-independence. The analysis becomes, thus, formal and ahistorical. Even in Durkheim's approach to comparative analyses, some compatibility among structures being analyzed is required to validate the results. Furthermore, in a historical-structural approach, the specificity of concrete situations is a precondition for any analytical formulation. Nevertheless, Chase-Dunn does not take into account the basic distinctions between class and political structures in an enclave type of economy, a nationally controlled export economy, and an associated-dependent industrialized one. Mixing data drawn from distinct situations of dependency, he intends to validate or to criticize statements that

have been presented as characteristic of specific forms of dependency. I am not arguing against the use of statistics or empirical (historical) data as a means of validation or rejection of theories. I am criticizing the inadequate use of them, in methodological and theoretical terms.

Some other papers present mistakes similar to the above, with an additional characteristic: they replace the theoretical views of dependentistas by the "common sense meaning of the term" (dependency and imperialism). The pretext for this is the lack of precision in the literature. By precision these authors mean a positivistic approach. After redefining the "theory of dependency" according to their own conceptions they intend to submit it to "empirical test," confronting hypotheses with data. Which hypotheses, how to categorize data, and who are the authors submitted to proof depends, of course, on the arbitrary choice of these empirical and objective cultivators of science. See, for instance, Raymond Duval and Bruce Russet, "Some Proposals to Guide Research on Contemporary Imperialism," unpublished.

13. See *Dependência e Desenvolvimento*, last chapter, "The New Dependency." Dos Santos took these ideas and developed the characterization in *El nuevo carácter de la dependencia*. Nevertheless, several critics and commentators have not realized the implications of what is new in the dependency situations of industrialized Third World countries. Bodenheimer, for instance, kept the perspective of the expansion model of one phase of imperialism as the main feature of "la nueva industrialización": "The international system *today is* characterized by: advanced industrial capitalism . . . the dominant nations need raw materials and, more important, commodities and capital market" ("Dependency and Imperialism: The Roots of Latin American Underdevelopment," in K. T. Fann and Donald C. Hodges, eds., *Readings in U.S. Imperialism* [Boston: Porter Sargent, 1971]), 161. Moreover, Bodenheimer's concept of the "infrastructure of dependency" relates basically to the multinational corporations. Thus, again, the external forces are supposed to reshape internal structures without internal mediation: "The infrastructure of dependency may be seen as the functional equivalent of a formal colonial apparatus," sustained by client-classes which play, in "modern" Latin America, the historical role of a "comprador bourgeoisie" (see 161–163). In this approach the functional-formalistic method is alive again, not because of the use of the expression "functional equivalent" by itself, but because Bodenheimer is comparing situations (the "colonial" and the "modern capitalist") constructed without historical content, as Gunder Frank sometimes does when he refers to feudalism and capitalism.

14. In this respect, the most influential essay was Osvaldo Sunkel, "Transnational Capitalism and National Disintegration in Latin America," *Social and Economic Studies* (University of the West Indies), 22 (1) (March 1973). Celso Furtado wrote some recent articles on contemporary capitalism, stressing the reorganization of the international market under the control of multinationals and its consequences for international political domination.

15. The importance of state bureaucracy and state enterprises in Latin America was stressed by several dependentistas. See, dos Santos, "La crisis de la teoría del desarrollo," and "Dependencia económica y alternativas de cambio en América Latina (*Revista Mexicana de Sociología*, 32 [2] [March–April 1970]: 416–463). My own views on the subject can be found in *Autoritarismo e Democratização* (Rio de Janeiro: Paz e Terra, 1975). See, for more recent developments in the discussion of the role of the state, the insightful essay by Guillermo O'Donnell, "Reflexiones sobre las tendencias generales de cambio en el Estado burocrático-autoritario" (Buenos Aires: CEDES, 1975; in *LARR*, 13 (1) (1975)). Marcos Kaplan published pioneering essays on the nature of the state in dependent societies. See, especially, his "Estado, dependencia externa y desarrollo en America Latina" (*Estudios Internacionales*, 2 [2] [July–September 1968]: 179–213). Francisco Weffort published a well-known, illuminating essay on "State and Masses" (*Revista Latinoamericana de Sociología* [Buenos Aires: n.a., 1966]).

16. This is not the occasion to recall the discussion on "marginality," to which Aníbal Quijano and José Nun have contributed. Recent research and criticism seem to reorient the discussion by assuming other hypotheses with respect to employment marginality, and industrialization. See Paul Singer as well as Elizabeth Balan and Lucio Kowarick in various issues of CEBRAP's *Cadernos* and *Estudos*. Vilmar Faria in his Ph.D. dissertation, "Urban Marginality as a Structural Phenomenon: An Overview of the Literature" (Harvard University, 1976), not only summarizes previous discussions, but proposes new approaches to the subject, taking into consideration empirical evidence and theoretical elaborations on the question of employment and capitalist development, without the "stagnationist" bias.

→ 6 ←

Development: The Most Political of Economic Issues

I am delighted to be speaking before an audience like this today—an audience that is given not only to reflection, but also to formulating strategies of action. I am particularly pleased to see some old friends here from my years in academic life.

I believe I am somewhat familiar with the subject I would like to discuss today: development as the most political of economic issues. You will pardon me if I begin my remarks by quoting myself, but it will soon become evident that in this particular case, I am not trying to be boastful. It is simply an analytical tool. One of the books I wrote, which was an attempt to come up with my own version of dependency theory, is entitled *Dependency and Development in Latin America.* The "development" perspective I dealt with in this book was soon forgotten. At that time, in the mid-1960s, development theory had identified itself with the functionalist theories that my book with Enzo Faletto had criticized. As such, analysts concentrated on "dependency" in order to make the distinction clear, since that was the novelty—the specific contribution of Latin American researchers to sociological thought.

I am not going to propose that we resurrect the theory here. It was important at a given time precisely because it clarified the limits and possibilities along with the characteristics of Latin American development. My objective today is more direct: I will attempt a comparative exercise to demonstrate the changes in development perspective since the 1960s.

Of course I will not be speaking merely as an analyst concerned with the direction of the Latin American development process, as I did in the 1960s. For me, development today has been transformed into a series of concrete questions, and it is integrated into the political process. In the 1960s, I sought analytical precision; today, this

Adapted from Fernando Henrique Cardoso, "Desenvolvimento: o mais político dos temas econômicos," *Revista de Economia Política,* 15 (4) (October–December 1995): 148–155. Originally presented as a lecture at the Center for Strategic and International Studies, Washington, D.C., April 21, 1995.

is still a goal, but I would link it to options whose costs have been closely scrutinized by all sectors of society.

My personal trajectory, first as an intellectual and then as a politician, has taught me that the most difficult problem faced by the state is to see to it that greater analysis actually clarifies choices. Merely pondering issues without considering reality leads to an isolated viewpoint. As Weber said, "politics is made with the head, but not with the head alone." Taking action without exhaustively examining all possible options and their consequences would be, in my case, sinning against Weber, against the ethic of responsibility. In sum, what I have learned is that the effectiveness of government management is strongly conditioned by the quality of the ideas that are its inspiration.

THE CONCEPT OF DEVELOPMENT

I would like to return to my comparative exercise. A first theme is that of the notion of development itself. In the 1960s, development may have been identified primarily with material progress and economic growth. The analysis of its implications had a certain simplicity: it was acknowledged as central to the social process. For some, material progress would lead spontaneously to an improvement in living standards. For others, the so-called dependentistas, the relationship was more complex. Politics intervened, and depending on how it was organized, growth would take different paths, with varying effects on social structures.

Today, I see two parallel phenomena. First, development seems to be a fragmentary process. It no longer has the basic force it had in the 1960s. This has resulted in a plethora of notions of development, which are not always easy to follow. There is sustainable development; social development, as in Copenhagen; human development; and development with equity.

Although this tendency risks overgeneralizing from the specific, in my view it is clearly an improvement. Economic growth is now understood as part of a larger process, and its results do not automatically translate into benefits in the environmental or social area. Moreover, some reflection on the problem of the environment is one of the factors that have challenged the simplicity of the original hypothesis. In fact, it has become clear, even in the developed countries, that growth itself has caused real problems that make it difficult to "sustain" progress. To be precise, it has become essential to think about the type of development we want.

At the same time, the authoritarian experience in Latin America has amply demonstrated the gap between growth and equality. Income distribution has deteriorated in some cases. It has become clear that development policies must be framed by values other than those simply related to the economy.

INTERNATIONAL INTEGRATION AND DEVELOPMENT

A second theme articulated in dependency theory was the influence of a country's mode of international integration on its concrete development approaches. In principle, this is the most original aspect of dependency as such. A comparison between the 1960s and the 1990s is very instructive here: It is clear that, in the last thirty years, capitalism has become more complex. The globalization phenomenon we saw in the 1960s was more on the production level, with the expansion of multinational companies. It has now broadened to an extraordinary extent, especially in the financial area. I need only to refer to well-known statistics on the volume of trade on the world's major stock exchanges in one day alone to demonstrate this.

So, countries are now more "dependent" on what happens elsewhere in the world, not only in defining their development projects, but also in the day-to-day management of their economies. A significant difference, however, arises from the fact that, on a differing scale, the globalization phenomena do not choose those they "affect." This means that developed and developing countries both win and lose with globalization. Here is an example: The need to create "defenses" with respect to the speculative currency game is not confined exclusively to the developing countries. Since both rich and poor countries will compete for capital flows whose fluctuations offer specific short- and long-term opportunities for profit, all countries will thus share an interest in this issue. The international community thus has a common interest in equipping itself with mechanisms to prevent the adverse effects of globalization, and to preserve the possibilities of generating greater wealth on an international scale that globalization includes.

Another current aspect relates to the assumption that dependency would be a leveling factor providing the developing countries with opportunities to overcome their state of poverty. As I recall, supposed differences in the modalities of growth basically would depend on who controlled the process of capital accumulation. But, in essence, capitalism at the center and capitalism at the periphery were far apart. Even if a peripheral country developed—and my book was controversial because it suggested the possibility of dependency and development occurring simultaneously—its growth would be distorted. It was as if the fact of being on the periphery condemned the country to an unjust fate.

Today, we know that this is not true. Countries that have successfully managed their economies by paying careful attention to transformations in capitalism's modes of production as well as to social issues have developed in a more propitious direction than others. The case of the Asian tigers is well known. What was left of "determinism," which was perhaps a vestige of Marxism in dependency theory—and I was a critic of determinism—will certainly have to be reformulated from the beginning. Political choices have a greater influence on the structure of the economy than they appeared to have in the 1960s.

In historical perspective, the situation is paradoxical. The effects of globalization seem to increase dependency in an indiscriminate fashion, while improving conditions bring benefits from greater international integration, depending on whether countries make the right choices. Awareness of international developments has become an essential requirement for modern politicians. In addition, the structural aspect of globalization itself requires that this awareness be applied to long-term issues. More than ever, economic policy choices have to be made with an eye to the future.

The stimuli we apply today will be decisive in defining the long-term possibilities of progress.

PRODUCTION MODES AND DEVELOPMENT

Continuing with my comparison, I would like to touch on the consequences for society of the third industrial revolution. When I wrote my book, it was already clear that the central element of development was the ability to accumulate scientific and technological knowledge. Perhaps my view was naive, since the problems caused by progress were not yet clear at that time. That is, they were not anticipated to be as serious as they actually are. I am referring specifically to the unemployment problem, which has become the central issue in the social dilemma of developed countries and is also causing severe problems in the developing world. The unemployment problem we are experiencing derives from the modernization process, and at the same time, is born simply of backwardness, of a lack of opportunity. A broad agenda exists for dealing with this problem. There are policies for education and for addressing social inadequacies. But let me reiterate that they require a clear definition of the type of society we want to live in.

THE PROBLEM OF THE STATE

In the 1960s, we still strongly believed in the ability of the state to shape progress. It was a promoter, a stimulus, and above all, a possibly autonomous force. For many dependency theorists, the solution would be found only by enhancing these attributes and, at the limit, turning to socialism itself.

Today, this view has radically altered. In the 1980s, the positive identification between the state and development has weakened, and the state is almost seen as an obstacle to progress. It is not only that neoliberal ideology is temporarily predominant. More than this, both in rich and in poor countries it is the objective failure of the state that has led to reform efforts that may not be framed in ideological terms. Another basic factor is the failure of ideological models. The state has to resolve concrete problems, with the concrete means at its disposal. The secret of a fair division of labor in society cannot be found in some ideological fantasy world, but is rather the fruit of negotiated compromises, based on consensus. If this were not the case, they would not be effective. The state is the fundamental actor, but its role changes. Because it has more limited means, its course of action must be carefully chosen. This represents another paradox: precisely because it must reduce its role, the state becomes a more relevant actor in society.

The end of the Cold War has led to a transformation of the very standards on which the development models would base their legitimacy. It is no longer only a question of the sound application of an ideology, but rather of a complex combination of values related to morality, justice, social well-being, and their actual achievement. Ideologies, especially when they were in conflict as in the 1960s, allowed one to take the sometimes perverse position that the solution of social problems could be demonstrated in the future. What I mean by this is the following: If in ideological terms, the choices made were "correct" today, the project's success would be guaranteed tomorrow. Unfortunately, we know that anticipated successes have led to illusions about the real performance of some economies that ended by collapsing.

THE POLITICAL SYSTEM

Perhaps the crucial difference between the 1960s and the 1990s in Latin America is the question of the political system. Dependency theory arose in a context of authoritarianism. The analysis was based on an examination of how countries would integrate themselves into international capitalism at the limits of authoritarianism. This led to unbalanced development, that gave no attention to the real social needs of the population. Democracy radically changes the dependency equation.

In the 1960s, the difference between authoritarianism and democracy was clear. For us intellectuals, at that time, the purpose of the basic political struggle was to end the restrictions on civil and political rights. We assumed that democracy would almost automatically improve social conditions. After all, on the theoretical level, we had acknowledged that authoritarian regimes distorted economic growth.

Today, there are two new views on this question. First, we no longer believe that democracy is limited to a set of laws, an institutional framework. These continue to be the underlying assumptions of democratic life. Beyond these, we know that democracy must be rooted in social practices and must become, as Tocqueville described it, part of the very culture of a people. I believe that in Brazil, we are reaching this stage, which makes the process of governing enormously complex, especially in a society that is still as full of contrasts as Brazil is.

I would say that there are now many more actors enthusiastically participating in the process of articulating their demands. The political realm has opened up and now includes, aside from political parties, nongovernmental organizations, which have proliferated to an extraordinary extent in Brazil; the press, which plays the role of spirited critic; unions and their organizations; business groups; and various community groups.

This fact leads to consequences for the very nature of the democratic process. The democratic dialogue between the executive and Congress, limited by the judicial branch, is transformed and becomes a complex balancing act among the exigencies of political negotiation; social demands, organized around strong themes like human rights, the environment, and indigenous rights; and pressure from the mass media. To a certain extent, the political environment is strongly influenced by the media, which deal with events and are required to produce results on a daily basis, while government actions, especially in the social area, achieve results only in the long run. This creates a permanent and creative tension. One of its consequences is that the level of scrutiny by society is so high and so varied that governments make fewer mistakes. It is also understood that it is impossible "to achieve democracy" without establishing creative partnerships: to govern, between the state and society; to produce, between the state and the business community; to advance social demands, between the state and nongovernmental organizations; and to improve working conditions, between the state and the unions.

We no longer believe in social classes that will unilaterally lead the development process. Today, development is a problem that requires broad social mobilization.

Democracy does not "resolve" social problems, but it is a necessary condition for dealing with them. The idea of "transparency" means no more than this: society understands itself better, has a better grasp of its vulnerabilities and difficulties, and knows its actual ability to transform itself. Utopias gain a realistic sense. The desire to change is more clearly outlined. It is no longer born of the inexorable design of history; it will emerge from the difficult and routine struggle of people everywhere.

INTERNATIONAL RELATIONS

Dependency theory did not pretend to develop a new view of international relations or explain diplomatic choices in the strict sense. Nevertheless, it would still be worth recalling that it reflected some elements present in the international milieu. The 1960s saw the beginning of negotiations between the North and South, and the view that, behind the negotiated arrangements conditioned by some criterion for justice, poor countries would not be bound by reciprocity criteria—international disparities in income would be reduced. We believed that governments could transform economic relations between the developed and developing countries. This was the counterpart to a sort of "underestimating" of the need for reform within each country, derived, as I said, from an almost magical belief in the liberating power of democracy.

There was another factor. Underlying dependency theory was a psychological "fear of the outside." This existed because in various ways we still paid homage, hidden it is true, to the theory of imperialism. In addition, there was a hard fact: The establishment of authoritarian government in Latin America, especially early on, had been made with the collusion of the Western powers.

With increasing global economic interdependence, the international rules of the game have changed. Although the state is still an essential actor in defining the very rules under which the processes of interdependence take place, its control of variables that affect development projects, as I have already mentioned, has lessened to some extent. On the other hand, international negotiations have become tougher. The UNCTAD "nonreciprocity" rules have practically disappeared for a country like Brazil. In the trade area, UNCTAD has been replaced by GATT, and now, by the WTO. Countries must now create economic power to achieve positive results in their international negotiations. The basis of the regionalization strategy—and I would like to mention Mercosul here—is fundamentally linked to this new view of the ways in which nations may project themselves in economic terms. In the end, if the game is about reciprocity, one must have something to offer, and market size is the first trump card.

However, we understand that the challenge of development requires intensive work at home. The reforms are well known: economic stabilization within the framework of a balanced budget; privatization; trade liberalization; the creation of the appropriate infrastructure and of a flexible and modern financial system; the availability of management capability; and the redirecting of the state to the priority areas of action, such as providing basic services in the areas of education and health.

We know that the success of countries in this global right for investment and markets depends to a great extent on the degree of progress in achieving these goals. In sum, the "psychology of fear" in the international realm has been transformed, because today no one doubts that international competitiveness is based on the establishment of internal conditions that determine the way each country becomes integrated into the international economy.

I would like to emphasize that this should not "disarm" the state. We can neither reject the international arena as we did during the 1960s, nor adopt what comes from abroad as the unshakable truth. The problem is precisely how to strengthen the state so that it broadens its own margin of choices among the opportunities offered by the international system, and consequently, eliminates its vulnerabilities in facing concrete problems.

Given the consequences of globalization, implementing policy in a responsible manner and with ever more prudence, is fundamental. We cannot be complacent and inactive abroad and react to events rather than dealing with them or preventing them. In this sense, I believe that Brazil—faced with the recent financial crisis in emerging markets—set a good example of responsible action when it adopted preventive measures based on careful analysis of existing alternatives.

CONCLUSION

It was not my intention to make a nostalgic trip back to dependency theory. Rather, I wanted to call attention to the central problem of our time: development.

More now than in the 1960s, this subject has become political in the strongest sense of the word. The fragmentation and broadening of the concept of development; the new dilemmas faced by countries integrating into the international system; the diffusion of the unemployment problem between rich and poor countries; the reform of the state; and the complexities of state management are all elements of the central question: What do we want our societies to be in the future?

Today, there is practically universal convergence around the values of democracy, social justice, and economic freedom. These are values that guide us and that clearly establish what we do not want. The return to authoritarianism, in any of its forms, is unthinkable in Brazil and Latin America; disregarding calls for social justice would be irresponsible; and retreat from our understanding that economic growth depends on an open economy and the strong presence of private initiative is out of the question.

Nevertheless, this understanding is just the first stage. The other stages—that would mean the expansion of these ideals—will unfold with political efforts, through day-to-day negotiation. We cannot, however, lose the impetus to change, improve, and achieve development and social justice.

I think that my utopian disposition, perhaps tempered somewhat by realism and responsibility, has not changed. And because this tendency is also strong in Brazilian society, I have a real mandate to transform Brazil.

→ 7 ←

Structural Bases of Authoritarianism in Latin America

Almost everyone, victors as well as vanquished, was taken by surprise by the ease with which the Brazilian populist regime was overthrown in 1964 and by the nature and extent of the subsequent military rule. In the impassioned aftermath of 1964 much of the discussion concerning the nature of the new military regime revolved around the rather sterile debate as to whether the military movement was a "coup" or a "revolution." Later a more serious analytic discussion ensued as to whether the 1964 coup should be seen as a "restoration movement," as one very able foreign observer, Philippe Schmitter, has called it.

Those who emphasize that the current authoritarian regime has many roots in the Estado Novo period are correct in some respects. However, a central thesis of this chapter is that the regime established in 1964 is not simply a return to the past. I will attempt to demonstrate that the regime represents a fundamentally new political restructuring of the polity and that this restructuring is closely interrelated with basic economic and social changes that became significant in the late 1950s and are now occurring at an even more rapid rate.[1] Furthermore, I contend that most analytic discussions concerning the nature and future of the current Brazilian regime have neglected or incorrectly interpreted the implications of these changes and that all too frequently analysts do not take into account, either theoretically or empirically, the dynamic, mutually shaping, interrelationship between politics and economics.

This chapter thus has three main goals:

1. It attempts to analyze the context in which the new regime emerged and to emphasize what is particular to it. My analysis stresses the dynamic process by

Adapted from Fernando Henrique Cardoso, "Associated-Dependent Development: Theoretical and Practical Implications," in Alfred Stepan, ed., *Authoritarian Brazil: Origins, Policies, and Future* (New Haven, Conn.: Yale University Press, 1973), 142–178. Used by permission of the publisher. © Yale University Press.

which new forms of national political power and new international economic forces have interacted and resulted in the emergence of what I call the new "associated-dependent development" in Brazil.

2. It attempts to show that some of the major analytic interpretations of the new regime, such as those found in the writing of Celso Furtado, Hélio Jaguaribe, or Cândido Mendes, have (despite their frequent brilliance) contributed to the conceptual confusion concerning the regime and its relationship to the "associated-dependent" model. I argue that these interpretations give overly static, mechanistic views of the relationship between the economy and the polity. They err either on the side of excessive economic determinism, which does not take into consideration the full implication of "associate-dependent development," or on the side of excessive political voluntarism, which does not take into consideration any economic constraints on political elites or sufficiently consider internal contradictions within the political elite.

3. Keeping in mind the dynamic interrelationship between politics and economics, it attempts to suggest the range of possible futures for the Brazilian development model and to offer some useful insights both for people actively involved in politics and for analysts.

THE NEW MODEL OF "ASSOCIATED-DEPENDENT DEVELOPMENT": POLITICAL AND ECONOMIC IMPLICATIONS

As I asserted before, the new bureaucratic-authoritarian political regime is closely related to the changes in the pattern of economic development in Brazil and in the balance of political forces on which that development was based.

During the Kubitschek administration (1956–61) the older model of economic development was undermined and lost its force. That model, which had emerged in the 1930s—with the Volta Redonda steel plant, if one wishes to refer to a landmark and a symbol—gained momentum during World War II and became the predominant policy in the second Vargas government (1950–54). In essence that policy orientation concentrated on strengthening the role of the state as investor, particularly in the expansion of heavy industry and in the formation of an infrastructure for the production of durable consumer goods. That policy orientation, as has now been well documented, was more a short-term response to practical problems than a coherent set of projections based on a nationalist ideology. Yet it had important effects on the style of economic development. It helped shape a development pattern in which, in descending order of importance, the state, native Brazilian capital, and foreign capital (mainly to finance public undertakings) were the main propellers of economic growth.

With Kubitschek's policy of rapid industrialization and the expansion of the urban middle-class market for manufactured goods, a redistribution of influence began to take place. There was a noticeable change in the groups attempting to influence economic policy decisions, as well as changes concerning the control of the investment process. The social bases of the populist regime (whether in its authoritarian stage under the Estado Novo or in the later democratic periods under Kubitschek, Quadros, and Goulart) began to correspond less and less to the class sectors controlling the productive forces. To this increasing incongruence in the internal arrangements relating the economic structure to the social and political structures, one must add the effects of changes in the organization of the capitalist economy at the international level. To put it succinctly, international corporations began to diversify not only the lines of production and economic activity under their control, but even the geographical distribution of their plants. For the purposes of our argument, the essential factor is that international capitalism became more interested in establishing productive units such as factories and plants in the periphery, that is, in the underdeveloped countries.

In the three largest countries in Latin America—Brazil, Mexico, and Argentina, all of which have sizable domestic markets—United States direct private investment has gone increasingly into the manufacturing sector.[2]

In Brazil, the level of foreign private investment in the dynamic industrial sectors has been so high and so sustained that the state sector and national entrepreneurs clearly no longer play a dominant role in such key decision-making centers as the capital goods and durable consumer goods industries.[3] This growing industrial power of foreign-owned manufacturing firms which sell to the domestic market also means that foreign firms are the main advertisers in Brazil. According to a 1967 *Visão* article, for example, the twelve major advertisers in Brazil (as measured by the accounts of the principal advertising agencies) were: Willys Overland, Sydney Ross, Volkswagen, Gillette, Gessey Lever, Nestle, Ford, Rhodia, Fleishman and Royal, Coca-Cola, Shell, and Colgate Palmolive.[4] They thus have a great potential influence on organs of opinion such as newspapers, weekly magazines, and television, much of whose revenue is dependent upon advertising.

The general consequences of these new trends in international capitalism have been (1) increased interdependence in production activities at the international level, particularly if we look at the world economic system from the standpoint of influence on decision centers, and (2) a modification in the patterns of dependence that condition, or set constraints and limits to, the development policies of the countries located at the periphery of the international capitalist system.[5] It is true that the state, public enterprises, and local capitalists have retained some role and influence.[6] But there has been a basic change in the main axis of the power system. The dynamic basis of the productive system has shifted. The result of these basic changes is that groups expressing the interests and modes of organization of international capitalism have gained disproportionate influence. From the perspective of our argument, it does not matter greatly whether the industrial firms are owned outright by foreigners or are owned by Brazilians associated with foreign corporations, for in either case they are linked to market, investment, and decision-making structures located outside the dependent country.

Another crucial factor in understanding the current political-economic model in Brazil is that the antipopulist sectors of the military and the technocracy, which had been relatively uninfluential in the populist model of development, gained in influence as the new economic trend emerged. Given their ideological affinity to the new holders of economic power, and the similarity of their policy orientations, they have played an important and often decisive role in the creation of the present regime. The antipopulist sectors of the military and technocracy have taken upon themselves not only the modernizing function in administration, but also much of the repressive function in the social and political realm.

In the same process the older ruling sectors have lost their relative power position in the total structure. Not only the traditional agrarian sectors (*latifundiarios*), but even industrial and merchant interests that have not adapted to the changed conditions under which the expansion of the market is now being sought and to the redirection of governmental economic and financial policies have found themselves politically at a disadvantage in the new regime.[7] As a parallel process, there has been almost complete erosion from below of the power groups and structures on which the previous system was based. The more traditional, bureaucratic component of the middle classes has lost prestige and influence. The position of the career politicians, generally identified with the dominant classes in the previous arrangement, has also been extensively undermined. These politicians had served to express, at the overt political level, the class alliance in terms of which power had been organized since the Old Republic (1889–1930). This alliance had survived (though not without important changes in its internal structure) and had made the "national-populist" development model viable for some time. In the case of the other component of the alliance the more integrated sectors of the working class marginalization was no less marked. Consider the complete disappearance from the political scene of the union leaders who mediated between these workers and the state.

My main hypothesis to explain such sweeping changes in the relative power positions of all the major political actors is that the accumulation process required that the instruments of pressure and defense available to the popular classes be dismantled.[8] This the 1964 coup did immediately, through repression. The bourgeoisie paid a price. By accepting military intervention at first in order to destroy the influence of the workers, it ultimately contributed to the creation of a situation in which a return to civilian control of the political process proved impossible. In other words, in its attempt to contain the "pressure from below," the bourgeoisie supported measures that essentially destroyed its own direct political expression. It is true that the bourgeoisie never had effective political organization and pressure instruments. Now, however, not only the political party system, but all other forms of political action open to the bourgeoisie became dependent on contacts and alliances with the military and technocratic groups that alone controlled the state apparatus. Whatever the long-range implications, this much can be said: The bourgeoisie lost all leverage to shape its more immediate political interests.

However, in order to understand a political model, it is not sufficient to direct attention to the social and economic pillars that support it. It is also necessary to describe the particular mechanisms through which it generates and organizes power, the mechanisms that make it viable as a relatively stable political structure.

The current Brazilian development model has caused great analytic confusion. As we shall see in greater detail later, some analysts have asserted that the economic interests of foreign capital are now dominant and that this means that there is no room either for political maneuvering or national development in Brazil. Others believe that the military leaders have acquired a position of such great power that, free of external constraints or internal contradictions, they can and have imposed their own development model on Brazil.

I will attempt to demonstrate here that these observers are mistaken in their assumptions about the high degree of autonomy and internal coherence of the dominant economic and/or political interests. They do not understand the dynamics of the process that I call associated-dependent development when they assert that it entails stagnation.

Before discussing their work in detail, I should clarify what I see as some of the crucial characteristics of the model of associated-dependent development. The phrase was chosen deliberately to combine two notions that traditionally have appeared as separate and contradictory: development and dependence. In my view, changes in international capitalist organization have produced a new international division of labor. The moving force behind these changes is the multinational corporation. Assuming as it does the immersion of industrial capital into peripheral economies, the new international division of labor puts a dynamic element into operation in the internal market. Thus, to some extent, the interests of the foreign corporations become compatible with the internal prosperity of the dependent countries. In this sense, they help promote development. Because of this factor, the growth of multinational corporations necessitates a reformulation of the traditional view of economic imperialism, which holds that the basic relationship between a developed capitalist country and an underdeveloped country is one of extractive exploitation that perpetuates stagnation. Today, the massive investment of foreign capital aimed at manufacturing and selling consumer goods to the growing urban middle and upper classes is consistent with, and indeed dependent upon, fairly rapid economic growth in at least some crucial sectors of the dependent country. Development under this set of conditions implies, quite obviously, a definite articulation with the international market (the same thing happens, of course, in the relationships among advanced economies). Development in this situation also depends on technological, financial, organizational, and market connections that only multinational corporations can assure.

In many Latin American intellectual circles the idea that associated-dependent development is in some important sense dynamic will be considered a controversial, revisionist assertion. Let me add at this point that this path of development entails costs. The data generated during the Brazilian "boom" based on associated-dependent development support the hypothesis that this pattern of development is based on a regressive profile of income distribution, emphasizes luxury consumer durables as opposed to basic necessities,[9] generates increasing foreign indebtedness,[10] and contributes to social marginality and the underutilization and exploitation of manpower resources.

Having thus sketched out some of the most useful empirical and theoretical considerations for understanding the extraordinarily complex and complicated model that has emerged in Brazil, I will now examine in greater detail the works of the major Brazilian analysts, whose interpretations are basically at variance with mine.

THE INDETERMINACY OF ECONOMIC DETERMINIST MODELS: CELSO FURTADO AND HÉLIO JAGUARIBE

Much of the confusion surrounding the conflicting interpretations of Brazilian development since 1964 is rooted in the failure to draw fully the theoretical and empirical implications of the dynamic interdependence between politics and economics. This interdependence is implicitly denied in the linear arguments that are in essence economic determinist or political voluntarist. Oddly (but predictably, since interdependence is denied) the same theorist may shift from a position of traditional economic determinism (where he neglects the impact of politics) in attempting to describe the actual working of the system, to a position of political voluntarism (where he neglects the constraints imposed by the economic system) when he suggests a strategy for surmounting the present situation. The works of Celso Furtado and Hélio Jaguaribe, though often extremely valuable, are both flawed in precisely this way. In both cases these conceptual flaws are compounded because they cloud their perception of the process that I call associated-dependent development, and thus they do not take into consideration the full economic and political implications of the process.

Celso Furtado, in his analysis of the Brazilian political model, rightly points out one peculiarity of what he calls the military state: its bureaucratic character.[11] Yet his analysis starts from the assumption that the military state would have social stability as its major goal and that the consequence of preserving the status quo would be slow development. The economic model corresponding to this political project would be reduced to urban industrial investment in favor of agricultural production. Through a "horizontal expansion of the economy" ("pastoralization") it would be possible to absorb manpower without altering the production functions, that is to say, without continuing to absorb modern technology. Such policies would make it possible to keep social pressures at a low level.

When Furtado wrote his influential analysis he was undoubtedly reacting to an existing ideological tendency within the 1964 movement that could be interpreted as advocating such a model. Yet, as Furtado himself admits, the reality of Brazilian development was more complex. To begin with, the army bureaucracy, in control of the state apparatus was likely to be inadequately responsive to the pressures of a rather highly differentiated society with comparatively high interclass mobility. Precisely for that reason, he adds, the middle class—a particularly effective political actor in the new situation—would probably react in one (or a combination) of three ways:

1. Fight for a return to formal democracy.
2. Attempt to mobilize mass support, with a particularly effective appeal to youth and student groups as a starting base, but aiming especially at the rural masses, in opposition to the military state.

3. Infiltrate the military by means of an ideological appeal stressing "authentically national" development, which, of course, would also attract some sectors of the middle class.

The last alternative, authentically national development, is advocated by Furtado himself in his book *Um projeto para o Brasil* (*A Project for Brazil*).[12] His ideas, however, did not gain much influence among the groups controlling the state. There clearly has also been no significant movement either toward a return to democracy or toward the mobilization of massive opposition.

Within the structure of Furtado's argument we are thus left with the "pastoralization" model as an estimate of the probable course of evolution of the new Brazilian regime. It is an estimate following from the kind of economic determinism and linear reasoning we have alluded to. In essence, it contends that the military state's policies are strictly determined by the social groups, which its power is based upon. In the Brazilian case, Furtado is implicitly assuming that base to be oligarchical and dependent. This seems to be inferred from the fact that the sectors of the bourgeoisie prevailing after the coup favor a pattern of development that is both associated with and dependent on international capitalism. As a consequence, social stability is valued as a goal and ruralization is the means to achieve it. Caught in cross pressures from the latifundiarios, international capitalism, and local entrepreneurs, the military state chooses the line of least resistance, which it understands to be that which will cater to the pressures from all these groups while presenting the least danger to its own integrity. The latter part of the chosen course of action implies keeping order, and particularly the hegemonic position of the armed forces.

In fairness, it must be said that Furtado has not really relied on this kind of prognosis. He estimates that the degree of social and economic differentiation already attained would make much more likely a model that is economically more dynamic and politically more flexible. That is why he then turns to speculation on the chances of a pattern of development that would be economically autonomous and politically more open. In the model he proposes, development would be based on the ability of the state, fueled by the middle class, to contain the excesses of international capitalism and promote development along national or autonomous lines. What he is really suggesting then is a return to the earlier nationalist development model politically adapted to a situation in which the other element of the coalition, populism, has been wiped out. The new coalition and its policies would be nationalist and technocratic. A major prerequisite for its viability would be the enactment of an income redistribution scheme that would broaden the market without endangering the accumulation process.

Furtado's proposed development model found few powerful supporters. The key middle-class actors in the model—the local entrepreneurs—and the sectors linked to the state have chosen a different path, as we shall see shortly. Any model comprises, of course, an analysis of the existing situation and a set of goals to direct action. However, Furtado's propositions lean much too heavily toward the latter. They neglect the economic realities of the new model of associated-dependent development and place almost exclusive reliance on political voluntarism. Its lack of appeal must be attributed to anachronistic undertones of his version of a national-developmentalist ideology based on the assumptions that a politically capable middle class exists and that it would be interested in supporting that ideology or model of development.

Before discussing in greater detail the issues raised by Furtado, let me turn to Hélio Jaguaribe, another important political analyst who has also explored the possibility of an authentically national route to development.[13]

According to Jaguaribe, there are three fundamental political alternatives for a development process under optimal conditions. Each, to be applicable, is dependent upon a specific set of conditions:

- "National capitalism." This depends on an alliance among the progressive sectors of the national entrepreneurs, the middle class, and the proletariat, under a neo-Bismarckian style of leadership by the head of state and unified into a national party for development.
- "State capitalism." By means of a coup, power comes to be controlled by the progressive sectors of the military and technocracy, which weld themselves together into a coalition approximating a "party of national revolution." Their leverage in this process is the state apparatus itself.
- "Developmental socialism." This presupposes a revolutionary takeover by an elite willing to mobilize the masses and to resort to socialist means of accumulation and control.

Before 1964, it seems that Jaguaribe's prescription for Brazil, given his judgment of the existing social and political conditions, was the national capitalist development model. After that date, by virtue of the changes that had taken place, he seems to have inclined toward the state capitalist model.

However, the political model that Jaguaribe believes will actually become institutionalized is "colonial-fascism." Unfortunately, since his main purpose is to argue how unviable this trend is, he has not fully elaborated the colonial-fascist model. He did, however, suggest some of its characteristics in the Brazilian case.[14] Colonial-fascism, he says, depends at least on the following:

1. Strengthening the state, not in order to make possible a significant extent of interference and control of the economy, but in order to preserve stability, which of course depends on maximum use of coercion capabilities.
2. Close integration, political as well as economic, of Brazil with the Western system as it is being structured by the United States.
3. Reliance, under state supervision, on the market: control of the economy must be, as far as possible, in the hands of private economic units.

This model would permit as it did in fascist Italy and Germany economic development without changes in the social structure. However, given the dependent character of the Brazilian economy, the local bourgeoisie, unlike its German or Italian counterpart, would be unable to place the economy on a dynamic growth plane. It would also be impossible to establish an appropriate coalition between entrepreneurs and a middle-class party, which he sees as the political axis of the typical fascist model. Instead entrepreneurs ally with international capitalism. Hence the "colonial" in his description of this type of fascism.

In the Castello Branco government's economic policies and its concentration of coercive powers, Jaguaribe perceived a clear trend toward colonial-fascism. The fundamental prerequisites for this model's functioning were apparently being deliberately prepared by government policies. Yet Jaguaribe does not think the model can work in Brazil. For one thing, "the colonial-fascist model would in a few years aggravate the disequilibrium, between population growth and the opening up of new employment opportunities, at all occupational levels, to such an extent that the new ruling classes would soon be compelled to enforce some sort of apartheid, that is, to prevent peasant immigration into the cities, where they would become explosive marginal masses." Secondly, "the dominant economy needs raw materials from the dependent economy . . . and cannot induce any dynamic effect on it . . . as long as the dependent economy does not develop a domestic market. . . . Yet the colonial-fascist model aims precisely to prevent the social changes required for the development of such an autonomous and endogenous economy."[15]

In short, Jaguaribe believes that the military regime will not be able to maintain itself if it keeps a colonial-fascist orientation, since this makes it impossible to overcome the structural impasses just mentioned. Thus, given that, in the long run, the military regime is incompatible with the complexity of the urban-industrial sector, political and socioeconomic changes will certainly take place once the fear that led the industrialists and the middle class to accept the colonial-fascist model vanishes. The options will then probably be limited to two: either the military will reinstate into power-controlling positions the social groups that are presently marginalized (in which case, of course, some will wish to assume civilian political roles through the political parties and so on) or the military themselves will transform the fundamental nature and meaning of the regime.

Initially, in 1967, Jaguaribe believed that the first hypothesis was more likely. Now he seems to regard the second—the regime changing itself from within—as a better approximation of reality.[16]

Let us now take a closer look at the two analytical schemes we have discussed thus far. Both start from the assumption that the economic model now being developed is not (or is insufficiently) dynamic. Celso Furtado speaks of pastoralization and stagnation, while Jaguaribe describes the Brazilian fascist model as colonial. According to Jaguaribe, today's metropolis-colony relationships can still be described in terms of an international division of labor in which the colony specializes in exporting raw materials, and such a relationship must be seen as an obstacle to development. Viewing the Brazilian economy as non-dynamic suggests two consequences. One is that the guarantors of the regime, the military, pursue a goal of social stabilization that requires economic stagnation. This follows from the assumed correspondence between the regime's social basis—the agrarian oligarchy—and its economic interests. The military, then, is nothing but the instrument of the oligarchy, regardless of the military's own corporate interests. The second consequence of this view is that the solution to the impasse must be to come back to a pattern of authentically national development, based, of course, on the assumption that the system's lack of dynamism derives from its dependent character. However, once it is realized that the Brazilian bourgeoisie, or its hegemonic sectors, has opted for the pattern of associated-dependent development, the basis for autonomous development must be sought somewhere else. Among the other possible candidates, the middle class is the strategic actor. Certain functional groups, specifically some sectors of the military or the governmental technocracy, both identified with the middle class in their social characteristics, come to be seen as decisive. These, then, would be the actors charged with the responsibility of carrying forward the project of authentically national development.

It is time to pause and ask: how much of this is an objective attempt to analyze real, existing tendencies, and how much is simply the preferred, normative model? An objective analysis would show, in fact, a very different picture. Associated-dependent development is not without dynamism; it is not based on ruralization at the expense of industrialization; it does not reinforce the old division of labor in which some countries only exported raw materials and imported manufactured goods. On the contrary, the distinguishing feature of the new type of dependency that is evolving in countries like Brazil, Argentina, and Mexico is that it is based on a new international division of labor. Part of the industrial system of the hegemonic countries is now being transferred, under the control of international corporations, to countries that have already been able to reach a relatively advanced level of industrial development. I have elsewhere called this process an "internationalization of the internal market," in contrast to the previous stage of import substitution industrialization.[17] The latter was significantly controlled by the local bourgeoisie and by the state.

It is clear that both Celso Furtado and Hélio Jaguaribe are familiar with this process. They have not, however, come to terms with all of the implications, as one can perceive from their description of the major political actors and the policies they should be willing to carry out. The model of associated-dependent development does have a dynamic character. It does allow for economic growth and social mobility, at least for the urban-industrial sector. Undoubtedly it does not prevent class attrition, it does almost certainly have a "marginalizing" effect, and it does not reduce inequality; on the contrary, it is based on concentration of income and increasing relative misery.

The task of the informed critic is not to deny or obscure these characteristics of the associated-dependent model of development. Instead, he must take them fully into consideration to make realistic assessments and identify the social groups that might be able to carry through an alternative model.

In Furtado's and Jaguaribe's analyses, the hope for an authentically national pattern of development, once pinned on the nationalist entrepreneurs, is now pinned on the middle class, and particularly on the military sector of the middle class. However, my analysis of associated-dependent development shows that the middle-class groups have, if anything, exerted pressure toward associated-dependent development. Rather than looking forward toward a "capitalism without capitalists," they have in practice favored growth through private capital, whether Brazilian or foreign, while other investment areas are reserved for the state itself. What is the role of the military in this process? What did they initially intend and what has actually happened? Is there any reality to the idea that they might themselves replace the dependent-associated, bureaucratic-authoritarian models of development and rule with other models as is occasionally suggested by such authors as Furtado and Jaguaribe?

The Castello Branco "project" was politically and economically liberal, though its liberalism was qualified, of course, by the circumstances of an underdeveloped country: a strong executive, political party representation (appropriately purged to prevent pressures from the Left), and a combination of market mechanisms with strong state regulation, strengthening private business, and opening the national economy to international capitalist investment and connections. The model had not foreseen either bureaucratic modernization or the steep rise in the participation of the public sector in the economy. Governmental policies of the Castello Branco period seemed to expect a massive contribution of foreign investment, which did not materialize. The government clearly intended to abide by its promise to restore democratic forms after purging the populist element. An illustration of this intention was Castello Branco's pledge to respect the electoral calendar, despite the risks this might imply for the regime. Finally, the Castello Branco model called for the army to refrain from exercising its overwhelming corporate influence on political decisions. This model in theory would benefit the party system and therefore the bourgeois sectors represented in it.

However, the military did not implement this model. They did, of course, share the goal of a strong executive, but they placed it under their direct control. This was accomplished, for example, by changing the organization and role of the military and civil offices of the presidency; broadening the scope of the National Security Council and particularly the latter's General Secretariat; creating a national intelligence service; and establishing security departments in all the ministries and state enterprises. In short, the aim was to establish ever-tighter linkages between the planning and control agencies of the executive and their counterparts in the armed forces, especially the chiefs of staff. Through these coordination devices, they sought to achieve greater control over all the key economic sectors and to accelerate economic growth. Thus the military came to accept as their own the goals of centralization of the administration and the repression of all forms of social protest. Making the state apparatus more efficient and increasing repression developed side by side. Both were justified by the doctrine of national security. Dismantling workers' organizations and achieving a high degree of "political tranquillity" should, quite naturally, make it possible to catch up again on the development process or, if you will, on capitalist accumulation on a greatly amplified scale. Thus, pursuing what at one level can be seen as their own policies, the military have in fact placed the model of dependent-industrial development on a sound, dynamic basis.

The military's actual policies, then, can be appropriately characterized as social stability with economic change. Yet even here one must qualify what is to be understood by stability. The term does refer, of course, to the maintenance of a class society, but it does not preclude mobility. Mobility occurs and is in fact ideologically encouraged, as long as it does not become associated with political mobilization. The policy is, in this sense, one of modern conservatism. Its aim is to keep socially open a politically closed society, while trying to accelerate capitalist economic growth through a combination of public and private enterprise.[18]

The main features of the present power arrangement, then, are the disproportionate amount of power held by the military (and, in a subordinate position, the technocracy) vis-à-vis the internationalizing bourgeoisie and the military's implementation of policies that entirely satisfy the internationalizing bourgeoisie's interests. This explains the complacent apathy of the urban middle class, not to mention the contentment and euphoria among those members of it who are beginning to enjoy the benefits of development through their employment in large private or public enterprises.

Thus an agreement has been reached between the Brazilian bourgeoisie and the state. The former has momentarily relinquished its political-control instruments (political party system, elections, and so on) as well as the instruments of symbolic ideological definition and diffusion (freedom of the press, habeas corpus, doctrinaire pluralism, liberal education), all of which have become rather closely responsive to state pressures and military control. In the trade-off, civil society has contracted and the state has mushroomed, particularly with respect to the regulation of economic life. But in the process, the military implicitly assumed an identity between the economic interests of the entrepreneurs and the general interests of the nation. They defined some areas in which private business would be preferentially encouraged to act. Thus structured, this system does have a dynamic element built into it; the question of its durability does not concern us here. The system does have considerable social costs, but it has also opened up very promising opportunities for the absorption of the modern sectors of the middle classes, linking them through self-interest to the international bourgeoisie. This is an important political fact.

Can this situation be described by seeing the state as an "executive committee" for the international bourgeoisie and the military as the latter's armed hand? If this description were accurate, political analysis would be simple. The social process would be conceived as a non-contradictory continuum or at best as a continuum in which the only contradiction would be that between the dominant classes, harmoniously integrated with the state, and the dominated classes, excluded from the state and hardly a part of an ongoing society. It seems more accurate, however, to underscore that the relative degree of stability achieved in the alliance among the military, the bourgeoisie, and the middle classes is the contrivance of a development model and a political regime in which their interests are balanced as against more serious enemies. This balance could be achieved, quite obviously, because their internal contradictions were not as antagonistic as the threat of a development policy generally favorable to the popular classes.

Let us come back to a question raised at the beginning of this chapter. Are we justified in inquiring about the possibly revolutionary economic consequences of the 1964 coup? Would it not seem more apt to describe it as a victorious counterrevolution? The answer is not simple. Clearly, the 1964 movement, through conscious intention and by virtue of its own dynamics, did seek and was able to impose its conception of order through repression. In this sense, its consequences were clearly reactionary. Was it, however, integrally counterrevolutionary? It is interesting to note here, despite the appearance of triviality, that some of its main actors assert this to have been the case, since they regard the previous regime as revolutionary. It is true that, from 1963 to March 1964, the Brazilian situation could be described as pre-Revolutionary. The state seemed to be in partial decomposition, and the level of mobilization might have reached a point where the existing capabilities of the political system would have been unable to control it. Yet, it is quite unlikely that the final outcome would have been a fundamental social revolution, given the lack of adequate means to achieve it: clearly defined goals, a non-opportunistic strategy on the part of the left-wing groups prevailing at the moment, organization to capitalize for its own benefit on the decomposition of the state apparatus. The populist alliance through which some sort of attempt was made to bring together the masses, middle-class groups, and the national entrepreneurs was itself dependent on the state. It was caught up in a web of interests and relationships ultimately based on an economic foundation that was not only intrinsically nonrevolutionary, but also backward. Furthermore, one of the structural anchors of that alliance was the nonincorporation of the rural population, leaving it politically unorganized and economically overexploited. This made it possible to count on the support of the conservative clientelistic parties, particularly the Social Democratic Party (PSD).

The 1964 coup forced out the national-bourgeois sector as well as the statist developmentalist groups that had until then been in a hegemonic position. The deposed groups were replaced with the bourgeoisie's internationalized sectors, which are necessarily more dynamic and more "modern," because they are in essence part of the international capitalist system of production. The new economic policies and administrative reforms unleashed the productive forces of "modern capitalism," and the entire economic system became intimately linked to the international capitalist system of production. In other words, the relationship between the hegemonic world centers and the dependent economy was, and is increasingly being, restructured in accordance with new patterns of international economic organization. As emphasized at an earlier point in this study, however, this situation does not preclude the possibility of industrial and financial development in the peripheral dependent state. The urban-industrial pole, which had been growing at a fast pace since the Kubitschek period, now became dominant in the development of Brazilian capitalism.

It is hardly necessary to point out that primary exports of raw materials and agricultural products still retain a major place in the economy. But even in these areas, new, associated forms of production involving international monopolies and local enterprises have appeared. Not even public enterprise is excluded from this new scheme of things, as attested by the mining consortia in iron and manganese. Other characteristically subordinated aspects remain, particularly foreign indebtedness and technological dependence, and foreign firms have acquired greater control over the private industrial sector.[19] The internal market has become essential to foreign businesses themselves.

In addition, the policy aimed at diversifying exports has produced a reduction in the relative weight of the traditional primary items (almost exclusively produced by local entrepreneurs) in favor of industrial or semiprocessed minerals, both expressing the new patterns of association. Public enterprises function more and more like private corporations, enjoying the same freedom and aiming at the same results. The role of PETROBRAS (the state oil monopoly) in the establishment of the petrochemical industry is suggestive in this regard: PETROBRAS works in association with international and local firms, although it acts as the lead partner in the consortium. Association mechanisms like this have reduced conflict between public enterprise and private business. It has thus been possible to forge a modus vivendi, if not an effective political alliance, between functional middle-class groups (such as the military, the technocracy, and the bureaucracy), despite their nationalistic values, and the representatives of the international and the Brazilian internationalized bourgeoisie.

Given the picture just sketched, is there any meaning in reviving, as Furtado and Jaguaribe do, nationalist ideals based on the assumption of an active, local entrepreneurial sector bound up with a state structure that serves as a bridge to the popular masses? Is it not true that the economic assumptions of the nationalist model autonomous state enterprise and equally independent, native, private capital no longer hold? Is it not anachronistic to go on thinking of the Empresa Publica (public enterprise) as the moving force behind that model? And if what I suggest is true, what can we now conceive as the political role, present and potential, of the nationalistic middle-class sectors? One answer suggests itself promptly: unless they confine themselves to an ideology that cannot be expected to offer any effective political choices, they will be compelled to redefine the content of their nationalism. That redefinition is already under way. In all likelihood, we will soon be unable to understand, in the light of the pre-1964 experience, what is now meant by nationalism.

It is in this limited sense that we are entitled to refer to the dynamic economic consequences of 1964 as a revolution. A bourgeois economic revolution did take place, brought into being by a reactionary political movement. It was economically revolutionary to the extent that it pushed the local bourgeoisie to adapt to the beat of international capitalist development, thereby establishing an effective subordination of the national economy to modern forms of economic domination. Modernization of the state machinery and the changes introduced in the public sector of the economy fall into the same context of integration into the international capitalist system.

Undoubtedly those who believe that the native bourgeoisie in dependent countries can carry through a bourgeois revolution, infusing the latter term with the meaning it has as a description of the French or American revolutions, will call attention to still existing "structural obstacles." These, they will claim, reduce the scope and meaning of the economic changes that have been occurring in Brazil since 1964.

I do not believe that the Brazilian bourgeoisie, a child of dependent capitalism, can stage a revolution in the strong meaning of the term. Its "revolution" is limited to integrating itself into the scheme of international capitalism, to associating itself with international capitalism as a dependent and minor partner. The Brazilian bourgeoisie will, and does, struggle to make the most of it. But it faces an objective limitation: capitalist accumulation in dependent economies does not complete its cycle. Lacking "autonomous technology" as vulgar parlance has it and compelled therefore to utilize imported technology, dependent capitalism is crippled. Dependent capitalism must thus bear all the consequences of absorbing capital-intensive, labor-saving technology; but that is not the main problem. It is crippled because it lacks a fully developed capital-goods sector. The accumulation, expansion, and self-realization of local capital requires and depends on a dynamic complement outside itself: it must insert itself into the circuit of international capitalism. The latter, of course, does develop the capital-goods sector without which the expansion of the consumer-goods sector (including durable goods) in dependent countries can hardly be imagined.

It was this limited transformation to a dependent capitalist economy that the 1964 coup made possible. In order to accomplish it, it was necessary to repress the working class, to keep down wages, and at the same time to broaden the channels of accumulation. In the process it removed, even though some instability may remain in this respect, the ideological and organizational factors that tended to work against the formulation of policies of association between the state, local private enterprise, and international trusts.

THE FRAGILITY OF POWER-ELITE MODELS: CÂNDIDO MENDES

To claim that a new economic power base has come into being and that a political modus vivendi among the dominant classes is again possible is not to say that political conflicts among the groups in power have ceased to exist. Even less does it mean that opposition forces have altogether disappeared. But here again, the more ambitious attempts to analyze the present Brazilian regime have failed, and once more this failure must be credited to an underlying linear construction of events. Or it may be attributed to what looks like the opposite error: the analytic models proposed have been so heavily based on the apparent power relationships prevailing in each particular presidency that the models crumble and must be rebuilt after each political zigzag that forces the government in power to alter its political or economic program. More often than not, political changes have been neither foreseen nor desired by the actors themselves. And yet they must bear some relationship to the more basic, underlying structures and constraints. To make them explicit wherever possible is the task of political analysis.

Thus, rather than inquire into the conscious purposes or manifest strategies of succeeding governments, we must attempt to identify political forces, to trace the contours of the framework within which they operate, and to weigh the outcomes of their actions. Before I present my own views, I will look first at the contributions made by another major political analyst in Brazil.

Cândido Mendes, who has made perhaps the most consistent attempts to lay bare the working models of political development in Brazil, seems to have been compelled to alter his explanatory scheme at each change in government. His revisions are explained by his attempts to capture the manifold political facets of the regime through ad hoc interpretations. Thus, the Castello Branco government was for him a "paradigm" of the power-elite model.[20] That elite, so the argument ran, had been formed among the members of the Superior War College, which trains both military and civilian personnel. These men formed a homogeneous group, conscious of its historical responsibility and armed with an effective political ideology inspired by the "doctrine of national security." Thus it was able to formulate, and started to implement, a national development model. That model corresponded to the notion of a modernizing autocracy, and as such it implied a consistent program of social and economic reform. For Cândido Mendes, the power-elite model, as practiced by the castellistas, prevented personalization in the exercise of power. The president had preserved for himself maximum coercive capabilities, but he did not in fact apply them, limiting himself to skillful use of threats rather than actions. Thus the model made it possible to avoid a thorough, formalized dictatorship.

According to Cândido Mendes, the power-elite type of regime, as exemplified by Castello Branco, has two main characteristics. First, it refuses to broaden the scope of political compromise through incorporation of other groups into the limited circle of power holders. This maintains the circle's own "purity" and prevents it from being disfigured or diluted. Second, the regime rejects consensual legitimation, which it might achieve through the manipulation of symbols with strong mobilizing appeal.

Thus the Castello Branco regime must be seen as a specific instance of the power-elite type, with regard to its structure or mode of exercising power. It consciously adapted that pattern to the task of instituting a democratic, technically reformed governmental structure. It sought to achieve this goal through strategically conceived economic and political reforms. That is why the military elite allied itself to the technocratic elite. This, as Cândido Mendes puts it, "made it possible for the castellistas to insulate themselves as a ruling group . . . from any objective determination, whether of class or any other social denominator, in order to retain exclusive access to the highest level of governmental decision."[21]

In an earlier study, Cândido Mendes had described the Castello Branco regime in more realistic terms.[22] Though emphasizing its characteristically power-elite type, based on a military technocratic alliance, he also called attention to the fact that the army, particularly after Costa e Silva became the presidential candidate, began to take an active role in the shaping of major decisions. Thus, he wrote, the political model "could be described as a 'technocracy' in an authoritarian state." Its overall function was "to provide the necessary institutional conditions for economic planning development."

The power-elite model became less tenable when Costa e Silva came to power. Therefore Cândido Mendes reinterpreted it. Of course, Costa e Silva's election was "inevitable, given the inner logic of the existing system."[23] The election served to legitimate the regime's natural course, in the sense that Costa e Silva's candidacy "was identified with the military's consolidation of their own position, as a strengthened and restored force, ready to take up a competitive and polarizing role in the exercise of the power functions which, taken together, make up the present Brazilian state."[24] Thus continuity was assured, despite eventual differences about policy coloration and even despite the fact that Costa e Silva's coming to power had "from a technical point of view, a populist cast, as a rigorously objective representation of a given stratum of the nation, namely the army." Despite all of these departures from the power-elite model as posited before, "he should find no difficulty in placing himself formally within the previously established line (or policy range)."[25]

In short, despite the obvious difficulty in reconciling the new features of the Costa e Silva period with the power-elite model, the ambiguity in the quotations above seems quite telling. Cândido Mendes continues to insist that the interpretation remains valid. The role of the army, he says, supports his contention. Acting as a status group and keeping major policy within its range of control, it guarantees the necessary conditions of the power-elite model's applicability. Yet, according to Cândido Mendes, the Costa e Silva government could evolve in the direction of a Bonapartist regime. That is, a populist caudillo could spring up from the military. A change in this direction would imply a drastic policy reorientation, involving a scheme of income redistribution and an extension of the power pact to incorporate other actors. The latter element in Cândido Mendes's speculation is accounted for by the existence (at the time he was writing) of the Frente Ampla, which was quite active as long as it managed to maintain itself. Incorporation of other political actors would also require some way of preventing a return to tutelary intervention of the dutrista type.[26] On the other hand, a Bonapartist solution would only make sense if it implied a deeper commitment of the armed forces in the regulation and management of the society. That is, it would require an extensive utilization of the military's "managerial" inclination (as exemplified, among other things, by General Albuquerque Lima's performance in the Interior Ministry at that time). Were these conditions to come about, it could well be possible for the military to shape the regime into a Nasserist pattern.[27]

Again, we seem to have the kind of analysis that starts with the intention of constructing an analytical model and then moves toward a rationalization of de facto situations, evolving into a thinly disguised normative view. In this case, hopes are pinned on military nationalism as an alternative to the development model that has already been put into practice. Yet, as mentioned before, Cândido Mendes did stress (probably too much) the privatizing character of economic policy under the Castello Branco government. He had also attempted to describe the "power vacuum" that led to the emergence of the military regime.[28] What social forces, then, would give the nationalist alternative the support it would need?

Here the misconceptions regarding the political process have their roots in a much too serious reading of the actors' political platforms and ideologies. Unlike the authors discussed in the first part of this chapter, who tended to overstress structural constraints, Cândido Mendes seems to think that the power-elite regime functions in a social vacuum. Hence his fundamental assumption that the elite—the president, technocracy, and military groups at the top—operates "technically." Celso Furtado and Hélio Jaguaribe tended to exaggerate the weight of the socioeconomic basis of political life. In Cândido Mendes's interpretation, on the contrary, the political actors act out a story that is purely ideological. The political logic that they follow is assumed to have nothing to do with the social and economic structure.

An analysis of the Castello Branco government and its "paradigmatic" character, however, should not take as a starting point the ideal-typical coherence of its purposes, but rather the insurmountable difficulties it faced in its attempt to convert them into actual policy. An important case in point is the Second Institutional Act, issued in October 1965 in response to government defeats in key state elections. There was an external conditioning factor (external to the power elite, that is), and it was this factor that made the act necessary. The troops, opposed to the idea of abiding by a self-imposed electoral calendar, imposed a ukase on the president. He had little choice but to accept the situation and broaden the "power pact"—broaden it to such an extent that the package bargain included military imposition of the Costa e Silva candidacy as successor. Why? Why is it that the Castello Branco governing elite insisted on elections and legality? Which forces pressured the president in this direction? Which opposed it? Perhaps by asking simple and straightforward questions like these, we can bring back into the picture the real nerve of the political process—conflict.

Any view that rationalizes de facto political processes, picturing them as the unfolding of an elite's conscious will, bears the burden of subjectivity. A more objective approach stresses the conflicts among groups within the arena of organized power as well as the conflicts between these groups and those located outside the arena who attempt to make their views felt and to change prevailing orientations. Let us keep in mind, for a moment, only one aspect of the contradictions faced by the Castello Branco government. The political outlook that was identified with his own personal views and that found considerable support in the political parties focused attention on "institutionalizing" the Revolution. In other words, the Revolution aspired to some sort of legitimacy that would ultimately reflect itself in a rule of law, or lawful state. In the army, however, there were groups—so-called hard-liners—who pressured for radicalization, for carrying the repressive anti-corruption measures much further. Given their aims, they naturally wanted strict military control over the decision-making machinery. Very likely these groups embodied two broad tendencies, which might or might not coincide in the same persons. Both were anticommunist, but one was nationalistic while the other was more concerned with moralizing. Both placed themselves together to the right of the government, and both were constantly on the watch for occasions to hold the government in check. Their faits accomplis were often sufficiently vigorous to threaten a crisis situation. In addition, there was, outside the centers of power, the "opposition." Toward the end of the Castello Branco term, it was made up of the MDB (the Brazilian Democratic Movement, which had been created to act as an opposition in the political-party game) and of various remnants of the pre-1964 regime and party system.

After the election of Costa e Silva, as mentioned earlier, a trend became clear. The army acted more and more as a corporate group, seeking to occupy the state apparatus, which had been modernized by the Castello Branco government. At the same time, the regime admitted into its ranks parts of the once assertive "national (local) bourgeoisie." This group was represented in the government by virtue of the prestige enjoyed by some nationalists (who were apparently partly responsible for the movement favoring the Costa e Silva candidacy). The most significant feature of the period, however, is neither the marshal—the president's paternalism—nor his populistic impulses. There was no change, despite official declarations to the contrary, in economic policy on the arrocho salarial (tightly keeping down the wage level). The insignificance of the self-styled Nasserites is underscored by the fact that their main representative, the minister of the interior, lost his post as a result of a clear and direct confrontation on economic policy with the minister of finance. The issue involved far more than a mere question of official roles, because the latter was known to represent an opposite developmental model, namely, strengthening entrepreneurial organization through association of private Brazilian, public, and foreign capital. Rather, the distinguishing feature of the period is that, once more, the president sponsored a strategy of "democratic opening" (abertura democrática).

The president sought to reactivate the party system, reassert political freedoms, and appeal to national union. Once the overall situation began to change, opposition and protest mounted (as exemplified by the rally of "the 100,000" in Rio de Janeiro, initial scattered guerrilla actions, the MDB's beginning to act as a serious opposition party, constitution of the Frente Ampla, and so on). And again, an opposition force inside the power system checked the government's course; the "young officers," nationalist and ultra sectors of the army, brought pressure to bear on the top officeholders, and the Fifth Institutional Act was issued. Now the situation changed drastically. The act virtually transformed the president into a dictator, under surveillance by the military. Now it was the army, as an institution, making its own pressures initiated by the ultra sectors.

The scene was repeated once more during the Costa e Silva period—without, of course, public demonstrations of opposition and protest—when attempts were made to "reconstitutionalize" the regime. These attempts originated within the cupula palaciana (the presidential inner circle) and were apparently supported by the "political class"—civilian politicians and remnants of the previous regimes. Reconstitutionalization did not come about, seemingly because of Costa e Silva's illness and immediate succession. Be that as it may, opposition to the new attempts at reconstitutionalization had already grown and another political crisis was gathering, quite aside from the president's illness.

In the meantime, two other factors emerged that completely changed the stage. One was economic—essentially the resumption of a steady rate of economic growth. The other was distinctly political—armed opposition beginning toward the end of 1968 and increasing in 1969.

In a sense, however, the picture remained the same until the end of Costa e Silva's period. The government, with some support from the army and from the political parties, aimed to institutionalize the Revolution. At the same time, a chain of actions and reactions from left and right, mutually conditioning each other, functioned as a veto on the strategy sponsored by the governmental leadership. Behind these pressures and counter pressures, economic policy decisions followed a relatively autonomous course. Interest groups somehow got the governmental favors and decisions they needed and returned them in the form of support, if not specifically to the governmental leadership, certainly to the regime itself.

Now, let us ask, what kind of regime is this? Costa e Silva's succession, through the election of Medici, made it possible to see quite clearly the way the system works. Despite nationalist pressures and despite the prestige enjoyed within the army by Albuquerque Lima, the fundamental decision to put aside the latter's candidacy had the following features:

1. It was limited to the upper stratum of the military bureaucracy (four-star generals).
2. It was based on bureaucratic criteria of hierarchy and corporate representation.
3. It was intended to prevent a crucial risk to the army arising from fragmentation caused by the proliferation of tendencies and factions. This risk would clearly have existed had the nationalist tendency prevailed; by the same token it would have led to the crystallization of an opposition.
4. It was, therefore, a mechanism to reconcile diverging tendencies within the army itself.

And, most significantly, once the decision was made, it was accepted in the name of hierarchy, discipline, and cohesion by the losers, even though they probably had a majority among the lower echelons.

Thus it was the armed forces, as an institution, which increasingly came to control the state. That is, a military bureaucracy came to control the state apparatus, itself a bureaucracy, which had been modernized in previous administrations. The result of this process was the consolidation of a relatively stable model of bureaucratic domination.

I have emphasized relatively stable, and with good reason. It is true that the regime has been able to generate effective policies and to keep order. It has not, however, solved its fundamental problems, particularly those of a distinctly political nature. It has not devised means to broaden and firmly establish its legitimacy in the society at large. For the time being, the risks of bureaucratic rigidity can be compensated for by the fact, discussed above, that the economy, including its public sector, has been cast into a more clearly entrepreneurial pattern. Administration has become more "technocratic." And, more basically, the bureaucratic-authoritarian nature of the regime does not mean that it fails to pursue the policies in which various social groups are interested. Not only the internationalized bourgeoisie, but also the military as a group and the rising middle classes (that is, professionals and skilled white-collar workers) have benefited from them. As long as the economy maintains its present growth rate, it is even possible that some sectors of the lower strata (workers in the more modern sectors, and so on) will share in the prosperity. This, of course, is quite likely to the extent that the government decides to pursue redistributive policies. The situation of these workers may be ameliorated even to the point of increasing their relative share of the total income.

The overriding goal as conceived by the military is to strengthen the state in order to guarantee national security. I have argued that there is no direct and necessary conflict between this goal and the development model that is being put into practice. The scheme even allows some room for nationalist pressures, as long of course as the "associated" nature of development is maintained and as long as a strong state is agreed upon as one of the major elements in the model.

To sum up: the regime is autocratic; its mode of organization is military-bureaucratic. It does have a dynamic economic foundation. There are undoubtedly limitations in both respects. There are political limitations and fundamental political problems that the regime has not solved. There are also economic limitations, for the model can be no more dynamic than the measure allowed by the dependent-associated development pattern.

AUTHORITARIANISM AND DEMOCRACY

This association between an increased growth rate and authoritarianism has encouraged the notion that they bear an intimate and necessary relation to each other. In this view, authoritarianism is seen as a prerequisite for economic development. It is not important to examine the whole argument nor review the evidence at this point. There is no doubt, however, that this belief has been enthusiastically adhered to in many quarters. As one can easily imagine, it has found supporters among the military, but it is by no means limited to military circles. Entrepreneurs, technocrats, and various segments of the rising middle classes have also found these notions congenial to their own interests and experience. Among the generally nationalistic ultra groups the authoritarian argument sometimes takes the form of a self-styled Nasserism. Ranged against these views, generally speaking, we find the remnants of castellista groups, as well as opposition groups without access to the government (part of the Left, intellectuals, the Church, and so on).

Given this picture, it seems particularly interesting to review briefly the argument against the authoritarians. The most eloquent defense of the politically democratic, economically dependent-associated development model has been put forward by a former member of Castello Branco's cabinet, Roberto de Oliveira Campos.[29] Borrowing language, model, and intention from such American political scientists as Apter, Almond, and Verba, he wrote: "The political option appropriate in our case which is in fact the one accepted (consagrada) by the Revolution of 1964 is a combination of participatory democracy and a strong executive. A reconciliation model is the most appropriate, considering that our society, at least in some regions, has already reached beyond modernization and has entered the phase of industrialization."[30] This model, he goes on to say, requires a strong executive, a functioning party system, and mechanisms of "popular reconciliation," the basis of which is elite-mass information and communication. It would thus be possible to avoid the risks involved in mobilization and autocratic systems. Information would replace coercion, making it possible to avoid committing the mistakes and paying the price entailed by either "distributive populism" or "nationalist excitation." The basis for a new consensual regime would be economic pluralism, which is the necessary condition for political pluralism and for an open society. Through the improvement of the channels of social mobility, such as the educational system, this society would come into its own.

Once more, we have an argument that conceives of the political sphere as strictly conditioned by the economic (if there is a pluralist economic structure, there must be political pluralism), associated with a normative perspective. Simple as they are, the facts of the matter indicate that the regime relies more on coercion than on information, despite economic pluralism.

Let us now turn to a final question. Does the existing level of coercion indicate that the Brazilian regime is not only bureaucratic, but also totalitarian? Tendencies in that direction do exist, but they are not dominant. The state officially sticks to a "democratic" doctrine. In this sense, the present situation lacks two fundamental components of the totalitarian model: an ideology and a mobilizing political party. It remains an economically developmentalist military-bureaucratic autocracy. Will it undertake the big leap forward toward a totalitarian state?

Once again, looking for an answer only at the ideological level will not do. If we emphasize the actual power balance instead, an important fact to be taken into account is the tendency for the older political interests to regroup themselves. They place themselves around the stabilizing axis of the military and state bureaucracy, in the political parties consented to by the regime. They of course submit to the centralizing and stabilizing tendencies of the regime, as the nomination of state governors by the president has clearly shown. On this occasion, the state legislatures perform the same ritual function as the national Congress, which elects the president after the choice has been made somewhere else. Yet economic policy decisions do seem to be made in a circle enjoying considerable autonomy vis-à-vis the political power centers. In that circle, entrepreneurs do participate, on a quasi-corporative basis.

This decision-making system, taken as a whole, is therefore both bureaucratic-centralized and accessible to the entrepreneurs. It has been able to generate policies and to define goals quite effectively and simultaneously to legitimate itself in the society at large through the symbolic appeal of strengthening the Fatherland. At another level, perhaps a more basic one, the regime seeks to gain legitimacy (or, as Cândido Mendes would put it, authentication) through economic achievements. In a peculiar parody of those analytical schemes that posit a strict conditioning effect between economy and polity, the only answer given to protests against repression comes in economic development figures. The language of human rights is in this sense translated into GNP growth rates.

However, the system does have potential destabilizers, two of which must be mentioned. One is internal: the system's inability to control the forces of repression within its own structure. The other is external: sporadic armed opposition. Most important of all, the regime has not created an effective institutional form, so that each succession is bound to become a crisis point.

At the beginning, from the Castello Branco period on, there were the veto groups, the ultras. Their actions, as mentioned before, almost invariably have a critical, conditioning effect on the political process as a whole. In addition, there is now the repressive apparatus and the left-wing armed opposition groups. Neither of these extremes seems capable of generating viable political strategies and goals. Yet both can and do reciprocally condition the regime's course. They are able to hold it in check under specific circumstances. To the extent that they make a more open political arena rather unlikely, they reduce the regime's ability to absorb opposition groups. They lessen the regime's ability to generate policies satisfactory to those interested in "critical" or "qualified" participation, that is, those who oppose the regime but would rather retain some diffuse influence than propose clear-cut policy alternatives.

The possibility that coercion increases at the expense of information, to put it euphemistically, does exist. The possibility of keeping that tendency within limits will depend on the ability of some groups within the government, or of outside groups like the Church, to neutralize the spiral of political violence. Let me assert that I do not believe in inevitability. If totalitarian tendencies exist, they can be reversed.[31] But I have no doubt that reversing them will require a vigorous reaction, within and without. The regime may well be coming to an impasse. Despite the economic accomplishments and despite the well-meaning disposition on the part of some who support it but would like to see it evolve toward "reconciliation," the fact is that forces opposed to this course of evolution have placed themselves in strategic locations.

I do not think that the outside opposition, armed or verbal, has any ability to cause the regime's breakdown. Quite the contrary, the regime is gaining strength. It benefits from the economic accomplishments, so that the situation can be described as bourgeois consolidation in the context of a developmentalist-bureaucratic regime. Behind all this lies the tragic fact that the power elite, as well as the opposition intellectuals, are unable to formulate realistic alternatives to the basic problems. Economic and urban development has mobilized the "masses," but it has not filled the historical vacuum of a society and culture in which they have never been organized, never politically educated, never enabled to claim their fundamental rights on an equal footing: bread as well as freedom. If this is true of that part of the population that has already been reached by the benefits of economic growth, it is of course even more so of the vast majority, which has thus far hardly been touched by the transformations of the last decades.

A long march awaits the Brazilians, a slow, patient march, before the nation will be able to be rebuilt politically for a people whose symbols, organizations, and hopes were crushed by the same power elite which, from the heights of its vision of the state and the nation, thought that, launching an autocratic process of development, it would bring the country one step closer to a regime of reconciliation. We have all paid the price of this elitist vision. It is to be hoped, at least, that the intellectuals will not invent other myths, whether Nasserist or not, which are as incapable as the present ones of producing viable policies for the participation of the popular classes in politics. Without this participation, any "technical" formula for mass mobilization will lead to mass manipulation, and perhaps to an increase in the accumulation of wealth, but will not bring about political development favoring the majority and increasing the quality of life.

NOTES

1. This essay was already written when I received Alfred Stepan's book on the changing pattern of military intervention in Brazil. In his book Stepan shows the effects of the overall changes I discuss on the military institutions and consequently on the type of intervention they exercise at present.

2. See F. Fajnzylber, *Estrategia industrial y empresas internacionales: Posición relativa de América Latina y Brasil* (Santiago: Naciones Unidas, CEPAL, November 1971), 204. This study is based mainly on official U.S. figures published in Survey of Current Business.

3. See unpublished research study prepared by ADECIF in Rio de Janeiro and published in *Jornal do Brasil*, 20 April 1970.

4. *Visão* (São Paulo, September 1967), cited in Fernando Magalhães, "El perverso 'milagro económico Brasileño,'" *Panorama Económico*, no. 265 (Santiago, Chile, November–December 1971): 34.

5. On the new patterns of dependence, see my study (with Enzo Faletto) *Dependencia y desarrollo en América Latina* (México: Siglo XXI, 1970). For an up-to-date analysis on the effect of the policies adopted by the multinational corporations on the Latin American economies, see F. Fajnsylber, *Estrategia industrial y empresas internacionales: Posición relativa de América Latina y Brasil* (N.p.: CEPAL, 1970) and *Sistema industrial y exportación de manufacturas: Análisis de la experiencia brasileña* (N.p.: CEPAL, 1970). Also, Anibal Pinto and Jan Kñackál, *El sistema centro-periferia veinte años después*, 3rd ed. (N.p.: CEPAL, 1971).

6. See table 5.1, based on data in F. Fajnzylber, *Estrategia industrial y empresas internacionales: Posición relativa de América Latina y Brasil* (Santiago: Naciones Unidas, CEPAL, November 1971, 204); this study is based mainly on official U.S. figures published in Survey of Current Business. [The original version of this article had several tables.]

7. For an analysis of these changes, with particular reference to the ideological expressions of the whole process through which some sectors redefined their interests, see my *Ideologias de la burguesia industrial en sociedades dependientes* (Argentina y Brazil) (México: Siglo XXI, 1971).

8. I am making only general remarks about the structural roots of the 1964 crisis. Of course, the picture is very complex and could not be adequately sketched within the limits of this chapter. It is, however, appropriate to point out the factors behind the institutional crisis, which has been called the end of the import substitution process. It had become necessary to restructure the mechanisms of accumulation at a higher level, one that would be better adjusted to the advances already accomplished in the development of the productive forces. This restructuring would require, among other things, keeping down the wage level and therefore dismantling an array of union and political organizations through which, in the populist period, the wage earners were able to resist part of the pressure for accumulation. In this sense, Morley and Smith's statement in this volume that from the economic point of view repression is not necessary is a purely formal one. Historically, it was necessary. Of course, once a regime has become established and accepted, and as long as it seems that it will go on functioning without social and political pressures, it is possible to imagine, idyllically, that repression is unnecessary. However, this is a naive, static view of an historical process. Without repression those pressures may grow, eventually affecting the very "rationality of the system." For an analysis of the structural process underlying the political crisis of 1964, see the essay "Raizes estruturais da crise política brasileira," in my book *Mudanças sociais na America Latina* (São Paulo: Difusão Européia do Livro, 1969), originally printed in *Les Temps Modernes* (Paris) (October 1967).

9. See the table based on data developed by IPEA (Brazilian Ministry of Planning) and ANFAVEA (Association of Brazilian Automobile Manufacturers), cited in Fernando Magalhães, "El perverso 'milagro

económico brasileño,' " *Panorama Económico* (Santiago de Chile), no. 265 (November–December 1971): 205–213.

10. See the table in Banco Central de Brasil and *Visão* (Rio de Janeiro, September 1971). Cited in Magalhães, "El perverso 'milagro económico brasileño,' " 16. As of April 30, 1971.

11. Celso Furtado, "De l'oligarchie à l'état militaire," in *Les Temps Modernes*, no. 257 (Paris) (October 1967), it appeared in Portuguese in Celso Furtado, ed., *Brasil:Tempos modernos* (Rio de Janeiro: Editora Paz e Terra, 1968), 1–23.

12. Celso Furtado, *Um projeto para o Brasil* (Rio de Janeiro: Editora Saga, 1968).

13. Hélio Jaguaribe, "Stabilité sociale par le colonial-fascisme," *Les Temps Modernes*, no. 257 (Paris) (October 1967). Quotations in the text are from the Brazilian edition "Brasil: Estabilidade social pelo colonial-fascismo?" in Furtado, *Brasil: Tempos modernos*, 25–47.

14. Jaguaribe, "Brasil: Estabilidade social pelo colonial-fascismo?" 25–47, especially 33–34.

15. Ibid., 43, 44.

16. See, for example, his "Enfoques sobre a América Latina: Análise crítica de recentes relatórios," presented to the Bariloche meeting of the Consejo Latinoamericano de Ciencias Sociales (CLACSO), November 1970.

17. See Cardoso and Faletto, *Dependencia y desarrollo en América Latina*.

18. It is necessary to keep in mind the objective difficulties involved in the institutionalization of this model. First, there is the limited room afforded for social mobility by such an intrinsically marginalizing development process. A second difficulty involves the position of rural workers. The populist phase was not very different in this respect. It too managed to keep its unstable equilibrium and to go on with accumulation for some time thanks to the economic overexploitation and political marginalization of the rural workers. The present bureaucratic-authoritarian regime, however, will find this problem to be an even greater obstacle to the maintenance of its chosen course of development.

19. See tables in the text, where evidence for some of these assertions can be found. However, since my purpose here is to emphasize a process of qualitative change in the development model, understanding the policy approach to development problems is more important at this point than any figures to indicate concrete results. It is necessary to observe, for example, that the public enterprises have "privatized" themselves: they issue stock shares, aim to make profits, and associate themselves with other, private business. In this context, indicators or conjectures (like those of Morley and Smith in this volume) concerning actual purchase of local businesses by foreign businesses, or the evidence that net foreign investment has diminished, which seems questionable, do not in any case invalidate my argument. The point at issue is that, in the present phase, it is the internationalized sector—whether it is made up of Brazilian, foreign, or mixed businesses, does not matter—that experiences the fastest growth. Moreover, foreign businesses utilize a substantial amount of internal, i.e., local savings for their expansion. Consequently, incoming capital is not a clear-cut indicator to measure the internationalization of the market.

20. See Cândido Mendes, "Sistema político e modelos de poder no Brasil, *Dados* (Rio de Janeiro), no. 1 (1966): 7–41. See also the articles cited in note 16.

21. Cândido Mendes, "O governo Castello Branco: Paradigma e prognose," *Dados* (Rio de Janeiro) nos 2/3 (1967): 63–111. Note that in his more recent study, "Elite de poder, democracia e desenvolvimento," *Dados* (Rio de Janeiro) no. 6 (1969): 57–90, Cândido Mendes insists that the Castello Branco government did not attempt to "authenticate" itself, that is, it remained faithful to the particular form in which legitimation does or does not occur in power-elite regimes. Precisely by doing this, the government was caught in a situation in which political validation became exclusively a function of its economic development model, which in turn depended on a number of factors lying outside the country's boundaries.

22. Mendes, "Sistema político e modelos de poder no Brasil," 9.

23. Ibid., 17.

24. Ibid.

25. Ibid. By "formally" Cândido Mendes means effective policy choices, since "this formal element would even include the commitment to uphold the economic models followed by the Castello Branco government."

26. After the name of Army Marshal Enrico Gasper Dutra, Vargas's war minister under the Estado Novo and later president of Brazil (1946–50).

27. See Mendes, "O governo Castello Branco," especially 110.

28. See Mendes, "Sistema político e modelos de poder no Brasil," especially 14–15.

29. In a series of articles published in *O Estado de São Paulo*, one of Brazil's major newspapers, under the title "The Brazilian Model of Development," 7–24 June; 1, 8 August 1970.

30. This quotation is from the article printed in *O Estado de São Paulo*, 17 June 1970, 5.

31. This is not to say that the alternative to totalitarianism must be a democratic overture. It may well go only so far as stabilizing itself as an authoritarian regime. In any case, even those who talk about "opening up" toward democracy seem to conceive of this only in terms of broader and more effective participation of the bourgeoisie and of the middle classes in the political process. They do not seem very interested in allowing the reconstitution of popular representative organizations. The latter therefore seems only a remote possibility in the present horizon of political choices.

→ 8 ←

Characterizing Authoritarian Regimes in Latin America

In recent years (the 1960s through the 1970s) there has been an accentuated tendency toward authoritarianism in Latin America. In itself, authoritarianism is hardly a new phenomenon. For a long time, caudillismo and militarism have been dominant features of political life in the region, and, in this context, democracy has been more an exotic plant than the expected result of a long-term trend. However, traditional caudillismo and militarism were products of societies in which the hacienda and the agrarian or mineral export economy was predominant. By contrast, what strikes us today is precisely the resurgence of authoritarianism in societies that could broadly be described as in a process of "modernization."

What are we to conclude from the fact that a whole region is becoming simultaneously both more modernized and more politically authoritarian? Did not the theory of modernization postulate a discontinuous but global process of democratization stimulated by the spread of democratic and egalitarian attitudes and values in all spheres of social activity? There is clearly a contradiction between the political consequences of economic growth postulated by this theory and the actual course of political history marked by military coups and flourishing authoritarian regimes.

If the theory of modernization provides little help in explaining this new authoritarianism, how is one to explain it? Another approach is historical. We must not forget that in the history of Latin America respect for political rights or even the subjective existence of such a notion and for the formal rules of political participation has been far more an ideology for the use and enjoyment of dominant oligarchies than a common practice. However, the recognition of a history of arbitrary rule does not serve as an explanation for contemporary authoritarianism.

Adapted from Fernando Henrique Cardoso, "On the Characterization of Authoritarian Regimes in Latin America," in David Collier, ed., *The New Authoritarianism in Latin America* (Princeton, N.J.: Princeton University Press, 1979), 33–57.

Still another approach to explanation, and for some people to moral justification, focuses on the specific needs of rulers and of the state. Yet even those people most disposed to accept the facts of life as if they were moral rules and to believe that the politics of princes necessarily implies the exercise of violence have difficulty in recognizing torture and kidnapping as legitimate means in the defense of the established order. If their doubts do not arise from a healthy human reaction against such practices, at least they know that obedience without consent is a weak foundation for a stable and durable political order.

Others who are not inclined to justify the new authoritarianism take still other approaches to explaining it. Yet they do not face such an easy task either. Even a brief survey of the already ample bibliography on Latin American authoritarianism leaves the reader perplexed. The state is defined with a whole range of adjectives such as "dependent," "bureaucratic," "corporative," "fascist," "bonapartist," "militarist," "police state," and so on. Needless to say, this proliferation of adjectives is hardly a substitute for coherent explanation.

In light of this state of the literature, I must make a plea for clemency. If the character of the authoritarianism dominant in Latin America has not yet even been precisely defined, it would be presumptuous on my part to produce a detailed theory of authoritarianism now. I can do no more than suggest in a very schematic way some of the problems outlined by the authors who have dedicated themselves to the subject and perhaps put forward some ideas arising from my own direct experience of one or another of the authoritarian situations. I shall therefore examine a number of issues concerning contemporary authoritarianism in Latin America, without suggesting that by so doing I shall have exhausted the subject or even touched upon all the central points.

BUREAUCRATIC-AUTHORITARIANISM

When one looks at Chile since the fall of Allende, at the Uruguay of Bordaberry and more recently, or at contemporary Brazil—which has already experienced a decade-and-a-half of military government—one should not be surprised that some social scientists have proclaimed the existence of a new and homogeneous form of regime: a military and authoritarian regime. The temptation to do this is even further reinforced by the recent history of Argentina, which has seen both the resurrection of Peron and his death, together with the fleeting days of magic and terror of Lopez Rega, only to be replaced by generals who, although eager to exorcise the magicians of Isabelita's court, did not flinch from using the rack and dungeon against the threat of subversion of the existing order.

But the Southern Cone of South America does not have the dubious privilege of a monopoly of military regimes. Though in other parts of Latin America the influence of the military and its bureaucratic efficiency may not be as great as in the south of the continent, there is the long-standing military regime in power in Paraguay, as well as the self-proclaimed revolutionary military government that came to power in Peru in 1968, although in the latter case there has been little or no torture. Moreover, military men control Ecuador, Bolivia, Panama, Honduras, and El Salvador. And even though the government of Guatemala has called elections, it is hardly possible to characterize it as other than a military regime. To do otherwise would mean that the Brazilian regime (always ambivalent in dealing with the difficult problem of legitimation) would cease to be a military regime with every controlled election that it holds.

Though military regimes rule in most of Latin America, it is essential to make distinctions among them. In classifying such diverse situations we must avoid confusion between the caudillismo of the old Latin American militarism (as in the case of Paraguay) or family-based caudillismo (as in the case of Nicaragua), and the more institutional control of power by the officer corps as a whole that exists in some other countries (such as Argentina, Chile, Uruguay, and Brazil).

It was in order to make effective distinctions of this type that the social scientists who first tried to characterize the new South American militarism added another adjective: "bureaucratic." It has been argued that the characteristic feature of the types of regimes implanted in Latin America in more recent years has been precisely the fact that in these regimes it is not a single general or a colonel who, like the caudillos of the nineteenth century, imposes a personal order by decrees. Rather, it is the military institution as such which assumes the power in order to restructure society and the state.

We must not underestimate the importance of this contrast. The bureaucratic-authoritarian regime is different from the old forms of caudillo domination whether civil or military. A new phenomenon has emerged in contemporary Latin America. The armed forces take power not as in the past to maintain a dictator in power (such as Vargas or Peron) but rather to reorganize the nation in accordance with the "national security" ideology of modern military doctrine. In contrast with the traditional forms of military domination in Latin America, contemporary militarism likewise stands out because of the already mentioned rule by the military institution as an organization. In the past, this phenomenon was not possible, given the less fully developed professional structure of the armed forces and the much greater power of the civilian oligarchies, which needed only occasional military intervention in order to exercise their domination.

The initial preoccupation of the authors who have tried to characterize the new authoritarianism in Latin America has been to distinguish it not only from authoritarian regimes of the past, but also from European fascism and corporatism. With regard to this second contrast, the differences are subtler. In the first place, Latin American authoritarianism is different from the typical forms of fascism because it aspires, above all, to produce apathy among the masses. It fears the mobilization of followers, even if they could be recruited from the middle, rather than from the lower strata of society. In consequence, it dispenses with political parties as organizational links between civil society and the state. The army, as guarantor of the authoritarian order, prefers a "technical," supportive relationship between the state and social groups, rather than a relationship based on alliances with broad social groups. Thus bureaucratic-authoritarianism diverges not only from the democratic model of bonds between representatives and electors, but also from Italian or German fascism, in which the mobilization of the party forces and the use of its extremist members as a repressive force was essential.

It does not fully approach the form of Spanish corporatism either, for in the sphere of civil society it allows the representative organizations of liberal-capitalist classes to survive without organic bonds with the state, declarations from Ongania or Pinochet in favor of corporatism notwithstanding. The state tends to exclude class organizations (although not class interests) from the decision-making process, preserving a rigid hierarchical structure that is bureaucratically controlled by various national security agencies and by the commanders of the armed forces. As in the past, corporative links are established within the trade unions (between workers and management) and between them and the state, and where these links were historically weak (as in Chile), the military regimes encourage them. But the state does not adopt a corporative form. It does not try to stimulate class organization, to promote a doctrine of organic harmony among social groups, or to establish corporative links among them that could form a base for political domination. Rather, the links between civil society and the bureaucratic-authoritarian regime are achieved through the cooptation of individuals and private interests into the system. Under these circumstances, stable pressure groups are unlikely to materialize, and a truly corporatist network of links between society and the state is unlikely to emerge.

Regarding ideology, we may observe in typical fascist regimes an ideology of national superiority based on a belief in the virtues of race and in the people's destiny. This "ideological cement" was in accord with the orientation toward economic and territorial expansion. Such nationalism could not be an ambition of Latin American authoritarian regimes, given their economic dependency. Instead, official ideologies favor a conservative and hierarchical mentality whose vision of grandeur has been confined to the reinforcement of the state apparatus. Hence, the ideological claims made in Latin America differ from those prevailing under classic European fascism.

Apathy and lack of mobilization; a mentality that is statist and hierarchical, rather than a broadly nationalistic ideology; state but not party; hierarchy and no representation—these all form part of the particular ideological and organizational instruments of contemporary military authoritarianism in Latin America. It would appear, therefore, that the characterization of the emerging forms of political domination in Latin America as bureaucratic-authoritarian has something new to offer the typology of political regimes in general.

In thinking about this new type of regime, we must note differences and similarities in relation to other regimes in Latin America that have many bureaucratic-authoritarian characteristics, but are not military regimes. Some authors have extended the term bureaucratic-authoritarian beyond the cases of strictly military regimes to include countries such as Mexico. Yet, if all these regimes are bureaucratic-authoritarian, what is the value of such a concept? If this term covers such a range of regimes, from the Chilean junta (or any military junta for that matter), through Peru,

Panama, Ecuador, and even to Mexico, what is the analytical content of this concept? Its degree of abstraction may be too great. I would argue that the notion of bureaucratic-authoritarianism should not be used in such a wide sense. I would restrict it to situations in which military intervention occurred in reaction against leftist movements and in which the policies that served to reorganize the state and the economy in such a way as to guarantee the continued advance of capitalist industrial development were implemented by military regimes, as in Argentina and Brazil. The reason for this restricted application of the concept is not an analytical whim but rather the need to underline the crucial fact of the militarization of the state. It is essential to differentiate these decidedly military authoritarian regimes from others such as the Mexican regime, which, although not completely bereft of bureaucratic-authoritarian traits, is undoubtedly civilian in its mode of control. How are we to conceptualize these obvious differences between Mexico and the military regimes of the Southern Cone?

POLITICAL REGIME AND STATE

To clarify the characterization of contemporary authoritarian politics, it is essential to distinguish between the concept of political regime and the concept of the state. By "regime" I mean the formal rules that link the main political institutions (legislature to the executive, executive to the judiciary, and party system to them all), as well as the issue of the political nature of the ties between citizens and rulers (democratic, oligarchic, totalitarian, or whatever).

The conceptualization of the state is a complex matter, but there does exist a certain degree of agreement that at the highest level of abstraction the notion of state refers to the basic alliance, the basic "pact of domination," that exists among social classes or fractions of dominant classes and the norms which guarantee their dominance over the subordinate strata. When Marx and Engels referred to the state as the "committee for the management of the common interests of the whole bourgeoisie," they characterized it at this level of abstraction: the capitalist state is the "expression" of the capitalist mode of class domination. To avoid metaphysics, this "expression" ought to be conceived of in organizational terms; that is to say, the dominant classes must make a continuing effort to articulate their diverse and occasionally contradictory objectives through state agencies and bureaucracies.

The need to distinguish between regime and state in this sense becomes quickly evident if one begins to compare Latin American countries. It is commonly argued that bureaucratic-authoritarian regimes enforce rules of political exclusion for the benefit of the private sector of the economy. It is understood that the predominant economic interests that support these regimes favor accelerating capital accumulation through controlling the labor force—a measure that appears to be an important concomitant of successful capitalist development. But, in this respect, there are obvious similarities between the Mexico of the PRI and the Brazil of Institutional Acts imposed by the army. In both cases, the policies aim to achieve rapid capitalist development, while the governments feel in the long run that continuing worsening of income inequality and dependency do not affect the historic destiny of their respective nations. Indeed, using these criteria, even such democratic countries as Venezuela and Costa Rica have the same type of capitalist state. In these two countries, there is likewise a socio-economic exclusion of the majority. There are similar models of economic accumulation (control of wages, patterns of income distribution) and even similar favorable policies toward multinational corporations. Thus the state, when seen as a basic pact of domination, is a comparable capitalist state in all of these countries.

A major shortcoming in the discussions of authoritarianism is that they have not focused adequately on this distinction between the state and the political regime. An identical form of state capitalist and dependent, in the case of Latin America can coexist with a variety of political regimes: authoritarian, fascist, corporatist, and even democratic. One line of economic reasoning looks for a one-to-one causal relation between state and regime. It presupposes that for each "stage" of accumulation there is an appropriate type of regime. However, the same historical difficulty that this reasoning produces in the case of mature capitalist countries (i.e., the absence of fascism in Anglo-Saxon countries, which made the most substantial contributions to the early development of capitalism) occurs in its application to Latin America as well. Brazil's growth under Kubitschek and the present Venezuelan boom are clearly cases in which dependent capitalist states have sustained democratic regimes.

Nevertheless, though the idea of a simple economic determination of politics is best discarded, there is room for exploring the degree of "compatibility" between different forms of dependent capitalist states and different types of regime. For example, what are the conditions under which a democratic regime can coexist with class domination based on a form of economic accumulation that imposes increasing inequality among social classes? Are not the roots of the crisis of all three Southern Cone democracies (Argentina, Chile, and Uruguay) to be found in the contradiction between a system of wide participation and political representation of the masses and the need for accumulation and control over the work force? I doubt that one can answer this question affirmatively, much less generalize an affirmative answer to the whole of Latin America. As I pointed out, the economic achievements of contemporary Venezuela and of Brazil during the Kubitschek period, among others, remind those who hastily proclaim the inevitability of military dictatorship in opening the way to the "current phase" of capitalist development that history is more capricious than it may appear. Further, it is hard to believe that exclusively economic motives were behind the right wing political and military mobilization against the Allende government or the post-Peronist administration. There is therefore a need for more careful analysis and further interpretation in the study of the relationship between a dependent capitalist state and different forms of political regime. To date, most of the gap created by the lack of research on this relationship has been filled by highly polemical interpretations generally insensitive to the variety of historical experience.

At this point, it should be obvious that I find it most useful to use the term bureaucratic-authoritarianism to refer, not to the form of the state as such, but to the type of political regime. The relationship between the two is far from clear and, given that this is a complex and rather controversial subject, it might be wiser to advance modestly along the unambitious path of the political description of the institutions of bureaucratic-authoritarian regimes.

THE INSTITUTIONS OF AUTHORITARIANISM

Almost by definition, bureaucratic-authoritarian regimes organize the relations of power in favor of the executive. It is the strengthening of the executive and the reinforcing of its technical capabilities (of its formal "rationality") that stands out in these regimes. The strengthening of the executive involves increased centralization that undermines the federal tradition, where it existed before. It also involves the elimination or sharp reduction in the role of the legislature. Moreover, the judiciary is controlled in practice, if not in theory, by the executive.

The non-democratic procedures for selecting the president and the bureaucratic expansion of the central administration in these regimes are, nonetheless, subject to a counterbalancing system. On the one hand, formal rationality requires the strengthening of a bureaucratic body of technicians, especially in the economic field; on the other hand, these regimes express the political will of the armed forces as an institution. In this way, the executive depends on the technocratic bureaucracy and on the only real party, the armed forces.

The institutionalization of mechanisms to solve conflicts between the executive and the techno-bureaucracy is relatively simple. The relationship between the executive and its real base of power, the military, is more complex. One might think that in these regimes the distinction between the executive and the armed forces is non-existent. However, as soon as the military bureaucratic systems become stable, the armed forces as such do not determine state policies or implement them. The military have veto power over the "big decisions"—the most important being control of political succession—but they are not necessarily involved in decision making regarding the economy or other important issues. It is for this reason that problems arise regarding the functioning of these regimes and lead to clashes between the executive and the armed forces. Once civilians who are independent of the armed forces begin to play a part, however small, in the decision-making process, the executive becomes the center of these decisions, and clashes with military "hardliners" are inevitable.

The success of the regime depends in part on the type of delegation of military authority to the executive that is adopted. There have been cases of military juntas and military presidents that are directly responsible to the officer corps. When the president is a general, the alternatives regarding the length of his mandate are few. These range from situations—transitory in general—in which the president is the commander of the armed forces, to the pretense of a presidential legitimacy defined by rules that are not exclusively military. In the Brazilian case there is an attempt to preserve something of the electoral presidential tradition: the president is a general nominated by the supreme command of the armed forces, but ratified by congress. He receives a mandate for a limited number of years. In other cases, the question of the presidential term is left open, provoking crises within the high command concerning the limits of the mandate and the course of succession. In Brazil, the succession is a traumatic event, but rival military factions have time and hope on their horizon, given the limited mandate of the general president. It may be due to this factor that military crises just prior to the completion of the presidential terms have been avoided, despite the fact that, to this date, Brazilian military presidents have been unable to have any of their own candidates nominated as successors.

The appearance of a strong, near dictatorial presidentialism sometimes hides the effective control that the military institution exercises over those in government, whether they are civilians or generals. There is, however, great tension between the strengthening of the executive and the control by the armed forces. In regimes controlled by military establishments that are less professional, and therefore less apt to accept the rules of the hierarchy, as in Bolivia or Ecuador, the threat of new clashes is constant. But extreme tension between the armed forces and the presidency has also occurred in Argentina, while in Uruguay the crisis between Bordaberry and the high command exemplifies the lack of institutionalization of such regimes. In a more discrete way, presidential power in Brazil has sometimes been opposed by the power of the high command. Paradoxically, the strengthening of the executive, combined with its lack of an institutional base, continues a characteristic feature of bureaucratic-authoritarianism in its military form. This is an important difference between such a form of government and the type of civil authoritarianism prevailing in Mexico, where the president has perhaps more power than any general-president of a military government in the Southern Cone countries.

Another important dimension of authoritarian regimes relates to the question of political parties. The official ideology (or mentality) accentuates the non-party character of military governments, as well as the aim of putting an end both to "politics" as an expression of conflicting ideologies and to the existence of parties that undermine the "national unanimity" desired by the military governments. Yet it is obvious that in practice the activity of political factions reappears. The relationship between interest groups in civil society and the state is based more on the criteria and mechanisms of cooptation than on the mechanisms of representation. In other words, those who control the state apparatus select various people to participate in the decision-making system, a selection process that will be extended to include even the most powerful of social forces, and even sectors of the lower classes. But they will never subscribe to the idea of representation. The delegation of authority from below is not encouraged. On the contrary, the decision regarding who will be called to collaborate, and for how long, is made at the apex of the pyramid of power.

The interest groups within civil society will naturally attempt to penetrate the decision-making circles. Once they have achieved this, they seek to further their own interests. However, they are not legitimized as representatives of their own constituents. It is the bureaucrats or people controlling top positions in the state apparatus who decide that this or that person may participate. The people who are selected may occasionally speak on behalf of other persons or groups, but they do not form a delegation as such. Hence, they are never recognized formally as "representatives" or delegates. Thanks to this mechanism, civil servants can "defuse" any pressure simply by dispensing opportunities to participate by their own selective means. In other words, in bureaucratic-authoritarian regimes, the representation of groups or factions—the political parties—is not legitimate per se. The interests that social groups manage to articulate in authoritarian regimes have to be defined inside the state machinery, while political parties in democratic systems tend to be rooted in civil society. The mechanism of cooptation allows private interests to establish their roots within the state, but only through committees or special advisory groups controlled by state officials (civilian and military). These may later become the leaders of semi-political organizations which I have described elsewhere as bureaucratic clusters or "rings" that constitute the links between the interests of civil society and the state, involving bargaining between private and state interests. Even though they may resemble the classic format of the lobby, these bureaucratic rings are different in that they do not involve genuine, autonomous pressure groups, but rather are part of the state apparatus itself and normally are under the formal leadership of a state official.

We cannot apply this characterization to all authoritarian regimes or even to all phases of a single regime. The degree of liquidation of representative mechanisms and parties depends on the degree of distrust that these institutions inspired in the dominant classes and especially in the military establishment during the phase preceding the rise of authoritarianism. Populism, as much as democracy, permitted the existence of left-wing parties and also permitted alliances between them and reformist forces. In the climate of the Cold War of the 1950s, the Cuban revolution in 1958 and the spread of guerrilla movements in subsequent years generated a political challenge at the local and international level. It was the reaction against the possibility of socialism that culminated in the present "Thermidor" in Latin America. The armed forces adopted and adapted the Franco American doctrines of internal warfare and became increasingly preoccupied with internal repression. They also became preoccupied with the necessity of implementing policies that promoted accelerated economic growth in order to pass quickly through the initial phase of economic "take off" in which, according to counterrevolutionary strategies inspired by the writings of W. W. Rostow, there is a greater likelihood that social revolution will occur.

The timing of the implantation of contemporary authoritarian regimes, as well as the degree of their economic and political achievements, has varied greatly among countries. The gradual establishment of a military bureaucratic order in Brazil carried with it the inheritance of a multi-party system. A second coup in 1965 created the present two-party system. In Chile and Uruguay, bureaucratic-authoritarianism emerged with more devastating force than in Argentina and developed an emphatically anti-party orientation. It was no coincidence that before the arrival of militarism in these countries, a wide range of left-wing groups, from the violent revolutionaries to the supporters of the peaceful road to socialism, had constituted themselves as a powerful threat to the established order. To the dominant classes and to the armed forces in these countries, "representative democracy" sounds only marginally less frightening than opening the front door to the devil, an appropriate metaphor, given that the military see themselves as the defenders of Christian and Occidental values against the world wide menace of communism.

To the disappointment of collectors of neat labels and monocausal explanations, the characteristics of the purest bureaucratic-authoritarianism are not always found in the most reactionary political and economic regimes. For example, from a formal point of view, the so-called "Peruvian model" of reformist tendencies has some similarities to countries governed by the military authoritarianism of the south. It would be wrong, therefore, to believe that the formal characteristics I have been discussing will always appear in an orderly and predictable fashion in conjunction with other important features of authoritarian regimes.

THE FUNCTIONING OF AUTHORITARIANISM

It seems obvious that the presence or absence of a party system will open alternative paths to authoritarian regimes. It indicates, at least, a different degree of relative autonomy in the political organizations controlled by social classes. As far as I know, there are no studies concerning the way in which preexisting political parties have survived under military authoritarian regimes. In the case of Peru, if there is some form of party still surviving, it is APRA, some of whose program and ideology were adopted by the post-1968 government in an apparently successful attempt by the military to neutralize this party. To assure success, the military added to their movement a tinge of nationalism and reformism, and even attempted certain forms of political mobilization through the Sistema Nacional de Apoyo a la Mobilizacion Social. However, because of the inherent difficulties that bureaucratic-authoritarian regimes have in developing any form of popular mobilization, this has now been diluted. In Chile, the prevailing militarism, having destroyed left-wing organizations, went on to dismantle the other political alternative in civil society, the Christian Democrats, but it is likely, given the Chilean social and political tradition, that the parties will just hibernate and eventually reemerge almost intact. The same can be said of Argentina under Ongania and Lanusse, and in the state of near civil war which is evident in Argentina today there is a withdrawal from political life toward a pre-political society: "man is wolf to man" once more. However, although in these circumstances it is difficult to imagine how political parties can be reconstituted, I do not believe that either the trade union organizations or the political parties of the popular sector and the middle classes (previously semi-organized under Peronism and Radicalism) will simply be eradicated. I would not be surprised if, in the not too distant future, the armed forces in Argentina have to face political demands too great for the narrow limits of militarism.

In the analysis of Latin American authoritarianism, one of the most interesting contrasts would appear to be between Brazil and Mexico. In these countries, it might be said that civil society is rather weakly organized in comparison to the civil societies of the Southern Cone countries. A tradition of a strong state plus elitist political control (in the case of Brazil) and of a bureaucratic hierarchy (in the case of Mexico) increases the likelihood of success for these authoritarian regimes—despite differences between them in form and content. Nevertheless, we have recently seen in Brazil how the one of the two parties created by the military regime to fill a purely formal role of opposition has actually become an effective opposition party. In the general elections of November 1974, the opposition won sixteen of the twenty-one seats for the senate. In the following months, the strong resulting impact gave the ironic impression that this military regime had made a rather original contribution to modern forms of authoritarianism by creating a party system almost exclusively based on the opposition. It is true that the dominant political system soon reacted, using whatever tools were available to deny the opposition any possibility of gaining power through the electoral system. In any case, the significant point is that the goals of the military have by no means been fully accomplished. In civil society there is an awareness of the illegitimacy of the regime and a conviction that sooner or later the political organization of society will have to be reconstituted.

Mexico, a civilian regime, provides an example of great stability, a stability that has much to do with the origins of the regime. The Mexican regime was born of a revolution that partially incorporated broad sectors of society into national life and established a political system more open to pressures and suggestions from the bottom, although still controlled from the top. Moreover, the Mexican bureaucratic elite has a capacity for control regarding economic and social matters that secures a certain hegemony within society. An extensive system of bargaining with regard to economic interests, along with efficient financial and economic performance since Cardenas, turned the Mexican state into an effective instrument of domination and political control. Consensus without democracy was the logical outcome, in spite of the continuing use of the instruments of repression to stifle any threat to the political or social order. The repressive aspects of Mexican politics have been diluted by the well-known mechanism of massive cooptation of the opposition practiced by the state and by a tolerance of violations of the boundaries between private interest and public office. In consequence, it is a non-military and "inclusionary" type of regime that has achieved a greater capacity for endurance by giving social roots to an authoritarian system.

What factors affect the degree of autonomy of civil society in the face of authoritarian rule? One is clearly the presence or absence of a preexisting party system. Others include the degree of effective control that authoritarian regimes exercise over everyday life (and over the mass media as well as the peoples' reaction to this control. For example, Peruvian military authoritarianism is markedly different in this regard from the Argentine or Uruguayan regimes: Peru has not implemented a system of terror within society. Although it is true that in Peru there is state control of the press, the formation of public opinion does not face the obstacles that are characteristic in Uruguay, not to mention in Chile, or in Brazil during the more repressive phases of the Brazilian regime.

Political science in Latin America has advanced little in the study of the control capacity of authoritarian regimes—perhaps due to a certain repugnance at having to investigate the different types of malignant tumor that these forms of authoritarianism are considered to be. This capacity for control varies among different authoritarian regimes due to multiple factors. The first of these involves the circumstances under which the regimes came to power. In some cases, the military overthrew the constitutional order by means of a blood bath. In others, a radio announcement was sufficient to depose the previous president. In the second place, the degree of weakness or strength of civil society must also be considered in order to explain the capacity of the regime to control it. Obviously, it is more difficult for the regime to deal with autonomous and therefore potentially more defiant social groups (Chile) than to keep itself in power in a society where politics is the exclusive preserve of an elitist bureaucracy (Brazil). In the third place, there are technical factors that either expand or narrow the control capacity of these regimes. We must bear in mind that we are not analyzing cases that resemble Nazi Germany, which was able to implement and maintain much more complete forms of control. Latin American authoritarianism is still "underdeveloped": it may kill and torture, but it does not exercise complete control of everyday life. The state is sufficiently strong to concentrate its attention and repressive apparatus against so-called subversive groups, but it is not as efficient when it comes to controlling the universities, for example, or even the bureaucracy itself. It would be unwise, however, to underestimate the recent advances made in this field, although the lack of a party to monitor and denounce the enemies of the regime makes this control rather difficult. Up to now, repression has been a task for the police rather than for the politicians.

An additional word on the functioning of authoritarian regimes is in order. Authoritarian regimes that are not based on a political party (again, the Mexican situation based on an effective party does not correspond to the pure bureaucratic-authoritarian regimes in this respect) are sometimes too weak to cope with complex societies. Moreover, it would be incorrect to suppose that the state apparatus operates as a unified whole in authoritarian regimes in Latin America. The absence of a party that could bind the system together and of a truly totalitarian ideology prevents the techno-bureaucracy and office holders from becoming committed to the military ideology of state grandeur. On the contrary, a considerable degree of privatization of the state apparatus occurs in such regimes. The coherence of the regime exists more at the top level, through the ideological discourse of ministers and generals, than in the routine behavior of the state officials. Quite frequently, the latter control parts of the state apparatus almost independently of the government, pursuing personal objectives of an economic or bureaucratic nature.

These features make the functioning of bureaucratic-authoritarian regimes less consistent than it looks at first glance. Potentially destabilizing factors are almost always present, diminishing the capacity of the regime to absorb pressures. This leads to a continuing use of repression, with all the demoralization and alienation produced by the widespread use of violence, even in the name of the security of the nation against its hidden internal enemies. When these regimes face situations in which actual "subversive" groups are few, the reiteration of the same arguments about threats to national security will become less convincing to the entrepreneurs and dominant groups that support the regimes, and opposition from these groups may increase greatly.

Many forces may thus tend to undermine these regimes, including the eroding factors mentioned above, the possibility of a political reaction against authoritarianism, plus changes in the actual degree of censorship and in the degree of repression. Variations in the effectiveness of repression sometimes occur in the same political regimes with the change of governments, if not within the period of any one government. It is obvious that the form of regime does not solely depend on the mood of people in power; yet this is important. The chances that political action aimed at the transformation of authoritarian regimes will in fact succeed may shift with every particular conjuncture.

AND, FINALLY, THE SOCIOECONOMIC BASES

At this point we must turn to another difficult theoretical question in social science: the relationship between structure and conjuncture. I prefer to avoid theoretical statements that would with difficulty escape pedantry, and would simply like to address two or three basic issues that have arisen in recent discussions of authoritarian regimes.

After more than a decade of military authoritarianism in many countries of the continent and of various decades of civilian authoritarianism in some others, earlier interpretations of its social bases have been superseded by history. The tradition of a militarism conceived as the armed hand of landlords and latifundistas was displaced in part by the economic policies consistently oriented toward industrialization that bureaucratic authoritarian regimes have themselves undertaken. Sometimes these policies have even damaged agrarian interests, and almost always the military regimes have preferred to receive support from agro-business than to preserve ties of close friendship with the latifundia.

It seems less clear which groups have been favored by the industrialization policies of these authoritarian governments. To whom have the military addressed their policies and where have they looked for support? The immediate effects of monetary stabilization policies usually implemented by the military after the take-over (normally after a period of political crisis, inflation, and economic uncertainty) demonstrate clearly which social groups have not been taken into account: workers and wage earners in general, as well as people living on fixed incomes. However, when the two critical economic variables—inflation and capital formation—are controlled, it is difficult to argue that these bureaucratic-authoritarian regimes have adopted a significantly different set of wage or income distribution policies from those launched in Latin American societies by democratic regimes. Moreover, in Peru the ruling militarism, which clearly did not adopt socialist policies, at least cannot be envisaged as a deliberate supporter of an "income concentration" pattern. Apparently what counts in these matters is the character of the state rather than that of the regime, as well as the level of development of the economy and, above all, the strength of social pressures from below. It is to control these pressures and thus to facilitate capital accumulation that bureaucratic-authoritarianism becomes repressive and depresses the living standard of the workers and of the masses. Alliances between big capital and the state are often implicit, but they exist even in situations such as Peru, where the ruling groups explicitly seek to be perceived as the people's defenders. The consequences of such an implicit pact are, of course, the same as if it had an explicit character: after all, bureaucratic-authoritarianism was not launched to assure the well-being of the people. Even though sociological inquiries have found a low level of political consciousness among the lower strata, there is one thing that people do know: this type of regime does not correspond to the political model of their dreams. Whenever it is possible, the masses make their dissent known to the regime: voting against it, rioting, or just keeping to themselves.

It is likewise difficult to identify the beneficiaries of authoritarianism simply by looking at the industrial and development policies of the regime. Initial hypotheses stressed the affinity between authoritarianism and big business, and to my knowledge there is no strong evidence to reject this hypothesis. Nonetheless, we should not give a mechanistic interpretation of these links such as to argue, for instance, that only a military regime could be successful in setting up the production of capital goods and in assuming the control of modern technology in a developing country. The economic policies implemented in Venezuela, Mexico, Argentina, and Brazil are quite similar, but their political regimes are clearly distinct. Again, behind such a hypothesis there lies confusion between political regime and types of state.

Given these reservations, and taking for granted that all capitalist states must facilitate and guarantee the process of capital accumulation, the appropriate questions with respect to this problem are probably the following: which groups have gained advantages from the current authoritarianism? Which centers of capital accumulation benefited from authoritarian rule—the local private enterprise sector, the state productive sector, or multinational enterprises? It has taken some time to render the obvious answer acceptable: Bureaucratic-authoritarianism is politically profitable for the civilian and military bureaucrats that hold state office. The difficulty in arriving at such a truism comes from a theoretical analysis that sees the state just as the expression of class interests, without recognizing that such an expression requires an organization which, since it cannot be other than a social network of people, exists in its own right and possesses interests of its own. It is not correct to deduce from the formal character of authoritarian regimes what type of economic growth policies they will pursue. The acceptance of such an interpretation would involve precisely the opposite error from that which occurs when one ignores the fact that the state is a principal beneficiary of bureaucratic-authoritarianism. It would imply that the state and its bureaucracy are the only real historical actors. The fact is that even in authoritarian situations the state is linked in various ways to social classes and to their interests.

Another important variation in the economic orientation of these regimes involves the relative emphasis on promoting enterprises in the public, as opposed to the private, sector. The Chile of today (under the direct influence of the so-called

"Chicago boys") is making considerable efforts to undermine the state sector of the economy. The Chilean leaders are attempting to establish a peculiar kind of "liberal" economy in the sense that the state redistributes wealth to those groups of private interests that economically control the regime. The Peruvian generals, at the opposite pole, strengthened the state organization and increased its capacity for economic decision-making. This state building occurred much earlier in other countries, under the political control of the entrepreneurs and professional groups, but in Peru a military intervention was necessary to strengthen the state. Subsequently, from a position of greater strength, the military regime attempted to renegotiate the terms of dependency. The Brazilian generals, initially enamored of an economic ideology oriented toward private interests and eager to expand relationships with foreign capital, have in the end enlarged the sphere of state production and even clashed with the American government on the issue of nuclear technology. Thus, it seems impossible to identify a one-to-one correspondence between forms of authoritarian regimes and a set of homogeneous economic interests.

Obviously, the range of alternatives has some limits. Though there are important differences among cases, the fundamental character of this type of authoritarian state is nonetheless capitalist. Similarly, the decisions taken by state bureaucracies occur within well-defined limits. Up to now they have not tried to "change the model." That is to say, the general rules of the local and world capitalist system of production are maintained. However, it would be incorrect to replace the cliché that the military are the bodyguards of landlords with the cliché that they now form a militia to protect the interests of multinational corporations. Authoritarian regimes try to accommodate themselves within the international environment by taking advantage of occasional fissures in the world's economic system. They make deals with multinational enterprises that in some cases involve renegotiating the terms of dependency within narrow limits though, in some cases, as in Chile, they do simply accept local and eventually international private interests as if they corresponded to the needs of the nation and of the people. Yet as a rule, at the ideological and sometimes at the practical level, they try to reinforce not the nation, but the state—if not for other motives, then at least to protect their own interests as a bureaucracy.

In the space available, it is not possible to spell out in detail the implications of this formulation. Nevertheless, it is worth stressing that if in recent years there has been a significant feature in the behavior of civilian and military public bureaucracies, it is their role in the creation of a self-sustained economic basis for their own power. State enterprises are expanding in most countries, and bureaucratic-authoritarianism has been an important factor in this trend. I am not referring to the formation of an ideal "state capitalist" mode of production, but to the use of state enterprises to facilitate capitalist development and to reinforce the position of those in power. However, a trend toward nationalistic and anti-imperialistic ideologies and practices is not likely. On the contrary, in recent years joint ventures between state enterprises and multinationals have been widely encouraged.

The immediate result of this process in terms of the composition of the state has been the creation of bureaucratic strata endowed with entrepreneurial capacity.

Sometimes the top executives of state enterprises clash with a government which has to cope with interests and pressures that come from different social groups, and sometimes the government as such has to enforce policies that are not in conformity with the expansionist interests of the state enterprises. Thus there emerges a social stratum which is created within the state and yet which, paradoxically, achieves to some degree a separate basis of power and can eventually clash with the government under given circumstances.

The point of this argument is not to minimize the significance of the growing links between Latin American economies and the international productive system. But it is difficult to believe that dependency derives from the military authoritarian form of these regimes. If it is true that these regimes make possible new agreements with multinational enterprises, they paradoxically encourage as well aspirations toward more autonomy among the military and among the executives of state enterprises. Further, the few countries still ruled by representative democracies in Latin America can hardly be presented as proof of the argument that democracy by itself preserves a country from foreign penetration.

SOME INCONCLUSIVE CONCLUSIONS

I am afraid that this short incursion into complex matters may have provoked not just doubts, which would not be a bad consequence, but more complexities and ambiguities than clarifications. I started by trying to emphasize the utility of the notion of bureaucratic-authoritarianism for describing, though not explaining, contemporary political realities. However, I fear that I may have contributed to the belief that factors of differentiation among Latin American regimes are so deep that the broad notion of bureaucratic-authoritarianism is almost useless. Furthermore, I have not been successful in identifying a one-to-one link between authoritarian regimes and particular economic policies. It is true that some military regimes have strengthened economic systems based on multinational enterprises, as well as on state corporations, which they themselves control. But it is also true that multinational enterprises managed to survive and expand under democratic systems (not to speak of their achievements under civilian authoritarian ones), while they were weakened under military government in Peru, for instance.

It may well be that the inconclusiveness of my argument about the relation between economics and politics reflects some anxiety that my intellectual inclinations prevent me from expressing more clearly. I do not think that we search in vain when we look for sequences and coherence in history, provided that we keep in mind that there is no greater irrationality than the belief that history can be fully understood through formal rationality. The character of the state—i.e., the structure of class domination and the economic system which this structure rests—imposes some limits on the form of the political regime. For instance, the bureaucratic feature of these authoritarian regimes (civilian or military) cannot prevent the emergence of the entrepreneurial function that the capitalist economy imposes on them. Yet it is a hopeless effort to look at political events from the narrow point of view of economic factors alone.

It is simplistic to imagine that a dependent capitalist process of industrialization can take place only through authoritarianism. A military junta may not even open new roads to economic growth, as recent events in Chile or Uruguay demonstrate. But, whatever the regime, the dominant classes, given the increasing internationalization of production, are forced to make deals with foreign interests and to organize the internal system of economic exploitation in order to cope with new realities. This requires the establishment of an economic system based on state and private corporations and demands state policies to promote capitalist expansion. The assessment made by the dominant classes of the value to them of any authoritarian regime, and hence the actual support that they will give to it, depends primarily on the regime's effective capacity to enforce development policies. The Mexican and Brazilian political systems are similar in this respect. Both have up to now been successful in reorganizing society to cope with more complex forms of capitalist growth. To achieve this, relatively stable forms of labor control have been established and state bureaucracies and public enterprises have been expanded, thus laying a base for the peculiar links already described between private interests and the state. The state as a "pact of domination" thus shows similar traits in both countries. However, it would be quite misleading not to take into consideration the political differences between the two regimes: the military form of the Brazilian system represents a crucial contrast to the party structure that underlies the Mexican regime.

Less marked but still important variations are found among the military regimes in different countries. These variations are primarily the product of differences in the development of the class struggle in each case. In general, the current period of military rule is a response to the crisis provoked in the state by political movements and struggle before the military takeover. In several Latin American countries, ruling classes have been unable to control the political pressure launched by the workers and radicalized members of the middle classes. In such circumstances, the dominant classes cannot maintain their power without open military intervention and support. The price to be paid for this "help" depends on the extent of the political disintegration prior to military intervention, as well as on the capacity of the armed forces to control revolutionary groups.

Above all, when leftist political forces were strong and well rooted in society, the initial phases of the military regime are highly repressive. It is in this initial stage that the fascist components of militarism stand out. The entrepreneurial role of these governments, on the other hand, evolves gradually. Attempts to solve the economic and social problems faced by these countries, as well as the emergence of alliances between multinational, domestic private, and state enterprises, progressively confer upon the authoritarian regimes their peculiar entrepreneurial features. Repression continues to be a significant component of political life, but attempts have to be made to justify the regime in the name of a rapid process of accumulation. High rates of output growth are as important as repression in the process of creating and projecting the image of the regime and in its acceptance by dominant classes. Social order with economic progress is the slogan used to hide any questions about "progress for whom?" A final word might need to be said about the economic achievements of authoritarian regimes and their capacity to impose political conformity on society. It is commonly said that these regimes are "strong." If what is meant by strength is a capacity for violence, then this is tautologically true. But it does not necessarily follow that authoritarian regimes are by themselves able to resist any kind of political challenge. The most dramatic evidence that they are not is the "Cordobazo" that put an end to Ongania's attempt to build a stable authoritarian order. Apart from their "internal conflicts," the authoritarian regimes cannot avoid the elements of uncertainty that pervade all political life. The present difficulties of Brazilian authoritarianism exemplify this. Hence, in explanations of change, it is necessary to take into consideration two different levels of analysis. The first refers to the interplay between structural possibilities for action and the actual behavior of social groups and leaders. Structural possibilities and actual behavior do not necessarily coincide. The second refers to the fact that the actual results of political action do not necessarily coincide with intended results. For example, sometimes military coups are launched in order to preserve private enterprise, but eventually they give rise to governments which—in spite of themselves—expand state enterprise, creating unexpected contradictions.

It is better, therefore, to recognize frankly the ambiguous character of historical situations than to proclaim nostalgia for the logic and coherence of explanations that ignore the unexpected and contradictory aspects of real political life and thus reinforce the image that authoritarian military regimes are likely to cope successfully with any pew demands.

The ambiguities of politics give ground for hope. Sometimes they open roads favorable to change by generating forces within an established order that eventually undermine authoritarian rule. The very functioning of authoritarian regimes and the achievement of proposed economic goals create new challenges to the military and new forms of opposition. The military will not necessarily be able to overcome these difficulties. To a large extent, the likelihood of change may depend on the political capacity of opposition groups to propose creative alternatives of power that address these same challenges by offering different, and better, solutions.

✦ 9 ✦

Dependent Development and Democratic Theory

This return to the theme of democracy after so much discussion about authoritarianism is neither a defense nor a revision. In 1971, when I wrote my essay for *Authoritarian Brazil*, "Associated-Dependent Development: Theoretical and Practical Implications," I did not see any possibility of the Brazilian regime's metamorphosis.[1] Indeed, many considered the regime's persistence an irreversible tendency due either to the structural situation of dependency or to an authoritarian vocation inherent in the historical formulation of Brazilian society. On a central point, however, my essays in *Authoritarian Brazil* (see chapter 7) and *Democratizing Brazil* are consistent: in neither volume is my emphasis on reaffirming dependency. Rather, my task in both essays has been to explore new economic patterns, new social formations and, especially in this volume, new political contradictions and possibilities that emerge within this late twentieth-century structural-historical novelty, associated-dependent development.

So the consequences, as the old Counselor Acácio says in the novels of Eça de Queiroz, always arrive later, but they do arrive. And, in the Brazilian case, they have arrived. In the last two decades, we have seen an unprecedented transformation. Today it is useless to debate the nature of the development which took place in order to speculate about up to what point there has been a transfer of the productive system from the Center to the Periphery. It happened, and so quickly and significantly that dependency theory began to be subjected to a strong critique from the position that instead of dependency there was interdependence.

Naturally, for authors who confused dependency with stagnation, and development of the periphery with the renewal of traditional imperialist links, the example

Adapted from Fernando Henrique Cardoso, "Associated-Dependent Development and Democratic Theory," in Alfred Stepan, ed., *Democratizing Brazil: Problems of Transition and Consolidation* (New York: Oxford University Press, 1989), 299–326.

of Brazilian industrialization is enough to knock down their poorly constructed theoretical house of cards. However, in my judgment nothing has shaken the foundational observations of Raul Prebisch and the United Nations Economic Commission for Latin America (ECLA) about the "deterioration of the terms of trade," about the differential speed of the fall in the price of primary-export products relative to industrial products in a period of decline of the economic cycle, or on the inverse relation with regard to periods of expansion.[2]

Nor has the analysis of the new structure of the international productive system, which described the dynamic role of investment in the Periphery, been cast into doubt. Multinational firms have reproduced the asymmetrical link between the Center and the Periphery through control of technology (in the production of inventions) and of the financial system.

It is now obvious that economic development on the Periphery is real; it is not mere "economic growth" without redistribution of resources and without deep structural transformations. But the links of dependency are not broken, and we are not just dealing with a gigantic process of "interdependence." In other words, the process of *domination* among nation-states mediated by renewed economic channels persists in the international capitalist system, in spite of the internationalization of the productive process, and even though there has been significant transformation in the social structure of dependent countries and a significant increase in the internal productive capacity of some of these countries.

In light of these historical transformations and given the perspective of time, the old polemic in which my essays on dependency were critiqued on the claim that they substituted the primacy of the *nation* for the primacy of *social class* is reduced to what it always was: a fundamental theoretical and political error. My whole theoretical thrust was to demonstrate that dependency produces a specific class situation in which on the political plane the question of classes and their struggle is inseparable from the question of the nation and its political expression, the State. A theoretical perspective that emphasizes the autonomy of class is of little help in understanding the dynamics of associated-dependent societies. Conceptually, "autonomy of classes" only makes sense if it incorporates a prior understanding of the "double determination" of classes. The first determination of class is the productive system, which in this case is internationalized. The second determination of class are the forms of domination: internal, consubstantiated in the state; and external, exercised by the central countries and their international regimes, such as the IMF.

Given this analytic perspective, how do we explain historically the fact that an associated-dependent development process in Brazil has opened up a range of political possibilities that resulted in the weakening of the authoritarian order? How do we theoretically and ideologically advocate a democratic position in countries marked by their heterogeneity between and within classes (which many call structural), by the persistence of pockets of poverty, and by inequality?

As a theorist of dependency and as an active democratic politician I am often asked (by foreigners more than by Brazilians) how I reconcile dependency theory and democratic theory. Since I consider this one of the most urgent questions of our day I will put aside issues relating to the form, the nature, and the economic limits of the associated-dependent development process (while maintaining the concept as a necessary tool for describing Brazilian industrialization) in order to concentrate on this political *problematique*.

In the pages that follow I will confront this challenge by examining four questions. First: What is the structure of the new society that the economic transformations of associated-dependent development have wrought? Second: Given that I do indeed think there is a certain "elective affinity" between the structures produced by associated-dependent development and the centralization of power, how and why was there a departure from the expected in Brazil with the emergence of democratizing spheres within a new and strengthened civil society? Third: Since a modern democracy cannot exist without democratic political parties, the difficult question for the democratic parties in an associated-dependent setting such as Brazil is what should be the correct relationship between social movements and parties so that both can carry out their democratizing tasks. Fourth: Considering that different types of societies have mobilized different sorts of interests and ideological defenses for democracy in different structural-historical settings, what are the political arguments and concomitant actions within our context of associated-dependent development that are both appropriate and possible as vehicles for mobilizing and consolidating support for democratic institutions?

THE NEW SOCIETY

The widespread belief that Brazilian society, with rapid industrialization through multinational investment, would end up generating a "new duality" disappeared before the historical results. We have seen neither the crystallization of a Belgium of prosperity nor the ocean of misery and marginality of an India. We do, however, have many new structures in our society. A close examination of the data from 1950 to 1980 reveals that at least eight major new material realities related to our style of industrialization have emerged.

1. There was a sharp increase in the number of workers employed in the secondary sector of the economy. There were 2.9 million such workers in 1960, 5.3 million in 1970, and 10.7 million in 1980.

2. Industrialization was spatially concentrated in the Center-South, but this process did not take place without the appearance of "industrial spots" in the Northeast, such as the massive petro-chemical pole in Salvador, and some metal-working in Recife and Salvador. Even in the North there are major plans for extractive and transformative industries by such varied interests as state enterprises, Japanese capital and Alcoa.

3. The form which accumulation and investment took did not reproduce decades later either the "Prussian model" (of concentration of investment in basic industry) or the "American model" of incremental industrialism. What we actu-

ally have is a kind of development based on the combination of the form of "inverted industrialization" (which initially featured finished products of the "mass consumption" type, such as automobiles, televisions, and refrigerators, and was established through technology transfer in black boxes) plus a form of industrialization which involves domestic entrepreneurs in technical progress and opens up investments in capital goods sectors (which grew at an annual rate of 16% in the 1967–76 period), and, on a smaller scale, in the key sectors of the second wave of the technological frontier, such as computers and military exports.[3]

4. This type of industrialization set off a strong chain reaction between strictly industrial investments and investments in services, to such a point that the hypotheses regarding a malignantly swelling tertiary sector (considered in this case as "not modern" and as a simple expedient to disguise unemployment) become unsustainable faced with the productivity of the "modern tertiary" sector directly linked to the expansion of industrial products. What had led many analysts to make extrapolations predicting the exhaustion of the industrialization process was that from 1950–60 tertiary services grew at 5.4% while the secondary sector grew at only 1.9%. But 1960–80 saw a strikingly different pattern: the secondary sector grew at a rate of 6.7% while the tertiary sector grew at 5.0%.

5. There was also the rapid capitalization of agriculture (from 1960 to 1980 the number of farms with tractors increased by a factor of 9, while the number of farms that utilized chemical fertilizers increased by a factor of 17). This process was accompanied by a steep rise in the rural proletariat and the emergence of the "bóas-frias" phenomenon where many rural wage earners in fact live in squatter settlements on the periphery of urban cities and are trucked out to their work sites. This capitalization of agriculture has three axes of dynamism: (a) investments in pioneer areas; (b) capitalization of family-based property or productive units; and (c) the emergence of large agro-business firms in areas of traditional agriculture.[4]

6. The dynamism unleashed by Brazil's particular version of rapid associated-dependent development produced brutal income concentration with impressive trickle-down. In 1960 Brazil had one of the worst Gini indexes of inequality in the world (50% of the population received 17.7% of the income, and 1% of the population received 11.9% of the income). By 1980 the situation deteriorated further, such that the bottom half of the population received only 14.2% while the top 1% garnered 16.9%. At the same time, trickle-down reached such flood proportions that whereas in 1970 only a quarter of Brazil's households had refrigerators and televisions, by 1980 more than half did. The apparent paradox is resolved when we take into account that in 1970–80 real average income per family increased almost 89% for the country as a whole. Contradictions abound, of course. In 1980, 73% of urban households were linked to the world by television but only 58% had sewage link-ups.

7. This whole process took place in the context of growing participation—from the beginning—of foreign investment, and later required growing international

financial support with soaring interest rates, the world recession, and the consequent decrease in exports and their value, the expansion of the "external debt" was once again a necessary condition to sustain local economic activity.[5]

8. In spite of growing links with the exterior, the *internal* market absorbed most of the productive expansion and the "coefficient of openness" of the Brazilian gross, domestic product to world trade did not increase. In fact, if we exclude petroleum-based imports Brazil has one of the lowest ratios of imports to total Gross National Product of any major market economy in the world.

These then are some of the complex phenomena we must think about. Hirschman, with his heterodox talents, called attention to the unexpected in economic development: an airline, for example, could be better managed and more efficient in an underdeveloped country than a railroad.[6] Something like this happens in a generalized way with associated-dependent development. When we wait for the "inevitable" to happen (in general conceived as a tendency extrapolated from the history of the early developer), the "unexpected" happens.

This "unexpected" is basically a specific effect of the combination of structural forces which fuse the "old" with the "new," often in a contradictory manner and without a guarantee that the contradiction will result in a new synthesis. Brazilian society at the moment is an incomplete synthesis, between one dynamic set in motion by the internationalization of the productive system, and another involving successive and not always successful accommodations by economic and social interests which preceded this process. The command of social transformation lies unequivocally with the internationalized sector of the economy, to the point that the word "sector" is inappropriate, since the "economic whole" moves within the context of internationalization. The social effects of this, however, do not correspond to what we would expect on the basis of a mere "functional sociology of convergence," nor is it merely an adaptation to the resistance of the "old structure." Both terms of the contradiction behave, in part, like an unresolved tension, as something that is created in the Periphery, as an original trait.

In less abstract terms, associated-dependent industrialization is creating a specific kind of society. It is a copy, but to paraphrase myself, an original Copy.[7] And being a copy, it is also a "desired and programmed" copy. We are not witnessing a phenomenon of "irradiation" of a "cultural circle," à la Kroeber. Nor are we in the presence of a social and cultural dynamism which is a given because of "transfer of technology." On the contrary, there is a domestic debate on "the good society," a domestic strategy for reaching it (seen differently by the competing forces), and a will to plan, through the choice of policies, the steps to be taken.

It is this mixture of the "inevitable effect" of industrialism, the choice of forms of insertion into the "new world," and the dead weight of that which cannot be thrown away, which gives vitality, presents and, at the same time, opens intriguing perspectives for audaciousness in the interpretation of Brazilian society.

Just as an example: It is impossible to understand the patterns of social and geographical mobility, the aspirations for living and the form of social control in force, without considering that TV and airplanes are a fundamental part of the "new society." But it is also precarious to understand this society without perceiving that in the full dynamic of Gesellschaft—in the industrial heart of class society, the ABC region of São Paulo—the "ethical political" moment, as Gramsci would say, of assertion of choice by workers and the insertion of the new São Paulo working class, took place through the revitalization—momentary but significant—of Gemeinschaft. The solidarity of the commune—the transcendence of the everyday and the corporative confrontation—before going through the party, came through the Church and through fraternity in neighborhoods.[8]

To take one of the poles of the dichotomy and bet on it as if it were the expression of the essence of peripheral industrial society is to dissolve the dialectic which built it in a mechanistic manner. To maintain the relation between the two parts in permanent tension is to give up on understanding the next moment, possible synthesis. To believe that we know beforehand which of the two contrary poles will win out without seeing that there might just as well be an unexpected fusion or a momentary solution through the more "traditional" pole, is to introduce into the theoretical framework like that of the nineteenth century, which could leave the observer perplexed before an unexpected turn in history.

It is in this spirit, which at the same time seeks regularities and rejects models, but is willing to accept "structural fractures" which break the regularities that we have to understand contemporary Brazilian society.

Some observers have decreed that the multinational firm, with its international dynamic, will replace the presence of the State in production. The state has been condemned, by these same criteria, to the role of figurehead for external interests: from the political arm of the oligarchy, it would be transformed into the militarized arm of foreign capital. Fortunate mistake: State investment in industrial firms and services grew and the regulation of the economy by the State intensified, to the point where it produced a (false) reaction on the part of the local bourgeoisie itself, which came to see "Statism" as the root of its problems (which, in reality, when they existed, were due to the competition of multinationals and to the crisis).[9] By 1979, if we rank the size of non-financial enterprises in Brazil by net worth, twenty-eight of the thirty largest were located in the public sector. Moreover, in the mid-1970s, comparative data demonstrated that Brazil had one of the most profitable State enterprise sectors in the world.

The presence of the State in the economy became so strong that a sort of structural inversion of the old distinction between State and civil society took place. This distinction, which underwent radical reformulation in the Marxist tradition through the work of Gramsci, needs to be reformulated theoretically to explain the type of relation that exists in Brazilian society. In effect, Marx replaced, in the terms of Hegel but going beyond, the natural law distinction which opposed natural society to civil society (the State) with the dichotomy between political society (the State) and civil society (the social order, classes, producers); Gramsci returned to Hegel, opposing political society to the private order, embodying it, however, as something beyond mere economic relations. In placing the moment of hegemony at the level of civil society, Gramsci broke with the traditional framework of relations between infrastructure-superstructure (closer to Marx's thought), in which the State is a part of the second, while the primacy of the contradictions which lead to overcoming class domination is given by the first, that is, by the social relations of production. Gramsci began to dissolve this rigid distinction and to a certain extent reabsorbed the State into Society, through Hegel's "Ethical State."[10]

So in the situation of countries like Brazil, in which the State is an important part of the productive order, it is also necessary to break with the notion that links between the political and private order are lacking, suggested by the old civil society. But the rupture takes place in regard to the opposite pole. As suggested by Gramsci's analysis we must not only stress that hegemony is developed at the level of classes as a struggle *in society* but also show that the State, in becoming a "Producer State," becomes part of the economic order and ipso facto of civil society.

It is clear that all this cries out for new theoretical frameworks able to understand both the new society and the new politics. It also cries out for another phenomenology of classes, beginning from what I call the specific blend of dependent-industrial societies, and thus freed from the schematism of analogies with the early developers. It would recognize that while industrialization quickly creates a proletariat, however much this proletariat grows in absolute numbers it will not be one more class position which becomes generalized by its size, given that the new society is both industrial in the old way and also a service and "programmed" society, as described by Touraine. Likewise, in the agrarian structure the "typically capitalist" sector produces rural workers, who, in relation to the peasant economy on the pioneer fringe and with the family economy that is becoming capitalized, are not fast becoming the dominant form of rural occupation. And in spite of the vigor of the capitalization process, the "informal sectors" of employment (and the "marginals") are not disappearing. They reproduce themselves, at the old rate and at the new rate: for example, the "informal sector" of luxury crafts, which arises from an eventual combination of more sophisticated methods with a "liberal" employment of labor (as in the case of computer programmers, for example).

Moreover, in the real sense of the term, broad petit-bourgeois layers are becoming wage earners in services and in factories; former "liberal professions" are becoming wage earners; and the modern "putting-out system" is bringing about the rebirth of false wage earners—independents—who constitute a regular labor force for big industry, dispersed in familial productive units.

Returning the analysis to the top of the social pyramid, other surprises interrupt the placid vision of a society that reproduces the advanced economic order. A few examples: the managers of State firms become a significant layer of the dominant class; the old national bourgeoisie does not disappear, but forms a layer between the State and multinational enterprise, trying to reserve for itself relatively important economic spaces; big foreign capital appears socially as an international bureaucracy, made up of professional administrators, with a strong "structural presence," but with enormous difficulty in becoming a class for itself at the level of local politics.

Thus we can see that the society which associated-dependent development wrought broke in significant aspects with the images which the sociological literature elaborated to describe the "effects of industrialization" and of capitalization of the Periphery. In the face of this new situation, how could we imagine a politics that conforms to old paradigms?

BREAKING WITH THE EXPECTED: DEMOCRATIZATION

Once again, this part does not intend to describe the political process that took place; other authors and I myself, in other works, have already done so. It is primarily intended to point out paradoxes, and then to try to explain them.

The discussion about whether or not there was a "democratic opening" in Brazil is today a non-question. There was an opening, with various consequences. The "theorists" to whom I never subscribed of the inevitability of fascism (whose only alternative would be revolutionary socialism) lost prestige even in the most radical intellectual circles; the force of events buried badly formulated interpretive caprices.

Nonetheless, some problems need to be clarified, given that even those who did not support the point of view that social revolution was inevitable as the antithesis of military authoritarianism, affirm and reaffirm (as I do myself) that there is a certain "elective affinity" between the structures produced by associated-dependent development and the centralization of power. The concentration of income, oligopolistic investment, the breakup of trade union structures, the generalization of mass apathy induced by the central power, the control of information, and the most repugnant aspects of the authoritarian order (such as torture and the deprivation of citizenship) were understood as symptoms of the relation between this pattern of development and a particular form of bureaucratic-authoritarian regime.[11]

It is true, and worth pointing out, that some authors, most notably Juan Linz, restricted the extent of their characterization of Brazilian authoritarianism; this would be more an authoritarian situation than an authoritarian regime.[12] It is also true that I tried to show (when there were already signs of redemocratization) that the "political form" (the regime) is distinct from the "pact of domination" (an alliance of hegemonic classes) that gives the State its social base. And I argued that the same style of associated-dependent development was consistent with democratic regimes such as Venezuela and Mexico.[13]

Nonetheless, for many Brazilians one of the most puzzling aspects of our recent history is that without any breakdown of the State apparatus, without any loss of military coercive capacity, civil society grew stronger, and, most important, in a society with many layers of authoritarianism there nonetheless was a deepening, a quickening of democratic aspirations.

Why is our society breaking with authoritarianism? Broadly speaking, we can identify three explanatory/prescriptive schools of thought about Brazil's authoritarian-democratic dynamic. All three schools are heterogeneous but one has a *functionalist* core, one a *Statist* core, one a *grassroots* (*basismo*) core.

The first ad hoc "functionalist" attempt comes in the form of a paradox: beginning from two theories which note the anti-democratizing effects of the historical process of change in Peripheral societies—dependency and bureaucratic authoritarianism— they end up stressing the "unexpected" democratizing aspects of those processes. As a result, given that there was development and given that bureaucratic control expanded the State machine and absorbed the military into it, an unexpected "space of freedom" was produced in civil society, at the same time as there was an authoritarian condensation within the State. Between the two, State and civil society, there was a gap, a sort of buffer vacuum. Democracy therefore was sown on the virgin soil of society, leaving the State wrapped in its splendid authoritarian isolation.

There were various versions of this hypothesis. Some were inspired by "modernization theory": the democratic subproduct was the consequence of social differentiation provoked by economic development, by the growing specificity of social roles required by growing secularization and rationalization of society, and by the need for standardization of norms appropriate for a modern industrial society.[14]

To a certain extent, almost all the authors in this school have shaped their work around this broad hypothesis, because there were in fact convergent processes which encouraged the re-elaboration of aspirations, conduct, and regular patterns of behavior commensurate with the universal aspects of industrialization. In an attempt to explain the return to democratic practices on the electoral level, for example, more than a few stressed that the democratic form of regulating the distribution of power would necessarily re-establish the competitive system of parties and representative mechanisms characteristic of "any democracy." Allied to the modernization theory, liberal political theory again resounded not only in the major press but also in academic texts and even in party programs.

The "theory of the gap" (between State and civil society) leaves us without a solution, however, to the central question: if it is true that the subproduct of socio-economic development is the demand for the autonomy of the social, of political representation of classes, and of a liberal-democratic creed, political change is moving towards an impasse: either the citadel of the State is conquered by the furor of classes demanding democratic power and becomes democratized, or, in a counteroffensive, the State advances still more in the direction of authoritarian processes, getting close to a situation of authoritarian control of society (in a version of the political process which is close to "socialism or fascism" vision, but rewritten as "democracy or dictatorship." But, by postulating this kind of dynamic, what was clear in Marxist theory about civil society is hidden, that is, that it is ruled by domination, and that, taken by themselves alone, civil society and democracy have nothing to do with each other as such, given that the democratization of society requires struggles among competing classes and the overcoming of the contradictions between the exploited and the exploiters.

The hypotheses about the development of an opposition between society and the State outlined above are not the only ones sustainable from the point of view of a functionalist and liberal theory of democratic politics. Nothing prevents the conflict from remaining unresolved, with advances and retreats by the two opposed poles, or with a dialectic where conciliation of interests in specific areas and open conflicts in others are both possible. Such a hypothesis presumes slow and gradual transformation towards democratization based on the assumption of the effect of the spread of universalizing mechanisms of industrial society. Within the Statist school especially strong among the regime's ideologues a version of the same process was developed from another angle. Rejecting the pervasive effects of the renaissance of civil society, these ideologues returned to Oliveira Vianna, Azevedo Amaral, and, against the express thinking of the author, Raymundo Faoro. They went back to seeing the modernization of the State as the main guarantee for a process of political opening and democratization, which would escape the "pitfalls of liberalism." In this case, the emphasis was not so much on the gap between society and the State, but on the "emptiness" of society. They continued to interpret the country as if the only possible framework for a stable political order was one built upon the efficiency of the State machine, coupled with developmentalist policies and guided by an enlightened will which should moderate and conciliate, whenever pressure arose from "reasonable" private groups. The legitimacy of demands "from below" (and everything with roots in civil society, be it business, the press, or the Church, and not only the popular sectors, was "from below") would always pass through the filter of State will, the ethical-political collector of an unorganized people on the road to the constitution of the nation.

Obviously, the modernization of society by the State and the making of the people into a nation thought of in these terms is not part of "democratic theory." Nonetheless, as ambiguous and confusing as this Statist version of authoritarian ideology is, it is also "liberal-conservative." It postulates a series of transformations and a gradualism which do not in principle negate the legitimacy of a demand for a State of Law: they only postpone and attempt to conduct it on the "good road" to a "democracy without conflicts." But the logic of such an argument obliges its advocates to accept, as a thesis and as a principle, that a "good government," to be democratic, must break with authoritarianism.

The grassroots version of why Brazil is breaking with authoritarianism combines a radical vision of autonomy of civil society with a socialist critique of social domination. This version stresses the same process of constitution and autonomization of classes (an emphasis it has in common with the liberal-functionalist theory of political change). But it also views as essential the way in which the new capitalist-industrialist order, on the one hand, maintains class differences and, on the other, disaggregates those without class, the "poor," the "marginals," the "inhabitants of the periphery," or whatever name is given to the disinherited of the capitalist order. Real democratization will arrive (and is arriving, according to those who hold this perspective) as it is crystallized in the spontaneous solidarity of the disinherited. It lives as *comunitas*, experiences of common hardship which form a collective we based on the same life experience that is transformed only when, through molecular changes, the simultaneous isolation of the State and the exploiters—which will perish at the same time—comes about.

To those accustomed to Marxist literature these might sound like the old themes of Revolution and fusion between solidarity, equality, and democratic participation. But this is true only up to a point. In their most radical version (common among social movement activists) this reformist version that proposes the New Utopia is accompanied by a rejection of the State so strong (in theory) that it also excludes the party, which is seen as an institutionalizing force, and thus a cog of the State. In the radical formulation of this type of democratic theory there is a fusion of lay anarchism and Catholic solidarity thought.

Underlying these three schools (which simultaneously prescribe ideologies favorable to different types of democratization) there are explicit differences not only as to what "real" democracy is but also, and more important sociologically speaking, as to who are the "historical subjects" of the desired democratization. The distinction at the level of democratic ideas is simple:

- For functionalist liberal democrats (as anywhere else in the world) it involves establishing a competitive regime, which accepts differences of wealth and property (of classes), but which claims to identify the possibility of a Common Good (the Public Spirit) which would be exercised and controlled in particular spheres of the State (Legislative, Executive, and Judiciary) through explicit mechanisms of *representation* and *legitimacy* (delegation of powers, elections, etc.) which ensure the sovereignty of the citizen as "political being" *par excellence*, the individual as the subject of history.
- For Statist liberal-conservatives, the problem is to rebuild a political order founded upon the idea of a Public Good located in the Executive, whose excesses must be controlled on the one hand by the will of the Nation and by its "permanent aspirations" as perceived, expressed, and renewed by a privileged sector of the bureaucracy (the security apparatus), and on the other hand, by the existence of certain channels of representation (parties and assemblies) with the right to speak but not to act on the major decisions of the State. (In addition to this—as a concession—some of them add freedom of the press and, up to a point, freedom of organization in civil society [parties, trade unions, the Church] which, though they are controlled, exercise pressure and indirectly allow the guardians of order to correct the course of their policies.) The true subject of the political process is the State as enlightened bureaucracy, considered the incarnation of the metaphysical will of the people.
- For the grassroots democrats, the fundamental question is the autonomous organization of the population around concrete demands almost always within the reach of and with direct consequences for the well-being of deprived groups of people. These demands should be made on the Public Authority without the ostensible mediation of parties and, if possible, without delegation of responsibility to elected representatives. The general will, in this case, is presented as the incarnation of a partiality that in its totality expresses a goal or a desire. The subject of the political process becomes a "living community": neighbors, workers in the *same* factory, landless tenants who measure their aspirations around the control of an area, etc. More than the rather abstract solidarity of a "class,"

what is needed is the solidarity of a professional "branch" or a specific segment of the people to give substance to the demand for democracy.

This typology of the kind of democratization desired and the actors expected to bring it about demonstrates that, with the exception of the liberal-democratic school (similar to what predominated in the democratization processes of early developing countries), the other schools that are most evident in the contemporary Brazilian process are, at the very least, "heterodox." One side comes from reformed authoritarianism; the other from Christian solidarity thought to be penetrated by anti-statist anarchism.

It would be wrong to imagine that the spectrum of democratizing pressures has been limited to these. The classic socialist vision, with all of its considerations about the relationship between social revolution and true democracy, is just below the surface among followers of parties which are small, but capable, at times, of strategic action: the (pro-Soviet) Communist Party, the (pro-Albania) Communist Party of Brazil, and various Trotskyist groups, all of which maintain the classical set of ideas and emphasize the "historical role" of the proletariat in the advance towards democracy. But either they attached themselves to the liberal-democratic view, adjusting their revolutionary aspirations to a "stage" which would follow a full State of Law, or they joined (in the case of the Trotskyists and the Albanians) with the grassroots pressures for a more direct democracy.

In addition, in the concrete process of political action, when these tendencies came together in the creation of parties (especially after 1979) and in the action of specific social movements (as in the unions and the movements in favor of a United Workers Federation [*Central Única dos Trabalhadores*]), *basismo* was rarely immune to positions which supported the decisive political role of the oppressed under the leadership of the unions and the "working class" organized into a party; likewise, in the parties most influenced by an ideal of Western competitive democracy (like the PMDB and the PDT), the "Marxist-Leninist" ideological segments were sufficiently influential to give value to the idea that the "active presence of workers" was necessary for an effective redemocratization, thus compensating for the limitations of the liberal-democratic vision, which is more lenient about living with social inequality.

The reader versed in the history of political ideas will see in these distinct positions the debate between Locke, Hegel, and Rousseau, as (unwitting) inspiration of the existing polarizations. But the reader will also see that Brazilian liberals are willing to live with the presence of the State. The authoritarians with a liberal-conservative thrust are sprinkled with ideas not only from Montesquieu (each regime conforms to the nature of society, and in an industrial society there is a certain division and balance among powers), but from contradictory influences which go from the acceptance of a certain kind of planning to distorted Hobbesian formulations to authoritarianism. And the radically democratic, however much they make *basista* statements in favor of "direct democracy," incorporate a pinch of Gramsci, even mixing in a certain amount of Leninism, and cannot easily avoid the concern with the Party and the State.

But the society in which the political process is evolving has very little in common with the societies and the problems confronted by the classical theorists. This is the point where my perspective on "dependency" crosses with the debate about democracy.

NEW IDEAS?

It would be strange if authors linked to a tradition of structural-historical analysis, faced with authoritarianism and the process of its transformation into a more liberalized order, critiqued authoritarianism and defended democracy from a Lockean vision of the two freedoms—the economic and the political—both foundations of philosophical individualism. Likewise, it would be inconsistent if the justification came from the side of philosophical utilitarianism, from Bentham and the idea of optimization of opportunities in the "political market."

However, there are other branches in the history of ideas and, moreover, in the history of socio-political practice, which can help to ground and justify theoretically and ideologically the defense of the "sphere of democracy." I called attention to the real (not epistemological) inversion of the relation between State and society, which characterizes the countries whose development takes place in the associated-dependent form (and which also occurs in many "advanced democratic" societies). Making use of other arguments, various sociologists and political scientists have proceeded in a similar way. For example, the notion of "regulated citizenship" developed by Wanderley Guilherme dos Santos tries to show the similarity and the difference when we compare the process of formation of citizenship à la Marshall and the process that takes place in Brazil. A citizen, among us, would be the worker whose right is recognized by the State.[15]

The weight of entrepreneurial bureaucracy (what I have elsewhere called the "state bourgeoisie" in order to provoke reactions) is abundantly recognized in political analyses of contemporary Brazil.[16] And the key role of the National Intelligence Service (SNI) as a "party" of the armed forces and the upper bureaucracy was pointed out by Alfred Stepan.[17]

In other works I called attention both to the political form of the relation between the bureaucracy and the entrepreneurs (the bureaucratic rings) and to the fact that, unlike what happens in classical political philosophy, among us the subject to be constituted and justified is not the State, but the citizen and the class. All this means that implicitly and sometimes explicitly here is another paradigm of political analysis in process of elaboration.[18]

As before, I will cite a few examples to illustrate the argument. One example will relate to the formation of parties and the party system; another will relate to practical-epistemological aspects of the legitimation of democratic worldview in process.

PARTIES TODAY

At the most abstract level, the discussion of the specificity of parties was already posed by dependency theory: the birds that sing here do not sing as they do there. But they are birds, and they also sing. They seem the same, but there are differences. Through this prism, the polarization between Conservative party and Liberal party in the Empire would seem at the same time like a fundamental dichotomizing core of political ideologies, a shadow cast by a stronger and more real radiating center—

from the central countries—and almost mystified. An educated and intellectually nationless elite seemed to be using the struggle over *ideas* rather than the struggle over *interests* as its banners. In fact, under the clamor of parliamentary debates was the solid presence of plantations and slavery.

Meanwhile, at the same time as an engaged demystification should be able to show the extent to which the ideological prism was produced by the refraction of interests, it would have to show that the conservative and liberal visions also shaped decisions and adjustments which had an effect on the real. Thus we are not dealing with "mere alienation."

I think that from this angle today's party system suffers from similar vicissitudes. The ideological aspect, which was clearer in the polarization between ARENA and MDB, was real, however much on another level it deformed differences of interest, diluted distinctions, and encompassed concealed social accords. The current spectrum, which goes from the PDS to the PT, passing through the PTB, the PDT, and the PMDB, makes the differences more visible. It almost satisfies those who are always looking for an ethical Cartesianism which links the notion of "clear and distinct" with a categorical imperative: if someone is a worker he/she has to belong to such and such a party, and this will bring about the good of the universe. The party which represents this side will be able to establish a State of Virtue, which will be dissolved into the Community of the Future; if someone is a plantation owner, or a boss, he must purge himself of original sin, accepting responsibility for all the evils of society, and will become a prop for the founding violence of any State, because it is rooted in class society.

Moreover, as in Old Europe, each party would correspond, more or less, to a class situation, and if there be internal contradictions, they would correspond to an ideological nuance which expresses a class fraction. On the formal level, a center, a center right, and a right would confront a center left and a left. Insofar as the real parties do not fit the model, they are not authentic, are weak as organizers of social interests, are mere instruments of manipulation by the forces of order, and are fortified in the State, which rules by dispensing representation and democratic legitimacy.

Let us leave aside the discussion of whether the model worked in the paradigmatic historical situation, Europe. Let us not get lost in side discussions on the changes that took place in mass industrial society with the influx of internationalized monopoly capitalism and the action of the interventionist State. Let us assume that none of this affects the argument of the prospectors for party authenticity. Still, why should a dependent society, penetrated by international capitalism from head to foot, born from a colonial-capitalist-modern situation, based on slavery, organized around a State bureaucracy, end up with a class and political situation similar to the one which prevailed in societies organized by bourgeois-liberal and sometimes bourgeois. State dynamics, struggling on the one hand against the *ancien régime* and on the other against the plebes and the emerging working class? Only if the argument were anchored in a finalistic philosophy of history and overlooked the differences among historical situations could one expect that in Brazil the parties, the classes, and their struggles would take place in the image of the Single Mold of History.

Clearly there are differences. And it is not so easy to discard even the ideological arguments, à la Raymond Aron, about the equalizing effects of modern society. But the conception of the modern political party as "an organizing machine and a structured and articulated political program," like the one proposed by Umberto Cerroni, describes a historical situation and not History.[19] Cerroni opposes the notion of a party as "faction," born out of the electoral committee or club, which is discharged in Parliament. He takes as a model the European socialist (and Communist) parties, in which there is mass participation by members, and in which the organizational structure and a certain conception of the world (a political philosophy) constitute the vital core that animates them. However, as Cerroni says himself, the Social Democratic (Labor and SPD) and North American parties depart from this model insofar as they stress economic-corporative interests and separate these from the struggle for a conception of the world; "political operations" predominate in them over the overall political conception.

With this argument I am naturally reducing the extent of the classical (Marxist-Leninist) definition of the party: it is not always the expression of a class interest together with a transformational idea, a worldview. But I do not want to eliminate the idea, which also comes from Cerroni, or from Gramsci, that whatever its form, the party is the place of mediation between idea and interest, the Gordian knot of all politics. Rather, I want to say that this mediation takes historically variable forms, of which the idea of the party as "embryo of a state structure" and therefore revolutionary because in conflict with the prevailing state structure, is the result of a historically specific situation and not the matrix of all essential definitions of the party.

In Brazil the parties were not born only in Parliament, nor were they the expression of an organizational machine that was set up to allow the mass membership of militants. Still less were their struggles and differences based on a global conception of the world.

Literally and paradoxically, the arbitrary legislation of an authoritarian military regime had a crucial role (in spite of its intentions) in the formation of Brazilian parties. It was to obey legal dictates that the PMDB and the PDS, the PTB and the PDT, and even the PT had to emerge from their shells made of agreements among Congressmen and of party leaderships, which did not even have a bureaucratic structure because there was not a real party machine to be controlled.

Under the authoritarian regime, the MDB and ARENA were limited to expressing the will of the electorate in the choice of Congressmen and Senators, a will distorted by apathy, lack of information, and violence. The Congressmen, restricted by authoritarian law, opted between two parties whose leaders were also Congressmen. While there was not a "world view," there was a concrete opposition of ideas as to the form of government: democracy versus authoritarianism. Interests followed behind this dichotomy, without necessarily aligning themselves unequivocally with one "side" or another. But there was no articulated correspondence between society and the State, in which, if we consider the legislative branch to be a part, and a weak part, lay the roots of ARENA and the MDB.

The job of articulation within society (with its interests and its culture) was being carried out with difficulty during the years of authoritarianism. In Brazilian political language, everything which was an organized fragment that escaped the immediate control of the authoritarian order was being designated civil society. Not rigorously but effectively, the whole opposition from the Church, the press, the university, the professional corporations, to the unions, business, and the parties was being described as if it were the movement of civil society. And it was discovered, without anyone having called it scandalous, that what was happening here was the reverse of what Gramsci described with relation to Italy: we were returning to a Latin conception of civil society.[20]

Since this is not primarily a theoretical discussion, I will leave aside the (necessary) polemic on the relevance and limits of the Gramscian paradigm for the analysis of Brazilian politics. In his polemic against economism (and against the literal reading of the primacy of structure), Gramsci reintroduced the primacy of the party, just as in his struggle against the dictatorship he reintroduced the moment of the idea, within the discussion of hegemony. In this respect he was innovative and left a living heritage; but his re-elaboration does not help to describe the historical situation we are facing. The notions of the moment of hegemony and of the germination of liberty in civil society (no longer thought of as "natural society") are necessary and useful; but we must bear in mind that the boundaries of the old natural law distinction and also the Hegelian opposition between producers and the State have been blurred. The State produces, regulates economic relations, and is a key part of manufacturing and service society. There is a new amalgam, in which hegemony, the moment of freedom (ideas, intellectuals, the major regulative institutions) cannot be considered separately from political society. There is a pan-politicization of the social and a socialization of the State, as Pietro Ingrao has noted.[21]

Thus when a new moment of politicization erupted in Brazil, the parties were born at the same time as a state form; and, as an instrument or the organization of struggle, of classes, and of ideas, including anti-Statist ideas.

In this situation, some imagined that the party-form, to be authentic, had to incorporate the "social movements" and could be the incarnation of the liberating idea. And many, in their evaluations of the question of representatives, refused outright to consider that parties that were not born directly from "social movements" and which perhaps did not even aspire to include them and represent them were in fact parties.

But why not? If the new industrial society interpenetrates State and society, the real question about parties and their representatives does not lie in the polarization between the "society of producers" and the society of administrators and collaborators. It lies in the capacity (or not) of the parties to build movable bridges on both sides of the antimony, like the famous "forward and backward linkages" of economic development.

As spaces of mediation between interests and ideas, between cooptation, compulsion, and hegemony, between institutionalization and becoming, between administration, domination, and rebellion, contemporary parties are necessarily internally contradictory. Their capacity for articulation is always tenuous: the big corporative organizations (the trade union, business, the Church) do not dissolve into parties; on the contrary, the parties run the risk of being absorbed by them, as in the example of the Labor party. Nor are movements within society—the strike, the occupation of urban land, riots, the trade union and student movements, the Press itself—anchored in parties. The trajectory of parties and these movements may coincide; sometimes they will even be wedded, but soon after the wedding night will come nausea if not divorce. And they will have to propose unceasingly and routinely new adventures, whose result will be close to that of Bernarda Alba. Weak substitutes for the old parties, the nostalgic will say. *Too bad.* These are the parties we have, not those we want. Within this limitation, they carry on relevant political functions.

Returning to the factual: this was how, without many illusions, the parties we have today were formed, almost all of them. And in their eagerness to win a bit of power, they formed some relation with society.

I will not give many examples. Beginning with the PT (which in this respect is more like the old parties) it is undeniable that it built bridges in determined social sectors: the factory workers of ABCD, middle-class intellectuals, segments of the common people influenced by the liberationist Church. It did not capture the labor movement; it did not become nationally organized; it is penetrated by sectors of the "organized left." None of this in my view diminishes the fact that if it will not become the big mass party under the hegemony of workers, it will be, nonetheless, a party of sectors of workers and intellectual sectors able to propose an alternative society. There will be imperfections and contradictions in the proposal. But who does not have these?

If the thesis is clearest when we use the PT as an example, it remains weak: Wasn't the PT the party with the poorest electoral performance? There are two alternatives from which to choose: either this reference shows that the party closest (in its pro-posals) to the paradigm of authentic representation, by not doing well electorally, condemns the others to be the counter-proof of inauthenticity, or, on the contrary, one can argue that the PT, in spite of its enthusiasm for direct representation, man-aged to become organized in the Brazilian political system.

I do not want to go deeper into these hypotheses. But I would say that it was more in spite of the PT cut deep into those sectors (real and important, especially in terms of political renovation) sensitive to ideology. And it remained restricted, in terms of a more refracted, but diffused, style of representation, which was organized in view of the simultaneously eventual and central polarities of mass society.

In the ways that a party like the PT is weak as an expression of the collective will, the PMDB is strong. Observations that the latter party seems more like a "front" than a party miss the point: in mass societies democratic parties which are open to social variation are, in a certain sense, fronts. But they are nonetheless parties, on the con-dition that they take positions on the major questions, and are diffuse but capable of producing a political cleavage, which presents the voter with an option. And also on the condition that they have leadership able to promote simultaneously internal bar-gaining among the wings of the party (sometimes coopting, sometimes effectively opening participatory and expressive space), and demonstrating a symbolic consis-tency with regard to the major national questions.

Obviously, neither is the PT limited to the functions mentioned, nor is the PMDB organically disconnected from its base. I exaggerate the argument to stress differences. Suffice it to remember that there has never been a party in São Paulo with so many spontaneous members and so completely structured in *diretórios* (local party organizations) as the PMDB.[22] It is enough to look to the professions of the people in leadership positions within the party to verify that the PMDB is the political outlet of the middle class and of leaders of the popular sector: doctors, union lawyers, bank workers, teachers, social workers share power in the *diretórios* (grabbing the hegemonic positions) with the union leader from the interior, the president of a rural union, and the neighborhood leader.

The PDS itself, party born out of the clientelism of ARENA, political arm of the authoritarian bureaucracy, renewed itself partially and became somewhat more autonomous. This should not be denied. Today there are new leaders who are conservative but not immobilist, and who are having a certain amount of impact in the PDS. The 1982 victory of the party in the gubernatorial elections in certain states would not have been possible had it not been for the combination of official pressure, financial resources available, and the modernization of leadership.

With more trouble, the labor parties try to establish a profile of their own. Not so much the PTB, which, jolted by the personalism and inconsistent leadership of Janio Quadros and Sandra Cavalcanti, is prevented from being more than a "front of individuals" and risks becoming only a screen for governmental interest, like the PDT. The latter, trying to emerge as the force representing a "social democratic" party, ran into a major obstacle: its electoral strength derives from a personal leadership (Leonel Brizola) ballasted in a poly-class movement which rebuffs an alliance without a future in a state (Rio de Janeiro) where the working-class base is small. In São Paulo, where the working class counts, the PT and PMDB occupy the space which a social democratic party would want to occupy.

There is not room in this essay to do more than refer to these facts. I do not want to analyze each party, but rather to counter the widespread idea that the parties are "inauthentic" and incapable of serving as a filter for the aspirations of the electorate.[23]

Withal, I do not negate that party institutionalization is far from complete and that there are serious problems of representativeness not only at the level of each party but at the level of the party system. Duverger called attention to the importance of electoral and party legislation in the institutional crystallization of political regimes. It is striking, in the Brazilian case, the degree to which the current legislation arbitrary and conducive to the maintenance of interests in power since 1964 is an obstacle to democratization. The PT skidded and disappeared because of this legislation. The PT runs a similar risk if the district vote is established without a system of two turns. And the labor Parties, if they do not unite, have little prospect of supremacy.

Even worse, the electoral system distorts the popular will in an alienating manner. The opposition won an eight-million-vote advantage and it made very little difference in the House of Representatives. Not to mention the Electoral College that will choose the President of the Republic, if things remain the way they are. But we should not confuse the disturbing action of authoritarianism perpetuated in this legislation with the incapacity of civil society to organize itself into parties.

If parties are not what they used to be, it is because they are more attuned to another type of society. Even if the electoral legislation is changed to allow democratization to advance, the parties will continue to be only partial instruments of the popular and national will, will contain very different wings (not to mention the regional differences within each party), will be in permanent and insoluble tension with the social movements and with the renewing eruptions of mass society, and will experience creatively (or not, depending on the leadership and the circumstances) the dialectic between front and party, between the function of interest aggregation and the ideological function.

One final comment regarding parties: if I tried to show that there is no reason to demand that the parties adjust to a classical European paradigm (on its deathbed there since the 1950s), it would also be naive to imagine that the future of the Brazilian party system lies in the direction of a United States–type division between Republican and Democratic parties. In Brazil, after the populist siege in which the masses erupted in the State (and stagnated there), social and regional contradictions and the traditions of absorption of intellectuals into the parties would fortify the "ideological nuclei" in each party. This is to say nothing of the presence of Communists and, to a lesser extent, the socialists, which would be a constant.

It is therefore better to keep an open mind about the future of the party system. We are not condemned by any structural law to a two-party system (in spite of the bipolarizing tendency characteristic of contemporary societies), nor to politics without ideology. We will construct a peculiar blend, in which the meeting between a European historical tradition and a society which is remaking itself, beginning from a colonial–slave owning–exporting base and moving towards an industrialized and service society (but located at the periphery of the capitalist system), will deflect any tendency to convergence with Western societies. We will go in unexpected, but not inexplicable, directions.

THE LEGITIMATION OF THE DEMOCRATIC IDEA

There remain a few comments to make on the utopian-theoretical-ideological foundations of the idea of democracy in a mass society in a country with an associated-dependent economy.

It is evident that "possessive individualism" and the idea of citizen property owner as the basis for democracy is a weak basis for justifying the democratic struggle in an associated-dependent society such as Brazil.[24] What is at stake today is not the "freedom of the individual" versus the totalitarianism of the State. The subject of individual freedom (psychological, physical, political) is naturally an integral part of a political process which follows upon a struggle against a military dictatorship which oppressed and tortured. But the social inequality and the fragility of the individual before business and the bureaucracy calls for the legitimation of a "collective" historical subject that is the union, the community, the movement, and even the party which appear as actors in the making to oppose themselves to arbitrariness and exploitation.

This non-individualist foundation of embryonic democratic doctrine is difficult to create and pays a price for its legitimation. Its emergence, however, is detectable even on the level of vocabulary and semantics: for the previous "I" of the leader, today is substituted "a gente" ("we, the people") the indeterminate subject— expanded with the concrete sense of "those present." To the extent that the democratizing demand today comes drenched with this character, destabilizing politico-institutional consequences are nourished.

As a result, the classical theory of delegation and representation, closely linked to the conception of citizen-elector (individual and rational being), is put in check, often through the strength of the "collective we," the only thing capable of legitimizing a general will which is becoming concrete. The result of this attitude is transparent: difficulty with or even horror at the delegation of power and the designation of leadership. This process was visible, for example, in the strikes, especially in those job categories, such as public employees and teachers, where "assembly-ism" put in check the process of "bargaining through representatives."

This radically democratic and collectivist attitude produces mistrust of members of Congress by the masses, not to mention the already discussed gap between mass society and the State.

Nonetheless, it would be wrong not to recognize that in spite of the problems that such values pose for institutionalization of democratic life, they have a positive side. They demonstrate the emergence of a will to renewal on the part of civil society that rejects the notion that the "political opening" remains at the level of a redemocratization based on liberal individualist principles, which in the past safeguarded social injustice, class inequality, and traditional bourgeois domination.

There is also renewal on the opposite axis of thought about redemocratization. I am referring to the assimilation, in the sphere of participation and control of the State apparatus, of tendencies in the countries of European "advanced democracy."

If, on the one hand, the *basista* thrust and the constitution of a collective Popular subject so as to support a new historical subject of democracy breaks the confining bonds of past institutional forms, on the other hand the reform democratic thrust which accepts the contemporary reality of the pervasiveness of the State breaks the illusions about the possibility of a democracy "of civil society."

There has not been enough progress in this regard, in terms of political movement and reform-democratic ideas, but we are going forward. There is an embryonic democratic thought that is not restricted to accepting the party-parliamentary game (although it remains a fundamental part, just as the defense of the dignity of the person and his or her rights remains fundamental to democratic collectivism) as a form of justifying the democratic worldview. Without greater transparency of information and of the decision-making process in the firm (whether private or State) and in the bureaucracy (*idem, ibidem*), and without evolving mechanisms for participation and control both through parties and directly by the interested publics, the democratization process will be crippled and meet with little reception in a society in which the "private," in the strict sense of the word, is weak in relation to the organized, corporate, and State interest.

I do not believe that these ideas are rigorously "new." But their combination and especially their diffusion in Brazil are in fact new. I would not say that redemocratization, with the characteristics which it begins to show, can occur without there being at the same time a clash between an industrializing and urbanizing Brazil and the archaic set of practices and notions associated with the Authoritarian State. However, I would not say either that the current process of redemocratization was the "expected effect" of the general processes of social change to which I referred. At the intersection between unprogrammed "structural changes" and authoritarian practices sustained by groups in power, there were specific social struggles, universal currents of opinion which converged, leaders and political-organizational forms which became active, and "unexpected effects" all mixed together.[25]

The political process under way is the result sometimes planned, sometimes imposed, sometimes remade by social and political struggles of all this. Thus, certainly, it could not have been "any other"; but on the other hand, it did not have to be "this one." And in the future, perhaps it will be "another."

NOTES

1. "Associated-Dependent Development: Theoretical and Practical Implications," in Alfred Stepan, ed., *Authoritarian Brazil: Origins, Policies, and Future Implications* (New Haven, Conn.: Yale University Press, 1973), 142–178.

2. See Fernando Henrique Cardoso and José Serra, "As desventuras da dialética da dependência," *Estudos CEBRAP*, 23 (1979): 33–80; and Raúl Prebisch, "El desarrollo económico de la América Latina y algunos de sus principales problemas," *Boletín Económico de América Latina*, 7 (1962): 1–24.

3. For the capital goods growth rate see page 145 of the article by Vilmar Faria cited in Table 1.

4. The data of tractors and fertilizers are from the interesting article by Bernardo Sorj and John Wilkinson, "Processos sociais e formas de produção na agricultura brasileira," in Bernardo Sorj and Maria Hermínia Tavares de Almeida, eds., *Sociedade e Política no Brasil Pós-64* (São Paulo: Editora Brasiliense, 1983), 188–189. Also see Juárez R. B. Lopes, *Do latifúndio à empresa: unidade e diversidade do capitalismo no campo* (Petrópolis: Editora Vozes, 1981). Série Cadernos CEBRAP no. 26; Vinícius Caldeira Brant, "Do colono ao bóia-fria: transformações na agricultura e constituição do mercado de trabalho na alta Sorocabana de Assis," *Estudos CEBRAP*, 19 (1977): 37–91; and G. Muller, "Estrutura e dinâmica do complexo agroindustrial brasileiro" (Ph.D. dissertation, University of São Paulo, 1980).

5. See the essays by Albert Fishlow and by Pedro Malan and Edmar Bacha in this volume.

6. Albert O. Hirschman, *The Strategy of Economic Development* (New Haven, Conn.: Yale University Press, 1958).

7. Fernando Henrique Cardoso, "The Originality of the Copy: ECLA and the Idea of Development," University of Cambridge, Center of Latin American Studies, Working Paper 27 (Cambridge, June 1977).

8. Fernando Henrique Cardoso, "A crisma de São Bernardo," in *Álbum memória de São Bernardo* (São Bernardo do Campo: Prefeitura Municipal, Secretaria da Educação, Cultura e Esportes, 1981), 27–93.

9. For the extensive debate about the role of the State in the economy, see my *Autoritarismo e Democratização* (Rio de Janeiro: Paz e Terra, 1975); Sergio H. Abranches, "Empresa estatal e capitalismo: uma análise comparada"; and Luciano Coutinho and Henri-Philippe Reichstul, "O setor produtivo estatal e o ciclo," both found in Carlos Estevam Martins, ed., *Estado e Capitalismo no Brasil* (São Paulo: Editora HUCITEC, 1977); Luciano Martins, "Estatização da Economia ou Privatização do Estado?" *Ensaios de Opinião*, no. 9 (1978): 30–37; Werner Baer, Richard Newfarmer, and Thomas Trebat, "On State Capitalism in Brazil: Some New Issues and Questions," *Inter-American Economic Affairs*, 30 (Winter 1977): 69–91; and

Thomas J. Trebat, *Brazil's State-owned Enterprises: A Case Study of the State as Entrepreneur* (New York and Cambridge: Cambridge University Press, 1983). Trebat's book also contains a valuable bibliography.

10. See Norberto Bobbio, *Gramsci e la concezione della societá civile* (Milan: Feltrinelli, 1976).

11. Guillermo O'Donnell, "Corporatism and the Question of the State," in James M. Malloy, ed., *Authoritarianism and Corporatism in Latin America* (Pittsburgh: University of Pittsburgh Press, 1977), 47–87. See also his "Reflexiones sobre las tendencias generales de cambio en el Estado *burocrático-autoritario,*" *Documentos CEDES/G.E. CLACSO,* no. 1 (Buenos Aires: CEDES, 1975).

12. Juan J. Linz, "The Future of an Authoritarian Situation or the Institutionalization of an Authoritarian Regime: The Case of Brazil," in Alfred Stepan, ed., *Authoritarian Brazil: Origins, Policies, and Future Implications* (New Haven, Conn.: Yale University Press, 1973), 233–254.

13. Fernando Henrique Cardoso, "On the Characterization of Authoritarian Regimes in Latin America," in David Collier, ed., *The New Authoritarianism in Latin America* (Princeton, N.J.: Princeton University Press, 1979), 33–57.

14. See the summary of these positions in Fernando Henrique Cardoso, "Regime Político e Mudança Social," *Revista de Cultura e Política,* 3 (1980–81): 7–27.

15. Wanderley Guilherme dos Santos, *Cidadania e Justiça* (Rio de Janeiro: Editora Campus, 1981).

16. Cardoso, *Autoritarismo e Democratização,* chapter 5.

17. Alfred Stepan, "O que estão pensando os militares," *Novos Estudos* (CEBRAP), 2 (2) (July 1983): 2–8.

18. See, for example, Cardoso, *Autoritarismo e Democratização.*

19. Umberto Cerroni, *Teoria del Partito Politico* (Rome: Editori Reuniti, 1979), 13.

20. Umberto Cerroni, in his *O Conceito da Sociedade Civil,* argues that "in the whole natural law tradition, the expression *societas civilis,* instead of designating a pre-state society, as would occur within the Hegelian-Marxist tradition, is synonymous—in the Latin usage—with political society, or the State: Locke uses one or the other term indifferently. In Rousseau, *état civil* means State. Kant also, who—besides Fichte—is the author closest to Hegel, when he speaks of the irresistible tendency which nature imposes on man to construct a State (*nas Idee zu einer all gemeinen Geschichte in weltbuergerlicher Asicht*) calls this supreme goal of nature in relation to the human species *burgerliche Gesellschaft*" (São Paulo: Graal, 1982), 26.

21. Pietro Ingrao, *Massa e Poder* (São Paulo: Livraria Ciências Sociais Editora, 1982).

22. In 1982 in the state of São Paulo the PMDB had 400,000 inscribed members, and somewhere between 20,000 to 30,000 party members participated in the elections that produced the 600 local party directorates.

23. Fábio Wanderley Reis, "O Eleitorado, os Partidos e o Regime Autoritário Brasileiro," in Sorj and Tavares de Almeida, eds., *Sociedade e Política no Brasil Pós-64* (São Paulo: Editora Brasiliense, 1983), 64, 62–86.

24. C. B. Macpherson, *The Political Theory of Possessive Individualism* (Oxford: Oxford University Press, 1962).

25. I gave one example of "authoritarian electoral legislation" which animated more expressive parties; I could give another example: the rather surprising lack of interest on the part of the military regime in persistently manipulating (as opposed to periodically repressing) the unions; this situation allowed for a more effective use of that space by unions and their lawyers so as to have workers benefit from labor guarantees, as well as to allow the union space to be occupied in some categories by authentic union leaders.

⇥ 10 ⇤

On Social Change

During discussions held in preparation for the XI World Congress of Sociology, some people suggested, half in jest, that the keynote for the meeting should be borrowed from Daniel Bell's book on ideology in a more cruel version: "The end of sociology." Some of the sociologists on the ISA Executive Committee felt that very few novelties have emerged, in the field of Grand Theory at least, from a reading of sociological journals and papers published in the last ten years. Not without envy, this generation has seen anthropology bask in the limelight, with structuralism and Foucault's "critique of culture," leaving professional sociologists somewhat lacking in imagination, and without the necessary zest even to tackle "middle-range" theories. Esprit de corps has prevailed, however, and here we are with redoubled creative vigor, ready to discuss the most classic of sociological themes: theories of social change.

Suffice it to cast but a critical glance over these theories: it will easily be seen that in spite of everything there are new ideas to expound, and that far from withering away, sociology is pressing ahead with the task of delineating fresh programs for research and interpretation.

What then are these new ideas?

I shall proceed with my introductory exposition in two sections: the first deals with subject matter, and the second with modes of interpretation. I shall leave the section on techniques to more competent specialists in the field.

Originally presented as the keynote speech at the Eleventh World Congress of Sociology in New Delhi, India, August 1986, when Cardoso completed his term as president of the International Sociological Association. It was published as "Problems of Social Change: Again?" *International Sociology*, 2 (2, June 1987): 177–187. Used by permission of the publisher.

NEW THEMES IN THEORIES OF CHANGE

"Social change" or "change in society" or "of society" were constant recurring designations defined by conflicting and opposed theories during sociology's classical age. It was the summit of theoretical ambition to aspire to determine the "laws" of social evolution.

Underlying these notions was the old idea of "progress," revived by the Enlightenment and victorious in the nineteenth century. Sociology contemptuously ignored the skepticism of the historians as to "general processes" of change, and proceeded unruffled with its search for regularities that could explain global social changes.

More modest in their ambitions, the post-classical and post-critical sociologists (if I may thus designate the Kantians à la Weber) remained convinced of the nomothetic value of social science but were more emphatic in applying their passion for generalizing about change to partial aspects of society (changes in society, but not in the type of society). To a large extent, they focused on the transformational action of active social agents in processes of interaction (individuals and groups), rather than on action at the level of structures (reforms and revolutions) or even that of key institutions in society (such as property and the state).

Here we encounter a major change in the themes to which sociologists gave priority. While Durkheim had taken the social division of labor, a universal process, to study the more general and recurring aspects of change through his "average types" and to put forward "laws" which applied to each basic form of "transhistoric" sociability; while Marx had taken the grand historical transitions (from feudalism to capitalism, to socialism) as the theme of his investigation; since Weber (in this respect also a classic: "The rise of modern capitalism"), the sociology of action had redefined contemporary subject matter.

It may be Parsons, more than any other, who offers the major paradigm of post-war sociology. In him there is a unique combination of a general explicative technique (extracted from Weber's ideal types) with a highly specific focus on the object and the theme of study: the nuclear family, for example.

Here we have change, but not a theory of change; we have theories in the plural. And it as the structural functionalism of Parsons and Merton that gave sociology in the 1950s both its grand model to explain change (the sum of dysfunctionalities, incomplete socialization, unattained values and even contradictions seen as "incompatibilities" between the demands of the social situation and the actors' role-playing) and the scope of its explanation: delimited social processes.

The most significant work of this period refers to partial themes in society, even when it breaks with structural functionalism; and it makes no reference to the global analysis of processes and patterns of change from one type of society to another. Myrdal's *An American Dilemma*[1] is a brilliant example of non-functionalist analysis, but it is confined within these parameters. *The American Soldier,*[2] by Stouffer and Lazarsfeld, is more faithful to structural functionalism.

Exceptions: Parsons himself and his immense sociological retinue studying the "passage" from traditional to modern societies. In this case, though, there are no "laws of passage" as such, but a polar characterization, which is more à la Tonnies than à la Weber, distinguishing idealized types. No analogy not even remotely can, however, be made between these efforts and what could be called "scientific methods" for analyzing regularities and transformations of them. Whereas in Weber (or in Parsons' specific studies) there is in addition to typology an explanation (which fits in with both causes and meaning), in what it has become conventional to call "modernization theory" or rather in this theory's formal tradition there is no explanation proper but a characterization. The changes that occur are characterized by opposition, but there is no attempt to explain their causality, sequences or forms.

After the sixties, and especially during the seventies, sociology underwent a further inflection. A dual inflection. Neo-Marxism, on the one hand and, or the other, a renewed preference for themes linked to change in fundamental components of contemporary society, even in terms of the tradition of "empirical" or structural-functionalist analysis.

Neo-Marxism developed out of two non-exclusive origins: an academic rereading of Marx (Althusser, Poulantzas etc.), and the incorporation of the themes of economic development and dependence into studies of contemporary societies. While the return to themes on change was not global, it dealt with more general aspects of contemporary societies, and also started from two main sources: comparison (with divergings and convergings) between capitalist and socialist societies, and the discrediting of the gradualist version of changes in modern competitive societies. The former source includes a range of work, from the somewhat linear studies of the effects of industrialism, in unifying politically and socially diverse societies, to more richly nuanced studies such as those of Raymond Aron,[3] where the themes of liberty, power and the limits of reason are reclaimed for the purposes of analyzing industrial societies.

As to the second of these two sources, it would be more appropriate to say that two things became discredited concomitantly: the gradualist vision of social change and the vision of "class conflicts" as the privileged fount of change in modern societies. Though there was not properly speaking a systematic and consistent critique of the theory of social classes and revolution, sociologists gradually switched their interest from the analysis of the working class (as in Georges Friedmann[4] or Serge Mallet[5]) to the analysis of "new actors."

Here again we have change, but change brought about by factors and actors that had not been contemplated by classical sociology, with its overriding interest in global societal change. Replacing the Marxist notion of productive forces/social relations of production/superstructure, there arose the idea that change could emerge out of conflicts occurring at any level of society. Thus, the May 1968 revolt was said to be an embryonic struggle between the "producers of knowledge" and the masters of society, personified by the state. The bureaucracy and the state, rather than the bosses, were the "enemy" of society's new liberators, those who based their critique on a rupture with cultural values.

The sixties were full of new practical challenges and new sociological approaches. To a certain extent, there was a shattering of the self-confident idea of "progress," as formulated by Western (Judeo-Christian) civilization. Not for lack of the material presuppositions of this belief: the very accumulation of knowledge and technologies undermined the notion that human solidarity and moral and spiritual values would accompany the march of civilization and economic growth. The Vietnam War (the new horrors of war seen on TV all over the world), religious intolerance, and the rebirth of regionalism, rediscovery of the theme of inequality among races and between the sexes; and the obsession with the nuclear holocaust, in the shape of the bomb and of nuclear-powered reactors (Three Mile Island and Chernobyl)—all these factors combined to recreate social actors and nourish the contemporary world's fears and anguish.

The Western world's self-confident vision, with its tranquil theories of modernization or tempestuous theories of revolution, assumed, up to the fifties, that there was a degree of compatibility between "economic growth," "transformational social forces" and human well-being. Since the sixties, this serene confidence has broken down.

According to the more skeptical or pessimistic observers, such as Robert Nisbet,[6] for example, the five basic premises that turned the dogma of progress into the mainspring of Western civilization have now disappeared. They were:

- faith in the value of the past
- the conviction that Western civilization was noble and superior to the rest
- acceptance of the value of economic growth and technological breakthroughs
- belief in reason and scientific knowledge
- belief in the intrinsic importance of life in the universe.

Evidently, there is no need to go all the way with Nisbet's subjectivism. It is merely a symptom of the phenomenon I wish to explain. But it demonstrates that both the perverse effects of economic growth (not so much the maldistribution of its benefits, but only the destruction of natural resources, many of which are unrenewable) and the discrediting of "Western civilization," together with the other factors mentioned, undermined faith in reason, especially in the sense of essentially "Western" reason.

The new themes of social change have much to do with this process. New social actors: whether they be Alain Touraine's "social movements," women's demands, black struggles, grassroots movements, or Latin America's "ecclesiastical base communities," none of these appears in the classic texts of sociology or of any sociologists before World War II.

There can be no denying that even a Sartrean conversion to Marxism as the "ideology of our time" cannot diminish collective existential anguish: the fear of atomic death and the holocaust, the virtual horror of unintentional destruction caused by atomic energy, of the new white plagues (such as AIDS), or urban violence etc., coexist with the glorious civilization of space exploration, information technology and biogenetics.

When theories of social change are assessed in the light of contemporary reality, it must be admitted that the "Grand Theories" have suffered substantial blows. True,

Weber would seem to have hit the mark with his intuitions foreseeing disenchantment with the world and the spreading grip of bureaucracy. But neither entrepreneurs nor leaders with an authentic political vocation have rescued society from routine. And a more detailed examination shows that the theory of the Calvinist ethic and hence of values as the prime mover of capitalist accumulation has had to undergo Trevor-Roper's[7] transplant in order to survive a little longer.

Theories of modernization and the countless studies inspired by Parsons,[8] which set out to show how the gap between traditional and modern is filled by moving on from "ascription" to "achievement," or any other pair of formal oppositions, run up against research on all sides showing how history has been much more capricious.

Hagen's[9] work on Colombia or Olson's[10] on the "logic of collective action," to mention only a few examples, constitute formal models in the best of hypotheses, not explanations of real processes of change. Similarly, in political science, S. M. Lipset's[11] claim to explain democratic institutionalization in Latin America, or Rostow's[12] famous book on the stages of economic growth are thwarted in the most conspicuous manner by the sheer facts.

Marxist theory of social change cannot be said to be any better off: the long-awaited revolution has not occurred where it was expected nor in those countries where it has, has the proletariat necessarily been the class which has taken the lead in conducting social change. Not to mention the fact that religious conflicts and aspirations to national independence (the latter more pessimistically assimilable to the Marxist paradigm of change) have replaced the *sans culottes* and the workers since the war.

But it matters less to lament the disappointing failures of past theory to forecast the future than to reaffirm that current sociology has at least been able to delineate new themes and to try to understand the dynamics of contemporary societies with a perspective that is more open to the variability of historical processes.

It is as if anthropology had taught sociologists the vital lesson that, while the simplistic, abstract models of the economists are useful to create analytical categories which can help to describe and even to foresee market behavior, they cannot serve as a paradigm for describing and interpreting (let alone anticipating the future course of) social processes which are also cultural and therefore which have to be seen in the light of possible options and innovations.

In this context, rather than weeping with Nisbet for the loss of a dogma, it is better to understand that intercommunication among cultures and societies in today's world destroys any egocentric urge to see the Western world as the only model, and the road momentarily followed by some European countries or by the USA as the highway to freedom, equality and the general good. But this realization should not lead to the opposite conclusion: that the industrial civilization and the cultural models of the West lack historic weight and the capacity for action. The point is that in the clash of interests and values each society reconstitutes the process at a given historical moment (or perhaps particular segments within each society, in differential fashion). Solutions may be "amalgamated," and a duplicity or plurality of patterns of social structure, forms of organization and culture may be developed; Western solutions may even be utterly rejected (or almost, as in the Iranian case). Rather than "one single theory," theories of change. Rather than "the privileged actor," kaleidoscopic panoply of agents for change. Instead of "one single outcome" of a homogenizing, universal type, a more diversified distribution that is richer in historic alternatives. This would seem to be the lesson we have to learn from contemporary theories of social change.

TYPES OF INTERPRETATION

Studies of social change have also provided an especially fertile ground for the debate on the scientific foundations of sociological explication. To what extent is sociology equipped to enunciate "laws of transformation"? Is there determinism in the strict sense, or are there merely trends? What are the types of explication produced by these possible laws—are they imperatives for change derived from the structure of the situation or are they conditional laws? Is it possible to determine the causes of change? Raymond Boudon's *La Place du Désordre*[13] is a highly intriguing recent work that provides a framework for discussing these questions. Boudon says there are four distinct types of theory on social change and one of these types has an important variant. What Boudon is indicating is that these distinct theories are what Imre Lakatos,[14] the philosopher of science, calls "programmes," that is, general orientations followed by segments of the scientific community in their research work. These orientations, or this "programme," are based on the postulate that it is possible to enunciate interesting propositions concerning social change, and that these propositions are verifiable and nomothetic (i.e., their scope surpasses a given temporal and spatial context).

The first type of theory identified highlights more or less general and irreversible trends. For example, the passage from particularism to universalism in modern societies, as in Parsons. These "tendential laws" are often little more than intuitions that cannot be statistically proven. Or they may be more sophisticated and set out to define the existence of stages (as in Comte's laws of the three stages or, more modestly, Rostow's stages of economic growth).

The second type of theory of change takes the form of "conditional laws" structured along the lines of "If A occurs, B will follow." When Parsons[15] suggests that the effect of industrialization is to reduce families to the size of the "nuclear family" (parents and children), he is formulating a theory of this type. So is Tocqueville[16] when he says the liberalization of a despotic regime leads to a violent reaction against it and not to a gradual acceptance of the improvement obtained.

This second type of explication of change has a major variant, when element A is not a condition or a single variable but a system of variables. In this case, it is a question of looking for laws of structure, as for example when it is said that the semi-feudal system tends to be stable because the user of land, although formally free to sell it, tends to be constantly in debt to the owner, who is not favorable to the introduction of innovations which could raise productivity of the land or of labor. Another example is Nurske's[17] theory of the "vicious circle of poverty," which states that at a time *t* a poor country has every chance of remaining poor for *t + 1* unless there is an exogenous shock, because poverty entails a low capacity for saving and investment, preventing a rise in productivity.

The third type of theory does not set out to explicate the content of change but its form. Thus Michel Crozier[18] attempts to show that in France change is destined to take the form of long periods of blockage followed by periods of crisis; in Crozier's view, this is because cultural factors lead members of an organization to adapt to problems that arise without discussing or questioning them, until an explosion occurs.

The fourth type of explication of change in Boudon's classification deals with the causes or factors which produce it. Classic examples can be found in Weber and Marx, especially in the "dialogue" between them on the question whether values (as in *The Protestant Ethic and the Spirit of Capitalism*) are uppermost in the explication of capitalist accumulation, rather than social relations of production and the productive forces.

The mere act of listing these various types of attempts to explain change sociologically is enough to show the variability in the scope or range of each one as far as the theoretical precision attainable is concerned, as well as the complexity of the factors involved in what is to be explained. On the other hand, the "laws," "regularities" or "intuited sequences" arrived at have very different theoretical and epistemological statuses. Boudon[19] recommends, for example, that a "well-tempered determinism" should be adopted: "with regard to social change, determinism is therefore not an indispensable postulate but a 'constat' which it is suitable to adopt or not depending on the case."[20]

There are certain processes, Boudon says, where a state at *t + 1* can be determined on the basis of knowledge about the state at *t*. But this is no general property. For this to occur, a whole set of conditions must be present and persistent, and the actors (for Boudon it is a question of explaining interactions) must be in a closed situation. Now this is not always the case: there are open situations in which the actor faces a set of options without a decisive reason for choosing one or the other. And there are situations in which certain actors can innovate. This innovation in turn may derive from a specific, private demand or may be brought about by the demands of a system; or again it may be entirely independent. Thus, for example and I shall not go beyond a general indication to know the determining weight of values (or ideas) in a process of change, it is always necessary to see them in terms of the structure of the process in question, which may or may not accept them as a primum mobile. The same goes for so-called materialistic explanations.

Following this cautious line of interpretation, Boudon draws attention to the need to refer explication not to the broad overriding processes of change, but to specific temporal and spatial elements, and to the need to pin them down within global structures, which may well have their own rules of change, although these will be less susceptible to explication in a strictly scientific sense.

This is the final point to which I want to draw your attention in this paper. It is that, although they are not testable for scientific validity after the neo-positivist manner, there are interpretations of change that even authors in the Kantian tradition, such as Boudon, accept as being interesting.

Boudon in fact distinguishes a logical progression that runs from the enunciation of possibilities to conditional laws, via the enunciation of conjunctures that may be more or less likely to happen. These conjunctures occur when a given state of possible affairs is more likely to happen than another state of affairs that is opposite to the first; for example, Tocqueville's[21] formulation, quoted above, on the effects of liberalizing an authoritarian order.

As to enunciations of possibilities or conditional laws, these fit more directly into Popper's logic, in the form of questions for which there are answers whose validity can be scientifically tested. One example of this type of scientific "discovery" (similar in procedure to the logic of natural science) is Trevor-Roper's[22] correction to Weber's thesis on the importance of the Protestant ethic to modern capitalism. Starting off with micro sociological hypotheses, Trevor-Roper shows that the link between Calvinism and capitalism does not flow directly from the theory of predestination but from Erasmianism and from the fact that businessmen are the ones who have the best chance of adhering to the Calvinist ethic, rather than the other way round. Furthermore, if there are Calvinists in the business world in Lutheran regions, it is because there were migrations. In other words, Trevor-Roper explains a more important set of facts than those Weber explains, and the facts Weber explains are contained in Trevor-Roper's. What is more, the micro-sociological facts explicated by Trevor-Roper are comprehensible in the Weberian sense, and are linked to the macro-sociological facts placed in evidence by Weber. This shows that there has been an accumulation of knowledge.

Boudon concludes that, in order to belong to the "scientific genus," the data for which an explanation is sought must belong to a well-defined set. "This means that such theories can only be local and partial. . . . Analysis of social change, therefore, is by no means a necessarily inexact science which by the nature of its object is destined to surrender itself to the incommunicable procedures of interpretation."[23]

Moreover, Boudon goes on, a great number of theories of change are not empirical but formal. He exemplifies this with Hotelling's[24] well-known article on stability in competition, and with Hirschman's[25] reinterpretations of the same model for its application to politics. And the same is true of the well-known study by Parsons and Smelser[26] on institutional change, showing that when dysfunction arises in a business organization (or any other organization, or even in a social system), it can be solved by creating new social roles and hence by differentiating roles. This type of formal explication says nothing at all about the frequency of functional differentiation, for example, or about its concreteness; it can be applied to a vast range of social processes. It is thus a "formal theory," but not a theory in the proper sense, and it would be mistaken to apply it realistically in order to account for empirically observed phenomena unless complementary propositions and appropriate data were introduced.

CLOSING REMARKS

Why have I made such a comprehensive summary of Boudon's work?

Not just because it provides a critical review of the epistemological status of sociology's contributions to theories of social change, but because it shows an openness to acceptance of a less "scientistic" view of sociology. Also because at the end, and now I can add this, Boudon highlights the "spirit of adventure" of which sociological analyses are an example: room is left for indetermination and even for indemonstrable value judgments which glue together scattered pieces of explanations of change, constructed out of probability analyses, conjunctural analyses, formal analyses, empirical generalizations and even mere (and often rich) interpretations.

With this broad horizon, sociology does not lament its failed forecasts but enriches itself. It is unafraid to venture into fields where there may not be much scientific rigor but where it may be possible to find the propositions, not the dogmas, human anguish needs to break through into light and fresh air.

To return then to the main thread of my argument: as I showed in the first part of this exposition, there are new challenges facing those who wish to understand change in the contemporary world and there are new actors to face them. And I want to wind up by coming back to the challenges of the present, many of which are far from having been submitted to any of the exercises in explicative rigor which I mentioned in the second part of this exposition, which has now become a long one.

The first challenge, which is the basis for our contemporary feeling of a dying civilization, is the menace of extermination of all life on the planet: fear, of war and atomic catastrophe, perhaps more than sociologists believe, are at the core of a future theory of change. "Occidental" or "Oriestern" civilization, which rebuilds the world, will have to change in order to respond to this challenge, or else it will reach the brink of extinction.

The second challenge refers precisely to the reformulation of the idea of "progress." If the kernel of this idea is the possibility of a holocaust (and hence the very negation of "social progress"), there can be no surprise when such "progress" is no longer seen as a guarantee of social change. Both Marxian versions of the "productive forces" as the dynamo of history and ingenuous versions of theories of modernization based on industrialism have to be criticized and fall into discredit. But this is no reason for adhering to Nisbet's metaphysical pessimism. On the contrary, Third World countries above all continue to believe in economic growth, providing the theme of equality among regions and among classes tempers the pace of accumulation.

The third major challenge of contemporary change undoubtedly resides in a return to Montesquieu, or in a vision of modern anthropology which relativises cultural and civilisatory differences. There is no sense in an arrogant Occident and a humiliated Orient, or a pretentious North and a head-hanging South. Because of the real oneness of communication systems and the prosperity which the planet as a whole has already accumulated, it may be possible to envision an "Occidental" or "Oriestern" world, as I said above, in which cultural dimensions coexist, now interpenetratingly, now existing as optional pluralities. This is the richest of challenges for the construction of a theory of change that does not assume that the destination for developing countries, the safe haven already found by the developed countries can be known in advance. After all, the developed countries have not stopped developing, and, moreover, the changes that occur there are affected by the social processes occurring in the developing countries.

Finally, another grand value enhanced by the nineteenth century is still intact and can be solved by our own century: the question of equality. For changes to occur powerfully, it is not enough to have a dogma—a utopia is needed. The utopia for our own time, which is the end of a millennium, exists and is flagrantly obvious: the struggle to abolish poverty.

It is highly likely that these themes or challenges are not susceptible to rigorous scientific treatment, but as Boudon points out, without a pinch of subjectivism and unless the possibility is admitted that the unexpected can happen, history can neither move forward nor be understood. These may not be strictly scientific themes. But they are indispensable if theories are to be not just exact, partial, or well-grounded, but relevant and interesting as well.

NOTES

1. G. Myrdal, *An American Dilemma* (New York: Harper and Row, 1944).

2. S. A. Stouffer and P. Lazarsfeld, *The American Soldier* (Princeton, N.J.: Princeton University Press, 1950).

3. R. Aron, *Sociologie des sociétés industrielles* (Paris: Centre de Documentation Universitaire, 1962).

4. G. Friedmann, *Le travail en miettes* (Paris: Gallimard [Idées], 1964).

5. S. Mallet, *La nouvelle classe ouvrière* (Paris: Seuil, 1969).

6. R. Nisbet, *History of the Idea of Progress* (New York: Basic, 1980).

7. H. R. Trevor-Roper, *De la réforme aux lumières* (Paris: Gallimard, 1972).

8. T. Parsons, *The Social System* (London: Tavistock, 1952).

9. E. E. Hagen, *On the Theory of Social Change: How Economic Growth Begins* (London: Tavistock, 1962).

10. M. Olson, *Logique de l'action collective* (Paris: Presses Universitaire de France, 1978).

11. S. M. Lipset, "Values, Education, and Entrepreneurship," in S. M. Lipset and A. Solari, eds., *Elites in Latin America* (New York: Oxford University Press, 1967).

12. W. W. Rostow, *The Stages of Economic Growth* (Oxford: Oxford University Press, 1953).

13. R. Boudon, *La place du désordre: critique des théories du changement social* (Paris: Presses Universitaire de France, 1984).

14. I. Lakatos, "Falsification and the Methodology of Scientific Research Programs," in I. Lakatos and A. Musgrave, eds., *Criticism and the Growth of Knowledge* (Cambridge: Cambridge University Press, 1970).

15. Parsons, *Social System*.

16. A. de Toqueville, *L'Ancien Régime et la révolution*, vol. 1 (Paris: Gallimard, 1952).

17. R. Nurkse, *Problems of Capital Formation in Underdeveloped Countries* (Oxford: Oxford University Press, 1953).

18. M. Crozier, *La société bloquée* (Paris: Seuil, 1970).

19. Boudon, *La place du désordre*, 192.

20. Boudon's *constat* is opposed to *postulat* in his words, because "determinism is not a condition for knowledge, but a particular quality of the process in which presence or absence depends on the very structure of the process." See Boudon, *La place du désordre*, 192.

21. Toqueville, *L'Ancien Régime et la révolution*.

22. Trevor-Roper, *De la réforme aux lumières*.

23. Boudon, *La place du désordre*, 207.

24. H. Hotelling, "Stability in Competition," *The Economic Journal*, 39 (1929): 41–57.

25. A. O. Hirschman, *Essays in Trespassing* (Cambridge: Cambridge University Press, 1981).

26. T. Parsons and N. Smelser, "A Model of Institutional Change," in *Economy and Society* (New York: The Free Press, 1956).

→ 11 ←

Social Science in Latin America

If we have accomplished something in our search for the universal in Latin America in recent decades, it is because we have been capable of constructing something that is basic in life: a spirit of community and togetherness, in spite of distance. In the last forty years, dialogue has been permanent and alive, even between people who often did not even know one another directly. But there have also been many who have known one another, who have found in direct relations the motivation to continue moving ahead with their intellectual projects. This is something that I want to emphasize: that there is original thought in Latin American social science and that this thought grew in an environment greater than that of a single university, or a single country, and that the spirit of community is maintained in spite of distance.

These have been decades of companionship, often at a distance, between tens, or maybe hundreds, of people who together elaborated a vision. Or perhaps there were many visions, but ones that always revolved around the same themes: what it means "to be" American; what we mean by development, dependency, authoritarianism, the possibility of overcoming difficulties, and the new dimensions of development. Without a doubt, the dialogue was not confined to the universities of our continent. We have always had points of reference in Europe and the United States. We have always paid homage to our great predecessors, to the great founders of the social sciences. Weber, for example, has always been a point of reference, as have Marx, de Tocqueville, and many others. In the same way, we cannot forget all those who imagined other realities in North America, in Germany, and in other countries: Habermas, to

Excerpt adapted from Fernando Henrique Cardoso, "A Nova Agenda Sociológica da América Latina," in *A Utopia Viável. Trajetória intelectual de Fernando Henrique Cardoso* (Brasília: Secretaria de Documentação Histórica, Gabinete Pessoal do Presidente da República, 1995), 31–44. Originally presented as a lecture at Central University of Venezuela, July 6, 1995.

cite someone more contemporary, Talcott Parsons, Robert Merton, and many other Anglo-Saxons in the social sciences.

We used these names as a reference, but never allowed ourselves to be captured by a spirit of imitation. In a work that I wrote many years ago, "The Originality of the Copy," I held that in many of our reflections, including the core-periphery theory that was the central axis of the thought of the 1950s, there were perceptible points of contact with what had already been said by others. But the copy was original: it was a "building upon," not only an "interpreting." It was not repeating, but was growing, and in growing, was transforming.

I want to come back to the theme of the historical evolution of Latin American thought on the economy in the last forty years. I do not mean to make this a nostalgic exercise, but to look at the knowledge capital that we have accumulated as intellectuals, elements that will help us to face up to the contemporary challenges of our continent. They are not trivial. I am encouraged when I find many of my academic friends no longer in their academic halls, holding chairs at universities, but rather in posts in government or in parliament. Perhaps we can examine, with different eyes, what we thought, and from there draw lessons for the present.

In a schematic way, I think that in recent years Latin American thought has had three marked phases: that of elaboration and affirmation (1950s–1960s), of the crisis and criticism (1970s–1980s), and the renewal (1990s).

I am going to look to elaborate on the theme without the commitment—pardon me, colleagues—of academic precision. These are preliminary references, more a memory of one who lived the problems and dilemmas of sociological reflection in our universities and centers of study than a meditated review, with the necessary distance and criticism, of Latin American thought.

My first observation is that we should be proud of the production of the social sciences in the 1950s in Latin America. Allow me to explain. For this, I am not going to recall the principal content, which are well known: the origin in ECLA (CEPAL), the vigor of the thought of Prebisch and Echevarria, the theory of the core and the periphery, the idea of import substitution, the incorporation of social themes, the ideas on integration, and many others. I can refer also to a Brazilian, Celso Furtado, and to a Chilean that had enormous influence here in Venezuela, Jorge Ahumada. But I do not intend to expand on this by listing the names of our masters. I intend to underline other aspects that these days appear, with more clarity and power, as truly permanent lessons.

In the first place, there was scientific caution. It was precisely the respect of the scientific bases of inquiry that gave vigor and credibility to our sociological and economic reflection. We were perhaps the first generation of social scientists, in the strong sense of the word, in Latin America. I do not wish to disrespect nor forget previous reflections, which reached notable heights. We had eminent predecessors. However, we succeeded in creating a school of thought. We elaborated theories together, with constant reference to that which was being produced, benefiting from and incorporating research and knowledge. In this sense, the theoretical references to Ricardo, de Tocqueville, Marx, Weber, and Schumpeter were essential. We went back to the origins to give consistency and, above all, originality to our reflection.

Exactly for this reason, we could engage in critical thought, going beyond socio-logical impressionism, going beyond stereotyped versions of reality. We understood that it was not sufficient to transport the visions and interpretations of other realities, European mostly, to Latin American life. The respect of fundamental theories, which brought necessary methodological frameworks, ensured that their transposition to our world was not done in an automatic and simplistic manner. The revision that Prebisch made of the theory of comparative advantage, understanding that it was fundamental to distinguish economically and sociologically the countries that, in different ways, were inserting themselves into the world of international commerce, is perhaps one of the most brilliant and finished examples of this process. The theory did not push us away from reality, but introduced us to its most problematic aspects. We did not force the doors of interpretation before we enriched the interpretations with an open vision of what Latin America was. If we parted from the class dynamic in capitalism, we did not fail to understand that in our social space there were differences given, for example, by the relations between the dominant classes and the state, which demanded specific meditation.

A third aspect is the fact that in many of our works, we showed the interpenetration of economic thought with social questions. We avoided—in this, dependency theory had some merit—reducing the explication of social questions to the merely economic. We accepted that, between the infrastructure and the superstructure, outcomes were not given, and solutions should be sought carefully in every social formation, and in every national scene. The comparative exercises were rich.

Another central theme was the incorporation of the international, initiated by Prebisch, which gained various important analytical additions. We knew that international factors shaped our reality, affecting our economic and social life directly, and the important thing was to understand how. Classical imperialist theory always appeared insufficient to understand the variety and peculiarity of Latin American situations. The solutions that we forwarded sometimes underlined the diversity of economic constraints and sometimes pointed to the social and political implications of diverse models of insertion into capitalism. If they did not replace Leninist suppositions, they certainly showed that, in concrete analysis, other elements and variables beyond the mechanisms of exploitation should also be taken into account.

Finally, I would emphasize that the sum of these aspects gave Latin American thought countless possibilities in their application to reality. In the first place, there was, especially in ECLA, the preoccupation that thought serve the development and modernization of Latin American countries. Theoretical innovation would justify itself in the measure in which it brought together conditions to mold the reality of social practices. The multiplication of government policies inspired by developmentalist thought, especially on import substitution, is a historical fact. The thought gave body, direction, and modern content to an actor that historically had been decisive in the life of the countries of the continent: the state. The theory justified actions that would promote processes of industrialization at the same time that it examined the limits and conditions of this process. In sum, the substrate is the perspective of change, its possibilities, and its limits.

Paralleling this, the same general characteristics of Latin American thought (the scientific sense, the originality, the critical power, and so on) led to its being expressed in diverse ways. The inclinations are diverse and one of the riches of the moment is precisely the debate between them. If you allow me a personal example, it would have been difficult for Enzo Faletto and I to formulate our dependency theory had we not had, as a backdrop, the more orthodox Marxist visions of Latin American reality and the more nationalist perspectives (in the style of the ISEB) of our continent. In this sense, I hold that we were developing, in diversity, a school of thought, in which the rule was internal debate and critical respect of the different elaborations. We were not lacking in utopian visions. For some, revolution and socialism; for others, a strong state, capable of changing the very nature of social relations; for others, rational capitalism. But always the idea was that we could be better, and more socially just, than we were.

When one reads a text of some theorist from that period, rarely will one notice a preoccupation with the social dimension. The exceptions are few and among them I will mention the principal one: Albert Hirschman. Not by chance, because every time I can, I seek some inspiration not only in Weber, but also in Hirschman, because the latter proposes an exit from the contradiction that Weber mentioned between the political and the academic vocation. When Hirschman goes looking into Kierkegaard for a citation to say that it is necessary to have "the passion for the possible," it may appear to be an unimportant find. But in truth, what he wishes to say is that a possibility (or will, in the political dimension) must be a discovery made with passion, and that it must take structures into account. Hirschman thus also added this political possibility to economic analysis. But what was proper to the 1950s and 1960s in Latin America, in the thought of many people, was precisely that thought was not about purely economic aspects and structure; it also considered that in order to change, a dimension of will was necessary.

This will, in the 1950s and 1960s, was seeking the solid ground of the state. At that time, no importance was given to what is today called civil society. Social movements, the forces of change that were not contained in the will organized by the state, were not considered much. In the 1950s and 1960s, we highlighted the power of the economic. The need for a political dimension was insinuated, but the political dimension was summed up practically in the organization of the state, in planning, in the capacity to anticipate that which could occur and to orient oneself through concrete objectives. In that phase of elaboration and affirmation, it was for this that we really had a passion.

The 1950s and 1960s were optimistic years. Intellectual creativity was strong in Latin America at that time. Utopias varied and the debate was intense, but few doubted that the future would be better than the past. The two subsequent decades were another story. The political environment turned authoritarian—the economic environment became dominated by the crisis of the growth model. Frustrations multiplied. Socialism was blocked and the hope of the ballot box was frustrated with the fall of Allende. The state, where expectations of rational direction were invested, became strong, but with the wrong orientations and configurations;

in fact, authoritarianism disguised its real failure, so corrupted was it in its lack of legitimacy. Capitalist penetration and its perceived advantages were, in the debt crisis, also shown to involve high risks.

Thus, in the 1950s, though we recognized the difficulties of change, we believed that the changes would be within reach, and that the problem was to unravel which social actor would lead to a better Latin America. We found in the 1970s and after new situations that added obstacles to our utopias.

In a necessarily simplistic general characterization, I would say that we abandoned our attempts at general theories, at least in the medium term, and were obligated to sharpen our capacity for more modest criticism—many of us came to write in journals and opinion papers—that sought above all to solve the internal mechanisms of a state (which was showing unexpected potential in its capacity to obstruct criticism) and an economy that appeared to obey the solutions of a perverse logic. Development was occurring, but the social costs were incredibly high. The association between thought and politics was dissolving before a reality in which many sectors were increasingly marginalized and questions of social justice deferred. It can be said that in the 1970s and 1980s, intellectuals rediscovered democracy. One returns to de Tocqueville, and rediscovers the power of the press, of the church, and of labor.

How do we treat these themes? The perspective is that of understanding the fundamental importance of democracy for the development of our societies. It is not that the question had been forgotten in the previous period, but, in truth, we were more interested in the dynamics of class than in institutions, as if once the ideal social institution were defined, the best institutional solution would naturally result. The ideals of justice and equality were prevalent over those of liberty. The suppression of democracy pointed us to the clear necessity for formal guarantees for citizens, for human rights, and for freedoms. Another point is the paradoxes of modernization and the theme of the political power of trade unions, now sustained in modern industry, which took on new dimensions. Authoritarian capitalism, in not modernizing aspects of its productive apparatus, was creating the bases of its own decline.

What were the consequences of this perspective for sociological reflection? We already saw that, in many cases, it led to a shift from the structural to short- and medium-term questions. However, I think that two thematic strains coexist.

In the first place, it was necessary to reveal the inner workings of the state; in this sense, the institutional problems appear more clearly. It is easy to perceive the autonomy of the state, even including examples in the area of foreign policy (as in the 1970s, a country like Brazil opened various conflicts with the United States in the commercial as well as the strategic and political domains). The difficult thing was to know the limits of this dynamic. In this sense, the "internal" knowledge of states, the alliances that it constituted, how these influenced their decisions, the social sectors with which it formed alliances, the mechanisms of bureaucracy, and the forms of maintenance of authoritarianism and of democracy (as in the case of Venezuela) are current themes. The military question is as well. In this sense, the North American contribution—in the end, Latin American thought always knew how to enrich itself with foreign contributions, be they theoretical or specific analyses of our reality—

The Cardoso family: Fernando Henrique Cardoso (row 3, seventh from left, around age fifteen); Gilda Cardoso, his sister (row 3, ninth from left); Nayde Cardoso and General Leónidas Cardoso, his parents (row 2, ninth and tenth from left); Antonio Geraldo, his brother (row 1, third from left); Leonídia Fernandes Cardoso, his grandmother (row 2, seventh from the left), mid-1940s.

Teaching, early 1960s.

At the public defense of his Ph.D. dissertation,
University of São Paulo, 1961.

With Raúl Prebisch, José Serra, and Aníbal Pinto
at CEPAL (Chile), 1970s.

Workshop at the Catholic University (PUC) of Rio de Janeiro, with economist Edmar Bacha, early 1970s.

Speech at a meeting of the Brazilian Democratic Movement (MDB), first campaign for the Senate, 1978.

With labor leaders, first campaign for the Senate, 1978. At far right is Luiz Inácio Lula da Silva.

Honorary Doctor of Law at Rutgers University, with Albert Hirschman, 1978.

Final meeting during the campaign
for city of São Paulo government,
with his wife, Ruth, 1985.

At home in São Paulo, 1980s: a favorite place to write.

Visiting professor at Berkeley, with his wife, Ruth
Corrêa Leite Cardoso, early 1980s.

Investiture as president of the Federative Republic of Brazil, January 1, 1995.

First "state visit" to the United States. With President Clinton, 1995.

With ex-president Ernesto Geisel, who was invited to lunch at the Palácio das Laranjeiras, Rio de Janeiro, March 17, 1995.

Fifth Ibero-American Summit, Bariloche, Argentina, October 15–17, 1995. Cardoso stands between King Juan Carlos of Spain and Fidel Castro.

Meeting of the "Grupo dos 15" (Latin America, Asia, Africa), in Buenos Aires, November 5, 1995.

Meeting of Progressive Governance for the Twenty-first Century, in Florence, Italy, November 1999.

was decisive in renovating the themes and the methodology of political science research in Brazil. It is not by chance that the very difference between sociology and political science was more marked in the 1970s, when problems became more explicitly political and when many researchers returned from the United States; we, who were educated earlier, were mostly devotees of European sociology.

In sum, the theme of democratic construction simultaneously opens the fields of sociological reflection and political action to intellectuals. We wanted to know the origins of authoritarianism, the conditions that would maintain it, and where it would be vulnerable. We wanted to explore its fragility politically. We discussed its cultural roots and its class support. For some, authoritarianism was more than a political phenomenon and appeared to be a necessary destiny of a Latin America for which a corporatist and patrimonial history had negated the experience of liberty.

Second, there arose, in the economic field, localized and structural concerns with the effects of an authoritarian political economy. The conjunctural themes were not explicit in the 1950s. In the framework of an argument cut from structuralist cloth, we preferred to analyze models of economic organization through their interactions with social and political models. Now, the challenge was about getting down to the concrete, and studying the implications of policies and orientations selected by governments. To refer again to the contributions of a Brazilianist, I recall the pioneering analyses of Albert Fishlow on patterns of income distribution.

At the end of the 1980s, these analyses and their questions flow into the understanding of the exhaustion of the import substitution model of development. I think that the critique of the model was done in stages. Initially, as I have just pointed out, the deficiencies of the model were raised as a channel for social justice. Next, when the debt crisis came about, it became clear that conditions for sustainable self-financing were lacking—from the moment in which foreign savings were exhausted and the fiscal capacity of the state weakened, there were simply not the private savings to continue growth. The weight of the state machinery, in which business and regulatory activities were multiplying, was shown to be inefficient and incapable of accompanying the changes in the world and in Brazil. Control over macroeconomic variables was lost with the high inflation, and in some cases hyperinflation, of the 1980s. Finally, it was recognized already at the end of the 1980s, above all when compared with the Asian experience, that the model was simply putting a brake on the competitiveness of the economy as a whole.

I will make a parenthetical comment to say something that is well known but is presently being forgotten. The import substitution development model had undeniably positive effects, above all in establishing foundations for the future development of Latin American countries. The fact that today we recognize that it "spent" itself should not preclude an understanding of the important role that it played. We know that the exigencies for jump starting modern development on an industrial base may require the state to assume the function of a businessman, filling lacunae that corresponded to the stage of development of Latin American societies at that time. Ideas are not absolute, they always express historical content.

To conclude, there is already in this period a decreased importance of the classic ideological debate sustaining social thought. For a simple reason: Through the imposition of the political struggle centered on the democratization effort, adversaries became allies, and it is evident that this had consequences in the field of reflection. In a certain manner, we anticipated in the struggle for democracy the effects of the "de-ideologization" of thought that became clear with the fall of the Berlin Wall. The preoccupation with current circumstance and the need for a more limited critical focus are other factors that pushed us away from the greater utopias and induced us to seek possible ones. We no longer wanted to transform societies radically but we knew that, without transformations first and foremost in the political system, our peoples would not have the conditions for a decent life. The critique of authoritarianism was not only political. We never deluded ourselves about the fact that democracy would simply be the first step in a long journey. We knew that authoritarianism was not simply the choice of one group, but was historically embedded, and had profound social roots. Perhaps for this reason, we came out of the authoritarian experience more conscious of what was necessary to transform Latin American societies.

Throughout these four decades, Latin America constructed solid bases to "conceive of itself" and to "conceive of itself in the world." More specifically, in the 1950s and 1960s, we designed the methodology that allowed us to understand the structural relations of different modes of insertion in the capitalist system. We created the sensibility for change as a routine that marks contemporary capitalism. In the crisis years, we returned to institutions and to the critical analysis of conjunctures. From shared structural bases, we got down to the world of specifics and differences.

Now, we initiate another phase in which the demands of understanding new structural relations are added to the need to interpret new political realities and, above all, an equally new society. The agenda is vast and challenging. But I believe that we are supported by the history of a rich body of thought, and, therefore, are capable of understanding what we are and what we want to become.

I will not be extensive in the description of the sociological agenda at a moment when, for me, the challenge is less to think about Brazil and Latin America than to overcome the daily difficulties of a governor of a developing country still marked by countless inequalities and injustices. I will permit myself to return to my first position of professor, and propose inquiries without obliging myself to answer, as governors must.

I will point out some central questions.

What does development mean today? We know that the concept has broadened, that it involves questions of the environment, of social justice, of minority rights, and at the same time, presupposes macroeconomic stability and the predictability of rules. The problem is knowing the internal relation between the various aspects, in such a way that the growth process be effectively modeled by values that we believe to be universal and that have continuity. The weight of science and technology, two intellectual aspects, is the other decisive factor and raises difficult problems about how to "overcome backwardness." In the contemporary origins of Latin American thought, theoretical propositions and policy proposals, reflection and action were intertwined. Today, this relation is more intricate, but cannot be lost.

How does the insertion of Latin America into the world take place? In the vision of dependency theory, we learn that international factors shaped Latin American societies from within. Today, the process continues, though with globalization the effects may be much more bruising. In the 1960s, we thought of the structural consequences of insertion that today have become more complex and to which have been added effects of extraordinary impact. It is the idea of the "omnipresence of flows" (studied by Manuel Castells), not only economic or financial, but also of a wide variety, involving modes of behavior and movements of culture and information. The rise of two processes—structural and historically specific—and their interconnections must be revisited, and with great care. We must revisit them in order to define the ideal forms of societal reaction to the international system, the best ways of profiting from inescapable globalization.

Still on the consequences of globalization, I would like to call attention to two items. First, the need for a reflection on the international process, especially on something that we social scientists did not attempt with due importance in the 1960s: the theme of foreign affairs. We saw foreign relations, as a reflexive action of the mode of insertion into a capitalist system that did not merit its own theorization. Not just because I became foreign minister do I say that options in foreign affairs must be analyzed. There are historical, strategic, and cultural factors, and many others that directly affect relations between states. By studying them, we understand diplomatic options that are becoming increasingly relevant to the analysis of modernization in our societies.

Another theme that was not part of our traditional repertoire—simply was not on the agenda—is the drug trade and the "narcoeconomy" (*narcoeconomia*). It is evidently a global phenomenon of extreme gravity. Yet we are still far from knowing its full manifestations and its dynamic (even its reach is yet unknown), and we still do not know what it means socially. Is it a social disease? To what is it related? To the transformation of values, or the exacerbation of individualism, or escape? It is a central question for us to understand not only the criminal side of the problem, but also its true social significance.

How do we define the role of the state? The liberal critique of the Latin American state probes into ideological patterns for what must be found elsewhere. To a considerable extent, success in facing the forces of globalization depends on strengthening the state, which must create effective mechanisms for change that it lacked. Government legitimacy does not exist if our people do not understand that they can attain conditions of security, of adequate justice, health, housing, education, and social security in the foreseeable future. The question for researchers is the manner in which a poor state, plagued by fiscal deficits that hinder its capacity to act, can reconstruct the conditions of effective actuation. We must learn how to realize the ideals of equality, still a pillar of thought to better the human condition.

How do we govern democracies? Our countries are renewing themselves. They have ceased to be the simple societies in which it was possible to understand them by referenced to a game of a few classes. Incidentally, when rethinking the problem of class in Latin America, marking the differences between national societies is the first step. Globalization—as in fact dependency already showed in a more simple capitalist system—has dialectical implications, since it simultaneously homogenizes and differentiates. Of singular interest is the growing role of the mass media. These and other means of electronic communication change the social metabolism and call into question the classic forms of representation. Democracy is becoming more alive, with demands multiplying in response to governments. What is the appropriate theory for countries that are still largely unequal, but that are marked by behaviors typical of mass democracies? What is the meaning of left and right in today's world?

I could go on with my inquiries. I should mention, for example, international questions such as integration—that is, the reassertion of Latin America as a space for cooperation. What directions do we take henceforth? How can we complete the work of integration? How will Mercosul and NAFTA coexist? How can we overcome the archaic dichotomies, such as those that opposed inflation and recession, domestic and foreign markets, state and the private sector, and growth and income distribution? How can we attain stability and transform it into a base for sustainable growth? How can we avoid an economic model that concentrates incomes? A sociological reflection on the judiciary is fundamental, as it is another forgotten theme in social science that is so decisive for the daily lives of citizens.

But, I will stop here. My previous discussion points to the need to reflect on processes of change. In this at least, Latin American thought has not altered itself since the days of Prebisch. As thinkers, we wanted to learn to change a reality that we saw as unjust. Today, we try to generate change, oriented by viable utopias.

⇥ 12 ⇤

Academia and Politics

The relationship between political and intellectual activity is an enduring theme among social scientists. On this occasion, when we pay homage to my dear friend Ignacy Sachs, I would like to remark on some concerns and personal reflections from my own experience as one who has been a politician and a sociologist, a statesman and a professor. I would like to speak as an intellectual, maintaining a certain distance from my life as a politician. But this is not easy. When politicians speak, what is important is not so much what they say, as how they say it. The message and the messenger are inseparable. Regardless, I am going to try to speak more as a researcher than as a politician.

Without a doubt, the most common criterion used for assessing this relationship between the academy and politics, between the chair and the pulpit, is the Weberian distinction between the two activities. In this sense, one finds oneself faced with two distinct and separate mindsets, which correspond to a separation between facts and values. Scientific thought about society is guided by the ethic of liberty, the *sine qua non* condition in the search for truth. Political action, on the other hand, is submitted to a logic of necessity linked to the world of values, and is necessarily contaminated by ideologies and interests, while it is also linked to a constant concern for consequences.

This distinction does have a certain power, and provides instruments of analysis that, without a shadow of a doubt, play an important role in thought about the differences between the two types of activities. In the evolution of social thought in Brazil—and I am sure one could say the same of other countries—there has been an

Excerpt from Fernando Henrique Cardoso, "L'utopie et le politique: du professeur au président," in Solange Passaris and Krystyna Vinaver, eds., *Pour aborder le XXIème siècle avec le développement durable* (Paris: Centre International de Recherche sur l'Environment et le Développement, 1998), 29–35 (Série "Développement, croissance et progrès," F [36], *Économies et sociétés*).

181

opposition between the purely academic outlook (based on scientific rigor and research) and a mindset more engaged in the transformation of social structures (where the political project of social change was the priority, and where scientific rigor took a back seat). This was the case in the beginning of the 1960s, for example, in the different currents of thought of the University of São Paulo, which was cautious about its scientific purity, and the group of intellectuals brought together at the Advanced Institute for Brazilian Studies (ISEB), which was more engaged in the elaboration of a national project.

With the benefits of hindsight, it is clear today that, in a certain sense, those on both sides of the debate were "right," since they were all confronted with real problems. On the one hand, it was, and it remains, necessary to give a greater role to an intellectual understanding of reality, to benefit from the criteria of greater rigor and to improve the scientific quality of research. But from a different and equally legitimate perspective, it was, and still is, impossible for an intellectual to distance himself, as if he were looking down from Mount Olympus, from an unjust reality where inequality is the rule and where authoritarian modes of rule prevail.

To give another example, the development of Latin American social thought at CEPAL (the Economic Commission for Latin America), in particular starting with the reflections of Raúl Prebisch, were oriented towards the establishing a rigorous analysis of Latin American economic reality. Nonetheless, these studies were simultaneously framed by a necessary project: starting with the deterioration of the terms of trade, we concluded that import substitution would be necessary. In this case, knowledge preceded the political project.

However, other cases are different. The question of which comes first—knowledge or political action—hides a complex reality in which the two are dialectically united in the very structure of human action. And yet, if we try to synthesize these two opposing cultures—that of the intellectual in his ivory tower and that of theory as a necessary ideational springboard for political activity—we arrive at some interesting questions:

- Is it possible to reconcile scientific rigor and politics? What role does the rigor of learning play in the political project?
- Is it possible to know objectively which policy will be the best for a given set of historical circumstances? Does knowledge predetermine the policy?

These are questions that I will not try to answer. I will limit myself to recalling something that is already well known: there is a complex interrelation between learning and social reality. This complexity seems particularly evident when one looks more closely at the question of social change and the transformation of societies, which is a central theme for sociologists and politicians in Latin America. It is a subject that dialectically links reflection and project, thought and action. Every time one speaks of transformation, one speaks of the values and the objectives and the directions of the transformation. Values are what can mobilize people politically, and articulate the social basis of change.

In the context of the relationship between the academy and political action, one might wonder: What are the parameters of change? How are the ideals that guide the transformation effort defined? If we confront these questions in the light of our practical experience, we realize that quite often the attitudes of intellectuals and politicians, paradoxically, invert the separation between facts and values. In many cases, we see that intellectuals present themselves as advocates of objective values, and as morally superior to the hazards and contingencies of political life. Through this lens, politicians are condemned to act in a world where cruel facts leave no place for truly ethical considerations. The academy is thus, in Weberian terms, representative of the ethics of conviction, whereas politics resides in the domain of responsibility, taken in the abstract sense of the term, as something separate from and opposed to pure conviction.

If we look more closely, however, this perspective is also insufficient. In a democratic society, there are not and there cannot be "monopolies" on values, truth, or ideals. If those who act in politics had a monopoly on the definition of values, academic political thought would be reduced to a sort of technical knowledge that one could use indifferently in any policy for social change. On the other hand, if intellectuals and universities held a monopoly on ethics, if the purity of the academy were a unique space for the affirmation of true values, political activity would be reduced to a technical optimization of defined interests, without any reference in the least to ethics. Politics would thus be alien to any utopian dimension.

Whatever the hypothesis, the result is unsatisfactory: we would see degradation either of academic work or of political action. The different perspectives—that of the intellectual and that of the politician, as well as those of the leaders of social movements and NGOs—must all take part in the political debate in order to create a balance between the ideal and the possible, in order to reach what one might call a "viable utopia."

It is precisely because dialogue is an indispensable step towards the construction of democratic legitimacy—according to Habermas—that the positions of those who participate in the public sphere cannot be limited only to the defense of unrealizable values or to the objective of obtaining short-term advantages from popular mobilization. The risk of a purely intellectual perspective is to transform ends into tactics, and converting ends into tactics means divorcing values from political action.

The risk of a purely political perspective is forgetting values and treating political action as an end in itself, as something that restricts itself to attaining positions of power, to the gain of individuals or specific groups. In this sense, politics would be converted into a technical domain, where practical "consequences" would prevail over the objective of the common good.

In my personal experience in political life, I have noted that the beneficial aspect of intellectual reference is precisely in allowing us to be conscious of these risks of political activity, and to avoid them. I find that maintaining a constant dialogue with values is what allows, or rather pushes, politics to look beyond the game of power, to look for an ethical orientation, and to ask when faced with a decision: is it possible to do this in a more satisfactory manner, in a way that benefits more people? I also think that the intellectual can learn from politics that human and historical limitations are also values in their own right, and this is important for changing the facile understanding of voluntarism.

This does not mean, in any sense, that one reduces the ethical impulse, that one puts aside the will to fight for a better world. On the contrary, it means looking for the conditions that allow this will to find concrete forms of expression in reality. It means understanding that this will, whether it comes from a man or a certain social group, is but one aspect of reality.

Conviction and responsibility are not necessarily in opposition to one another. Confronted with the uncertainty that characterizes political decision making, conviction—on the condition that it does not get transformed into a dogma that is out of touch with reality—can play a key role in assuring that society remains oriented.

I would like to conclude with a few observations on more recent tendencies in our societies and in the international context. These tendencies, in my view, accentuate the importance of a constant dialogue and a close interaction between the academic world of the intellectual and the political world of the governor.

In the first place, the consolidation and deepening of democracy in Latin America has given a greater importance to the ethical dimension in our political life. At the same time, this process has made daily political life more difficult and complex. Democracy broadens the space for social demands, which multiply and take on a greater urgency to the extent to which social movements are more protagonistic in their participation. Societies recognize their injustices more clearly and demand urgent treatment of long-standing social problems. At the same time, the instruments for solving these problems must be "negotiated."

Because of the effort at conciliation made by different sectoral interests, expressed through the growing forms of participation that democracy comprises, a political dialogue capable of producing the universal from the particular is a most important task. Thought, the reference to the universal, thus takes on a new importance in the search for the common good.

In this context, the reflection of Montesquieu—on the necessity of civic virtue as a motor for political action in a republican framework—takes on a new meaning. In a democracy, being a citizen means something more than voting periodically. It also means debate, reflection, and a certain political wisdom, without which political action could not be distinguished from conduct based on individual or group interests.

Of course, this does not mean disqualifying or ignoring interests. All things considered, the rights of social groups, in the framework of the laws, to improve their station in the economy and the society, is a perfectly legitimate aspect of democratic life. However, just as the market, while being an essential part of economic reality, cannot orient the economy (since it does not in itself reflect ethical values), so too political competition and the game of power are not everything, since they do not solve all the problems of a democracy.

This shows, in the first place, that good political practice necessarily brings reflection and knowledge. Not only a technical knowledge, but also moral knowledge, and a reflection oriented on the universality of the *res publica*. If this were not the case, there would be no way to avoid the risks of corporatism, and the public sphere would be seen as "sequestered" by private interest groups.

At the same time that we see these characteristic changes in the consolidation of democracy, we are witnessing rapid transformations in the forms of social interaction, within countries and on the international level, due to technological innovations that have radically modified modes of production, communications, and transportation. The acceleration of the processes of change has reached such a rhythm that our capacity to react to it can very often be insufficient.

What importance does this have for reflections on politics? Of fundamental importance is the fact that today, perhaps more than ever, government decisions must be "enlightened" by intellectual thought. They should also benefit from a long-term vision that is the comparative advantage of universities.

Not reacting to change, and I would even say not anticipating change, is a luxury that we cannot afford. In times of war, where knowledge of the terrain means the difference between life and death, cartography goes from being an academic art to being about the very priorities of state security. So too, in our time (which is not a time of war, but is a time of important change) the cartographic knowledge of the terrain before us, the rigorous analysis of the opportunities and risks presented by novel situations, can make the difference between development and marginalization, and between successful and failed societies.

Thus, knowledge must "enlighten" political action more every day. We cannot allow ourselves to have a static vision of the relationship between theory and practice. And, sadly, we find this type of vision all too often in our universities, as we do among those who dedicate themselves to politics.

At this point, we can no longer use Weber as our model. The challenges of the current situation demand a sort of fusion (but not confusion) between the two mindsets I have mentioned above: that of knowledge and that of action. In the framework of democracy, in looking for a synthesis between thought and action in the fundamental concept of civic virtue, the republican tradition shows itself to be more productive and more current than some abstract distinction between facts and values, or between conviction and responsibility.

→ 13 ←

In Praise of the Art of Politics

It is particularly meaningful for me to return to Stanford University, where I have served as a lecturer and visiting professor, to deliver the Robert Wesson Lecture and to announce the establishment of the first chair in Brazilian Studies at any U.S. university. The chair's name honors Joaquim Nabuco (1849–1910), the great politician and diplomat who fought for the abolition of slavery, a goal that Brazil achieved in 1888. Nabuco's worth as a true statesman is attested by the clarity, originality, and modernity of his ideas, as well as by the commitment to justice and values that informed his actions. Nabuco's writings continue to be essential for anyone who wants to understand the genesis of contemporary Brazil. He shows us that the covenant that must exist between intellectuals and truth should be paralleled by one between politicians and reality. Nabuco's example is my lodestar: he taught me never to dissociate problems from their analysis, nor careful reflection from the desire to solve such problems.

Nabuco concerned himself with the great movements of history, the dramas of humanity and civilization, and the common good. He had a keen understanding of the social effects and consequences of political actions. In the case of abolition, for instance, he saw that simply freeing slaves would not be enough; slavery had become too deeply rooted and had colored too much of Brazilian life. The abolitionist movement was "capable of destroying a social state built on privilege and injustice, but incapable of designing the future edifice on other foundations." The triumph of abolition, said Nabuco, was not followed by "complementary social measures for the benefit of those freed, nor by a strong movement from within to refashion public awareness."

From Fernando Henrique Cardoso, "The Art of Politics," *Journal of Democracy*, 7 (3) (1996): 7–19. © The Johns Hopkins University Press and National Endowment for Democracy. Based on the lecture at Stanford University, March 11, 1996.

If we were to apply Nabuco's analysis to the situation in Brazil today, we would see that like the abolition of slavery, the restoration of democracy is only a first step necessary to be sure, but, in and of itself, insufficient if we are to correct the serious social inequities in our country. There has been undeniable progress; Brazil now enjoys democratic political institutions. Still, the reconstruction of the political system remains incomplete. We are just beginning to see the first glimmerings of the true "refashioning" of public awareness advocated by Nabuco, and even more importantly, of the revitalization of the public sphere as a possible locus for the rational discussion of interests. Thus we face a double task: one political and another, intertwined with the first, which is of a more sociological sort and which has to do with the modernization of society.

We must not only reshape the structure of the state and the relationship between state and society; we must also transform the pattern of income distribution in order to meet the fundamental goal of increasing the fairness of Brazilian society. These prodigious challenges are not going to be met overnight. Still, we have no excuse for forgoing measures that are both possible and necessary here and now. The importance of politics in meeting such challenges forms the theme of my remarks today.

REPRESENTATION AND ITS PARADOXES

The need to inject new life into representative democracy has become manifest in every country that has adopted this political system. It must contend with the growing lack of interest in politics, low voter turnout, and even more seriously, hostility toward professional politicians that has reached the point where "opposing mainstream politicians" has become a winning electoral strategy.

Paradoxically, it is the very success of democracy as an idea and a principle of near-universal legitimacy that has drawn this fire, not only from democracy's critics but even from its defenders. In Brazil, such criticism is being heard at a time when the country is undergoing a series of rapid transformations that pose new dilemmas every day. Democratic institutions have remained essentially unchanged since the era of the founding of the United States more than two centuries ago, even though the world itself has changed dramatically. The relatively simple societies of the recent agrarian past have given way to the complex mass societies of the present. Our task is to enhance and update democracy so that it will continue to prevail as an ideal while the institutions inspired by it function effectively.

Societies are less homogeneous than ever. It is no longer possible to divide society neatly into two classes, the bourgeoisie and the proletariat, roughly equivalent to capital and labor. Economically speaking, individuals can be found in a broad spectrum of possible combinations in the new relationship between capital and labor. For example, workers now partake in capital via pension funds, thus reducing their interest in confronting capital, the returns on which will serve as the basis for their retirement. In contrast, labor has become differentiated, with knowledge now accounting for a growing share of the aggregate value of the world economy.

Those who possess knowledge will be in a position to attract the abundant capital available in the world today. The Silicon Valley companies that surround us here in Palo Alto, California, offer a poignant example of how knowledge-based work now commands better pay than in the past because it has become scarce vis-à-vis capital. This stands in sharp contrast to the earlier industrialization process that was contemporaneous with the rise of the classic democracies, where labor was abundant but not highly skilled. Conflicts over income distribution between the bourgeoisie and the proletariat, which were crucial to the history of the last two centuries, have lost much of their force and now have little capacity to mobilize public discussion.

Today's social fabric is exceedingly complex, with groups and individuals pursuing a wide range of goals. Progress is defined in terms of diverse (even divergent) objectives and the very idea of "quality of life" becomes more refined and elaborated each day. Moreover, these objectives are now often drawn from demands that arise out of a global framework, meaning that they are projected from abroad onto national societies that may or may not be prepared to deal with them. An example of this is the environmental legislation that the more advanced countries have adopted. Such standards are undoubtedly an important achievement, but they cannot be applied to developing countries without more efficient and generous international cooperation.

The waning of the classic dichotomies between capital and labor, bourgeoisie and proletariat and, in ideological terms, right and left has led to what Alain Touraine calls the "disappearance of social categories, indeed of social protagonists themselves." Individuals and groups are no longer defined by the roles that they play in the social relations of production, but first and foremost by their regional (this is typically Brazilian), racial, cultural, or religious identities. The exercise of civil rights guarantees that there will be a proliferation of such newly mobilized identities. Thus to Touraine's observation that "rather than defining ourselves by what we do, we have come to define ourselves by what we are," I would add "not only by what we are, but also by what we desire." These desires are varied indeed, and the objectives of politics have broadened to match them. Politics now gives groups of citizens an opportunity to rally around causes such as the fight for human rights and the preservation of the environment.

In sum, we are experiencing the fragmentation of society into groups or "ghettoes." This has made it seem as if only the market or mass culture is left to unite citizens in a single national identity. Values crumble, both those that formed the glue holding national societies together and those that guided the relations among social classes. People all over the world are so fascinated by the new and by television's distorted image of reality that they risk forgetting what really constitutes a nation's identity: a common history, a cultural heritage, a collective journey (with all its triumphs and difficulties), and a shared sense of the future.

Within the public sphere it is becoming ever more difficult to harmonize the actions of social agents with their cultural identities. Here is the essential difficulty besetting the classic mechanisms of representation: many social demands, however legitimate in and of themselves, no longer reflect a broader set of values tied to an economic and cultural identity. The polity has been shattered; political mediation, the foundation for the very idea of representative democracy, fulfills its function of transforming individual interests into collective interests only partially, if at all. Public opinion polls show that political mediation is increasingly being shunted aside and discredited.

It is natural for the public to judge governments according to Max Weber's "ethics of ultimate ends" or results, in line with people's increasing demands in terms of the economy, justice and security, environmental protection, and human rights. These broader demands become the very fabric of politics; in order to remain legitimate, governments must respond to them. But how can we reconcile them with the responsibilities of officials who must face the difficult and complex task of allocating perennially scarce resources? How can we find the means to cover this enlarged set of demands?

Thus public debate tends to focus less on what must be done than on how to allocate limited resources in order to satisfy demands that certainly compete for attention even when they do not directly clash with one another. We must achieve results, to be sure, but in a responsible and well-balanced fashion. The words of Nabuco on the principal attribute of politicians are worth remembering here. Politicians, he cautioned, must "adapt the means to the end and never jeopardize the greater social good because of a doctrine or an aspiration."

THE FRAGMENTATION OF THE PUBLIC SPHERE

One result of this fragmentation of both the polity and the political agenda has been the sapping of the traditional role of political parties. In the past, political parties achieved a high degree of consistency because they identified with a set of ideals that reflected the interests of certain social classes or groups. Parties made an ideological choice, and then translated it into a program of action. In an era in which ideological differences are fading and in which interests have become less clear and more dispersed, parties run the risk of losing some of their capacity to mobilize the public. Parties therefore need to find new forms of mobilization that can transcend narrow issues and that can keep real collective interests in mind, interests that are no longer identified with ideologies as much as they were in the past.

A politics dominated by narrow interests is one in which the distinctions between parties will blur while politicians hop freely back and forth among them, with little sense of respect for or loyalty to their original party. There is also the risk of government by precarious suprapartisan majorities that ultimately place politicians and parties on the same undifferentiated plane. This makes it difficult for voters to choose; they will react, in most cases, by tending to see politicians as if they were all parts of an institution that, in the final analysis, focuses exclusively on its own interests as a closed group. If parties succumb to immobilize and fail to curb power when it is wielded to the benefit only of particular interest groups, then they will have ceased to accomplish their mission of serving as key players in the public sphere.

Another source of the dilemmas confronting representative democracy is the very scale of some modern states. As Robert Dahl reminds us, when representative democracy first appeared, it was adopted to govern smaller societies, where interests were simpler and less diffuse, and where more direct contact was possible between representatives and their constituents. In mass democracies, this link has become more tenuous. Casting a vote is sometimes compared to writing a blank check. This is true, in part, because in most representative systems the power of voters to punish representatives is limited to the refusal to reelect them. Yet these limitations of representative democracy have paved the way for the progress of participatory democracy. Actions taken in defense of group identities or by nongovernmental organizations (NGOs) dedicated to specific issues have led to new types of activities that make political mediation more difficult. Interest groups address executive-branch officials, the business community, and other sectors involved in the decision-making process directly, without mediation.

The increase in participatory democracy means a growing partnership between government and civil society. This is good, but it is not enough. Direct participation is no substitute for representation. More importantly, in a state ruled by laws, representative institutions must assemble and fine-tune the legal framework that governs social and economic relations. Movements based on direct participation cannot simply disregard current rules; when changes are called for, it will always be necessary to look to the legislative branch to change the laws. In Brazil, the state has always played a decisive role in the relationship between capital and labor. Classical economic liberalism has never been prevalent. The state was the driving force behind the industrialization of Brazil from the very beginning, whether through direct investment, tariff protection for domestically produced goods, or the granting of monopolies and market reserves. The Brazilian state has always mediated and shaped the conflict between capital and labor. On becoming a "member" of the business community, the state also acquired a direct interest in conflicts over income distribution. Herein lies one of the principal causes of the unfortunate Brazilian penchant for corporatist arrangements.

Such arrangements have become embedded in every branch of the federal government, in states and municipalities, and in the state-owned companies. Various categories of civil servants, for example, enjoy special retirement schemes. Paternalism marks labor legislation that has been on the books since the dictatorship of President Getúlio Vargas in the 1930s. A separate labor court system whose magistrates are chosen from among the representatives of various interest and class groups was set up to judge labor-management conflicts, thus strengthening the notion that the state is the arbiter par excellence of all conflicts, including individual conflicts, in labor-management relations. With the government now backing away from the obsolescent development model based on protection for local industry and a direct state role in production, Brazil needs to refashion the underpinnings of its legal system.

None of this is to say that the problem of relations between capital and labor is off the national agenda. Rather, the problem has taken on a new shape that demands new mechanisms for conciliation. Discussion should focus on how to provide genuine, long-term worker protection through a model that can transform conflict into partnership and avoid repeating past mistakes.

Even though information flows freely, democracy suffers because public debate on broad issues often lacks substance or quality. What seems to be missing is citizen interest in assimilating more detailed and higher-quality information. Are the issues of the day being adequately debated? This is a question not only for those directly involved in politics, but also for ordinary citizens. What is truly in the public interest? How can demands for change best be framed and change best be brought about? An informed citizenry not only asks these questions as it makes demands, but also monitors the performance of political actors and institutions to gauge their compliance with voters' wishes.

Problems related to the quality of public debate are exacerbated in mass democracies, particularly in those with great social inequalities that are no longer limited to developing countries. In such countries, a large segment of the population is typically passed over in the political process: some because they do not feel encouraged to participate, others because, although they are interested, they cannot set up the appropriate channels of communication. If we want democracy to remain strong, we must find a way to include these non-participants in the sphere of public deliberation. The press has an important role to play in this respect, and I will come back to this issue later.

The growing process of globalization and the concomitant weakening of the nation-state are exacerbating the problems that I have been describing. The nation-state's scope for independent action in economic policy is diminishing, while other issues by their very nature transcend national boundaries. The state must cope with limits on its ability to cover all the social demands that it once was able, at least in part, to meet. These demands, moreover, are on the rise as populations become more diverse, life expectancies increase, and rapidly changing technology aggravates unemployment. Because the state is temporarily unable to respond to growing social demands, it is seen as ineffectual, and politicians as a group fall out of favor.

We must foster greater realism about state capabilities if we are to restore the viability of democracy and make citizens realize that they, too, must take responsibility for addressing our problems. It is incumbent upon the state to take actions in strategic areas to show that it is still a positive, high-quality political instrument. This is a key concern of my government, and the reason for the leading role I have tried to play in the implementation of reforms in Brazil.

REPRESENTATIVE DEMOCRACY IN BRAZIL

It should be remembered that in Brazil representative democracy had to overcome a major obstacle that never existed in the United States: the "exceptional regimes" and authoritarianism that interrupted the rule of law twice, and for very long periods. During the 1980s, with the country undergoing a transition toward democracy, we believed (perhaps somewhat naively) that the exercise of democracy would lead automatically to the perfection of the mechanisms of mediation and of the relations between representatives and constituents. Going even farther, we hoped that democracy would lead to the solution of social problems. Things did not work out quite that well, of course, but over the past few years we have made progress in consolidating democracy and the rule of law. There were pitfalls along the way, but we sidestepped them with maturity and equilibrium.

This is cause for pride, but not complacency, about the functioning of our institutions. Ample room for improvement remains. Nothing exempts us from the nettlesome paradoxes of representative democracy. Brazil as a society has advanced, in political terms, more rapidly than the state. Society's capacity for self-organization has become the driving force of the political process and conditions the actions of the state. Evidence of this capacity can be seen in the increased number of NGOs, the force of social movements, and the use of press freedom to expose injustices and abuses of power.

In Brazil, the dilemmas of representative democracy are epitomized by the large number of political parties that the public sees as ideologically fuzzy. Under such circumstances, people tend to vote for a specific candidate rather than a party. Weak parties make change twice as hard to achieve. Gathering a majority for a bill becomes a case-by-case exercise requiring negotiations that become ever more arduous as the bill at stake becomes more narrowly focused. Of course, there are some questions that are almost plebiscitary in nature, where clear popular desires reign and consensus is relatively easy to reach. The liberalization of monopolies and the lifting of restrictions on foreign capital fall into this category. Other issues, however, are tougher. As we face the problems of reforming our social security and civil-service systems, we must combine the short-term sacrifice of personal interests with the expectation of long-term collective benefits. In the area of tax reform, meanwhile, negotiations have bogged down over the question of how to distribute tax revenues among the various regions of the country.

Reforms can prosper only insofar as the citizenry participates in their design. In the final analysis, it is essential to bridge the well-known gap that separates the legally constituted Brazil from the real Brazil.

Since the 1970s, certain political players, such as the new labor unions and business associations as well as NGOs and various grassroots organizations, have come out from under state control. Their emancipation has been twofold: on the one hand, most of these players have tended to look away from the partisan system of mediation when defending their interests and demands, preferring instead to establish direct relations with the executive branch. On the other hand, these groups began to play a role in complex issues formerly arbitrated by the state, such as in the recent negotiations on flexible work contracts. There is a risk here for democracy, since such activities may encourage people to think that society can do totally without the state, and that the legally constituted authorities "hamper" progress or create a needless barrier impeding direct dealings between parties to a contract or a dispute.

Each country has to find a balance between society-wide participation and the role of the state. On the one hand, too dominant a role for the state vis-à-vis society leads to authoritarianism, technocracy, political patronage, and paternalism; on the other hand, disorganized pressures from society on the state can create the impression of a government adrift. Although there is no ready recipe to ensure the right balance, we know that such equilibrium is indispensable.

As Nabuco put it, "a government, unless it is unaware of its mission, cannot favor one interest to the detriment of the other interests of society: the great problem in public administration lies in being able to combine all the interests."

I would like to point out one last thing regarding the dilemmas of representative democracy in Brazil. It pertains to the pace of decision making at the current juncture, which is one marked by sweeping and dynamic transformations. Legislative progress has been slow, it is true, but this is not because of gridlock and inefficiency. Rather, it is because Congress's agenda is overloaded with highly complex issues. The judiciary, likewise, is laboring under a huge caseload that is causing enormous delays in the handing down of decisions. This is a grave problem, for "justice delayed is justice denied." The spectacle of clogged courts and a seemingly paralyzed Congress is precipitating a loss of confidence in the government. The solution lies not only in convincing the citizenry that such delays are natural and that the updating of institutions takes time, but also in speeding up the pace of deliberations within such institutions.

THE MEDIA AND DEMOCRACY

In contemporary mass democracies, it is impossible to improve the political system without taking the media into account. Manuel Castells rightly affirms that the political sphere has been "captured" by the media, by their flow of information and images. Today, a policy that does not appear in the media simply does not exist. According to Castells, this does not mean that public policy is subordinate to the media. What it means is that without the media, facts alone cannot start the process of popular mobilization. Politics, in short, cannot do without the mass media in today's world.

The enhanced role of the mass media does, however, present certain challenges to democracy. The media are no substitute for the public sphere, but simply one of its many components. The basic function of the media must not be to engage in the constitution and construction of events, but rather, by disseminating and analyzing facts, to help citizens make judgments on issues. In doing this, the media will be providing a public service. The risk is that facts may be oversimplified, that the part may take precedence over the whole, the phrase over the full text, the interpretation over the facts, the image over the rationale, and most especially, that a particular aspect of a given event may be highlighted to the detriment of the process that led to it, simply because it plays better. The danger lies in treating news in a fragmented way, in not taking the greater care required for a broader understanding of events. The desire for immediate results can lead to situations in which the real news of the day is often not properly emphasized, and may even be ignored in favor of some petite histoire, a case of wheeling and dealing, a bit of gossip, or the "he said she said" type of story.

The speed with which news is transmitted is the great trump card held by mass communications, and its very raison d'être. Yet we must ensure that in carrying out their legitimate functions, the mass media do not influence public opinion through the dissemination of a simplified, negative agenda, dissociated from the real problems that affect us.

Democracy is not built on the public's impulses alone, since these can change, and they tend to be expressed in a generally simplistic way. Democracy depends on solid and hardy institutions that take their own time, usually at a pace that is necessarily slower than the flow of information. To take advantage of a neologism, it is wise and prudent to avoid the press's simplistic "plebiscitization" of complex issues that must wend their way through our institutions in a context of public dialogue.

In saying this, I do not in any way want to detract from the importance of the mass media in denouncing abuses of power, corruption, and the improper functioning of government at every level. I acknowledge the important role that the press has played in the fight against authoritarianism in Latin America. Nonetheless, the press must be more than a forum for whistle blowing, particularly in Brazil, a country that, after all, is enjoying full democracy as well as a period of optimism and the renewal of sustained economic growth. The press needs to move beyond an "adversarial" attitude. The power of the press to mobilize public opinion can be decisive in overcoming problems and in consensus-building itself.

BROADENING THE PUBLIC SPHERE

As a true believer in democracy whose political career was largely forged during daily discussions in Brazil's Senate, I must strongly voice a firm, passionate, and yet reasoned defense of Congress as the locus par excellence of the consensus-building that is needed if we are to move forward while simultaneously safeguarding the values most dear to our sense of nationhood, the values without which no nation can recognize itself.

I am proud to be a politician. It pains me to see the loss of prestige that politics as a profession has been suffering throughout the world. I fail to see how one can organize any broad, constructive program without the growing participation of the citizenry; without an active legislature; without political parties; without mass media that are aware of their heavy responsibility toward the public; without striving to improve relations among various interest groups so as to go beyond the mere and reprehensible "give-and-take"; without taking time to think critically and consider new ideas; and, above all, without political leaders capable of looking to the common good.

The revitalization of the art of politics can follow several paths. Let me suggest some guidelines, and then elaborate on a few of the possible paths. In *Democracy in America*, Alexis de Tocqueville writes, "Government loves what the citizens love and naturally hates what they hate. This community of sentiments in democratic nations constantly joins each individual and the sovereign in one thought, and establishes a secret and abiding bond."

If the system of political representation is ever to be perfected, the rules that define it must constantly evolve. The number of parties, the requirements for their creation, the methods of securing party loyalty, and the electoral system itself all need to be reassessed in light of the new demands made by mass democracy. Nothing would do more for the credibility of politicians than the establishment of mechanisms to make elected officials more accountable to voters. Voters need a reason to reelect their politicians, and politicians should court such favor by providing full accountability for their acts and decisions to those who have elected them.

An opposition is necessary; it should be vigorous but responsible, and it must always be guided by the pursuit of the public interest. One way to increase the level of accountability among politicians and to bring those who are representatives closer to their constituents is through a district-based system that would link voters more closely with those who represent them. Examples of such a system exist in several countries. At any rate, it behooves our legislature itself to implement measures through which its own functioning may be improved. Congress will know best what such measures might be.

It is essential that the public sphere be broadened so as to encompass more and more of those who today are voiceless. By the same token, it is necessary for everyone to be ready to sacrifice his or her personal interests to the benefit of all. Global development will eventually enhance the life of each and every one, not in answer to mere demands for immediate action, but rather over a longer period of time. Herein lies the essence of a democratic republic.

The broadening of the public sphere is also essential if conflicting interests are to be dealt with transparently, freely, and above all rationally. Jürgen Habermas is right to say that in any public debate, only the proposal supported by the best arguments should prevail. Any case should be argued in such a way as to convince and persuade one's interlocutors. Convincing and persuading through reason is a sure way to broaden consensus. Consensus breeds legitimacy. Public ethics—which should fuel the ideal of virtue in politics—are the fruit of reason, not the expression of force.

The success of the anti-inflationary Real Plan, for example, had much to do with the credibility established when we decided that each step in the plan's implementation had to be presented as part of an exercise in persuasion and explanation.

And yet it is not enough to improve Congress and the system of representation. Nor is it enough to broaden the public sphere. Citizens must also be better prepared for the exercise of democracy. Here education is paramount, and the teaching institutions should, in tandem with the press, ensure that citizens will be in a better position to distinguish between alternatives, to understand them, to propose new options, to choose those representatives who will defend their interests, and to demand results and cogency. Citizens cannot expect the state to address their priorities if such priorities are only murkily expressed, or if the citizens themselves are not willing to collaborate in making proposals a reality, to the benefit of the majority. In this regard, I have borrowed from an important legacy left to us by traditional conservative thinkers in referring to the responsibility that falls upon elites, by which I mean those in each segment of a populace who exercise some type of leadership or play some role in public representation.

In counterpoint, let me turn once again to Alain Touraine. Touraine feels that we cannot expect the players alone to rebuild society and, I would add, politics because the players also need, to a certain extent, to be reconstructed. In what sense? It is not that social protagonists have "disappeared." On the contrary, one trait of modern societies is precisely the proliferation of social movements and organizations. The range of topics under public debate has broadened. Now it is essential to find points of convergence among these extremely variegated objectives themselves the result of the fragmentation of demands in contemporary society and to develop the political capacity that can give these points of confluence direction and meaning.

In the case of Brazil, and primarily because of the struggle against authoritarianism, democracy has taken root in society even before it has in the political system, thus demanding a reassessment of the way in which social and political issues mesh. Political activity must perform two functions. First, as an opportunity for dialogue, political activity must be capable of ensuring that demands will be expressed democratically, that any topic can be discussed, without constraints. Second, as a means to promote the public weal, political activity must make scattered objectives somehow cohere and point them in a direction that will be in the interest of all.

Negotiation is the key art in politics. It stems from tolerance, from the genuinely democratic acceptance of differences, of plurality; it also stems from the idea that one reasons to conclusions by debate, by consensus building. It is through negotiation that we can overcome the traditional dichotomies that have been frayed by the passage of time, concepts such as "left" and "right," "progressive" and "reactionary." It is only through negotiation that we will be able to promote those changes that will be so necessary if we are to attain development with justice.

I realize that my comments and proposals include a generous dose of determination and idealism, but these traits are part of the essence of politics itself. Joaquim Nabuco acknowledged this with the sensitivity and acuity of a great statesman, asserting in *Pensamentos Soltos*, "Purely ideal politics can be compared to an architecture that holds the laws of mechanics in contempt. Nonetheless, such politics will forever be the most popular of all, while similar architecture would collapse instantly."

I will conclude by saying of politics what Octavio Paz says of history in his book *Corriente Alterna*: "[It] is a daily invention, a continual creation; a hypothesis, a risky game, a wager against the unpredictable. Not a science, but rather a skill, not a technique, but rather an art."

→ 14 ←

Freedom for the Have-nots

In Brazil there has long been a profound conviction that democracy is a political system that does not easily take root in underdeveloped countries. And yet for long periods in its history Brazil itself has had a formal democratic system. In the nineteenth century, the Empire coexisted with parliamentary government, and in the present century, except for the periods between 1937 and 1945 and 1964 and 1985, there have always been elections and a plurality of political parties. The facts remain that people have always tended to emphasize the problem of democracy rather than its stability and the strength of its roots. The noted Brazilian historian Sérgio Buarque de Holanda liked to say that democracy "is a delicate plant, and has great difficulty growing in the tropics."

In the so-called Third World countries, even when a regime has had leaders chosen on the basis of elections between representatives of different parties, it has always been criticized by someone, not without justification, on the grounds of its "elitist" or "oligarchical" character. In such cases, fragile democratic institutions were confronted with political realities such as patronage, lack of real freedom for society's underdogs, and the artificiality of political parties.

These criticisms contain an element of truth. But in the light of world events during the last ten years, I wonder whether it is not the dictatorships and authoritarian regimes rather than the democracies that have turned out to be fragile. Dictatorships, as recent history shows, end up being less durable than democracy, which is increasingly becoming a universal value.

In his "Dictionary of Politics,"[1] Norberto Bobbio reviews the various meanings of the word democracy from ancient Greece to the present day, and concludes by emphasizing the dichotomy between democracy as an egalitarian ideal and democracy

From Fernando Henrique Cardoso, "Freedom for the Have-nots," *UNESCO Courier*, 45 (November 1992): 21–24.

as a method, in other words, between democracy as a value and democracy as a mechanism. But his comments were made before the current great debate about the transition to democracy in Eastern Europe. If he were writing now, he would perhaps comment that it is vain to think of merging these two meanings of democracy.

Nevertheless, I think he would primarily emphasize the role of freedom, both in theory and in practice. It is freedom, far more than a definition of new rules of democracy, that has fostered the democratization process in Eastern Europe, led to the downfall of anachronistic dictatorships in Greece, Spain and Portugal, and encouraged the fight against authoritarianism in Latin America. It still motivates the struggle for democratization, particularly in Asia and some of the newly industrialized countries such as the Republic of Korea.

All the same, we need to analyze rather more deeply the different processes of transition to democracy that are taking place today. I shall confine myself to those in Latin America, with which I am directly acquainted, but I shall compare them with those in Eastern Europe. Apart from the aspiration to freedom that is common to them both, I see only differences between them.

In Poland in 1981, I observed at first hand the final stage of the events that led to the Gdansk agreements between Lech Walesa and the management of the Lenin naval shipyard. I drove to Gdansk from Warsaw, where I was attending a meeting of the International Sociological Association, in order to take a closer look at the strike. I remember that what surprised and even shocked me were the symbols displayed in the streets—effigies of the Pope, Polish flags from pre-people's democracy days, and lighted candles. Was this a return to the past?

Then I remembered the events of May 1968 in France, which took place while I was a professor of sociology at the University of Nanterre just outside Paris. On the barricades in Paris, at demonstrations by students, workers and others, the *Internationale* was always sung. *"Debout, ô damnés de la terre!"* ("Arise ye starvelings from your slumbers!") intoned well-fed crowds led by young people waving black anarchist flags.

The antecedents of the two movements, like their socioeconomic contexts, were different. But they shared the same mixture of symbols, simultaneously contemporary and anachronistic, which sought to express a message that still lacked a vocabulary and a fixed grammar. In each case there was a powerful reaction against ossified structures and a tremendous longing to turn over the page of history.

MAKING THE TRANSITION TO DEMOCRACY

But the quest for greater freedom is not the only factor in contemporary history. There are others, including components of what I call substantive democracy (to distinguish it from formal democracy), which implies health, education and general welfare for the masses. Yet both in eastern Europe and in Latin America, despite their different situations, efforts to build a democratic political system come up against the same agonizing problem: can democracy exist in a society paralyzed by an economy in which penury is rife?

Before answering this crucial question, we need to be clear about the differences between the forms of transition to democracy found in the two regions. In Latin

America, the transition has neither jeopardized the market economy nor sought to change it; indeed the changes that have occurred there have strengthened the market. In Eastern Europe, the situation is totally different: as well as acquiring more freedom and more democratic rules, society and the economy must also be rebuilt. In the Latin American countries, attempts to reform society and the economy take in the context of an already existing civil society, competition between companies, and efforts to move away from a system of patronage which pervades the world of politics. Latin American societies are much more like those of Western Europe and the United States than those of Eastern Europe where (particularly the ex-USSR, which experienced seventy years of communist government) civil society has to be recreated from scratch.

In order to move into the democratic phase, the first item on the political agenda must be to channel the urge for freedom into the construction of state and non-state institutions that fit into the Madisonian tradition of checks and balances. In a way, this is easier to achieve in Latin America, where the state, even if authoritarian, has not destroyed the market and non-state organizations have been preserved, than it is in Eastern Europe, where the democratic drive comes from limited sections of the intelligentsia and groups within the dominant party "contaminated" by the new ideas. But what really set the ball rolling was the aspiration of the masses for freedom and consumer goods.

In Latin America, since major economic reforms had not been introduced and the back of the dictatorships (i.e., the military) had not been broken, the transition boiled down to a mammoth negotiation between the old masters and the new and there has been no real break in continuity. In terms of institutions, Argentina, Brazil, Chile, Uruguay, and even Paraguay, had to revert to democratic practices and curb the influence of the old rulers without excluding them altogether.

The forces working for democracy in Latin America met resistance from within the state, but found support in the already (existing) civil society that coexisted with the dictatorship (trade unions, universities, companies, the media and even political parties). In Eastern Europe, on the other hand, when the party-state broke up, civil society had to be completely reinvented, not reinstated.

Here I should like to mention a thesis that is relevant today, although many democrats dislike it. It is based on the theory of elites of the Moravian-born U.S. economist Joseph Schumpeter, who believed that democracy exists when rival groups struggle for power and compete for votes. Voting not only has to be introduced, but competition has to be organized by elites, which identify objectives and put them to the people, who make a choice. Rules made by the majority are observed and minorities respected. Continuity and alternation in what the Italian sociologist and jurist Gaetano Mosca calls the "political class" are not only guaranteed but prescribed by electoral competition.

FREEDOM EVEN ON AN EMPTY STOMACH

Now in both Latin America and Eastern Europe dictatorships have wrought havoc in the sense that they have destroyed elites. Reconstructing these elites is a necessary precondition for the revival of democratic institutions. Learning how to manage social groups and get them to express their feelings and interests without falling into blind corporatism is a long and thankless process; but it is the essential tool for any democratization.

This brings me to the crux of the matter: the rising tide of popular demands. Democratization by definition opens the floodgates of society. What happens then? In Eastern Europe, where totalitarianism was stronger and inequalities are less pronounced, popular demands are for more freedom and participation and so are aimed mainly at the state and government. In Latin America, where inequalities are glaring, demands are for better jobs, better pay and better public services.

But in both cases, penury is intolerable when it goes beyond limits set by the people and by the capacity of productive forces to satisfy demand. Here the debate about substantive democracy and formal democracy crops up again, although in different terms. The prospects for constructing a democratic political system in which people enjoy a full range of freedoms are reduced where there is no prosperity. In Eastern Europe libertarian aspirations have until now meant that democratic values have been preserved even on an empty stomach; but in Latin America, where inflation and unemployment are rife, and crises, exhaustion of public funds and a large external debt are commonplace, the maintenance of an open and democratic society is a tour de force.

This is the finest lesson the twentieth century can pass on to the next millennium. We have discovered the fragility of dictatorships, and also that peoples nowadays want freedom. They are ready to endure penury because they realize that lack of freedom offers them only an ersatz prosperity and robs them of the benefits of citizenship. But beyond a certain threshold the necessary correlation between formal democracy and substantive democracy becomes unavoidable.

NOTE

1. N. Bobbio, N. Matteucci, and G. Pasquilo, *Dicionário de política* (Brasília: Editora Universidade, 1986).

→ 15 ←

Caesarism in Democratic Brazil?

In Brazil, as we moved from a military authoritarian regime, we suffered the tragedy of the death of Tancredo Neves, and were faced with the fact that the new president, José Sarney, had been the head of the party that supported the military regime.

The redemocratization was undertaken with personnel that belonged to the ancien régime, with a much more profound degree of change and confusion than what happened, for example, in Spain. It was not easy, in these circumstances, to propose to the citizenry the idea that we were founding a new regime.

It is certain that in Brazil, curiously, there is not this "foundational passion." People simply do not believe that, from one day to the next, everything will change. There is always a sort of accepted continuity of a past that more or less renews itself. Nonetheless, there were concrete facts: elections, a new constitution, and so on, to mark the transformation.

The country discovered that that which is called "civil society," and not only in the sense of "popular movements," already existed in Brazil. Or rather, with all its differences, with all its imperfections, there existed a possibility of societal representation.

The Brazilian military regime always held elections. In that era I used to joke, at conferences outside of Brazil, that the great contribution of the Brazilian military dictatorship to contemporary political theory was the creation of a single party regime with opposition. In fact, the regime allowed the creation of the old Brazilian Democratic Movement (MDB), which was a large opposition party, while the official party, the Aliança Nacional Renovadora (ARENA; National Alliance for Renewal), was sustained by the government and not the other way around, as would have been normal.

Adapted from Fernando Henrique Cardoso, "La construcción de la democracia: desafíos y dificultades," in Julio Cotler, ed., *Estrategias para el Desarrollo de la Democracia: Perú y América Latina* (Lima: Instituto de Estudios Peruanos/Fundación Friedrich Naumann, 1990), 195–210.

In 1974, the opposition won the majoritarian elections in the Senate, but did not win in the lower chamber (Chamber of Deputies) because this was run under the rules of proportional representation. Thus it is that still in 1982, under the authoritarian regime, the Congress (i.e., the Senate and the chamber together) was still predisposed to say "yes," and very rarely a "perhaps no," to everything the government proposed.

THE CONSTRUCTION OF DEMOCRACY: CHALLENGES AND DIFFICULTIES

With the indirect election of Tancredo Neves by the electoral college in 1984, and later with his tragic death, Sarney took over the presidency. Political conditions were already so different that the pressure of society could not be contained. The Congress, which had been a "rubber stamp Congress" ratifying executive decisions, became a place of debate. Even if it was not deciding anything, at least it was realizing that society was being represented not by parties, but by opinions. For this reason, it was very difficult to predict the behavior of any congressman as a function of his party membership. In the Constituent Assembly, it became clear: In the voting on the fundamental issues except for the representatives of the parties of the extreme left, party membership was not a predictor of the behavior of the representative. In the corridors of the Congress there was a very intense movement, then a wide fringe of society was organizing in a corporatist manner to pressure, especially in the middle strata: judges and lawyers, more the former than the latter; the police; professors; women, and occasionally a women's social movement; trade unions; military leaders; and so on. Military leaders ceased to be the lords of power and began negotiating with us their future participation in the state and their limitations, including calls for limits on military power from within the military itself. To be sure, the military did not intervene in all initiatives, but they did defend their own interests very strongly.

Insofar as the democratic system progressed and the work of the Constituent Assembly advanced, starting in the second half of 1987, the whole of society made its presence felt in the parliamentary arena. Bankers were the last to arrive, but they arrived; the big bankers, who had never set foot in the Parliament, came because they feared that limitations on financial capital would be written into the constitution. Nonetheless, some such limitations were approved, including some that were a little disingenuous, such as placing a legal limit on the interest rate. Industrialists also came. Multinationals came with much greater difficulty, because they do not have local channels of representation, but in the end they were represented through industrial federations. Peasants arrived, large confederations of peasants; at last we recognized that society had much more active channels of representation than we imagined. But, I repeat, it was not through parties that they were present: they came directly, through unions, corporations and the like.

In short, every sector of society tried to write into the constitution something that was a lever for its own interests, which resulted in an excessively detailed constitution, which many people have criticized, but which corresponds to the reality of the country. People do not much believe in laws, and perhaps the constitution has more value than law. Hence, items that certainly are not constitutional became articles in the constitution. Any professor of constitutional law would become nervous upon seeing these in the constitution; but the reason they are there can be understood. It is because the different social segments want a strong legal apparatus to protect their interests.

We thus recognized that society had ways of saying what it wanted. To be sure, not all of society was able to act. The countless numbers of marginalized people in Brazil did not have these channels of representation. The other groups, in one way or another, made proposals and applied pressure. This put parties in check, in establishing a direct relationship between interest groups and representatives, with the representatives seen as capable of vocalizing the specific interests of the groups. Obviously, it was not parties as such, except those of the left that drove the political readjustments in society.

The principal party, the PMDB, which had an absolute majority in the assembly, went to pieces with each specific theme. The representatives that had leadership functions (I was the leader in the Senate), and especially the leader of the Constituent Assembly, Senator Mario Covas, had the huge task of processing all of these demands and implementing the agreements. In the end, we had to use a demoralizing tactic: we did not say that the PMDB votes in such and such a way, but rather said, "the leader advises the deputies of his party to vote this way," because we no longer had control of the party. Interests were very strong, and the leadership had no way to make a confused party, such as the PMDB, vote for a law that, for example, would allow the state to expropriate land and pay it over a period of twenty years, with a low interest rate.

INSTITUTIONAL PROBLEMS

Once the Constituent Assembly was completed, we confronted a situation in which parties, with all the weaknesses mentioned already, had to act in a new system of government that perhaps functions poorly: a system that did not become parliamentary, yet is not, in the strict sense of the word, presidential.

There is no doubt that democracy exists in Brazil. Nevertheless, in order for democracy to be perceived as valuable by the people, there are two basic conditions. First, the "rules of the game" cannot be separated from social interests. Second, efficacy and governability must prevail.

We have a hybrid political system in Brazil. At the beginning of the democratization process, we replaced an authoritarian president with Sarney, who for all his formal powers did not have a majority, since he did not truly belong to the PMDB. To be sure, Sarney was officially a member of the party, because the legal rules obliged him to be in order to be elected vice president. However, his preparation, his mindset, and his interests were not to be found there. He held formal power; we held the majority in Congress. The result was that in discussions about the form of government, various political sectors proposed that we adopt a parliamentary regime and that the presidential mandate be reduced. During the final phase of the Constituent Assembly, this was the big battle.

Sarney said that he would accept a shortening of his term of office by one year, but he did not want to preside over a "transition government." Rather, he insisted that he was a president equal to those of the past. He did not, however, accept the parliamentary regime. We wanted a parliamentary regime in order to have an opportunity to remake the state apparatus. It was not so much the regime in itself that was important, but that a sort of shock therapy for the state seemed necessary.

However, we believed that a very strong presidential system, in the Brazilian style, destroys parties. The consequences of this situation can be seen today in Brazil with the electoral campaign for the presidency. The candidate that has 40 percent of the vote (Fernando Collor) does not have a party, but created one for himself. Nonetheless, I am sure that, if he becomes president, on the following day there will be hundreds of deputies at his disposal. The deputies have no way of countering such a strong president.

Despite the opposition of Sarney, we drafted the whole constitution, as if it were to be a parliamentary regime. Then, on the day of voting for the system of executive power, the president, plus the military, plus businessmen, plus the press, applied heavy pressure, and the majority capitulated. The result was a constitution based in parliamentary presuppositions, save for the chapter on presidential powers. We created a system that functions with great difficulty; the Congress holds too much power, yet the regime is not parliamentary. This could generate an impasse, especially if the new president is elected by a majority of the eighty million voters, while none of the major parties have more than a million members.

The president, in the Brazilian system, rises like a Caesar, a national savior. But when this man takes power, he will recognize that he will have to confront a Congress in which he will not necessarily hold a majority. We may thus have an unstable political situation.

We have created a plebiscitary democracy that also has strong congressional representation, based on a traditional system, and parties without organic links to society. Thus, the worst is that the Caesar is in fact not a Caesar, since the constitution has added a strong Congress to the presidential system.

Moreover, the new republic has heavily damaged the more or less competent bureaucracy and technocracy, which the military developed. In this aspect, the two dominant parties (the PMDB and the PFL) have returned to the pre-1964 era, taking up charges and functions without a sense of meritocracy. The division of state positions between the two parties strengthened a bureaucratic system that responds to the interests of parties, which do not in turn necessarily support President Sarney. Similarly, in the Congress no one is ready to fight for the president. Ministers have little solidarity with one another, nor with the president, as happened in parliamentary cabinets. There is no real cabinet of ministers. When the ministers meet with the president, a sort of spectacle is played out. On it, the president gives the floor to the minister of finance, who, already through common agreement with the bureaucracy and the president, distributes or appropriates resources and speaks as if he were a great demiurge. The act continues. The other ministers, who say nothing, upon leaving the office of the president, go to the Congress or pace the floor of the minister of finance, who in practice has become the caricature of a prime minister. This is the system that exists today. If it is not reconstructed in a way that allows us to ensure governability, we will face growing difficulties and conflicts in the Brazilian political system, since the elected president will have to obtain a parliamentary majority. If he does not obtain it, conflicts are inevitable.

I repeat, there have been great changes in this country. Society has the capacity to represent itself, not necessarily through parties but directly through the Parliament. As a consequence, the system that we have is a "false Caesarism," because Caesar does not have as much power as the public thinks he has. The new president, who will not even be elected so much through a "plebiscite" as through "publicity," will have enormous difficulties in imposing his political will.

→ 16 ←

Reforming the State

These notes refer only to a few processes in effect in Brazil to ensure both that the government increases its capacity to make its proposals effective through public policy and that the people gain greater control over the decisions and actions of the government. I will not, therefore, refer to the fiscal crisis of the contemporary state, nor to the debates of the 1980s about neoliberalism that proposed a "minimalist state." Nor will I address questions of "governability" (or rather the political capacity to sustain governments), nor what international bureaucrats call "governance" (i.e., the administrative and managerial capacity to implement the decisions of the government). For treatment of these themes, as well other aspects relevant to state reform, one can consult the multifaceted work of Luis Carlos Bresser-Pereira.[1]

However, before entering into the nitty-gritty of what the current government is doing to reconstruct the bases of Brazilian society, I believe it will be useful to make some more general reference to the political and ideological climate that predominates at this fin-de-siècle, or rather, this dawn of a new millennium. The presence of this climate in Western countries enabled the formation of the nation-state and the transformation of the state that are necessary to face the challenges of a new era of international capitalist development and the emergence of what sociologists called, in previous decades, "mass societies." These became viable thanks to new modes of mass communication and information, and the universalization of the citizenry, giving strength to civil societies.

I am referring to what, in the journalistic jargon of Europe, is being called the "pink wave." This echoes the predominance in American popular sentiment (which apparently has not yet reached Congress), for new forms of solidarity that minimize

Excerpted with permission from Fernando Henrique Cardoso, "Notas Sobre a Reforma do Estado," *Novos Estudos* (CEBRAP) (50, March) (1998): 5–12.

the effects of the increasing vulnerability of labor, the cost (or lack) of health care, and, in general, the scant attention paid to contemporary social and environmental questions.

Curiously, despite the diverse traditions of the United States, of Continental Europe and England, the Anglo-Saxon "stateless societies," like the nation-state societies of the Continent, have been criticized for their proposals. On the one hand, these proposals are not neoliberal, reflecting a minimalist state. Nor, on the other hand, do they advocate a welfare state that nationalizes the economy and is an integral provider of social welfare.

In place of this, Americans, with the proposals of Robert Reich before them, will attempt to reinvent the state, or, as they put it, "reinvent government."[2] Europeans are also proposing a new paradigm in government, be it the New Labor of Tony Blair, or the successful pragmatism of the Portuguese Socialist Party from the time of Mario Soares to the present, with Jorge Sampaio and Antonio Guterres. Or be it through the efforts of Romano Prodi and his former communist allies to place Italy within the Maastricht convergence criteria, or even the Socialist government in France under Lionel Jospin.

To be simple and direct, all of these new paradigms start with an observation: the market is an inescapable reality; and it allocates resources and profits according to capitalist notions of efficiency, rationalizes organization and productive processes (merging science, technology, and the organization of production), and accumulates wealth. But it is not the market that guarantees, as some by-product, a redistribution of rents, social welfare (such as security, health, social services, and social security), or the cohesion of society. These elements are also inescapable, not only as a moral imperative of contemporary society, but also as factors that lead to social cohesion and balance. They require public action. Nonetheless, "public action" is not the same thing as "state action," or bureaucratic action. Nor are the worthy objectives of redistribution of profits and property best reached through "nationalizations," or state control of production.

It is obvious that the new ideas (which, alas, are not all that new) follow different trajectories from country to country. We could not expect that the French Socialist Party, which was elected against certain liberal proclivities, will wear the same hat as Labour in England, which won from another political position.

Following the argument of Samuel Beer regarding New Labour,[3] such it is that Blair, in opposing himself to John Major, faced a Conservative Party that since Margaret Thatcher had tossed overboard the oldest Tory tradition. The Tories now appropriated the ideas of Gladstone more than other conservative currents, and thus, it was no longer "statist" or nationalizing. In France, statism never suffered a similar shock, and it would not be Jospin who would take up against it. But in practice, Maastricht and the single currency continue to be a "compass," and even the workers' demands against Renault-Belgium, or the protests of the jobless, are curtailed by the rationalizing power of the market.

Meanwhile, in Italy, as in Germany (despite the fact that in the latter the governing party has not proclaimed its support for any English-style New Labour or even the Clintonian "New Democrats"), the question of rationalization comes up against corporate interests and even the general interests of a society accustomed to a state that, in the eyes of the people, represents above all a way of accommodating social interests through pensions and very generous retirement guarantees.

What I wish to underline, at any rate, is that the new theme is not "ours." It has to do with the consequences of the internationalization of production, and with the all-encompassing pressure of competitive markets. But it also has to do with the fiscal crisis of the contemporary state and, principally, with a profound change in the means and the actors who provide the social safety nets that are indispensable for the functioning of modern societies. It is in this sense that I believe we are arriving at a political moment that is "postideological": postliberal, postsocial welfare–statist, and so on. For the lack of concrete understanding of the new ways, we speak of things as new: "New Labour" or "New Democracy," for example, much as Roosevelt once spoke of a "New Deal."

For reasons of politico-ideological struggle, and due to limited information, many people confuse, or try to confuse, this new posture with the old "neoliberalism." However, the truth is that in any one of the situations I have cited, as well as in Brazil, this is about the reconstruction of the state. This will enable it to attend to the calls for solidarity and new forms of behavior with the same devotion, while respecting the limits of the market. This is not about the destruction or minimization of the state and government action. But, and I repeat, in the new social conditions, public action is broader and more efficient than state action.

At this point, I want to make my last additional comment on this principal theme. Tony Blair (and the people who inspired him, like Anthony Giddens) called attention to something meaningful—to the responsibility (or duty) of every citizen, and not only to his rights. The idea of rights makes the state and government responsible and active in the social process, but this idea can also alienate, if the responsibility and solidarity of each citizen are not well established.

Of course, this does not excuse us from seeing the citizen (above all the mass with incipient citizenship, as in Brazil) also as a carrier of rights, and this must be assured by the state. But recognizing responsibilities breaks the traditional expectations of a state that acts (or should act) and a passive citizenry that receives and becomes a client who makes demands, but is not constructive.

Having these considerations as a backdrop, I now will comment on the reforms that the government is undertaking, with the support of the Congress and public opinion, in the Brazilian state.

To begin, our state, in the form in which it was crystallized by governmental practices and by the constitution of 1988, is a hybrid result of heterogeneous tendencies. Generally speaking, it is the confluence of at least three distinct situations and rationalizations. The first was that of the Vargas era, which had various aspects, but that fundamentally signified the strengthening of the interventionist state on the economic front, with some opening for "social protection" in the domain of workers' rights and social security, and a certain inattentiveness to the democratic representative processes. Second, the constitution of 1946, with its emphasis on the political and representative aspects of democracy. Finally, the bureaucratic-authoritarian era of military government, which emphasized an interventionist tendency on the economic front (while absorbing the presence of private capital, especially foreign capital) and gave space to a certain developmentalist technocracy, but that obviously regressed in the democratic and representative aspects, while perhaps having accentuated the "social protection" of specific groups in society.

It is clear that every government can either accentuate or reduce these tendencies. Juscelino Kubitschek gave emphasis to economic development, broadening the national and international private sector in the productive system, and enlarged the democratic space. In the postauthoritarian period, governments began to implement policies based on the constitution of 1988, which, if it tended to maintain interventionism in the economic terrain and even stimulated autarkic tendencies, is essentially democratic and accepts the notion of political as well as social rights.

As simplistic and incomplete as the above characterization may be, it remains clear that with these delineations, the Brazilian state would have—as it has had—difficulties in adjusting to the homogenization of markets and the need to solve the problems of generalizing social benefits and attending to the citizenry.

A reform of the state, then, becomes imperative. In what sense should it be undertaken? In the first place, in the present-day world, if we do not want the minimalist state, governors must not be only representatives (who correspond, through the vote, to the will of the people), but must also have the capacity to make decisions. As such, reforms that give fiscal rigidity and governability to the state become necessary.

The question of fiscal rigidity, in our case, took place (as it still takes place) through the maintenance of economic stability, through budgetary balance, and through the creation of mechanisms that make state accounts transparent. This movement began with the Real Plan, under the government of Itamar Franco, and with the renegotiation of the debt, both the foreign debt and that of the states to the Union. At the same time, the transparency of information implied the construction of a more adequate system for controlling public expenditure. This began also in the Itamar Franco government, with the "White Paper" on Central Bank accounts, which sorted out its relations with the National Treasury.

Starting with the creation of the Social Emergency Fund, the Union began to gain better control over public expenditure and developed greater sensitivity to public opinion on questions related to the fiscal crisis. In terms of the rationalization of management and its detachment from the clientelist and partisan game, we saw the flexibility of monopolies, the concession of public services to private initiative, and privatizations. It is noted that the privatizations began with the Collor government, continued with greater impact and greater transparency in the Itamar Franco government, and continue today with this new transparency and accountability to society.

With this, the state began to regain the conditions necessary to act in consonance with the challenges already referred to. Why? Because economic stability and the better organization of public finance gave the government space to start an ambitious program of infrastructure investment: privatization and broadening of the railway system; repair and widening of roadways, or the opening of new ones; use of waterways; new ports and private management of the old ones; making the cost of doing business in Brazil cheaper; an increase of 40 percent in hydroelectric energy generation up to the year 2000; construction of gas pipelines in the Amazon, in the south, and between Bolivia and Brazil, and so on. We are also taking up social projects once again: generalization of attendance in primary school; increased salaries for primary school teachers; reestablishment of the Federal Economic Fund (Caixa Econômica Federal) for the construction of housing and sanitation measures; an increase in health expenditures, thanks to the Contribuição Provisória sobre o Movimento Financeiro (CPMF); reaching settlement on agrarian land reform, to such a point that in four years more families are being settled than in the entire past; and so on.

We are, therefore, making the state more robust. But it is worth calling attention to three points:

- In infrastructure programs, the budget of the Union accounts for only a small part of the total funds, and rather stimulates private investment to realize that that was planned.
- In social programs, wherever possible, administrative decentralization to the states and municipalities takes place, and social control is increased, and priority will be given to projects generated with the participation of community groups.
- Regulatory agencies with public responsibility take the place of old fashioned bureaucratic control, which was frequently tied to the particularist interests of patrimonialist clienteles.

These innovations are vital for a reform of the state. They take two basic paths, conforming to the nature of the questions treated:

Regarding government actions relative to infrastructure and public services, regulatory agencies are being constituted that replace ministerial bureaucracies—and the old lobbies encrusted within them—with a group of people selected by the executive, on the bases of technical expertise and administrative competence, and approved by the Senate. Examples include Anatel, for telecommunications; Aneel, for electric energy; and ANP, for petroleum. These "regulators" have a mandate to protect them from undue political pressures. They must act in the interest of the public and the consumer, who are also present in consultative councils. They control the seriousness, the efficiency, and the universalization of the services in order to attend to all sectors of society, and not only those who are best integrated. As such, in privatizing and giving concessions for public services, the state, no longer in a bureaucratic way but now with new personnel, continues to be present in its social and regulatory function. This same approach will extend to other sectors of the society, such as transportation, in the near future.

With regard to government action in social policy—education, health, housing, and so on—as I have already said, the goal of the reforms is to break clientelism and bureaucratism. For example: in education, a parent-teacher association will control funds distributed directly to the schools. Or, as already noted, the distribution of FGTS resources for sanitation and civil construction will be under the generic control of the Ministry of Labor and under the specific control of councils in which the opposition, unionists, beneficiaries, the Church, and other social actors must be present.

Obviously, all this involves a series of processes. It is not merely a question of the "political will" of the federal government. We must improve the quality of management at the three levels of government (federal, state, and municipal), and must have communities that participate more actively in the decision-making process. All this requires time, learning, and organization. But the direction is already traced out.

The Brazilian state, with the characteristics presented, has a history of centralization, of attention to "big players," and of inefficiency. The efforts to change that we are undertaking work in a direction contrary to this tradition. Unfortunately, the tradition is already being defended with tenacity by some political sectors that claim to be progressive.

Thus, for example, the big financial agents of the government (the Banco do Brasil, the Caixa Econômica, BNDES, and Banco do Nordeste are among the principals), without ceasing to finance large projects and big capital, began to finance small- and medium-sized businesses, small-scale rural producers, and even, through the "bank of the people," the informal sector.

To give only one example: the Banco do Brasil and the Banco do Nordeste handle the resources of the Pronaf—which was created by the present government—that is intended to provide agricultural financing to small family production units. It began with thirty thousand contracts in 1995, and reached more than five hundred thousand last year. This is a rotating credit program, like a credit card, whose interest rates (of 6.5 percent with an inflation of 4 percent, or 2.5 percent per year) are only charged on the amount disbursed, for loans of close to 5,000 *reais*.

The reform of the state also requires a reform of management. In place of bureaucratic management, we seek a somewhat more professional management. This requires training of the bureaucracy, the possibility of state careers based on merit, flexibility in the forms of payment, and performance criteria. In certain cases of proven ineptitude, there will be a possibility of firings—the "rupture of stability"—not with the purpose of downsizing (for in truth we will have to increase the number of functionaries and provide better remuneration in the future), but to maintain the idea that the functionary is a public servant. In this context, the objective is to obtain results that universalize public access to government services, in education, in health, and so on, and at the same time create in the public bureaucracy a spirit of meritocracy—which indisputably exists in many sectors—and not of privilege.

It would be an error and a profound injustice to judge the entire past and the entire bureaucracy as mistaken, incompetent, and lazy with relation to public objectives and the social responsibility of the state. While there are sectors that require such a severe judgment, it is not to correct this that the reforms are being undertaken. The reforms are designed to put the state in harmony with time, to let it coexist with a more informed society, which increasingly wants accountability in government. To let it coexist with a more dynamic and entrepreneurial economy, which requires a more competent state to support it and orient it. And to let it coexist with a citizenry that is more active and feels greater solidarity, that wants not only to enjoy the exercise of its rights, but also to find public spaces where it can exercise its duties. It is for this that the government is taking up the task of democratizing the state, through the whole of the reforms alluded to and through many more actions in addition to these, that are already in course or have been planned.

At this point, the question may be asked: Who does a reformed state serve? I recall my footnote, which distinguished the state from government. Despite the formalism implicit in this distinction, I do not imagine that the transformations in process will change the pattern of current domination. But I do believe that, in mass democratic societies, such as Brazilian society increasingly is, the old interventionist and patrimonial state has become an uncomfortable fit.

It is certain that in the old state, midlevel actors, including the civil-military bureaucracy, accommodated themselves and took advantage of the state. From there, we can consider the mechanisms of appropriating resources and advantages that served a certain type of enterprise, not only state-owned, but also private, national, or foreign firms associated with state-owned enterprises or with the state structure. There existed a mechanism of privilege for specific social categories not directly linked to capital. It suffices to look at the abuses and privileges, ideologically transformed into "rights," in social security or in health.

Also, it is certain that even the old state pattern opened itself to the presence of disfavored groups, as for example, in the case of rural social security. So from there, the proposed reforms and the path of implementation became constituted interests. It not being possible to generalize privileges or "rights," given the fiscal crisis, new participants were blocked from entering the state distribution machinery. Particularism was defended even by some unions that, in theory, should be defenders of the public interest, of the generalization of services to the marginalized popular sectors.

With reform, the guiding principle of the state becomes the universalization of access. Priority is placed on basic education, health (not only curative and hospital services, but also preventive care) with a criteria of basic minimum assistance, and the elaboration of retirement rules based on the contribution and not on the unequal repartition of the cake for the benefit of those who possess special retirement plans.

In this sense, state reform provides incentives for the formal rationalization of the public machinery and criteria of open competition to the detriment of powerful bureaucratic registries. Above all, it is a democratizing movement to establish the state as a presence in a society that—while it has millions of socially excluded citizens—no longer tolerates the existence of social exclusion.

Another question, of a different nature, is to know where a reformist government can find support when it looks to accelerate democratizing transformations and finds political difficulty in obtaining, if not the support, at least the understanding of the so-called progressive sectors. For these sectors, the horizon for progress is often delineated in the past, when Labour, for example, nationalized the mines, China launched the Cultural Revolution, and the Soviet Union transformed bureaucratic oppression into a working class virtue.

From all of this comes my support for reforms that, with time, will cause political signals to cease functioning in a distorted manner, and will make it possible to accelerate state reforms with greater support. Then, we may further celebrate democratization and better social attention to those who most need it.

NOTES

1. Luiz C. Bresser Pereira, *A Reforma do Estado dos anos 90: Lógica e mecanismo de controle* (Brasília: Ministério da Administração e da Reforma de Estado, 1997).

2. In this article, I will refer, at times, to the state and government as if they were one and the same, as in the Anglo-Saxon literature. Nonetheless, in precise terms, government is the set of institutions, mechanisms, and people that exercise power, whereas the state refers to the institutions and mechanisms that assure domination. Through the adoption of specific policies, governments can impose different directions on the apparatus of the state. The state reflects in a more lasting manner the class interests of the organized segments of society that give form to the structure of social and political control.

3. Samuel Beer, "Liberalism Rediscovered," *The Economist*, 7 February 1998, 23.

⇥ 17 ⇤

Farewell to the Senate

We have seen the task of transition through to its end. Looking back at the obstacles we have overcome, we can say to ourselves and to the country, without boasting, but with satisfaction: mission accomplished. But this is not the time for congratulations. It is time to think about the future. To sketch out, with the ruler and the compass of democracy, the kind of country we want to build for our children and grandchildren. And it is time to put hands to this task, to shrink the gap between dream and reality.

In my mind, the path to the desired future requires us to settle the score with the past. I firmly believe that we have turned the page on authoritarianism in the history of Brazil. It remains, however, a piece of our political past that stalls us and retards the advance of society. I am referring to the legacy of the Vargas era, to its model of autarkic development and an interventionist state. That model, which in its era assured progress and enabled our industrialization, began to lose vigor at the end of the 1970s. We crossed the decade of the 1980s blindly, without perceiving that the specific problems that were tormenting us—the hangover from the oil price shocks and the foreign interest rates, the decadence of the authoritarian regime, hyperinflation—were simply symptoms that masked the structural exhaustion of Vargas's model of development.

At the end of the "Lost Decade," the more lucid political and economic analysts, of the most diverse persuasions, were converging on the belief that Brazil was experiencing not only a collection of discrete crises, but also the end of a long-term cycle of development. They sensed that the complexity of the existing productive stock

Excerpt from Fernando Henrique Cardoso, "Despedida do Senado," farewell address to the Brazilian Senate by the president-elect, Brasília, December 14, 1994. From the web site: <www.planalto.gov.br/secom/colecao/desped.htm>. Last accessed: December 2000.

precluded a deepening of industrialization through import substitution. The pattern of protectionism and statist intervention was suffocating competitiveness, reducing economic efficiency, and leaving Brazil ever farther behind in the flow of technological and managerial innovations that were revolutionizing the world economy. A new cycle of development would necessarily place on the agenda the reform of the state and the insertion of the country into the international economy. What was lacking was the transposition of this agenda from specialized intellectual forums into the national political arena. This change began to happen in the government of Itamar Franco. Unfortunately, it happened in a messy manner, in a political environment polluted by an atmosphere of folly.

I am preparing myself to assume the presidency, not with a Messianic attitude of one who imagines himself the bearer of some unprecedented mission. I do it, rather, as a proud follower of the work of President Itamar Franco. I will propose an agenda of change that is now ripe and that is largely familiar to the political powers. Allow me, senators, to speak once again of the fundamental points of this agenda, underlining those for which a partnership between the presidency and the Congress will be indispensable for the successful change.

MACROECONOMIC STABILITY

The first point is the continuity and deepening of the process of economic stabilization, not as an end in itself, but as a condition for sustained economic growth and for the amelioration of the social divide. My government, recognizing the massive manifestation of popular support for the Real Plan, is absolutely committed to the preservation of the national currency and to economic stability. This modernization agenda has nothing in common with the old developmentalist project based on heavy state intervention, whether through expenditure or official regulation.

The performance of the economy since the implementation of the *real* has exposed the fallacy of the "recessive plan," which held that the fiscal austerity necessary to control inflation is contrary to growth. Continued economic growth will require investment rates above 20 percent of the GDP, such as we had in the 1970s. Confidence in the country's economic stability and the construction of an institutional framework that permits private initiative to take full advantage of its creative talents will be the foundations of an increase in investment, especially investment in infrastructure. This institutional framework will emphasize the growing autonomy of the Central Bank as the guardian of a stable currency.

The installation of a true economic and social democracy will mean that state action must become more effective for the majorities that have not or cannot be organized: consumers, tax payers, and above all the poor and the economically excluded. For this reason, it is necessary to rescue the state from pillage by corporatist "strategic interests" who seek privileges that distort the distribution of profits. The return of growth and the reduction of the social divide point to a decisive attack on those public expenditures that exist only to support corporatist arrangements.

The deepening of the stabilization program also demands that we further de-index the economy. The future government will have to rise to this task, without tricks or confiscations, but with caution and with determination.

Another error exposed in reality was the idea that stabilization would require a "social squeeze," that is, would have high social costs. In reality, in place of the squeeze, what we see since the implementation of the *real* is a noticeable recuperation of the average wage and consumption among the poorest social strata. In plain language: the people are eating more. They are better clothed. They are consuming in a way that was impossible before due to the corrosion of salaries through the inflation tax.

Faced with this, it is amazing that trade unionists and politicians that claim to defend the interests of workers did not have anything better to propose, at this time, than a return to complete monthly indexing. As if the merry-go-round of prices and wages had not already proven to be useless in defending the purchasing power of wage earners!

THE OPENING OF THE ECONOMY

At this point, stabilization policy crosses with another item on the agenda for a new model of development. This is to move ahead with the opening of the Brazilian economy—including, as appropriate, the financial and service sectors—and their integration into the global market.

In 1990, when commercial opening was gaining velocity, with the abolition of many nontariff barriers to trade and the beginning of the timetable for the reduction of import tariffs, there were many who predicted a "meltdown" of national industry. In place of this, what we have seen is proof of the vitality of our industrial stock. Despite high inflation rates, which made recourse to bank credit practically unfeasible, industries of all types and sizes responded to the challenge of openness with enormous vigor. They restructured; they sought out modern technology and management; they succeeded in improving their productivity and product quality. A good indicator of this dynamism is the nearly five hundred Brazilian enterprises that hold the international quality certification ISO 9000. But the crucial indicator, obviously, is the performance of exports. Exports have increased more than 14 percent in the past three years, and they are closing 1994 with an annual growth rate of 13 percent.

The commitments that Brazil has just made at the intergovernmental Summit of the Americas in Miami, project a hemispheric free trade zone in 2005. That is, in ten years from now. Mercosul will function as a customs union starting on January 1. And the cooperation agreements among South American countries, the Latin American Free Trade Association (LAFTA, or ALCSA), are rapidly being defined. Integration into the global market suggests we will maintain our increasing rate of external sales.

From here on, however, our motto must be clear: export more to import more. We will not export to continue producing gigantic commercial balances and to accumulate reserves on the order of the 43 billion dollars we have deposited in international banks. Export to import: that is the rule that must preside over the new cycle of growth. Import capital equipment and capital inputs to accelerate the modernization and expansion of industry, of agriculture, and of domestic services. Import consumer goods, yes, maintaining moderate tariff protection such that domestic prices approximate world prices, and so that the gains in productivity that have already occurred and will occur get transferred to the whole of society. It is in this way that growth and income distribution are mutually reinforcing in mature capitalist economies.

In this perspective, the government must be attentive in order not to commit the performance of exports and production to the domestic market by an artificial appreciation of the *real*. It must also be attentive—indeed, it must be well prepared—to react promptly to attempts at dumping and other illicit commercial practices in imports. We are prepared to push forward the necessary technological development in our industries, and we will finance it with interest rates approximating international rates. But in no case will the government cede to pressures that would result in a return to protectionism, through reindexation of exchange and an equally artificial devaluation of the *real*. The dollar must not return as an index of domestic prices.

Therefore, we will maintain and improve the competitiveness of our exports, but remain consistent with the politics of stabilization and with a strategy of economic openness. We will do this through these measures that, on the one hand, allow new gains in productivity to firms, and, on the other hand, improve the systemic efficiency of the economy, reducing the so-called "Brazil tax" (*"custo Brazil"*).[1] This covers a wide range of measures, from the elimination of taxes that hinder exports, to the improvement of roadways, transportation, and the ports, whose poor state makes domestic production more costly. This brings us to two other fundamental items in the reform agenda.

A NEW STATE-MARKET RELATIONSHIP

One of these concerns is the new relations between the state and the productive private sector. In the cycle of development that is being initiated, the dynamic locus of production passes decidedly from the state sector to the private sector. I have repeated this to the point of exhaustion, but it does no harm to insist: this does not mean that the action of the state ceases to be relevant to economic development. It will remain fundamental, but its nature will change. The state-as-direct producer passes to the back burner. Enter the regulatory state. Not a regulatory state spreading rules and special favors to everyone left and right, but one that creates an institutional framework that assures the full efficacy in the system of relative prices, creating incentives for private investment in productive capacity. Rather than substituting for the market, a general principle of regulation will be guaranteeing the efficiency of the market.

Cheap labor and abundant raw materials will cease to be relevant comparative advantages in the world market. What makes the difference today is efficient links between production and commercialization. It is essential that Brazil offer its domestic industry conditions similar to those of our foreign competitors. For this reason, we must undertake a revision of our tax system and the rules regarding the capital and labor markets.

The opening of the economy implies the elimination of anachronistic restrictions on foreign investment, and requires clear rules for the movement of capital into and out of the country. We will also have to go a long way toward dismantling old regulations that gave official protection to certain sectors. The removal of these wasteful inefficiencies of the old model will increase enormously the global efficiency of the Brazilian economy. It will reduce costs to firms. It will reduce the costs of economic policy for the government itself, as it is today overburdened with subsidies and the administration of its regulatory paraphernalia. And it will translate into lower final prices, both for the domestic consumer and for exports.

Alongside this, with the control of inflation, the financial system will be able to return to its basic function of capturing domestic and foreign savings, and efficiently channeling these funds into financing for productive activities. The measures to reduce the "Brazil tax" must be accompanied by a decline of domestic interest rates to levels that approximate international rates. All this must be done without losing sight of the central objective: the reaffirmation of the industrial vocation and technological base of the Brazilian economy.

ECONOMIC AND SOCIAL INFRASTRUCTURE

The fourth point that I would like to emphasize is the composition of the economic and social infrastructure for the new model of development.

In this age of global competition, the most successful countries accumulate two types of assets that are characterized by low international mobility and that figure heavily in calculation of comparative advantage. First, physical infrastructure in energy, transportation, and telecommunications and second, that which is called, inappropriately in my opinion, "human capital."

Brazil's investments in economic infrastructure, aside from enabling a reduction in costs and a growth in production for the domestic market, must still take into account the expansion of external commerce. A part of these investments will be financed by the state. For this, the recuperation of public savings is essential. However, partnership with private initiative will have a decisive role. The process of privatization must be accelerated and extended to other activities and firms in the sectors of energy, transportation, telecommunications, and mining.

Keeping in mind the essential criteria of transparency and adequate valuation of public assets, the very conception of privatization must be broadened. There are several different modalities of privatization that the future government will see adopted, within the parameters defined by the Congress, and monitored by the Congress.

These will include: the sale of firms with direct or indirect control of shares by the federal government; the sale of minority shareholdings; the sale of frozen assets; the concession of public services, including the responsibility for new investments; administrative service contracts with private firms; and outsourcing of activities.

I have no doubt that the advance of privatization will improve the overall efficiency of the economy, as long as it is accompanied by—and I will be attentive to this—the strengthening of the public authority with regulatory and fiscal functions in each sector. Today, those government bodies charged with controlling the state-owned enterprises control them. In truth, the state-owned enterprises and their "controlling" agencies are in a gray zone, where neither the logic of good business management nor the logic of the public interest reigns. Both wind up being overrun by political mismanagement, by spurious concessions to private interests, and by corporate "capture." It is necessary to separate these two domains—the public authority and the private firm—in order to strengthen both of them. We must give each autonomy of management within the clear boundaries of social welfare. This is as important for private enterprises as for those that remain state-owned. But we will not allow ourselves to be excited by theoretical considerations about the intervention of the state in the economy. The immediate reason to advance with privatization does not have to do only with administrative efficiency. It is also of a fiscal nature.

To be sure, privatization is partly about reducing the public debt, so that the recovery of "public savings" not be eliminated by the cost of previous "dissavings," that is, by the payment of interest. As an inheritance of the fiscal indiscipline of recent years, the Federal Treasury is burdened with over 200 billion *reais* in direct or indirect liabilities. The senators know well the difficulties of the states. The balancing of these megaliabilities will come through, among other measures, the sale of assets from the federal government and from the states.

The governments must divide with private capital the necessary investments in economic infrastructure. Using a conservative estimate of economic growth, Brazil must invest 20 billion *reais* per year for the next four years, so that bottlenecks do not arise in the supply of energy, transportation, and telecommunications. The public sector will not be able to finance this volume of investments on its own. And, in the new model of development, it has other priorities to which it should dedicate the windfall resulting from fiscal improvements. I am referring to social policy.

Partnership with private initiative in the economic infrastructure opens space for the state to invest more in other necessary areas: in health, education, culture, and security. In sum, such a partnership will enable Brazil to invest more in its people, which is the greatest strategic asset of a country. A task which, in our case, comes together with the moral imperative to incorporate into the development process the millions who are marginalized and living in misery.

In the social arena also, there is a gray zone between the public and the private. It is the gray zone of clientelism and corruption, where so many resources and good intentions have already been diverted. For this reason, partnership with the community is fundamental for the success of social policies. Not because the community can substitute for the action of the market, but because it is indispensable for giving efficiency to this action. The community can point out the correct priorities, monitor the application of resources, and participate directly in the implementation of them.

NGOs—nongovernmental organizations—have already proven their value in the defense of the cause. Rather than seeing them as threats to the sovereignty of the state, we must learn to consider them "neogovernmental organizations." They should be viewed as innovative ways of linking the state and civil society and, for this reason, their accounts should be available for public scrutiny. Why not deepen this NGO experience, and engage them broadly in the fight against poverty? Why not recognize that, in partnership with the state, they are an agent of the new sustainable development model, as much from an ethical as an ecological point of view?

The very state itself has to reorganize to embrace this partnership. The principle of reorganization is already a given: it is decentralization. We wrote in the constitution that it is up to the municipalities to execute public services in the local interest. What remains is applying the principle. Decentralization means partnership with the community. This will be the guiding principle of the actions of the future government in universalizing access to health services and high quality instruction in our schools. They are also general principles of the Community Solidarity Program, in which I hope to see the diversion of resources give place to articulate action on the part of the different ministries, states, municipalities, and NGOs in the areas where there is a high concentration of poverty.

Summing up, I believe in the following: macroeconomic stability based on fiscal and monetary discipline, with the continuation of the Real Plan; integration of the Brazilian economy into the world market; a preponderance of private initiative in the business sector, accompanied by the reinforcement of the regulatory instruments of the state; and the constitution of a modern economic and social infrastructure through new forms of partnership between the state, businesses, and communities. These are, in my understanding, the fundamental points of the reform agenda that we have before us, so that the reemergence of growth in the last two years in fact may be the beginning of a new long-term cycle.

BRAZIL IS IN A HURRY

A president of the Republic—even though he may only be the president-elect—should not venture far in the analysis of political risks, at least not in public. There is a tendency for mere conjectures, mere "plausible scenarios," to make headlines the next day, as if they were the announcement of some consummate disaster. That said, if I could break this rule one more time, before submitting myself to the rigors of the presidential liturgy, I would say that the largest risk that we run today in Brazil is the risk of success.

It happens that a succession of positive results—the victory over inflation, the return of growth, the free and fair elections, and even our fourth World Cup victory—all this has led the country to breathe a sigh of relief and to begin regaining confidence. This in itself is ideal. The danger is that society's relief causes us to lower our guard when faced with persistent problems. And they are not trivial problems. I will dispense with another walk through the horrors of the social reality that the senators know all too well and that they have anguished over as much as I have. The return of economic growth in itself is not going to change this reality; we must be clear on that. What will become of the millions of illiterate and semiliterate adults who are unemployable in industry, in services, and even in modern agriculture? Will their children at least have a hope for a better life?

The very stabilization of the economy, and with it the opportunity for sustained growth, is not guaranteed. The Social Emergency Fund, which is the fiscal basis of the stabilization, is a transitory arrangement. As everyone knows, it will remain in effect until December 1995. If it is not substituted with permanent measures, the precarious fiscal balance—the "controlled imbalance," as Minister Sérgio Cutollo called the accounts of the Social Security fund—will give place to an uncontrolled imbalance in January 1996.

I have never stopped repeating that the Real Plan is only the first step in a larger set of changes. It is a bridge to the necessary structural reforms that we lost the opportunity to put in place this year. Pardon me if I state the obvious: it is not a strong currency that makes the country; it is the country that makes the strong currency.

Brazil is in a hurry, and we, its elected leaders, have a window of time—a short window of time—to put in place measures that guarantee the continuation of stability and prepare the ground for a new cycle of development. The people, who today are attempting reconciliation with their governing power, will judge us harshly tomorrow if they suffer further disillusionment.

THE CONSTITUTIONAL AGENDA

I know that a large part of the responsibility for the conduct of reforms in the next four years will come down to me, as the head of government. While the reform agenda is not mine, insofar as I was not the one who invented it, it was I who came out in defense of it in the presidential contest. The results, then, will be first ascribed to me.

In the spirit of presidential rule, I will solicit discussion, with the Congress, of the legislative measures necessary to get the reforms on track. True to my parliamentary origins, I intend to take on this role in a democratic manner, with a scrupulous respect for the sovereignty of the legislative body, but also with enormous determination.

I propose that we start over from where we stopped in constitutional revision, by the removal, from the 1988 constitution, of the ties that bind the Brazilian state to the old model, and of some improprieties that we constituents added on our own account. In this matter, I have no cards up my sleeve. Despite the disappointing results, the process of revision served to put on the bargaining table the alternatives for every relevant subject. At this point, introducing new ideas matters less than finding the political will necessary to deliberate. I have dedicated myself to this since I was elected, and even before, in the search for alliances that would give a broader coalition and greater partisan strength to my candidacy.

In February, I will send to Congress a combination of amendments that were suggestions presented for revision by President Itamar Franco, and alternatives discussed in the context of the Congress on Constitutional Revision. Allow me to anticipate here the idea behind some of the proposed reforms, beginning with the two questions that in my mind are preeminent: fiscal reform and economic order.

The fiscal regime of the constitution of 1988 is economically inefficient, socially unjust, and intrinsically deficitary. The itinerary for the correction of these distortions includes looking at the mechanisms of the tax system, the division of competencies between the federal government, the states, and the municipalities, the federal budget, and security.

Tax Reform

The tax reform demanded by the country does not have as its objective the increase in the nominal tax burden, but the facility of tax collection, the efficiency of the economy, and social equity. This reform does not only involve changes in the constitution. Much can and must be done also through statutory law and Senate resolutions. Beyond that, it demands a cooperative attitude on the part of the states, which are responsible for the most important tax in the country in terms of revenue volume, the ICMS.

With a view toward the efficiency and the competitiveness of the economy, it will be indispensable, for example, to diminish the burden on productive investment and exports. With views toward employment and social justice, we will have to reduce taxes on payrolls and on the basic goods basket. With a view towards the diminution of the cost of tax collection and fighting tax evasion, we have to eliminate some taxes and integrate the national tax collection mechanism with that of the states and municipalities.

To find an equilibrium point between the different reform proposals is difficult, but I do not believe that it is impossible. Some alternatives discussed during the constitutional revision advanced a great deal in this sense. My intention is to put one of these, or a combination of them, to the Congress, as a base from which to take up the discussion once again. It will be much wiser, once the tax system we want is designed, to make a gradual transition, evaluating the effect of the changes at every step, and correcting eventual errors in projection on the behavior of tax collection. But we know that it is much more difficult and slower to correct errors in the constitution than in ordinary law. The ideal in this matter, as in many others, will be to tighten the constitutional text, leaving the details of the tax system to statutory and ordinary law.

Sharing Tax Revenue

Tax reform should not alter the distribution of revenues between the Union, the states, and the municipalities. The return to the previous centralism of the 1988 constitution is out of question. The constituents opted, correctly in my view, for the financial and administrative decentralization of the Brazilian state. It is now a matter of making this choice consequential. Rather than reconcentrating resources, we will look for a more balanced division of revenues.

I mentioned before that the general principle of decentralization is already written in the constitution. The Union should exclusively exercise the function of coordination and for actions of a purely national character. States and municipalities should provide the services of local and regional interest, including financial management.

This rule, which appears simple and logical in general, runs into enormous difficulties when we make the distribution of revenues concrete. This is due in the first place to the ambiguities of the constitution, and we can now eliminate these ambiguities. But there are difficulties that do not come from the constitution, which are the social and political realities. They have to do with the enormous heterogeneity of Brazil on the one hand, and with clientelism on the other, which thrives on the discretionary distribution of federal monies. Clientelism is almost a closed page in Brazilian politics. It may survive as a local reality, but I do not believe that it has the strength to continue setting the tone of federal relations. In this matter, the budget investigators have already done an autopsy on the politics of clientelism.

As to the economic and social heterogeneity of the country, this is truly present and must be taken into account for decentralization. For example, many municipalities—perhaps the majority—are ready to assume fully the management of basic health and education services. They only need transparent criteria and fixed timetables for the transfer of state and federal resources. Others, especially small municipalities in the poorest areas, may still need a more direct presence on the part of the state and the federal government. The constitution should, therefore, clearly identify decentralization as a principle, reserving a necessary margin such that the transfer of resources also take into account the specific situations of the municipalities and the states.

Truth in Budgeting

In the area of federal budgets, the big problem is the inflexibility of expenditures. Along with augmenting the automatic transfers of resources to the states and municipalities, the 1988 constitution created or embraced so many limitations on fiscal revenues, that it practically eliminated the freedom of the federal executive and the Congress to define priorities for public spending. As minister of the treasury (*Fazenda*), I experienced—and shared with the Congress—the anguish of trying to harmonize the most legitimate social demands within the strictest margin left by these restrictions and other expenditures that could not be compromised, such as spending on personnel and social security. It was an experience I would not wish on my worst enemy.

We could continue to flee from the problem by letting expenses shrink through inflation. The price we would pay, though, would be to sacrifice our power to controlling inflation. To face up to the problem implies making the public budget more flexible, eliminating from the constitution the excessive earmarks on receipts, and at the same time reinforcing the instruments that are adequate for the programming of expenses foreseen in the constitution: the multiannual investment plan, the law of budgetary directives, and the annual budget.

Reform of Social Security

Finally, among the fiscal concerns, there is the question of Social Security. I will spare the senators the diagnostic with which they are already familiar. I will pass directly to the fundamental realization: Our pension system suffers from a serious structural imbalance. The relationship between contributors and beneficiaries, which today is barely two to one, will decrease even more in the coming years.

If the current rules are retained, there is a probability of growing deficits, even assuming an improvement in structural factors such as economic activity, the efficiency of administration in the system, and the fight against fraud and tax evasion. As the Treasury must cover these deficits, the imbalance in the pension accounts is transmitted directly to the federal budget.

There is no way to conceive of a permanently balanced budget in these conditions. Nor is there a way to think about a real increase in the minimum wage, since the value of pension benefits is linked to it. It is possible to loosen this knot by improving revenues. But I do not see how to untie it without touching the distortions that the system shelters by way of the distribution of benefits.

The exclusive use of the single criteria of time employed—a case practically unique in the world—created a social and financial distortion that will deepen exponentially in the coming years, such that when people are retiring younger, but have an increased life expectancy. It will be indispensable to change the retirement criteria to a formula that combines time in service with a minimum age. While it is obvious, I wish to state the caveat that these changes will in no way affect current retirees, whose acquired rights will be protected. And yet, we should have a transitional rule that safeguards the expectations of rights, including a consideration of the time that would be necessary for the worker to retire by the current rules.

The correction of distortions cannot stop there. What authority would we have to shift the general rule of retirement by time employed, without touching the special pensions of civil servants, magistrates, legislators, and professors? Early retirement or multiple pensions, thanks to the reciprocal or simultaneous counting of time employed, have resulted in pensions constituting a growing share of federal personnel expenses. This, alas, explains in large measure the paradox that the spending with increased personnel, as the salary of the majority of active employees, remains low. Thus, the reform should be completed by the installation of a truly universal public pension system, with the guarantee that the benefits ceiling be compatible with self-financing over the long term. This will create an incentive for a complementary pension system, be it public or private.

I know that the question is thorny. Yet it is preferable to tackle it now, while it is still possible to conceive of ways of changing the system, that also preserve the rights that people have acquired and have come to expect. To cross our arms in the face of difficulty would signify, in fact, our complicity in the implosion of the system.

Foreign Capital

Moving from fiscal questions to economic order, I would like to underline two themes: foreign capital and state monopolies. The 1988 constitution went against the flow of history in relation to foreign capital. While governments throughout the world, including the socialist world, were trying to attract capital as an important development input, we placed unprecedented restrictions on its presence in the Brazilian economy.

It is notable that the majority of constituents, on the left and on the right, basically responded to the same antiquated vision according to which foreign capital was either an obstacle to national development or operated through trusts as an economic predator. By an irony of history, the criticism of this vision was rapidly generalized, beginning with the promulgation of the new constitution.

I believe that the moment has come to finish with these unfitting restrictions, to look again at the mechanisms that impede foreign capital from undertaking the mass of investments necessary to stimulate the energy, electricity, and mining sectors. We should eliminate the discriminatory distinction, which is more rhetorical than practical, between "Brazilian firm" and "Brazilian firm with Brazilian capital."

State Monopolies

The same vision that inspired discrimination against foreign capital resulted in writing into the constitution a state monopoly on petroleum, which had been in effect in common law since 1954, and extending it to telecommunications and to local natural gas services. It was justified in the name of the national "strategic interests," as if private exploration were an open door to antinational subversion. State monopoly, however, runs a different risk: that of being an umbrella of corporate privileges, of spurious associations with private interests, and an obstacle to the realization of the necessary investments in infrastructure and vital sectors of the economy. I defend the flexibilization of state monopolies, to permit partnerships with private concerns and private investments in the expansion of these areas.

The agenda of modernizing the country, as I understand it, must include other constitutional themes: the rights and obligations of civil servants; the relations between work and union organization; and the organization of the judicial power.

Last but not least, modernization includes political reform, and notably electoral reform. Circulating in the Senate is a bill I authored, which seeks to harmonize the constitutional principle of proportionality with the introduction of a single-member district vote, along lines similar to the German system. This project, I am pleased to recall, was approved by the Commission on Constitutionality and Justice.

I limit myself to flagging these subjects, Mr. President, due to the limitations of time. I will not neglect them. In the message I will bring to Congress in February, I will make explicit my proposals for a constitutional amendment on this matter.

REFORM WITH CONTINUITY

I conclude with a few observations on a question that seems crucial to me: that of our political direction. The amplitude of possible changes by constitutional amendment is less than in a revision by absolute majority in a unicameral session. I would look favorably on formulas that allow the Congress to accelerate the passage of the amendments, so long as this does not, however, raise a paralyzing controversy over procedure that could act to the detriment of a possible consensus over the tenor of the proposals.

Even recognizing the difficulties, I think that we should not restrain the order of the day beforehand. It is better to be ambitious at the outset, so that society and the political forces have a complete vision of where they want to arrive. And have a clear idea of the priority of the proposals, so that, if it were the case, they might distribute their time to their deliberations and not clutter the agenda of the Congress.

I insist that Brazil is in a hurry and has a small window for getting change underway. May haste not lead us, however, to run amok over either the juridical order or those that legitimately oppose a particular point of the reforms. A constitution is neither made nor changed with a steamroller, but through dialogue. It is or should be the expression of the deepest-held values of the nation; not the unilateral will of transitory majorities. For this very reason, all the discussion of constitutional amendments should have as a backdrop a concern with returning the constitution to its natural state as a document of general and permanent rules.

The detail in the 1988 constitution had the undesired effect of depoliticizing questions and sending excessive numbers of decisions to the courts. Matters more properly part of legislative action or a governmental program, once frozen in the constitution, remain excluded from the normal political process. This has terrible consequences, particularly in fiscal matters. What happens when the rigidity of constitutional norms comes up against the peaks and valleys of finance?

Judges should decide in accordance with the law. To make and adapt laws to the conditions of the country is the task of elected officials. When this possibility is negated by the constitution, we all end up, judges and elected officials alike, in the same dilemma, a "Sophie's choice," between juridical order and fiscal discipline. Constitutional rigidity worsens the inherent risk in the change of complex norms, like those relative to the tax system. For these reasons, to deconstitutionalize everything that it is possible to deconstitutionalize should be the basic criteria of the discussion of the constitutional amendments.

May the patient search for consensus not signify, however, giving up the obligation to decide. For there to be a true dialogue, and not mere obstruction shrouded in flowery rhetoric, it is necessary that the majority articulate what it wants, while respecting the minority. Brazil is in a hurry, not for miracles, but to feel that it is on the right track and that it is moving forward.

It is to the future president and to the majority of the Congress to blaze that trail and take the consequential measures, without undue haste, but with decision. I always said that the stabilization of the economy was a process of continuous actions.

It has nothing to do with halting inflation "in one fell swoop." It is also thus that I face up to the agenda of national structural reforms. I see it as a continuous process, less a one-hundred-meter dash than a truly profound test that demands as much vigor as enthusiasm.

Brazil needs change and Brazil needs continuity. Continuity in its change, and change within its continuity.

NOTE

1. "Custo Brasil" can best be described as the "cost of doing business in Brazil," and is not a tax as such. In common parlance, a "Brazil tax" may better capture the idea than the more directly equivalent "Brazil cost."

→ 18 ←

Inaugural Speech

I belong to a generation that grew up captivated by the dream of a Brazil that would be at once democratic, developed, free, and just. This dream comes from long ago. It comes from the heroes of independence. It comes from the abolitionists. It comes from the revolutionary lieutenants of the Old Republic. I saw this dream shine in the eyes of my father, Leônidas Cardoso, one of the generals of the "Our oil is ours" campaign, as it had once shone in the eyes of my grandfather, an abolitionist and republican at the end of the empire. For students like I, who placed all our enthusiasm in these struggles, petroleum and industrialization were the ticket to the modern postwar world. They assured a place for Brazil on the train of technological progress, which was accelerating and threatening to leave us behind.

For a time, during the presidency of Juscelino Kubitschek, the future appeared ready to accept us. We were developing. Brazil was industrializing rapidly. Our democracy was functioning, despite some setbacks. And there were opportunities for social improvement. But history takes turns that confound us. The "golden years" of Kubitschek ended in inflation and high political tension. Somber years followed, in which we first experienced growth, but at the expense of liberty. We could speak of progress, but only for the few. But it was all of us who suffered the inheritance of an external debt that melted the economy and an inflation that aggravated social wounds in the 1980s.

I myself saw my sons give birth to my grandsons, dreaming of and struggling for a day in which development, liberty, and justice would go hand in hand in this country. I never doubted that this day would arrive. But I never thought that day would find me in the position that I assume today, elected by the majority of my

Adapted from Fernando Henrique Cardoso, "Discurso de Posse," delivered in Brasília, January 1, 1995. Located at: <www.planalto.gov.br/secom/colecao/discurs.htm>. Last accessed: December 2000.

compatriots to blaze the path to the Brazil of our dreams. With humility, but also with absolute conviction, I say: This country will move forward together! We will recover that which must be the most precious possession of a people: its liberty. We will turn the page of authoritarianism that, under different names and different forms, tainted our Republic from its very beginnings. We will regain confidence in our development. Today, there is no serious specialist who predicts for Brazil anything other than a long period of growth. International conditions are favorable. The burden of foreign debt no longer suffocates us.

Our business owners have innovated, have rebuilt their factories and offices, and have overcome great difficulties. Brazilian workers have confronted the rigors of arbitration and the recession and have lived up to the challenges of new technologies. They have reorganized their unions to be able, as they are today, to stand up for their rights and their piece of a growing economic pie. The time has come to grow and to flourish. And most important: Today we know what our government needs to do to sustain economic growth. And we will do it. Indeed, we are already doing it.

The absolute majority of Brazilians have opted for the continuation of the Real Plan, and for the structural reforms necessary to banish, once and for all, the specter of inflation. As president, I will dedicate myself to this task with all my energy, counting on the support of Congress, the states, and all the vital forces of the nation.

We have returned to liberty, and we will have development. What remains is social justice. And this is the great challenge for Brazil at the end of the century. This will be the number one objective of my government. Joaquim Nabuco, the great spokesman of abolitionism, thought of himself and his companions as acting on behalf of a "mandate of the black race." A mandate that was not given by the slaves, since they did not have the means to assert their rights, but that the abolitionists themselves adopted, feeling in their hearts the horrors of slavery and understanding that its shackles and chains kept the whole country economically, socially, and politically backward. Similarly, we are horrified to see our compatriots at our sides as though they were not Brazilian, to see human beings subjugated by hunger, suffering, ignorance, and violence. This cannot continue!

As with abolitionism, the movement for reform that I represent opposes nobody. It does not wish to divide the nation. It wished to unite it and to look toward a better tomorrow for everyone. But, unlike Nabuco, I am well aware that my mandate comes from the free votes of my compatriots. From the majority of them, independent of their social condition. I think of the following in particular: a great number of the excluded; the most humble Brazilians who paid the price of inflation, without a way to defend themselves; those who are humiliated in lines at hospitals and at *Previdência*; those who earn little, but who give a great deal to this country, in factories, in fields, in stores, in offices, in the streets and on the sidewalks, in hospitals and schools, and in all forms of labor; and those who cry out for justice because they do indeed have the conscience and the character to struggle for their rights. It is in large part to these people that I owe my election.

I will govern for all. But should it be necessary to end the privileges of the few to give justice to the vast majority of Brazilians, let no one doubt: I will be on the side of the majority. With serenity, as is my fashion, but also with firmness. Searching always for the path of dialogue and persuasion, but without ever abdicating the responsibility to make decisions. I know that the majority of Brazilians do not await miracles, but do expect results from their government every day. This is because Brazilians have come to believe in Brazil again, and are anxious to see it improve every day.

We also note with satisfaction that interest in Brazil is increasing in other countries. Our efforts to consolidate democracy, adjust our economy, and attack our social problems are accompanied by very positive expectations overseas. One can perceive today why our transition was slower, and often more difficult than those of other countries. It is because it was the broadest and the deepest. In one transition, we restored our democratic liberties and initiated a reform of our economy. We thus constructed a solid base from which to move ahead. We have the support of society to effect change. Society knows what it wants and where we need to go.

At the speed of the communications age, as we open the Brazilian economy, we leave behind xenophobic attitudes that were more an effect than a cause of our relative closure in the past. None of this implies renouncing even the smallest fraction of our sovereignty, nor neglecting the means to protect it. As commander in chief of our armed forces, I will be attentive to our need for modernization, so that we may attain operational levels consistent with the strategic stature and the international commitments of Brazil. In this sense, I will confer new duties upon the general staff of the armed forces, along with those already established. And I will forward proposals, based on studies to be realized in conjunction with the navy, the army, and the air force, gradually to adapt our defense forces to the demands of the future.

In the post–Cold War world, the importance of countries such as Brazil does not depend only on military or strategic factors. Rather, it depends on internal political stability, on general welfare, on the vital signs of the economy, on the capacity to grow and create jobs, on the technological base, on participation in international commerce, and also on diplomatic proposals that are clear, objective, and viable.

For these reasons, the realization of a consistent national development project must strengthen us on the international scene. The time is right for Brazil to participate more actively in this context. We have an identity and we have permanent values that we must continue to express in our foreign affairs. Continuity means trustworthiness in the international community. However much drastic changes may satisfy our short-term interests, they will not allow us to construct the image of a responsible state if divorced from a long-term vision. We must not, above all, be afraid to innovate when our interests and values demand it.

In a phase of radical transformation, marked by the redefinition of the rules of political and economic interdependence between countries, we cannot simply turn our backs to the course of history. We must be attentive to it in order to influence the design of the new order. It is time, after all, to change our discourse and our external action to reflect the times, taking into account the changes of the international system and our new consensus with regard to our objectives. It is time to debate openly what Brazil's profile should be as a sovereign nation in this transforming world. This debate should include the chancellery, the Congress, the academy, unions, business, and nongovernmental organizations.

We will rid ourselves of the old ideological dilemmas and the old forms of confrontation, and will confront those themes which are the source of cooperation and conflict among countries: human rights and democracy, the environment and sustainable development, the great tasks of multilateralism and the challenges of regionalization, the rejuvenation of international commerce and the elimination of protectionism and unilateralism. Other central themes we must consider are access to technology, nonproliferation efforts, and combating international crime.

We will take full advantage of our global presence, both politically and economically. This presence will allow us to deepen our regional integration efforts, beginning with Mercosul, but also with regards to a united Europe, NAFTA, and the Asia-Pacific region. And we will continue to identify new areas for potential cooperation, such as with postapartheid South Africa. None of this will interfere with our traditional relations with the African continent, or with countries such as China, Russia, and India, which by virtue of their continental sizes are faced with problems similar to our own in their efforts to promote economic and social development. I believe that Brazil will be one of the most successful countries of the next century. I am convinced that the only obstacles that stand in our way are the problems of inequality between our regions and our social groups.

We know that the development of a country is not measured by what it produces. True development is measured by the quality of attention that a country gives to its people and to its culture. In a world of instantaneous global communication where peoples fragment and specialize, cultural identity is rooted in nations. We Brazilians are a people of great cultural homogeneity. Our regionalisms are variations of a basic culture, born from a combination of occidental-Portuguese tradition with African and Indian traditions. Our intellectuals, our artists, and all those who transmit our culture are genuine expressions of our people. I want to provide the conditions that will help us construct our citizenship. Because citizenship, apart from being an individual's right, is also the pride of being part of a country that has its own values and style.

The priorities I proposed to the electorate, and which a majority approved, are those that directly affect people's quality of life: employment, health, security, education, and food production. The creation of jobs will come with the return of growth, but not automatically. The government will thus initiate programs and take specific actions to ensure it occurs. It will accept that the challenge is to make it succeed throughout Brazil, not only in this region or that region, and that the challenge to reduce and ultimately eliminate our inequalities is a challenge not solely put to the disadvantaged.

Access to hospitals, respect in medical treatment, elimination of unnecessary waiting, and combating waste and fraud are as indispensable elements of health care management as adequate resources. Health issues must be confronted and my government will thus promote not only curative medicine, but also preventive medicine. A modern vision of health includes basic hygiene and sanitation, mass vaccination programs, adequate nutrition, and physical fitness for all.

Schools need to return to the center of the teaching process. School is not only the function of the professor and the recuperation of his salary, especially in primary education. It is much more. It is a community space, where national actions, social solidarity, and the participation of student and teacher converge to form citizens. As we cross the threshold of the new millennium, we must recognize that we can no longer live with pervasive illiteracy or functional illiteracy. It is a sad illusion that the mere consumption of trinkets will make us "modern," if our children continue moving through school without absorbing even the most minimal, indispensable knowledge to live in a modern society. It does not suffice to build schools fit for kings, and afterwards to fill them with poorly paid and poorly prepared teachers, together with unmotivated students who are without the physical or psychological materials necessary to gain from them.

To fulfill our promise to end misery, it will also be necessary to end spiritual misery. Modern modes of communication will help us in this endeavor. Alongside the news and entertainment, we will engage in a veritable national crusade for educational television, beginning with a strong push for literacy and cultural programming.

The priorities of the people will also be the priorities of the government. This will demand a substantial reorganization of the governmental machinery. The administration has deteriorated after years of disorder and belt-tightening. Clientelism, corporatism, and corruption claim taxpayer money before it arrives to those who should benefit from the government's social action. The Itamar Franco government began cleaning up this parasitic corruption in the last two years.

It will be necessary to go into many hornets' nests to end the fatigue and make the structural reforms necessary to create efficiency in the civil service. This does not frighten me. I know that I will have the support of the majority of the people. Including those functionaries who have a love for public service. The most important support one can give is not to the government, nor to the president. It is the support we are capable of giving to one another as Brazilians, and the support we can give to Brazil. This social revolution will only happen with the support of society.

The government has a fundamental duty, and I will do my best to discharge that duty. However, without congressional approval of constitutional reforms and legislative actions, some of which I outlined in my *Farewell Speech to the Senate*, and without a mobilization of public opinion, good intentions will amount to little more than words. We need to put together new forms of participation to cope with the seriousness of the process of change.

A fundamental part of this consciousness, of this revindication of the citizenry, and this mobilization, will depend on modes of mass communication. Our means of mass communication were fundamental in redemocratization, and have been essential in restoring morality to public life. Now they have a central role to play in mobilizing support for a just and fair society, while maintaining their critical independence and a passion for truth in information.

When Brazilians are better informed, when they can be more critical of public policies than of the folklore of daily life, and when they can put events in perspective and can acquire an ability to act coherently, rather than simply profess their intentions, then they are better prepared for the practice of citizenship. This collective support for the country is moved by a sentiment, and this sentiment has a name: solidarity. It lets us break free from the small circles of our own particular interests and help our neighbor, our colleague, or our compatriot, near or far. We, Brazilians, are a solidary people. Departing from this sentiment, we will form a national civic machine, uniting government and community to erase hunger and misery from the map of Brazil. We will assure decent lives for our children, getting them off the streets and, above all, putting a stop to the shameful massacres of children and young people. We will assure this with energy directed from equal to equal. To women, who are the majority of our people and whom the country owes opportunities in education and in the workplace. To our racial minorities and to our quasi majorities, namely to blacks, who hope that equality will become not just a word, but also a reality. To indigenous groups, some of who are living testaments of human archeology, and all of who are testaments to our diversity. We will make of our solidarity the basis of a citizenry in search of equality. And our hope of seeing a Brazil that is free, prosperous, and just will beat ever stronger, with ever more certainty, in the breast of every Brazilian.

➹ 19 ➷

New Approaches to Development in Latin America

B razilians have a family tree with Portuguese roots and Spanish branches, sprinkled with *mestizo* blood, and have always had a feeling of respect and admiration
for Spain. Every time I arrive in Rodrigo, coming from Portugal, or in Tuy, looking
for Santiago de Compostela, I get chills when I see in the secular stones the strong
mark of the Spanish walls, and when I can divine in the voluntarist design of these
cities the soul of a proud people that built civilizations.

I will never forget the pages of the great Brazilian writer, Sérgio Buarque de
Holanda, who compared Spanish and Portuguese colonization in America. In an admirable chapter of *Roots of Brazil* (*Raízes do Brasil*), he describes the Spanish colonial
city. The city obeyed a rigid architectonic design, whereas the Portuguese city spread
out lazily, following the flavor of the local geography. There is an enormous difference
between the "Plaza Mayor," from which point the roads spread outward geometrically,
and the "Paço Municipal" (with its prison on the side, of course) nested on the first el-
evation it came across and circled in a disorderly manner by alleys without a plan.

I have noticed this difference from having worked closely with José Medina
Echevarría, one of the most eminent Spanish sociologists of the generation that survived the difficult years of the civil war. Exiled in Chile, as I was, Medina was many
years my senior. We worked together at ECLA, at the United Nations headquarters
in Santiago.[1] His European (German-Spanish) background was so strong that the
contradictions of populism did not disturb him, nor did the cultural disorientation
of peoples who, in order to have an identity, begin by negating what they are and im-
itating what they are not, as we have done in Latin America.

Excerpted from Fernando Henrique Cardoso, "Alternativas Econômicas para a América Latina," presented
at the seminar, "Nuevos escenários y nuevas políticas para Ibero-América," Salamanca, Spain, July 20,
1990, and published in *As Idéias e seu lugar*, 2nd ed. (Aumentada, Petrópolis: Vozes, 1993), 227–244. Used
with permission of the publisher.

It is in this spirit, that of an Ibero-American, that I hope to present in this seminar some doubts and some alternatives for a Latin American economy faced with a world that once again appears new. So let us begin there, with the idea of a New World.

THE NEW WORLD

Latin Americans, who until the last generation had learned to consider ourselves a part of the New World, felt a shock in the 1980s: Had we not become antiquated? Had a New World not arisen at our sides, or even before us, without us even having a notion about it?

The feeling that we always had of belonging to the "new," in contrast to "old world" Europe or to the tired, old United States, was so ingrained in us that the very idea of economic development seemed to be our property. What is more, some countries of Ibero-America appeared to be the concrete expression of the impetus of growth that only the "young nations" possess. A recent study by Angus Maddison, comparing the five major OECD economies with the five major developing economies (USSR, China, India, Mexico, and Brazil), shows that the greatest performance in terms of GDP growth between 1970 and 1987 was Brazil's at 4.4 percent per year. Even taking into account a more rigorous indicator, such as growth per capita, Brazil's was second at 2.1 percent per year, barely outpaced by Japan's 2.7 percent per year. What was it, then, that changed in the 1980s? Why did a country like Brazil cease to be "new," compared to, say, Italy or Germany?

I am perhaps leaving aside the fundamental issue here: the technological gap. This works today as the "School of Sagres" worked, through discoveries. After the compass, improved cartography, and the new technology of ships capable of crossing oceans, what were outmoded galleys worth? Today, what is the value of an abundance of natural resources, or labor (however cheap it may be) after the advent of the information age, of microelectronics and biogenetics?

But alas, it was not the Portuguese, nor even the Italians with their curiosities, nor the Spanish with their Salamancas who most benefited from their technical inventions and conquests. The Dutch, for example, knew how to "be new" in the sixteenth and (especially) the seventeenth centuries, without having been the precursors, inventors, or discoverers of novelties. Rather, Dutch society "adapted itself" to the age. Was Protestantism capable of absorbing the rational pragmatism of Portuguese and Spanish Jews that permitted this modernization? Perhaps. But the fact is that the House of Orange plus the commercial companies, and not the Inquisition or the Cross, made Holland the splendor of Flanders. In commerce, in reason, and only secondarily in war were they the leaders of the New World. It was not what the Iberians planted in Latin America, but what Europeans did in Europe, with their triumphant capitalism, that created "modernity" and gave us the Golden Age of civilization, followed by the Enlightenment.

The "new" today is not "development." And it is not thought that scientific invention and technological patenting, in themselves, can build a new civilization. What is new is the combination between "organizations" (rationalization, as it were), public and individual liberties, and greater equality. It was this miraculous formula that turned "old" Europe into the hope of the future. Is it not perhaps this same sentiment that, here in post-Franco Spain (which buried and exorcised the nefarious "long live death," whose meaningful public repulsion came right here in Salamanca from the mouth of Unamuno), renews that hope? Was it not Spanish ability—the iron will and determination to reach its goal—that linked Spain to the EEC, that maintained respect for liberties, and that moved the country in the direction of greater social justice? Was it not this that makes us look at Madrid not as a capital of Castille, but as a pillar of an eventual "Hispanic-American world"? And did not even Portugal, though more modest in its economic dimensions, accept the challenge and throw itself into the competition of the Common Market, to once again board the ship of progress? One need only travel through the agrarian province of Minho, which is accommodating itself to industrial civilization almost in the mode of a putting-out system, to perceive that there pulses "another development." This is not only about growing economically and letting the trickle-down effect throw crumbs to the poor. In the fusion of organization, liberty, and social justice, the motor of the future is not only accumulation and the class struggle generated by it. There is a "new spirit" in all of this.

It was Warner Sombart, perhaps even more than Max Weber, who anticipated the vision of this "new spirit." Weber, stuck in his dialogue with Marx, did not break with the iron logic of capitalism generated by Marx's brilliant vision. He did not seek to invert it, but gave more weight to the competent "organizers" of capitalism than to its brutal exploitation. Sombart, on the other hand, underlined the essential. Let us say with a certain liberty, that it is not merely exploration (which becomes increasingly irrelevant with the successive technological revolutions) that matters, but a spirit of adventure combined with a method.

This "method"—science made into technology and the enterprise made into the international organization—is not a dogma. It comes from Descartes, and was tempered by Pascal (among others), who made it routine even for believers to have an anguishing doubt about the world. And "adventure," as distinguished from the "unknown" in the Age of Discovery, is a mental anticipation of stages to be conquered.

As in the period of great discoveries, all this requires courage and boldness. But it is no longer the individual courage of a leader that is required. The modern *Unternehmer*[2] is a social force rooted in the various levels of society, shared as a collective will, that requires motivation and new and always mutable objectives. The "new" spirit of capitalism is, however, this mixture of entrepreneurial spirit with scientific knowledge and with collective propositions of welfare.

The accumulation of capital is a condition for all of this. However, the accumulation does not occur automatically, that is, through a direct exploitation of the labor force that benefits individual capitalists. Contemporary capitalism presupposes a "specific socialization" that turns mere accumulation into a part of a broader civilizing process. This requires universities, rationalized (and not only nationalized) states, a bureaucracy dominated by political aims outside of business, and a societal will for liberty and social justice.

THE "NEW" GLOBAL SCENARIO

To put it in simple and direct terms, the basis of these transformations has to do with the exponential growth of productive forces and with the outcomes of the class struggle. Increases in productivity generated exceptional surpluses that could be channeled, through taxes and social policies, to social development, impeding the growing impoverishment of the masses.

In a postwar Europe faced with the challenge of communism, we saw in several countries the adoption of a type of "social democracy" that benefited wage earners and laborers. Enormous public budgets, a Keynesian vision that did not fear deficits, and the increasing power of unions and leftist parties saw the successive revolutions in production as instruments equally favorable to the accumulation of wealth and to the reduction of social inequalities.

In the United States and Japan (each of which has its own characteristics, even without the social-democratic élan), postwar politics was also "welfarist," albeit circumscribed compared to Western Europe. To such a point did the capitalist world embrace the idea of a social welfare state that in the last decade we underwent a sort of "ideological regression." This consisted of reiterating the values of the free market economy and reducing the power of the state to collect taxes. Capitalists feared that political will had shifted away from the demands of accumulation necessary to continue economic growth.

This tendency was most clearly expressed by the Reagan and Thatcher governments. However, in practice the notion of a "new capitalism" was already so culturally ingrained that even the United States continued sustaining a public deficit, which was in no way orthodox. Social policies, including unemployment protection, public housing, and resources for health and education, also remained in effect even in the England of Margaret Thatcher, despite the antistate and privatization rhetoric. Everywhere, the government continued supporting economic growth and social welfare. Meanwhile, the technological revolution made the globalization of the economy possible. Especially important were the changes brought on by the information revolution; these included faster and more secure means of communication, including transportation of people and merchandise, as well as messages.

Since the 1960s, and increasingly in the last twenty years, there has also been a decentralization of industrial production through multinational enterprises, as there has been an enormous, and consequential, increase in global commerce. This has grown at a rate two or three points higher than GDP growth. Alongside this, a massive revolution, affecting the whole network of production and services (from finances to telex, to fax, to satellite communications, and so on), created new sources of power and resources, permitting the decentralization of production and services while guaranteeing unified controls.

The result of this whole process (abstracting here from the strictly political questions) was the formation of institutional frameworks that established the contours of globalization. Among these were common markets, and bilateral and multilateral accords. These consequently gave rise to fears of a future marked by "customs fortresses," in which tariffs were substituted for nontariff accords in market protection. It is precisely against this that developing countries are now fighting as they look to strengthen the GATT in the Uruguay Round.

Paradoxically, these facts gave rise to the ideological notion that the contemporary world is moving towards a reaffirmation of the market and of liberalism. In truth, negotiations are conducted politically by governments, economic alliances weld together the interests of oligopolies in production and distribution, and these are ramified on a global scale. This has created a new system of "spontaneous prospective planning," which does not contradict the values of individual liberty mentioned above because they do not preclude the options of investment and consumption.

It is certain that the policies that gave rise to the "conquering bourgeoisie," and that in the nineteenth century integrated people into nation-states, are slowly being substituted by other more dynamic ones. The individual entrepreneur, the tycoon or *Unternehmer*, are now archaeological relics vis-à-vis the board of directors. On the one hand, there are corporate bureaucracies and the amalgamation between science and productive organization; on the other, the "mother company" and the network of its affiliates, which can include family businesses, or individual high-tech businesses. The diplomat, the typical representative of the "politics of power" and the national state, is weakened, giving way to direct action by negotiators and producers that act in the framework of agreements negotiated by governments at the technopolitical level.

This "New World" appears to have permitted the rise of localist forces, of national and cultural values such as language and religion, alongside the globalization of the economic means of production. The new conception of the firm and of production, including the idea of spontaneous global planning, permits not only more individual initiatives, but also more public space for the exercise of traditional cultural values. It is this challenge that perturbs Eastern Europe and Communist Asia, as much as Latin America and the countries of the Third World.

It does not fit in this speech to discuss the vicissitudes created in this situation by the Soviet Union, China, and the other countries with centrally planned economies. It hardly fits to say that this new phase of "Western capitalism," globalization of the economy with controlled dispersion, associated with practices of creativity and liberty, put an end to the bureaucratic conceptions of central planning in socialist economies. The technological superiority that served to support the potential of capitalist enterprise productivity, and that is not foreign to the question of liberty and individual initiative, has become evident.

Faced with this, some currents of opinion see in the disengagement of the Eastern and Soviet economies the resurgence of capitalism, the market, and nineteenth-century liberalism. If this were to become the case, the socialist countries would have lost the train of history once again. What they are lacking is not "capital" in the technical sense, and not individual appropriation of the means of production. More importantly, they are lacking an "entrepreneurial culture" (*cultura de empresa*), which involves discipline in work as well as an appetite for risk and competition. Specifically, they are lacking the new notion of "spontaneous planning," which does not substitute the market for the bureaucracy, but makes of the market a calibrator of the impulses of entrepreneurial groups.

It is through the market, through the reaction of other producers and of consumers, that enterprises dispose of instruments to evaluate their decisions. The "motor" of this system is competition, which leads enterprises to growing technological development and makes them dependent on it in order to profit. For this reason, the bureaucratization of the economy as well as its oligopolization—which results from a lack of countervailing public interest to preserve the functioning of the market—have fatal consequences for economic growth and the maintenance of welfare in a society. The "new" in the contemporary world consists in having transformed creativity—technological and organizational innovation—into routine as much in the enterprise as in society. And all this in a climate of liberty.

THE LATIN AMERICAN PANORAMA

While the world faced the alternatives brought by the globalization of the economy, Latin America, starting in the 1980s, has struggled with economic stagnation, foreign debt, and inflation. To be sure, the leaders of Latin American economies exaggerated in persisting with external loans, thanks to the abundance of Eurodollars and acceptable rates. The Asian countries that entered into the process of economic internationalization (the Asian NICs[3]) were more prudent with respect to the capture of financial resources in foreign markets, and applied bolder politics to correct for social inequalities, including, in some cases, land reform, and in all countries, a relative increase in wages.

When they already had worrisome signals in the international financial market, before the Black September of 1982, when Mexico declared a moratorium on its debt payments, the Latin American NICs continued to indebt themselves. They did nothing significant, however, to improve the quality of life for their citizens. It is important not to forget that the great leap (the "miracle," as it was called, which exaggerates the industrial and export power of these countries) of the Latin American economies in the 1970s occurred under the aegis of military authoritarian regimes. At that time, it was believed that a fundamental requirement for Latin America to enter modernity would be an alliance between local capital, the state, and multinational corporations.[4]

It is still possible that that strategy for economic growth was the most adequate to assure that the "new capitalism" did not asphyxiate in state corporatism, in protectionism, and in the idea of maintaining the economies in autarkic conditions of production. But the reality that resulted was a heavy debt burden, and an export orientation based more on the necessity to produce surpluses in the trade balance to pay the debt (with a contraction of imports) than the idea of a new global economy. It was, therefore, the reinforcement of protectionism to safeguard the foreign enterprises already installed. It was a social immobilism and the disproportionate weight of the oligopolies sustained by official policies.

In other words, industrial growth in Latin America followed the path opposed to that which characterized the new amalgamation of contemporary capitalism. With this, Latin America marked time, while Asia, or at least significant parts of Asia, assumed the entrepreneurial culture of the new age. It was only in comparison to Africa that Latin America came out looking good. In truth, the picture is even worse than this description makes one believe. The very perspective of "economic development" adopted in Latin America maintained an essentially "Rostowian" view of the stages of growth. Latin America was not embarrassed—in official circles—to even speak of "blessed pollution" when it came to attracting the "dirty industries" of the First World. With such a lack of perspective, it is no surprise that the alternative for competition that most prospered in recent decades has been traditional: realize the potential of the comparative advantages offered by natural resources, which were believed to be abundant, and the use of cheap labor.

At the moment in which contemporary capitalism was winning in the central countries, the new dimensions already referred to could only lead to tragic consequences. The greatest tragedy consists precisely in that the massive exploitation of labor was accepted as a pillar of economic growth and the degradation of the environment as a factor of progress.

Hopes were created by the Brandt Report, which illustrated a Keynesian vision on a global scale, valuing the consumption of the poor to sustain the production of the rich. It happens that, despite this, the contemporary economy can do without considerations of poverty. It needs investment and consumption, but from producers, not from the masses of the poor. In the vision of Keynes and Brandt, on the global scale, the poor (with the help of the rich) would cease to be poor, transforming themselves into consumers. As such, the rich, in helping them, would be helping themselves, creating the basis for global prosperity.

But the prosperity of the rich does not follow this path. Africa can suffer from famine without creating a "demand crisis" in Europe, and the same is said about Latin America with relation to the U.S. economy. Once it was recognized that this perspective was not realistic, only two options were left to First World thinkers who wished sincerely to rescue the developing countries: to criticize the international aid organizations, demanding more of the same style of development with a touch of moral solidarity (as in the case of the Brundtland Report), or to threaten "ecological catastrophe" and imagine preservationist alternatives for the poor countries, financed by the rich.

If, however, we wish to adjoin realism to goodwill, it will not be in this way that Latin America finds alternatives for its development. Accepting, in the interest of time, that there is a minimum of homogeneity in Latin America and that the solutions found by the continent's relatively larger countries can serve for the rest (or can, at least, create favorable conditions for them), I would say that Latin America will need to find a solution for four or five fundamental, interconnected problems:

- the foreign debt
- the fiscal and organizational crisis of the state, and states' inflationary tendencies
- technological capacity building and an increase in competitiveness
- the domestic distribution of income
- realizing an educational and social revolution

All this must be seen from a perspective quite different from that which marked the "golden years" of economic development on the basis of import substitution. In effect, for that proposition, the fundamental and sufficient ingredients for the "take-off into economic development" included: protectionist barriers; the building of a state capable of dynamizing the economy (and, therefore, capable of savings and investment); the formation of a domestic market as a catalyst of economic growth; and the belief in nationalism as a pillar of the national interest. If this, added to a certain distributionalism forced by corporations and regulated by the state, did not produce general social welfare, it did give roots to an entrepreneurial class, and provided access to the "urban-industrial" civilization to large numbers of the middle class, as well as to a more limited number of the working class.

In contemporary conditions, the dichotomy between domestic and foreign markets is losing strength, and the dynamic character of exports is being recognized as part of a country's development. The state, faced with an enormous fiscal crisis, is ceding space to private initiatives; the search for competitive niches for local production at the international level is becoming decisive for prosperity, and thus, so is technological training. At the same time, the clamor for greater social justice has replaced the nationalist fervor of the past.

I will not suggest at this time formulas or panaceas for any of the items that I listed above. But I cannot fail to refer, in passing, to some of these, since they constitute problems to be resolved in the search for an economic alternative.

On the question of the debt, two comments. First, it is necessary to know that a good part of the debt is due to the accounting for unpaid "variable interest" as a debit. Starting with, let us suppose, a loan of some 100 million dollars at an interest rate of 7 percent per annum, a fluctuation of the international rate of interest that raises rates to 15 percent per year (and indeed even 21 percent), makes it obvious that real investment will have enormous difficulties in amortizing the debt. The debt comes due without a counterpart in real investment. That, for the whole group of loans, debilitates the country's capacity to pay. So, by the calculations of the Banco Central do Brasil, of a debt of approximately 70 billion dollars to private banks, nearly 25 billion are accounting debts: they refer to interest on interest and the fluctuation of the interest rate, without reflecting resources invested in the economy.

Second, as the debt was "nationalized," private borrowers deposited in local currency the amount corresponding to the repayments to honor their debts. The state, which does not directly produce foreign exchange, except when it is the owner of export industries, needs to do two things to pay the debts: induce trade balance surpluses and produce local currency to buy the foreign exchange. The former implies policies that not only encourage exports, but also slow imports, and with them part of development. As the state could not surpass certain limits in the collection of taxes (and since, for other reasons, the state is bled by those who live at its expense, that is enterprises—private and public—or the bureaucracy) it ended up indebting itself internally in order to be able to pay the debt, even though the country held reserves. The foreign debt and the fiscal crisis of the state are linked as if by an umbilical cord. As a corollary, any economic alternative for Latin America must face these two problems, and how they interact. Mexico and Chile—and now Venezuela—renegotiated their debt and took advantage of the notion (which is more accepted today in international finance) of debt relief. In the case of Chile, as the state is the proprietor of copper, perhaps an adequate reduction of the debt service could permit the relief necessary for a return to growth. In Mexico, despite the advantages that integration into the Northern Hemisphere offered it, and even with the reduction of the debt, the chronic problems of imbalance in the public accounts will continue to devastate the country. It is quite true that the government succeeded in a sort of internal pact that cleared the horizon. It will have facilitated (and this logic holds for Venezuela) the challenge of reestablishing public finance to take up growth with more controlled inflation.

As I have already mentioned inflation, it is obvious from the perspective that I have adopted that the policies characteristic of the International Monetary Fund (IMF), of the "control the monetary base—squeeze social spending—balance the budget" genre, are insufficient. These do not deal with the principal question, which is the interconnected domestic and foreign indebtedness of the state. Moreover, they propose the impossible: that the debt be paid and, at the same time, that the budget be balanced.

These ponderings should not be understood to mean, however, that I dismiss the need for profound fiscal and tax reform, which are all the more necessary and more difficult in countries organized as federations, which have provinces with autonomy in public expenditure. Nor should one think that I consider the control of inflation unimportant. I only insist that this be done by reestablishing capacities for taxation, savings, and state investment (thus imposing conditions on foreign and domestic creditors for the payment of the debt) lest all our efforts be like those of Sisyphus.

In this panorama, the alternatives of economic development of Latin America should not count on the support of foreign capital as a decisive factor for the return of growth. Foreign capital will come in small proportion, in the measure in which the countries begin resolving their internal problems. This is because the international financial system has better alternatives and is fearful of investing in development, and because the negotiation of the foreign debt, if done justly, will augment the bad will of the banks.

This does not mean that Latin American countries can forego foreign investment. However, they will have to look for it through official international credit and through joint ventures that transfer technology in key areas in which every country can be competitive. As such, the formulation of a competent and serious policy of industrial and technological development is indispensable.

And at this point the logic becomes circular. If the states of Latin America do not get out of the fiscal crisis in which they find themselves, and if they do not reorganize themselves, they will have neither the political nor the social capacity to define and implement effective policies of economic growth, be it agricultural or industrial.

In other words, the alternatives for a new surge of economic growth on the continent depends on the definition of directions of the domestic politics of the countries that permit the cleaning up of their finances and the stabilization of the state. No longer should the state substitute for civil society, but rather it should permit a better articulation of the latter. By "better articulation," I mean two things: that the local entrepreneur finds conditions and incentives to invest and that governments sustain income policies that begin to overturn the current hyperconcentration of wealth. None of this will be done, I repeat, without an educational revolution and without welfare policies that lead to greater equality—which supports liberty—as well as to higher levels of technical competence and social organization.

We are, thus, in Latin America, in a paradoxical situation: In order to grow economically, countries first need political conditions, with a better organized state, which is not clientelistic and which is capable of social commitment. The growth, which will be propitious for better domestic living standards no longer, will be understood, as in the past, as having become "inward-oriented." It will be oriented as much by the domestic market as by international competition. However, in order to reach this level, a hard politics of renegotiation of the debt will be necessary, and this will probably arouse negative reaction in those sectors that always insist on valuing the foreign market: bankers and international investors.

If the pieces of the puzzle were easy to fit together, neither politics nor talent would be necessary. For this, the difficulties, which are many, for the return of economic development and for the entry of Latin America into modernity should not discourage us, but stimulate us. We have the lessons of "old" Europe, which renewed itself in thirty years. Latin American countries, instead of insisting on Rostow's "stages," should understand that they can make leaps. If they perceive that in order to be modern and competitive they need better domestic organization (of an entrepreneurial nature) as much in the state as in civil society, greater technological training, better education, a better distribution of income, and above all, that they need liberty for all of this to occur, they will greet the new millennium with a chance to succeed. Vamos apostar e torcer. Com muito compromisso.

NOTES

1. ECLA, the United Nations Economic Commission for Latin America, is more commonly known by its Spanish acronym, CEPAL, the Comisión Económica para America Latina.

2. Literally, "undertaker," meaning the person or force that undertakes to complete a task or achieve an end. Here, Cardoso refers to the anonymity of the social forces that propel social change.

3. NICs; newly industrialized countries.

4. See Cardoso and Enzo Faletto, *Dependency and Development in Latin America* (Los Angeles: University of California Press, 1979), and Peter Evans, *Dependent Development: the Alliance of Multinational, State and Local Capital in Brazil* (Princeton, N.J.: Princeton University Press, 1979).

⇥ 20 ⇤

Globalization and Politics

Globalization has become a sort of fashionable buzzword: Quite often said; seldom with the same meaning. It is in fact one of those far-reaching concepts that are used by different people to explain facts that are of a completely different nature. Even when qualified as "economic," globalization can still be associated with a variety of phenomena.

Possibly the first notion one relates to economic globalization is that of the ever-growing expansion of transborder financial flows and their impact upon the monetary and exchange policies of national economies. The effects of the financial dimension of globalization are somewhat disputed. If the mobility of capital flows across borders can be seen as an efficient way to allocate resources worldwide and to channel them to developing countries, their volatility and their possible use for speculative attacks against currencies are thought to pose new threats to the economic stability of countries. In other words, the virtually free movement of huge capital flows creates both opportunities and risks.

Another aspect is the globalization of production and the ensuing expansion of world trade flows. In the past, as a general rule, all stages in the production of any specific good were usually conducted in one country, and that good was either locally consumed or exported. This is no longer true. The domestic contents of most goods has diminished, and intermediate production stages now take place in different countries. Final products, specifically technology intensive ones, can hardly be considered to be fully "Made in" a given country. This is the result of the interplay of several new trends, including reduction in the costs of the mobility of

Adapted from Fernando Henrique Cardoso, "Social Consequences of Globalization: Marginalization or Improvement," a lecture at Indian International Center, New Delhi, January 27, 1996. Original available at: <www.planalto.gov.br/secom/colecao/globa.htm>. Last accessed: December 2000.

production factors and the economies of scale required by increasingly sophisticated production processes.

International trade of intermediate goods is conducted primarily among industrial units of the same company. Corporations frequently structure their activities to fit marketing and production strategies designed to enhance their global or regional competitive position. Countries are selected for investment by those companies on the basis of the overall advantages they present. This has led to increased competition for foreign investment among countries, particularly developing ones. As opposed to the sixties and even the seventies, when controls and restrictions were deemed necessary to discipline the operations by transnationals in their markets, developing countries have been reformulating their trade and economic policies, in part to offer an attractive domestic environment for foreign investment, which is needed to complement their generally insufficient rate of domestic savings.

Another dimension of economic globalization is thus a growing uniformity in the institutional and regulatory framework in all countries. For the globalization of production to take place, rules in different countries need to be made similar, so that no "artificial" advantages prevail in any of them. Examples of these rules are the introduction in the World Trade Organization of international standards for intellectual property rights and trade related aspects of investment measures. Matters that were once considered to fall primarily within the domestic jurisdiction of each State are now subject to multilateral disciplines. Naturally, there are limits to such uniformity, due to national differences. The interplay of global trends toward uniformity and national identities is a complex one.

Finally, economic globalization is linked to a revolution in production patterns leading to a significant shift in the comparative advantages of nations. The competitive position of a country relative to others is determined more and more by the quality of its human resources, by knowledge, by science and technology applied to production methods. Abundant labor and raw materials are less and less a comparative advantage, to the extent that they represent a diminishing share of the value added in virtually all products. This irreversible trend makes it unlikely for countries in the South to succeed solely on relatively cheap labor and on natural resources.

THE STATE AND POLITICS

Hand in hand with economic globalization goes a change in the role of the State. Globalization means that external variables have an increased bearing on the domestic agendas, narrowing the scope for national choices. I have already mentioned that requirements for external competitiveness have led to greater homogeneity of the institutional and regulatory frameworks of States, that these requirements have left less room for widely differentiated national strategies with regard to labor, macro-economic policy. Fiscal balance, for instance, has become a new dogma. The Maastricht Treaty of the European Union sets limits within the budget deficit of its members.

Both international public opinion and market behavior have also come to play a role in redefining the range of possible action by States. Information flows freely and rapidly. If, for example, the news is disclosed that any particular country is having difficulties controlling its budget deficit or is going to hike its interest rates, world financial markets make decisions based on that information which will have an impact on the country concerned. Countries, their leaders, and the policies they are pursuing are under the close scrutiny of the world public opinion. Any misdeed or step judged by these immaterial entities to be in the wrong direction may exact penalties. Conversely, developments or decisions construed to be positive are rewarded. International public opinion and above all markets tend to be conservative, to follow a certain orthodoxy in economic matters. They establish a pattern of economic conduct that admits of little variation in a world of immense variety of national realities. The complex process of adjustment must not ignore such diversity.

Globalization has changed the role of the State in another dimension. It has completely shifted the emphasis of government action, now almost exclusively laid on making the overall national economy develop and sustain conditions for competitiveness on a global scale. This does not necessarily mean a leaner State, though that too is quite often a desirable side-effect of this shift of emphasis, but it certainly calls for a State that intervenes less and better; a State which is capable of mobilizing its scarce resources to attain selected priorities; a State which is able to direct its investment to areas which are key to enhancing the country's competitive position, such as infrastructure and basic public services including better education and health-care; a State which is prepared to transfer to private hands companies which may be better managed by them; a State, finally, in which civil servants rise to the demands of society for better services.

And all this has to be made at a time when democratic values and a strengthened civil society compound the demands for change. This transformation of the State must also be conducted within an economic context of fiscal discipline and austerity in public spending, in which the State has fewer financial resources.

This is no easy task. It requires a change of attitude and a determination to fight against vested interests in the public sector. But there is no alternative. In the case of Brazil, we have, in a nutshell, to rebuild the State if we are to stand any chance of managing successfully the transition from an inward-oriented development model to one in which our economy becomes integrated into the world trade and investment flows.

It may seem paradoxical that this reshaping of the State in no way conflicts with traditional ideals of the Left (and I am proud to be a founder and member of the Party that represents Social Democracy in Brazil). By reallocating its resources and its priorities to education and health in a country with sharp social contrast such as Brazil, the new State will be contributing to something it failed to do in the past: to promote equal opportunity at a time when qualification and education are a pre-requisite not only for finding a job, but also for increasing the degree of social mobility.

Today, more than ever, long-cherished goals of the Left may be attained in conjunction with and because of our efforts to enhance national capabilities with a view to participating competitively in the world economy. In addition, this transformed State needs to be stronger in the discharge of its social duties and better prepared to regulate and control the newly privatized activities.

The difficulties of this process of transition in the role of the State are felt everywhere and cannot be underestimated. The reform of the social security system in France and the hard negotiations for the approval of the U.S. budget are illustrations of the obstacles governments must overcome, basically because there are no immediate and clear-cut answers to the challenge of transition. Abandoning the traditional practices of the welfare State does not imply putting aside the need for better living standards for our peoples.

POLITICAL IMPLICATIONS

From what I have said so far, one may be under the impression that the globalization process would respond only to market forces. From the perspective of both the allocation of financial resources and decisions concerning productive investment, the market is really a decisive factor. But we should avoid the mistake of drawing, from this fact, misleading conclusions.

The first such misleading conclusion would be to consider that seeing globalization as the result of market forces alone would exhaust the debate on the matter. This is not true. The framework within which the market operates is politically defined. The power game among nations is not absent. Neither is the possibility of economic co-operation among States. Foreign trade negotiations are still conducted through dialogue among States in foray created by them, in particular those concerning the definition of the rules in which competition occurs. Economic clout is a key factor in these negotiations, as well as in the settlement of bilateral trade disputes. In some cases, economic powers invoke their influence to circumvent the very multilateral disciplines they themselves have proposed. Subsidies in agriculture clearly illustrate this trend. On the other hand, the recent movements towards the creation of schemes of regional integration, which are a characteristic of the nineties, are also initiatives with which governments have tried to influence the direction of economic globalization.

The second dangerous conclusion would be to transform the market into a form of ideology, according to which everything that falls into line with market forces is good, positive, brings development, whereas every political decision meant to regulate competition forces is viewed as negative.

It is precisely the recognition that there are "limits" to the market that enables us, developing countries, to act politically in defense of our national interests. But the forms of such action, of regulating the globalization process, vary among different developing countries. Whether or not we want it, economic globalization implies a new international order. We must accept this with a sense of realism lest our actions be devoid of any effective impact. This does not imply political inertia, but a whole new perspective of how to act on the international stage.

We must also accept our differences. The South is not a single entity. Globalization has accelerated and deepened the differentiation among developing countries in terms of their capacity to take advantage of international investment and trade flows. When I wrote my books on the dependency theory, the underlying hypothesis was that the international process of capitalism adversely affected conditions for development. It did not prevent development, but made it unbalanced and unjust. Many considered economic inward-orientation was a possible form of defense against the alternative of an international integration regarded as risky and dangerous. This view has changed. We have to admit that participation in the global economy can be positive, that the international system is not necessarily hostile. But we should work carefully to seize the opportunities. Successful integration into the global economy depends, on the one hand, on diplomatic articulation and adequate trade partnerships, and, on the other, on the individual homework of each developing country based on a democratically built consensus.

But marginalization is by no means confined to those countries not yet integrated into the world economy. It grows inside otherwise prosperous countries. For globalization means competition founded on higher levels of productivity, that is to say, more output per unit of labor. Unemployment has therefore resulted from the very reasons that make an economy successfully competitive. The situation is particularly serious in Europe. Those who are laid off in rich countries may resort to social safety nets of different scopes. Some may be retrained to find a replacement job.

However, little can be done to alleviate the frustration of the young willing to enter the labor market without having been able to find a job. Hopelessness, drugs and alcohol abuse, family disruption are some of the problems brought about by unemployment and consequent marginalization. There is a sentiment of exclusion, a certain malaise in vast segments of the rich societies, fueling violence and, in some cases, xenophobic attitudes.

How to deal with the complex problem of unemployment is a challenge to which practically all countries participating in the global economy are faced with. The answer to it is certainly not to be found in a reaction to globalization, by either closing the economies to trade with foreign partners, which can only aggravate the marginalization of a country, or introducing unnecessary rigidities in the regulatory framework of labor relations, which is a step that runs the risk of preventing rather than stimulating job creation.

Though job creation is hardly a direct responsibility of governments, there is a wide range of possibilities for them to address the problem. The first and maybe more important measure governments can take is to promote sustained growth by adopting adequate economic policies. The second measure would be to promote programs both by the official agencies and the private sector aimed at retaining workers laid off by sectors in which they can no longer find a suitable job.

A third step is to make the regulatory framework of labor more flexible so as to preserve jobs, by, for example, allowing companies and workers to negotiate freely a range as wide as possible of issues such as the number of working hours and vacation days, payment of hours exceeding the normal working day, etc. Flexibility of labor relations should also result in lesser costs for the hiring of workers. Finally, there are some official instruments that can be linked to expanding job creation such as financing by State banks and tax incentives.

In countries with large populations such as Brazil and India, consideration must also be given to the operation of the so-called informal economy as far as job creation is concerned. To what extent does the informal economy reduce jobs in the formal economy and to what extent does it offer additional jobs? Better knowledge of this question is necessary for us to draw the right conclusions and take appropriate action.

INTERNATIONAL RESPONSE

Let me now conclude with some brief comments on what can be done by the international community to cope with the negative effects of economic globalization, which will influence our national options in the foreseeable future.

As I said, globalization has created exclusion of those poor countries that have not so far shared the fruits of the process. It has also created marginalization inside those rich and developing countries integrated into the world economy. But it has also multiplied wealth, unleashing productive forces on an unprecedented scale. Shall we renounce the positive elements of globalization, the possibilities of wealth offered by it, and turn back the clock of History, admitting we could do so? The answer to this question is certainly negative.

How then can governments and heads of state act to mitigate the painful side effect of marginalization at a time when the role of the State has changed and somewhat been reduced?

Just as States can correct social imbalances internally, so it is possible to think of a group of States being capable of proposing ways to attenuate the social consequences of globalization. This is not simple. We are aware that problems today are global in nature, such as international capital volatility, drug trafficking, protection of the environment, migration, etc.

The challenge is to make the transition from recognizing the existence of global problems to devising concrete instruments and establishing effective mobilization for change among all countries. Without having the pretension of offering a full answer to that question, may I suggest that a good beginning is for us to present proposals for change that can meet four conditions:

a. the first one is that proposals for change be universal, that they can build, through negotiation and example, some form of consensus of interests among States, rich and poor, developed and developing;

b. the second condition is that all proposals be feasible and do not exacerbate rivalries, that they be neither unrealistic nor naive;

c. third, that proposals be capable of mobilizing those States and other actors with a clear capacity to influence the negotiating process;

d. and the fourth condition would be that proposals incorporate an ethical content that makes them capable of overcoming the mystique of the market and the sheer power game.

It is time for us to try to re-instill the ethics of solidarity within the State dealings and, through them, to the whole of society. Governments cannot do everything. Nor can world leaders. Yet, because of the role they play, the example they can give, they can act as catalysts for change, for reintroducing ethical values at a time which lacks them.

At the international level, the ethics of solidarity can lead to new utopias, albeit more modest ones, to fulfill the ideological vacuum left by the demise of the great utopias of the past. The ethics of solidarity should reintroduce in the international agenda the subject of co-operation for development within a new perspective, capable of combating indifference towards marginalization, exclusion, famine, and disease, which are at the root of migration and violence worldwide.

Internally, in each of our countries, the ethics of solidarity should be put at the service of creating new forms of partnership between society and the government, of helping organize society through education in such a way that it becomes more self-reliant and less dependent on governments with fewer resources, of attaching added importance to community development and to nation-building. Citizens and above all the elites have a social responsibility they must exert if we are to live in a better world.

⇥ 21 ⇤

Globalization
and International Relations

First of all, I would like to thank Doctor Greg Mills, the director of the South African Institute of International Affairs, and Doctor Steven Friedman, the director of the Center for Policy Studies, for providing me with the opportunity to be here this afternoon.

It is with great pleasure that I meet South African colleagues in order to discuss some key international issues.

It is my wish that this lecture be an additional step to those already taken towards a more significant bilateral cultural exchange between South Africa and Brazil. We have already organized two initial seminars that sought to compare our respective realities, and I have learned that the results have been extremely useful.

The perception that we are experiencing some of the same problems, which thus may be "thought about" in the same ways, serves as an important step in bringing us closer.

I would like to propose several topics for an exercise of common reflection, without necessarily being concerned with closely examining them.

In the nineteenth century, research regarding capitalism was the core of sociological thinking and, in fact, its very foundation. Today, some of the central questions posed by social scientists pertain to globalization.

It is not a phenomenon that by itself provides the outline of a new scientific perspective to explain, as did Marx and Weber, the relationship between economy and society. It is still the heritage of the classics, however, that shapes the conceptual universe, the framework for understanding globalization, a phenomenon that, in fact, carries the tendencies of capitalism to the limit.

Excerpted from Fernando Henrique Cardoso, "Globalização e outros temas contemporâneos," a lecture at the University of Witswatersrrand, Johannesburg, South Africa, November 27, 1996. Available at: <www.planalto.gov.br/secom/colcao/globa.htm>. Last accessed: December 2000.

We know that classical methods are clearly not sufficient. On the one hand, they do not form a basis for an overall theory of globalization, as they did for capitalism in its origins. On the other hand, even if the current analytical findings warn about problems such as unemployment, "marginalization," and an increase in inequalities, they have not yet reached the stage of clearly offering overall political and policy solutions to these problems. The connections between science and politics, between analysis and the need for justice are somehow missing.

Aspirations for a more just society have not been laid to rest. On the contrary, they have become more encompassing. There is a growing demand for equity, for societies that are more just, ecologically balanced, and respectful of human rights, although the means available for achieving these aspirations are not always indicated nor even clear.

Globalization may or may not offer conditions for a more equitable world. It is a matter of making the right choices, both nationally and internationally.

This statement may sound paradoxical at a time when the prevailing trend is to focus the international debate on those social and mainly economic processes leading to growing uniformity. Such processes are accentuated by globalization and tend to be seen as inevitable, as though imposed by some kind of "determinism." The old subject of uniformity, which was in Comte, in Marx, and, more recently, in Aron, is now back, as if its positive "promises" were at the point of finally being fulfilled.

Globalization is a concrete reality that countries like Brazil and South Africa cannot overlook. However, from a sociological point of view, it is also important to examine what globalization does not explain. And it certainly does not explain why countries have different reactions when faced with the process itself.

This question deserves a few comments.

First of all, to the extent to which the central analytical concept is growing uniformity, the natural tendency is to believe that whatever does not fit perfectly into globalization is its opposite.

This view considers the forces of globalization as being opposed to the forces of fragmentation, and the capacity to adjust to economic realities as being opposed to failure to adapt to them. It establishes a divide between "positive" and "negative" values.

In that sense, the differences among countries would be explained within the framework of globalization itself.

Therein lies the danger of an "analytical reductionism" that would attribute the success or failure of each society, of each nation, to its ability or lack thereof to integrate itself into the international flows of trade, investment, and technology.

That ability would be defined in terms of several requirements deemed to be essential for a country to become a "success story," yet another fashionable concept. Basically, the emphasis is being put on the values of economic performance. Competitiveness becomes the key to having an increasingly prominent international role.

Against this background, there would be countries well or ill-prepared to confront the challenges posed by the international system.

Globalization has its own values in terms of policy orientation. There is a clear list of "good policies" that serve as a yardstick against which countries are measured and judged. Deviations from these "good policies" would ultimately explain failure and, therefore, differences among nations. There is a peculiar emphasis on what is seen as a sort of "social choice," but this is a poor basis for a sound sociological explanation. But the question remains as to why there are such deviations, either positive or negative, why some choices were possible in certain circumstances and others not. I will give two examples:

- The first has to do with the extraordinary "adaptation" by the Asian tigers, which was due to well-devised policy options, made at the right time, and also, in part, to modern ways of taking advantage of deeply rooted cultural values even though it is a fact that such values were also present when those countries were poor. It is this complex combination of culture and policies that will account, in the end, for their "success."
- A second example will show that using either the globalization process or a country's adherence to certain values of efficiency and competitiveness as a gauge fails to explain why South American countries cannot fully take advantage of their potential for exports of, say, agricultural goods.

The reasons for this include the European Common Agricultural Policy and a tradition of subsidized food exports by virtually all developed countries.

The European Common Agricultural Policy, in turn, cannot be understood without knowledge of the patterns of land occupation and social organization in most of Europe.

Simply taking what is "global," or some notion of "choice," as our reference will not give us a complete understanding of the complex interaction of the various forces on the international scene.

Here I will go back to the same methodological tool that inspired the "dependency theory," if I may. Capitalism expands itself in different ways. The central element in order to understand capitalism's rationale is to be found in the relationship between the dynamics of its expansion and the "concrete situations" of specific countries such as Japan or the United States.

The expansion of capitalism has gained more speed and strength. Yet, those "concrete situations" continue to exist. And it is necessary for us to take them fully into account.

Globalization is too narrow a framework to explain what is behind concrete and specific cases. Disregarding this, or the importance of a country's history, makes any analysis incomplete, flawed.

The interaction between what is universal and what is specific is lost, as is the possibility of identifying opportunities for integration, since those opportunities will only be discernible if they are based on a national perspective of the globalization process.

Globalization is clearly insufficient to elucidate the role the state has to play in the development of each society. In general terms, there is nowadays a tendency to downplay this role, as if the state could be seen simply as performing the functions of managing public accounts, at the domestic level, and of negotiating ever lower tariffs at the international level. At most, in view of the Asian tigers' success, "selective intervention" in certain sectors can be temporarily accepted.

In fact, there seems to be a good measure of confusion over the role of the state, and a simplistic reference to globalization does not help to clarify it. The size of the state, defined a priori by ideological criteria, is of less importance than the quality of its actions, in particular in the social area.

Today, the state that is needed in a country like Brazil is one that intervenes less often, but better, one that is capable of defining clear priorities and of mobilizing the resources necessary to implement them.

The role of the state has become much more complex in a democracy. In addition to its classic functions in the areas of law enforcement, health, education, and foreign policy, the state must now meet increasing demands for more equity, for more justice, for a sound environment, for respect for human rights.

A more demanding society has to be matched by a more sophisticated state. A well-organized and efficient state will be in a better position to meet those demands, many of them springing from globalization itself.

Furthermore, the state must also be well-equipped so that in the negotiation of the rules within which globalization is to take place the national interests are preserved.

The state has to become more refined, more perceptive of and responsive to the demands of the population, more transparent, since the array of subjects it has to deal with is now wider and more challenging.

We are far from the death of the state that many have predicted. Nonetheless, the state we need at present ought to be different from the one that has existed so far.

A related topic is that of the politics of globalization. It would be a serious mistake to consider globalization as being the result of market forces alone.

The boundaries within which the market operates are defined politically, in direct negotiations between governments in multilateral foray, such as the World Trade Organization. The power game is always present in such negotiations.

It is the clash among conflicting negotiating positions that gives rise to the framework of rules and parameters that will set the limits and the conditions for globalization to operate.

Real differences at the negotiating table have to do, primarily, with different stages of development and features of social and political structures. In a word, with each country's history such distinctions can hardly be explained by the forces that promote uniformity.

Furthermore, globalization does not eliminate the hierarchy among states. But there are two differences in the manner in which this hierarchy is now reflected in the behavior of international actors.

The first difference is that the hierarchy today is not expressed only in terms of military strategic power—although this continues to be a decisive factor, as evidenced by the Persian Gulf War.

It is established by a complex equation that includes as increasingly important variables both economic might and what is described as "soft power," that is to say, the ability to collect and process information, the power to create and disseminate worldwide cultural and social patterns, as well as international prestige and diplomatic influence.

That hierarchy becomes evident when one considers that countries have varying capabilities of influencing the outcome of international negotiations.

How then could we prevent such negotiations from deepening the hierarchy? How could we agree on common rules in the face of different national capabilities? How to build bargaining power in order to intervene more effectively in the negotiating process?

In any event, it is better for all of us to have a set of predictable and universally applicable rules that prevail over the sheer use of power.

The second difference in how the hierarchy manifests itself at present is that shifts and maneuvers within it no longer follow a preestablished pattern. There are several possibilities for countries having common interests to associate themselves. Specific subjects muster different constituencies. Each country is free to pursue its international goals in association with different groupings.

Paradoxically, then, globalization forces us to have a greater and keener awareness of our respective identities. For it is this increased awareness that will be the starting point for the outline of the range of options for the diplomatic action of each of us. It is based on our specific individuality that we will seek to integrate our economies into the processes of globalization.

Brazil and indeed South America as a whole are very much in tune with contemporary forces of change. Democracy and economic freedom are values already embraced by all countries in the region.

We look at globalization more through the lens of the opportunities it offers than that of the risks it entails. South America is accordingly engaged in fostering its own regional integration schemes such as Mercosul.

We know how necessary it is for us to widen our economic space, to have access to the expanded markets that are called for by the economies of scale associated with modem technology-intensive production processes.

But our integration is not being created in the void. We rely on a tradition that is linked to the thinking of the Economic Commission for Latin America, ECLA (or "CEPAL" as we refer to it in our region). This is certainly an asset.

ECLA was a pioneer in studying the alternatives and patterns for the integration of our countries into the world economy. Its thinking was instrumental in forging a sense of unity in our region, which still prevails and is behind the integration process now under way in South America.

Peace, democracy, and political dialogue are also distinctive traits of South America, elements of our historical evolution. Democracy is the best guarantee for effective change. Democracy ensures predictability, coherence in the transformation process, and continuity with accountability. We are committed to supporting democracy in the region.

In Brazil, we know that there is still a lot to be accomplished, that our reform processes are still somewhat incomplete. But we are working hard to get the necessary changes and reforms approved, within the timings imposed by our democratic institutions, by the pace of negotiations with Congress and society at large.

We have a difficult task to undertake in the social area in order to redress our historical imbalances in income distribution and to improve our social indicators. Redeeming our "social debt" to the poor is a task for more than one government, for more than one generation. And we will have to accomplish that task together with our efforts towards integrating Brazil's economy into international trade and investment flows.

A better knowledge of our strengths and weaknesses enable us to positively envisage the prospects of Brazil's participation in the globalization process.

Such a perception defines our options and our path, establishes priorities, and determines the selection of partners for joint efforts in particular areas on the international stage.

One of our key partners must be South Africa. We are at similar stages of development and share similar views on international questions. It is only natural, then, that Brazil and South Africa start acting more closely in defense of common interests in international foray. This is one of the reasons why I have come to South Africa.

Another reason is to add momentum to the development of our bilateral cooperation opportunities in every area. Geography does not separate us; on the contrary, the South Atlantic brings us together. Air and sea transportation links are already in place to help us intensify trade flows.

Hand in hand with trade goes investment. Mercosul offers South Africa expanded business opportunities, in the same way as South Africa can open the door to other countries in its region for Brazilian products and technology, through the Southern African Development Community.

It is incumbent upon us to translate this potential into deeds, thereby strengthening our assets to participate successfully into the global economy.

In concluding, I refer back to my opening remarks, when I said that the perception that we are experiencing some of the same problems is an important element in bringing us closer, including at the international negotiating tables.

I will be happy if I have succeeded in getting this message through—that joint actions by countries such as Brazil and South Africa are indispensable in the shaping of the globalization processes under way.

⇥ 22 ⇤

The Impact of Globalization on Developing Countries

I do not intend here to address globalization with the rigor of a man of science, among other reasons because in everything I have read about globalization, I perceive that there is as yet a lack of a "unifying theory" to explain in depth the genesis of the changes and the course of the rapid developments underway in contemporary economic reality. Academia, it appears to me, is still in the process of mapping and understanding the set of events that are changing the lives of nations at a heretofore-unimaginable speed.

But the timing and motivations of the politician are essentially different from those of the social scientist. The politician cannot wait for the sedimentation of knowledge in order to act. Should he do so he will be overcome by events. We have today but one certainty, and that is of the vast scope and depth of change—and this haunts and vexes us—in the awareness of the complexity of the challenges we must face.

The truth is that, irrespective of the theoretical gaps which exist, enough is already known about globalization for us to perceive within a reasonable perspective where the probable course of globalization will lead and in what fields we can act to mitigate some of its more pernicious effects, and at the same time, to exploit the full potential of the advantages which are arising so that, in the coming years, we can make great strides towards prosperity with greater social justice.

Globalization, in its various manifestations, has become an unavoidable component in the decisions of governments, conditioning both choices at the national level and actions abroad. This, however, in no way detracts from the fact that one of the most important missions of contemporary political action is to ensure that

Adapted from Fernando Henrique Cardoso, "The Impact of Globalization on Developing Countries: Risks and Opportunities," a lecture at Colegio de México, México, February 20, 1996. Original available at: <www.planalto.gov.br/secom/colecao/impact.htm>. Last accessed: December 2000.

development will be guided by values, in accordance with which economic gains only have significance if they bring greater well-being to the majority of citizens. Thus, starting from this premise, we must find the means and instruments needed to lead the effort to integrate our countries into the new standards of productivity and competitiveness, the only way to achieve the necessary sustainable economic growth in a globalized economy.

ANALYTICAL CONTEXT

A starting point for an improved understanding of the nature of the changes currently taking place in the worlds of economic and political reality would be to reflect on some of the reasons underlying the obsolescence of some of the theories which sought to explain in depth the dynamics of relations between Capital and Labor and their repercussion in the international scenario.

It is evident that I do not propose to exhaust such a complex theme in so short a time. My objective is merely to trace some lines whereby to allow us a better understanding of that which is taking place in the world today.

The extraordinary changes that have occurred since 1989, one of which has been the acceleration of the effects of globalization, reveal the limitations of the theories and hegemonic ideologies of this century. This is true not only of Marxism; both classical liberalism (by virtue of the changes in the theory of comparative advantages), and social-democracy (which suffers from the criticism of the exhaustion of the welfare state) require a radical reformulation that has as yet not been forthcoming. Obviously, the historical perspectives available to the founders of these schools of thought were quite different and were based upon the premises of certain specific forms of dialectic between the internal and external, and even between relations of capital and labor, which no longer exist.

The world has changed; the nature of Capital has changed; the nature of Labor has also changed. The instruments necessary for achieving increasing levels of social inclusion have likewise changed.

What History has not rendered obsolete in the ideologies principally of the left is a generous aspiration to the effect that change should have the objective of incorporating the weak, the disadvantaged. It is for this reason that the theme of inequality persists and occupies a necessary space in the reflection on globalization.

1. In the dimension of Capital one of the aspects to be highlighted is that we are witnessing a veritable atomization of its property. Today pension and investment funds, for example, hold a strategic position in the control of Capital and in the definition of its utilization. This is diluting and depersonalizing the relations between employer and employee in the most dynamic and modern sectors of the economy, though in Brazil, as in a great many other developing countries, most employment is provided by small and medium companies.

Even the relation between entrepreneurs and companies is changing: the "Schumpeterian" businessman, the visionary entrepreneur, is now being replaced by those who control some form of specialized and innovative knowledge, or otherwise, by the managers whose decisions are guided by standards of efficiency and competitiveness. The trend is not new and has been described since the 1950s, but it has most certainly become more marked in recent years.

To give but one example that confirms these trends: in Brazil, pension funds have become the greatest investors in the process of the privatization of the economy. The managers of these funds now retain vast power, in terms of the choice of options for investment in the economy. The majority of these managers have come from the staffs of State companies.

How then can one with any clarity speak of capitalist exploitation, of the attainment of surplus value in the classical Marxist sense if a significant portion of the workers are beginning to be Capital's partners? Undoubtedly, there are specific groups of workers who have been better at achieving means of access to capital precisely because they were capable of becoming organized in a modern manner.

And here we have a first question, more of a sociological than of an economic nature: does the differentiation of labor derived from the ease of access to capital (and as I shall point out, there are other determining factors in this differentiation) admit only modern forms of organization, or does it also serve those who, by political artifice, have managed to consolidate corporatist arrangements?

Another crucial element is the increasing mobility of international capital flows and their impact on the monetary and exchange policies of national economies. It becomes increasingly difficult to identify the origin of capital and, above all, the intentions of the managers who deal in it. An analysis of how profits are distributed and of who benefits there from also becomes a complex matter.

This does not mean that we are helpless in the face of the volatility of capital. The awareness of this trend cannot lead us to passivity. The internationalization of capital flows should correspond to new international arrangements to discipline them. And this is perfectly possible.

2. In classical economic theory Labor, Capital and Land were considered the three basic factors of production. The factor Labor was characterized as being static, homogeneous. Technology was associated directly with the factor Capital, not with Labor. Nowadays, as production has become more "knowledge intensive," it is the worker himself who possesses this knowledge to a far greater extent than the company. A significant example of this is the case of Silicon Valley in the United States, which grew from a knowledge base, to which capital flowed a posteriori. Though this example may be somewhat schematic, it serves to illustrate the point which I wished to stress: that in the terminology of Marx, variable capital rises in importance in relation to constant capital to the degree that the productive process becomes more knowledge intensive.

This fact has deep implications for our countries and economies. Knowledge has become a factor of differentiation in labor. Physical strength and general aptitudes have lost importance as elements that differentiate labor. High-level, qualified and creative manpower has become a "scarce" element, in comparison to the relative abundance of capital in circulation around the world. This is even more important for developing countries: any comparative advantage which peripheral countries might enjoy in terms of cheap and abundant labor has practically disappeared, or to be more precise, it is now located in the less modern sectors of the economy. This reinforces the difficulty of dealing with internal differences in complex developing countries, such as our own. It has become necessary to combine public policies that preserve areas that are modern and competitive by international standards, with a permanent effort to incorporate backward, more labor-intensive sectors.

There is another point that has had an extraordinary impact upon the relations between Capital and Labor. The modernization of the economy has led industrial manpower in Marxist terms the proletariat par excellence to lose ground to jobs to the tertiary sector; a sector which has a low capacity to mobilize (for the purpose of bargaining with the holders of capital), greater informality and greater differentiation in terms of variety in the types of jobs and in pay scales. It is as a result of this change in the profile of jobs that there has been a move towards greater flexibility in labor standards throughout the four corners of the world.

Many consider that this migration of jobs from the manufacturing sector to the service sector has been a negative phenomenon. Conceptually however, this is a mistake: it is a fallacy that only industry can provide high-quality jobs. Also equally outdated is the notion that only the manufacturing sector has the potential to generate exports, and thus, the capacity to promote growth more easily.

3. Some significant consequences stem from the implementation of the new forms of Capital expansion, the organization of Labor and the relations between Capital and Labor.

First: if on the one hand the mobility of capital flows across national borders may bring real opportunities for growth to emerging economies, on the other, the volatility of this short-term capital and the possibility of its being used in speculative attacks against currencies constitutes a real threat to economic stability and to the level of employment in these countries. (Mexico and all of South America, and even the more distant financial markets, are well aware of the undesirable impact that this volatility can cause).

Second: knowledge, as we know, has become a decisive factor in the differentiation between workers, rendering the position of those who occupy most of the least-qualified jobs vulnerable, especially in developing countries. On this question I would like to make an aside: this internal differentiation among the working class is reminiscent, at first sight, of the notion of a "proletarian bourgeoisie," which in Marxist thought is linked to imperialist exploitation. However, this is no longer the case: the rise of specific sectors may be a positive factor and represent productivity gains and the capacity to organize. The problem emerges when the benefits crystallize in corporatist mechanisms, resulting in unequal advantages that owe much more to the political skills of certain groups than to advances in methods of production. What had appeared at first sight to be modern may thus in reality be conservative, not healthy competition at all, but rather identified with the perquisites of political patronage. This occurs above all, in certain sectors of the State; in some countries this has led to the situation whereby the traditional left is used by these groups to defend causes that are paradoxically conservative, in that they preserve situations of privilege.

Third, and perhaps most alarming: in the face of this scenario of transformation, who are to be the new social protagonists for the construction of the future? No longer will it be the "conquering bourgeoisie," since capital has become depersonalized; no longer will the middle class act as the privileged bearer of democratic values; and neither will it be the proletariat, the orphan deprived of its revolutionary utopias after the downfall of real socialism. Further along I shall return to this theme, which I believe to be essential.

Parallel to the transformations which have occurred in the dimensions of Capital and Labor and in their inter-relations, other elements contribute to the obsolescence of the theories which sought to explain the system of economic and political relations on the basis of the Marxist concept of imperialism.

When Enzo Faletto and I worked on the building of a theory of dependence, the sub-strata of development on the periphery of capitalism, especially in Latin America, was the internationalization of the markets. However, at that moment, another phenomenon was emerging, one which was still hard to perceive in all its aspects from the conceptual viewpoint of the 1960s. While markets were being internationalized, in Latin America and the developed West production was also being internationalized, which was to cause an impressive expansion of the flows of international trade, which grew far more than did the growth rates of the national economies. Formerly, the prevailing rule had been that all phases of production of a given good took place in the same country. This merchandise was either consumed locally or else exported. Tariff and non-tariff protection, in association with the strategy placing priority on the development of the domestic market, fed a series of national development projects based upon protected industrialization, or import substitution, as the process became known in Latin America. (I recall that the Asian strategy was different since it was based upon a better income-distribution profile, and it was aimed at the domestic accumulation of capital and technology, which would, at a later stage, lead to more efficient models for meeting the issues of globalization.)

But let us go back to the model of import substitution: its exhaustion stemmed basically from the fact that the national content of the majority of goods diminished and their phases of production became internationalized. The more technologically advanced the product, probably the greater the number of countries that had participated, all the way from its conception and design up to its production and marketing. This trend grew stronger, and this was not only as a consequence of the lowering of production costs (resulting from the technical and technological revolution), of the greater mobility of the factors of production, and furthermore, of the fall of transport and communications costs.

It was also the result of the progressive reduction of tariff and non-tariff protection, in successive rounds at multilateral foray such as GATT, sponsored mainly by the developed countries, but which also began to engage the more recently developed countries, who craved new markets. In this particular, the countries that joined the GATT latest, as is the case of Mexico, had to consolidate their tariffs at a lower level than those who had joined in an earlier period. It is symptomatic that of late there has been a broadening of the themes treated by GATT, many of which were formerly restricted to internal jurisdiction.

As a result of the sum of these developments, there has been an exponential growth of intra-firm trade, which is today responsible for the most significant portion of international trade. If, a few decades back, what interested the multinational conglomerates was the legislation in force in the countries receiving their investments regarding the remittance of profits, now, they seek to give priority to the capacity of a given nation to produce intermediate or final products at competitive prices, within the framework of globally defined corporate strategies. Countries are now selected to receive investment from these multinational corporations on the basis of the estimate of the comparative advantages that they can offer, among which is qualified labor that has increasingly become a decisive factor.

These developments result in various consequences, the first of these undoubtedly being the weakening of the national development projects based on state-owned companies that had excluded the external market. The second was the intensification of competition among countries, especially of developing countries for foreign investments. To a great extent countries have reformulated their policies in the economic field in order to attract capital, to complement their own insufficient rates of internal savings, thus obliging them to offer a more attractive and predictable domestic environment.

This once again is nothing new. What is now occurring, however, is different from the 1950s, since the model has changed, and there is no longer "specialized" investment for the Third World, while local economic activity has become linked to these transnational chains of production. Not always is this link to the outside world homogeneous, especially in extremely large countries in which the process of modernization cannot reach the nation as a whole. "Separating" certain parts of the national territory for differentiated types of foreign links has been the solution adopted by some countries.

The intensification of competition between countries has not, however, excluded cooperation, which may take various forms. The main form has been regional integration. The creation of expanded markets, either in the form of free trade zones or, on a more advanced plane, customs unions, has become a fundamental instrument for developing countries within the context of globalization. In the case of Brazil, in less than a decade Mercosul has become the main project for national diplomacy. Mercosul today attracts to the region as a whole a growing volume of large-scale investments, which have a significant impact upon the generation of new jobs. I am thus convinced that regional integration projects can be an effective mechanism for combating the most pernicious effects of globalization.

The third consequence is the emergence of an increasing uniformity in the institutional and regulatory frameworks of all countries. For the globalization of production to advance, the hegemonic notion of the standardization of economic and commercial rules has begun to prevail, so as to impede the creation of artificial advantages in a given country. An illustration of this has been the introduction within the World Trade Organization of international parameters for intellectual property rights and the Agreements for the Protection and Promotion of Investments. It is evident, however, that a more homogeneous normative framework will only achieve its objective if, in the application of the standards, there is a greater sense of balance and, above all, if the unilateral abuse of economic power is stopped.

Also intimately linked to the issue of globalization is the limitation that is imposed upon the capacity of States to choose differentiated development strategies, to adopt heterodox macroeconomic policies, or even more, to support rigid formulas with regard to Capital and Labor. The capital markets then act as veritable monitors of national activities; any measure, however correct it may be from the domestic view point, which might signal a false step or upset foreign investors, leads to short-term capital flight, which in turn seriously affects the financial system of the country.

The orthodoxy or conservatism of this type of insubstantial though influential tribunal places constraints on the capacity of governments to operate, since, on the one hand, governments cannot simply ignore these factors which condition contemporary reality, and on the other hand, they are obliged to seek among the contradictions and inconsistencies, and also in the windows of opportunity of the emerging system, strategies capable of reaffirming the priority of the national interest, of strengthening the vocation of countries such as our own for sovereign self-determination and, above all, consolidating our capacity to influence the building of the future.

Globalization is far from being a phenomenon that advances in a uniform manner on the international plane. Its pace obeys a variety of movements. The financial paradigm, for example, is different from the commercial one. In the latter, the areas of resistance are much more pronounced, especially in the developed countries, as has proven to be the case in the issues of agricultural products, fish, and so many others. There is a clear contradiction between the discourse of globalization and what happens in practice, a reality in which the regulation of limitations is dictated by diplomatic negotiations. In the financial area, the opening is certainly greater, but this does not mean that it is exempt from regulatory mechanisms, which are normally established by the Central Banks of each country.

Globalization has also made a contribution to changing the role of the State: the emphasis of governmental action is now directed towards the creating and sustaining of structural conditions of competitiveness on a global scale. This involves channeling investments for infrastructure and for basic public services, among them education and health, and removing the State from the role of the producer of goods with primary responsibility for the productive system.

At several moments, I have mentioned that one of the sociological consequences of the modernization induced by globalization is the dispersion of interests, the fragmentation of Labor and of Capital. The core of political action today is precisely the creation of a political space in which these interests can be harmonized rationally. It is in this respect that I consider it essential to understand that, with globalization, the State needs to recompose its functions. Thus the mission of the State to provide steering capacity for development becomes much more important than the patently ineffectual attempt to take the place of private enterprise in the production of goods and services which are not of an eminently public nature.

This small grouping of contemporary developments in international economic relations, in my opinion, provides powerful elements that place in check all the theories that sought to explain reality, and above all, the traditional political and economic strategies which States sought to follow in their quest for growth. The challenges of facing a new reality are vast and increasingly complex, since it has become unfeasible to separate the internal and external conditioning factors. Besides this, a paradoxical situation is created, since while the demand for equity increases in democratic regimes, among other things as a consequence of the globalization of information, it is directed at a State which, due to its new role, should intervene less often and more effectively as it has increasingly restricted options in terms of economic policy, as a consequence of the necessary fiscal discipline and austerity in public spending.

Precisely for this reason, never has the quality of political work been so important. In what manner, and based on what values should governments combine the internal and the external elements; how to conciliate the scattered pressures with the imperative of defining clear goals; how to make the classical mechanisms of representation compatible with the growing desire for the direct participation of citizenry in the decision-making process; how to coordinate the thrust of transnational economic values with the need for a sovereign perspective? (I could provide a great many more of these dichotomies.) We know that today there are no ideological formulas which coherently spin the threads of a changing reality. A merely pragmatic attitude on the part of the government is an insufficient and simplistic attitude in the face of problems that involve complex options and values.

In this respect it becomes evident that the essential work of the politician in our respective countries is connected to themes of social justice. His or her principal mandate derives from those who possess little or nothing. In societies such as our own we cannot fool ourselves and accept globalization as being a natural fact of life, or as a new form of ideology, while allowing internal dichotomies to become aggravated. Inequality, though feeding upon the asymmetries and injustices of relations among States, is still basically a national problem. It is our capacity to overcome this, and with intelligent measures to adapt to the new situation, which mark the action of the modern statesman. Whether the proponents of neoliberal ideologies like it or not, the State is still an essential reference, as an instrument for organizing the transformations, and the modern politician cannot and should not abdicate this responsibility.

INEQUALITY AND STRUCTURAL UNEMPLOYMENT

For decades, developing countries have, without much success, tried to influence the construction of a new international economic order. The truth is that, to a certain extent unnoticed by them, this new order was already being forged and is now known as globalization. Without giving in to the illusion that this new order responds only to market forces, however decisive these may be, and that the power of nation-states has ceased to have the same impact upon the course of events, it is precisely the recognition of the "limits" of the market and the strength that some large countries such as Brazil and Mexico have to influence the course of the globalization of the economy, which allows us to adopt measures capable of counteracting the most negative social effects of the phenomenon, such as the growth of inequality and the increase in unemployment. To do this, however, governments have to accept, as I have already said, certain conditioning factors of the economic order currently being forged with realism and a sense of pragmatism. The novelty of the process and the speed of the transformations require entirely new forms of action in the international scenario.

1. As we have seen, globalization creates uniformity even as it differentiates. The trend among many analysts and ideologists is to praise the processes that create uniformity, as if they in and of themselves were sufficient to create wealth and equity. The themes of differentiation are, however, decisive and perhaps constitute the essence of the construction of a political perspective for globalization. In truth, the issue of the rise in inequality and social exclusion that globalization appears in some way to exacerbate is intricate and hard to combat. It is manifested both on the international plane and on the internal plane by both developed and developing countries. It is paradoxical, one might even say ironic, that the increase of inequality occurs precisely at the moment in which, with the end of the Cold War and greater opening to the world of the most hard-line socialist regimes, we move towards institutional uniformity and a greater universal convergence of values.

In the dimension of interpersonal relations, inequality can be regarded less as the fruit of "capitalist exploitation" or of distortions of the model of accumulation, than of the qualitative differences in labor and of innate or acquired skills and abilities. Material inequality is perversely identified as the result of a natural process of differentiation among individuals. This break in the sense of solidarity has serious repercussions on the very idea of national identity itself, as was pointed out by Robert Reich, the current Secretary of Labor of the Clinton Administration.

In the dimension of the relations between States, inequality is perceived not so much as a historical, political, economic or cultural phenomenon, but rather as an incapacity to adapt to the institutional and ideological framework which prevails in "nations who are winners." This waning of the economic, sociological, historical or ethical explanation for inequality leads to the growth of indifference and intolerance with regard to "losers," who are classified as the only ones responsible for their own backwardness.

Still on the plane of the relations between States, the concept that development requires that States "do their homework" satisfactorily, so as to establish the internal conditions of competitiveness has greater currency than the call for international cooperation for development, or for mobilization of the international community in the struggle against the segregation of the poorer countries. Perversely, the existence of inequality and exclusion is thus considered a natural datum reflecting reality, thus losing one of the most important elements of traditional "conservative" thinking, which as has already been mentioned, is solidarity; the protection of the weak and dispossessed in the name of the defense of a higher value, of the cohesion or of the harmony of the social fabric.

The real challenge is thus to go beyond conservatism. We know that it is indispensable to rediscover community values and recreate an ethics of solidarity. It is, however, no easy task to re-arrange the instruments and institutions that have the effective capacity to address inequality and exclusion.

2. The issue of unemployment is another theme that raises concern on the part of governments and citizens, especially because it is an aggravating factor in the process of deepening inequality and social exclusion.

Some preliminary statements are necessary so as to avoid our contemplating the future with our eyes turned back to the past. The first of these is that we have already come up against and we will have to increasingly face the extremely serious problem of so-called "structural unemployment" which is a consequence of both the loss of competitiveness of certain sectors of the economy which were formerly protected by almost unassailable tariff or non-tariff barriers, and the enormous productivity gains per work unit. The second, that was referred to earlier, has to do with the phenomenon of the outsourcing of the economy and has contributed to the transformation of the nature of work on a global scale. In Brazil, for example, the tertiary sector responds for more than 60% of the total of jobs in the economy. This is a fact of great significance in the decision-making processes of governments.

Even the developed countries are not immune to the problem of unemployment. Among OECD member countries, unemployment rose by a factor of three between 1970 and 1992, according to data published in the *1993 UNDP Report on Human Development*. And as a consequence of migratory movements, the problems of unemployment, both in the North and in the South, began to interconnect more clearly.

The fear of the worsening of this situation in the countries of the North was what led to certain attempts to "react" to the process of globalization, as was the case of more closed schemes of regionalism and the advocating of such theses as "social dumping" or of "green protection." Market shares which we had worked hard to obtain by being more competitive began to be subject to discriminatory or illegal surtaxes or, worse still, had to face mechanisms of unfair competition, in flagrant disrespect for multilateral rules, as is clearly illustrated by the issue of agricultural subsidies in the developed countries.

COMBATING UNEMPLOYMENT

I have sought to demonstrate that unemployment, like so many other social issues, has an international dimension. The very nature of globalized development generates dramatic effects, as is illustrated by the trajectory of some developed countries. One point that I have sought to emphasize is that we should not stand passively by in face of the problems that globalization has caused to emerge. The definition of the national strategies needed to combat these evils is absolutely imperative and urgent. For this reason, I shall now reflect briefly upon the manner in which we in Brazil are dealing with the theme of unemployment.

One of the main problems of government in a democratic country such as Brazil, which has vast social liabilities resulting from the historical neglect and negligence by its elites, is the misconception on the part of the population that the Federal Executive Branch can do anything, and has the capacity to overcome century-old distortions in the course of a single Presidential term of office. It is natural that this should be so, especially in light of the success that we are enjoying with the stabilization of the economy.

I am fully aware that the problem of employment, both in terms of the quantitative supply of jobs and of the qualitative aspect of the new jobs to be created, constitutes one of the most serious issues to be faced by political leaders throughout the world. This is because the preservation and generation of jobs are prerequisite steps not only for the success of any social policy, but also to ensure the very dignity of the citizenry.

Facing up to this complex theme, however, does not depend only upon governments, though some governmental policies may be essential to minimize the impact of structural unemployment.

I shall now focus upon the Brazilian case that, I believe, bears certain similarities to that of Mexico. Before pointing out some of the measures my government is adopting in this field within the context of a broader strategy for social development, it would be useful briefly to analyze some of the elements which prevail in the dimension of the labor force and on the side of the supply of jobs within the Brazilian economy.

With regard to the dimension of the labor force, we must be aware of the following aspects:

a. the demographic component will continue to exert strong pressure on the labor market over the next 15 years, the period after which the effects of the current drop in fertility rates will begin to be felt;
b. the socio-cultural impact of the rise of the participation of women in the labor force.

With regard to the dimension of the supply of jobs, it is important to stress that:

• as a result of the opening of the economy and the imperative of competitiveness and productivity, it is necessary to know what will be the sectoral composition of a peripheral industrial economy that is integrated into the new international division of labor;
• as I have already indicated, a profound restructuring of production is underway, as a consequence of new technologies which, on the one hand, devalue non-qualified labor, and on the other, demand great retraining efforts among the labor force; and

- an organizational restructuring of the productive sector will demand the abolition of certain intermediate categories of jobs, at the same time as there is a growing trend towards the "informalization" of the labor market, which is further exacerbated by the outsourcing of functions.

In light of these conditioning factors and given the limitations of the actions of the State, how best to seek innovative solutions which involve the different levels of government, civil society, labor unions and employers' organizations? It is not my task here to draw up a more detailed prescription to attack the problem. I merely mention some of the measures, both on the supply and the demand sides for Labor, which my government has adopted or is in the process of implementing.

On the side of the supply of labor, I am committed to two points which I deem to be essential: massive investment in primary education and wide-reaching training and retraining programs, the costs of which are to be shared with the business community.

On the side of the demand for labor, our actions are to be concentrated on:

- sustained economic expansion by means of policies to promote growth conciliated with stabilization;
- the development of specific policies for the generation of employment, with a resumption of large-scale investments in the infrastructure and social areas (the social area, though overvalued as a significant generator of jobs, has enormous potential for employment generation);
- technical and financial support for better training in labor-intensive sectors, such as construction, family-based agriculture, and tourism;
- tax incentives, improved conditions of financing for production, and technical support for small and medium companies, which provide most of the jobs in the country;
- the stimulus, through financing from State development banks, of programs which preserve and create jobs; and
- the reduction of the cost of the labor factor in negotiations between Capital and Labor so as to make labor relations more flexible, including measures which provide greater autonomy to unions for the celebration of collective labor contracts.

CONCLUSION

We are experiencing changes that will reorganize the policies and economies of the next century. The task of providing a human dimension to development in the era of globalization has become a major challenge, since all of us have to deal not only with a radically new reality, but especially with the ethical vacuum which the idolatry of the marketplace has caused and which the demise of the revolutionary utopias has exacerbated.

If, through globalization, the economy becomes the conditioning factor in the realm of production and management, the same does not apply in the realm of values. It is necessary to separate the concrete facts ushered in by globalization from a pseudo-ideology which is building up around the phenomenon, with nuances which range from the uncritical preaching and celebration of the "virtues" of the emerging system, to the affirmation of the inevitability of the loss of relevance of the nation state.

In this regard we need to reflect on how globalization, which signals the onset of an era of prosperity unprecedented in the history of Mankind, a new Renaissance, as I have already stated can be oriented toward the fulfillment of the demand for equity on the part of four-fifths of humanity which subsist in conditions of poverty and sickness. How can we reinvent the sense of community on the international plane, so as to avoid social exclusion and segregation? How can we strengthen the social responsibility of the cultural and economic elites?

This last question regarding the social responsibility or as some would have it, national responsibility of the elites requires, as I see it, a more pondered response. Independently of the "democratization" of Capital, of which I have already spoken, and even for precisely this reason, the mechanics of the reproduction of the elites has become more robust. At the same time, the elites begin to close themselves off in the defense of their own more particular and narrow interests, which threatens not only the idea of democracy but also the very concept of the Nation. This irresponsibility of the elites fosters an exacerbation of individualism and a culture of conflict that cannot be sustained. What can be done to revive this social responsibility of the elites is one of the great challenges of our times. The appeal for an ethics of solidarity, a redefinition of national values and, especially, the struggle against inequality, which the elites today consider as something quite natural and even acceptable, are ideas that only Politics, as the art of building consensus, can resolve.

I have the conviction that the developing countries can contribute, perhaps even more than the developed countries, to this conceptual passage from the realm of the economy to the realm of values. Because, more than ever before, we have to exercise our creative capability of responding simultaneously to the challenges of the new reality and the overcoming of a social legacy which grieves and shames us.

It is not a question of going back to the values of the past, reviving utopias which no longer explain the contemporary world nor mesh with the prevalence of democratic values and the market economy. The solution to contemporary problems goes beyond national borders and demands universal mobilization.

A key to the framework of thoughts that I have attempted to address in this lecture is the lack of definition, which prevails at the present time as to who are to be the social protagonists in the building of the future. I do not believe that it is any longer possible to identify a specific social class with this role of helmsman of the nation on the path to development, in the midst of the turbulence of change. Giving a human dimension to progress, strengthening the ethic of solidarity both in the national and international dimension, has increasingly become a collective, dispersed and fragmented exercise: a veritable composite of partial utopias. No single social class or group today has the monopoly over the demand for equity.

It is precisely for this reason I once again persist in saying that we must revitalize the essential values of humanism, of wise understanding and of tolerance. These are the distinguishing characteristics par excellence of modern legitimacy. A real engagement on the part of the government and society is necessary to counter the current climate of exacerbated and nihilistic individualism, which conspires against our very notion of national identity. Governments, intellectuals, the leaders of civil society all have a vital role to play so that the new renaissance may bloom with all its capacity to transform History.

→ 23 ←

Toward a New Dialogue in North-South Relations

Si el viejo proyecto socialista de las izquierdas no da más frutos, es que ha llegado ya la hora de construir uno nuevo—uno que no solo viva de la protesta, sino uno que esté animado por la utopia de un orden social más justo. [If the old socialist project of the Left is no longer bearing fruit, that is because the hour has arrived to build a new one that does not live by protest alone, but that may be animated by the utopia of a more just social order.]

—Oskar Lafontaine

In the epigraph above, I quote a sentence from Lafontaine's article in the first issue of the magazine *El Socialismo del Futuro*.[1] That sentence summarizes the political challenge the left faces today.

Indeed, since the libertarian wave of May 1968 until the fall of the Berlin Wall, socialism and the Left in general have found themselves cornered, placed "in the spotlight" (*en el banquillo*). An entire tradition, which once blended reason and utopia, enlightenment and revolution, saw itself displaced by an uncertainty about the idea of progress and a disbelief in the dialectical "negation of the negation": as history unfolded, the victorious Revolution could no longer be seen.

On the contrary, the postindustrial world had occasioned a new libertarian wave, driven by a kind of "anguished pessimism" which in turn had been brought about by that existential anxiety over the real possibility of the end of the world (or, at least, of mankind) which nuclear terror and environmental destruction impose. To the ecological protest (which in many dimensions was anti-modern, too, afraid of technical

Adapted from Fernando Henrique Cardoso, "North-South Relations in the Present Context: A New Dependency?" in M. Carnoy, M. Castells, S. Cohen, and F. H. Cardoso, eds., *The New Global Economy in the Information Age: Reflections on our Changing World* (University Park: Pennsylvania State University Press, 1993), 149–159. © 1993 by The Pennsylvania State University. Reproduced by permission of the publisher.

progress and incredulous about reasons of state, if not reason) was added an anti-institutional spirit, already evident in 1968 in the revolts on university campuses all over the world. From this political-emotional atmosphere arose the new intellectual currents: postmodernism; the fragmentation of knowledge (and of the world); distrust of the tradition of rationalism that had given birth both to liberalism and to the several versions of the socialist critique.

Certainly there were intellectual reactions. Indeed, the attempt to reevaluate the Frankfurt School (somewhat skeptical altogether and, in the version of the Kultur Kritik, full of anti-modernism) undertaken by Jürgen Habermas,[2] as well as the revision of Talcott Parsons undertaken by Niklas Luhmann, were attempts to anchor critical thought onto the old pillars of reason.

However, the path the socialist movement is now trying to follow (whether "shining" or not, I don't know) did not originate there. On the contrary, it originated in the shock that ensued when, at the last minute, the leadership of the Soviet Union under Gorbachev[3] recognized the enormity of the ecological challenge and the nuclear threat. It originated, too, from the perception that although we are now experiencing the Third Industrial Revolution, and are now living in what Manuel Castells calls an "informational economy" (Ch. 2 in Carnoy et al. 1993), important areas of the world and segments of society continue to be downtrodden.

That is to say, there is a risk of barbarism, both in the global dimension and in the societal dimension, and this risk will not be reduced either by a reliance on the inevitability of progress or by its denial through anti-institutional protest. It is this feeling of risk, of danger, of adventure, which, lacking the support of a belief in salvation (in revolution, in harmony, in certainty), makes any ideology (whether doctrine or "science") necessarily more humble, more "probabilistic," and less a wellspring of verities.

In this sense, the socialism of the future will have to adjust itself to a sort of "middle-range utopia," if I may put a new twist on Robert Merton's notion of "middle-range theories."[4] Nonetheless, Oskar Lafontaine's observation continues to hold: if socialism is incapable of offering hope, if it offers mere protest (ecological or anti-institutional), even if it is a "movement" and comprises other movements, it will still fail to pave the way for change that does not limit itself to mentalities and ideologies, but instead represents a political instrument for better days.

Accepting this weak version of utopia, we do well to accept the contemporary moment: that social justice and freedom are the pillars of the new socialism, that we all surrender ourselves to the supremacy of the market. But we must not accept its logic. The "invisible hand" (and even Karl Popper accepts this)[5] is not perfection; it exacerbates and accumulates injustices.

For hope to survive it is necessary to associate social justice and freedom with the political instrument. The latter will no longer be the union of state and party, even if both are reformed, for postindustrial societies and information economies are "decentralized": politics is not the center of all change; nor do the state and the parties constitute the sole instruments for reforms. The "polyarchization" of contemporary societies, as Robert Dahl has pointed out,[6] is a fact. But, either we build mechanisms and institutions with which the citizen can relate, at various levels of society, to the *res publica* (the "public thing"), or the paths leading to the new society will not be established. We can and we must discuss the place of the "public," the limits that mass society and organizational society impose on the making of "public opinion." We can even dream of a rational public discourse à la Habermas or destroy the myth of the public man.[7] But we cannot escape redefining the scope of politics and extending it far beyond state and party.

Finally, in this brief introduction, which may not seem to address the theme proposed, but which, as we shall see, is necessary to clarify it, the other pillar of socialism, the theory of exploitation (of classes and of nations), has been shaken by an earthquake of magnitude 8 on the Richter scale: the technological-scientific revolution has greatly reduced the mass of the exploited who are necessary for the health of the capitalist system both at home and among nations. That said, what can be done?

THE PRESENT WORLD

It was Gorbachev who most vigorously helped turn the page of history, reducing Marxist salvationism to its present scale. But with what arguments? Basically by recognizing the two great elements that constitute the fabric of hope in the contemporary world: (1) that nuclear war no longer represents, à la Clausewitz, the continuation of politics by other means, but rather the extermination of mankind; and (2) that "centralism," of whatever stripe, undermines creativity and hinders technical progress.

The consequences become obvious. Security systems must be collective, driven not by fear of the threat one bloc may represent to the other, but by fear of the "end of the world." From there to giving preeminence to global issues and thus to ecology is but a small step. And, on the other dimension, when the idea of the centralizing state, of the global economic plan, and the rest is destroyed to the benefit both of local decision-making and the democratization of society one must then address the question of the market as an instrument for regulating the economy as well as the matter of political pluralism as an instrument for guaranteeing justice and legitimacy. Thus, one arrives at the question of setting up new institutions on different foundations.

There remains the issue of equality. It is obvious that although in the first moment, in the face of the "crisis of the empty shelves," even the issue of freedom yields to the issue of supply (as Boris Yeltsin noted recently) soon thereafter, the former Soviet society having been democratized, the issue of equality will reappear. It will reappear, though, not as an absolute value to be guaranteed by the revolution, by the party, and by the bureaucracy, but instead in relative terms of "more equality." No longer will the issue be one of "less state," as in the neoliberal wave (now perhaps in decline after Margaret Thatcher and Ronald Reagan), nor one of "more state," as in Stalinist Sovietism, but rather one of a "better state," aimed at correcting the inequalities caused by the market.

The welfare state once again? Why not? On condition that it be imbued with the signs of the present that it be defined more as a "movement," creating new public spaces so that the citizen and the organizations of civil society may participate institutionally in social decisions, than as a collection of mere "social policies," supported by state bureaucracies animated by the doctrine of whatever party holds power.

In one way or another notwithstanding the opinions of those social theorists who have seen in the modernization produced by capitalism the creation of "institutional orders" which were different, from each other functionally (economy, culture, religion, society, technique, production, etc.) and which would interrelate in a rather hierarchical pattern under the state a new model of social organization has surfaced. The new order is "decentralized," less functionally integrated, more "systemic." Decisions at all levels are adjusted by continuous feedback. Such a system adjusts to conflict and sets up equilibrium between a desire for freedom and a fear of chaos (nuclear war, ecological disaster, etc.). And things can fall apart.

In regard to what we may call the "ethos" of this new world that has reached Soviet society, we may identify a strange victory of reason. When many thought that a postmodern era of total fragmentation was dawning, an era in which any sort of global view would be impossible, an era marked by the union of cybernetics and totalitarianism (the "brave new world" of 1984), what happened was a strengthening of freedom, the pursuit of understanding, and a proliferation of global issues.

Thus, classes and nations in vast regions of the planet, although their differences have not been abolished, are experiencing a spirit of globalism and enlightenment. And all this is now being mistaken by many as a victory for competition, for self-reliant individualism, the market, and neoliberal capitalism.

Sweet delusion or bitter disappointment? It is true that the Soviet world and Eastern Europe and even China have returned to modernity in almost classical terms: market plus freedom. However, behind this marriage (which is not only one of convenience) there is a revolution in the mode of production and living that brings together humankind in a way that is very different from what one might imagine if one's explanatory framework were that of the "end of history" with the victory of neoliberalism.[8]

The rationale that wins, as I said, is more humble and is hardened by the genuine risk of nuclear holocaust and chaos. The desired freedom is to be found neither in revolutionary salvation nor in the contest of private interests decided by the hidden god of the market. The new humanism, if I may say so, finds its proper subject more in humankind than in individuals and is therefore a collective humanism. And in the realm of practical action there is something new that rests neither on the individual nor on his soul, objectified in the state or in a bureaucracy, but on setting up "intermediary bodies," which are not, in fact, "bodies" but movements and new public spaces.

Behind these changes, I repeat, is the true revolution of twentieth century: the marriage of science, technology, and freedom; of university, enterprise, and public authority. This "marriage" made it possible for the great technological revolutions (from nuclear energy and the laser beam, to biotechnology, to computers, microelectronics, and robotics) to go beyond the factory walls and affect the organization of society. This is why Castells describes the new global society as an "information" society and not merely postindustrial. The contemporary revolution reaches beyond the chain of production and kills "Fordism" and "Taylorism"; it revolutionizes the organization of the factory and of management; it reaches the public sector, the schools, the churches, the unions and, eventually, everything—not only through the new methods of management it permits, but also through the establishment of great mass-communication networks; not only through conventional electronic media (radio and television), but also through computer networks, facsimile machines, modems, and the rest.

All this, added to (and made possible by) the proliferation of the great manufacturing firms, the banks, the trading companies, and so on, provides the foundation for a globalized economy. And thus, along with the marriage of science, technology, and freedom, the great trend of the modern world is the globalization of the economy.

The centrally planned (socialist) economies collapsed because they were unable to absorb these changes and were unable to establish the necessary conditions for the evolution of this "new spirit." Perestroika ("restructuring"), along with glasnost ("openness" or "freedom") became necessary from the very moment when the USSR vilified cybernetics as a "bourgeois science." Thirty years would pass, however, before Gorbachev could openly criticize that attitude. The "organizational revolution," moreover, was never of any concern to the dogmatists of the "Gross plan." They still saw the world through infrastructural lenses. "Production" was their watchword, and productivity was to be improved only by investment in the "hard" industries—nothing "soft," no "human capital," no telemetrics for them.

The world of today, then, represents the victory of a "new rationality," of the technological revolution wedded to decentralized forms of management and decision-making. It favors a plurality of decision levels, making feasible a "polyarchical utopia."

AND THE SOUTH?

However, the Great Transformation—which caused centralizing authoritarianism to fall, which altered completely the forces of production and created the "information economy," giving new characteristics to classes and to class relations—has not reached the whole of the planet. Worse, while globalization of the economy caused the formation of new economic blocs, destroying the old East-West polarity and with it the U.S–Soviet hegemony, it also had a negative and disintegrating effect on the Third World.

In other words, the new "democratic-technological" revolution not only "integrated the world economy," but it also paved the way for the emergence of larger and more powerful political and economic entities: the United States plus Canada plus (who knows?) Mexico; the European Economic Community; those parts of the East wanting to participate in the European experience; Japan and parts of Southeast Asia; and even incipient but promising agreements for the integration of the Southern Cone. At the same time, however, the old "Third World" fragmented along two or three main fault lines. What was once only a part of the Third World constitutes today a huge Fourth World of need, hunger and, above all, hopelessness. Other parts of the Third World managed to become part of the global economy: the old newly industrialized countries (mainly in Asia) and those countries which, though lacking a strong industrial base, have found niches in the world economy (e.g., Chile, the drug-producing countries such as Colombia, and, above all, the petroleum-producing countries). Finally, some countries of continental size such as India, Brazil, and (to some extent) Indonesia as well as (with other characteristics) China have been unable to make the entire integrating jump, but do have the necessary internal resources to escape the "quaternization" that leads to poverty without hope.

Therefore, we are no longer talking about the South that was on the periphery of the capitalist core and was tied to it in a classical relationship of dependence. Nor are we speaking of the phenomenon, described some twenty-five years ago by Enzo Faletto and myself in our book *Dependency and Development in Latin America*,[9] whereby multinational companies transfer parts of the productive system and the local producers are tied to foreign capital in the "dependent-associated" development model. We are dealing, in truth, with a crueler phenomenon: either the South (or a portion of it) enters the democratic-technological-scientific race, invests heavily in R&D, and endures the "information economy" metamorphosis, or it becomes unimportant, unexploited, and unexploitable.

So the South is in double jeopardy seemingly able neither to integrate itself, pursuing its own best interests, nor to avoid "being integrated" as servants of the rich economies. Those countries (or parts thereof) that are unable to repeat the revolution of the contemporary world, and at the same time find a niche in the international market, will end up in the "worst of all possible worlds." They will not even be considered worth the trouble of exploitation; they will become inconsequential, of no interest to the developing globalized economy.

On the other hand, those Southern countries that do succeed in finding a way to join the contemporary revolution, even partially, will face still another problem. They must define how they will integrate themselves (i.e., a selective policy of "opening up markets," an appropriate industrial policy, an educational policy that makes it possible to integrate the masses into contemporary culture, a science and technology policy capable of supporting economic growth, etc.) without being swallowed up by the globalization of the world economy.

The problem is that the South's great comparative advantage, which once ensured its integration into the international market, albeit in a condition of dependency, has lost its importance. Basically, that advantage was an abundance of arable land, mineral resources, and cheap labor. Thus, "quaternization" now seems to be the most likely outcome for those countries that can count only on such resources.

There has been, then, a substantial change in the dependency relationship between South and North and I would say, it is a twofold change: (1) certain areas of the earth are of greatly diminished importance to the world economy (even considering their exploited and dependent condition); and (2) in other parts of the South, the challenge is no longer solely "economic" but now involves the whole of society. Let me clarify. In the past, it was possible to respond politically to the old dependency relations by appealing to "national autonomy," by demanding more industrial investment in order to correct deterioration in the term of trade, and by expanding the domestic market in order to break the chain of "enclave dependency" and stimulate the internal distribution of revenue. Now the political response demands that the South, too, construct a new kind of society.

A future with dignity for the countries of the South will be achieved only with more education, a better state, enhanced productivity from its "human capital," and a great technological leap forward (information technology, new materials, environmental sense, and new modes of organization). Also required are a democratized society and state (necessary conditions, as noted above, for the marriage of production, university, and society in an atmosphere of freedom which is conducive to organizational and technological innovation).

A NEW DIALOGUE

So, we are back at the beginning. Paradoxically, in a world in which technique once seemed to generate the authoritarian control of everything, now this same technique presupposes freedom. In the advanced capitalist countries, as the failure of the socialist societies showed, without hope, without a utopia (even a " middle-range" utopia), there can be no continuation of "progress" (although progress is not inevitable, since both nuclear holocaust and error remain as possibilities).

In the Southern countries, priority must be given to societal reform. Otherwise, their positive integration into the world economy will not be possible. In this case, too, progress (hope, the welfare state, democratic socialism, social democracy) is neither the necessary consequence of the current challenge nor the only way to attain the democratization of society and state. But they remain as valid and contemporary options, provided they are brought properly up to date.

It should be noted that, in the face of the challenge of modernity and the impression that reason and the market are closely intertwined notions, the political concern in vast areas of the South is that the reaction against inequality can occur only through a strengthening of the national will perched upon the fortress of the state. Where this conviction finds the bases for its propagation in faith (as in Islam), cultural regression may be proudly presented as if it were an instrument of progress. In many areas of the South, discouragement seeks sublimation in new salvationist theses that substitute for blind faith in the inevitability of revolution (which was an attribute of the industrial world until the coming of the "information economy") through national unity against imperialism (or whatever epithet is now given to "advanced capitalism").

This regressive response, if not capable of shaking the foundations of the modern world (and it might well threaten them, as in the case of Iraq, forcing military reactions which are also irrational, even when aimed at wiping out evil) does absorb human energy. Indeed, this kind of response paralyzes vast sectors of the South, which, instead of seeking appropriate answers to their troubles (even more so in the Fourth World, which finds no answers at all), develop regressive ideologies. Skeptical about utopias, even those of "middle range," such movements create nothing but matrices for the local "counterculture," with only isolated repercussions in the hegemonic centers.

It is therefore necessary to redefine the dependency issue. This redefinition, however, so as not to yield only discouragement and a feeling that the South is either no longer of any importance or impossible to "integrate," will require a Copernican revolution of the kind proposed by Gorbachev. Just as the Berlin Wall did not begin to collapse until the moment when the former Soviet leader recognized the futility of war between the two superpower blocs and the impossibility of economic centralism beating capitalism, neither will the South, at least those sectors where nothing but hopelessness is to be found, escape its perverse isolation until its problems are considered in a global context.

The "new humanism," the "global village," and "spaceship earth," all these fine-sounding phrases become cynical slogans when they do not include poverty, backwardness, illiteracy, in short, the problems of the old Third World, as matters to be discussed and faced at a global level. This "globalization" of Third World problems cannot be approached as a unit, since, as we know, the South is not homogeneous. The term "new humanism" may mean, for many countries, something like: "renegotiation of the foreign debt in terms compatible with development, plus technology transfers, plus access to world markets." For other countries it may mean nothing less than the direct transfer of food, health care, and schooling.

What cannot happen is what has been happening until now: in discussions of the "crisis of socialism" and in reassessments of the effects of the "global economy," the South remains as a mere hindrance to which only lip service is paid. If the socialism of the future is to reclaim hope, it will be necessary to adopt a global approach and to treat as common issues, along with the environment, the problems of poverty and of rebuilding the societies, not just the economies, of the Third World. If this ethical dimension is lacking, the ideology now being prepared for a renewed social democracy will have the bitter taste of hypocrisy.

But it is not simply a matter of "ethics." Third World poverty, cultural regression in some areas, and the hopelessness all this brings will have an impact on the First World in various and menacing ways: migrations, disproportionate demographic growth among the "non-internationalizable" populations, terrorism, and authoritarian nation-states whose powers, though limited, can be menacing nonetheless.

Therefore, whether with a utopian vision or with a plan for preserving well-being already attained, the "new socialism"—or, more properly, social democracy—must address the North-South relationship in a new spirit. Just as there was a way to bring East and West together, there is now, in the new international order of the globalized economy, a gap to be bridged by a dialogue founded on realism and, at the same time, on solidarity, without which the populations of the Fourth World, at least, will continue to suffer in poverty and oblivion.

NOTES

1. Oskar Lafontaine, "El socialismo y los nuevos movimientos sociales," *El Socialismo del Futuro* (Madrid), 1 (May 1990).

2. Habermas's first important book in this genre was *The Structural Transformation of the Public Sphere* (Cambridge: MIT Press, 1989). See also *Knowledge and Human Interest* (Boston: Beacon Press, 1971) and *Legitimation Crisis* (Boston: Beacon Press, 1973).

3. Mikhail Gorbachev, *Perestroika: New Thinking for Our Country and the World* (New York: Harper and Row, 1987).

4. R. K. Merton, *Social Theory and Social Structure* (New York: The Free Press, 1949), especially the introduction.

5. For example: Popper's lecture under the auspices of Bank Hofman, Zurich, June 9, 1988, published as "Algumas Observações sobre a Teoria e a Praxis do Estado Democrático," *Risco* (Spring 1990).

6. See R. Dahl, *Polyarchy: Participation and Opposition* (New Haven, Conn.: Yale University Press, 1971) and his more recent *Democracy and Its Critics* (New Haven, Conn.: Yale University Press, 1989), especially part 5 ("The Limits and Possibilities of Democracy").

7. See Richard Sennett, *The Fall of Public Man* (New York: Alfred A. Knopf, 1977).

8. See Francis Fukuyama, "The End of History?" *The National Interest*, 16 (Summer 1989). Also see *La Fin de l'histoire et le dernier homme* (Paris: Flammarion, 1992), published in English as *The End of History and the Last Man* (New York: The Free Press, 1992).

9. Fernando Henrique Cardoso and Enzo Faletto, *Dependency and Development in Latin America* (Berkeley and Los Angeles: University of California Press, 1979).

→ 24 ←

Viable Utopia

The period of history inaugurated with the fall of the Berlin Wall has the conditions necessary to be largely a better era than the world of bipolar conflict. This idea may seem straightforward and virtually unquestionable. Nonetheless, there are still those who lament the end of the Cold War, perhaps because the Cold War made it easier to explain the world, and to a certain extent brought a greater degree of predictability to the international scene.

To be sure, the contemporary international system is characterized by greater uncertainty, and this situation creates mixed feelings. On the one hand, there are those who see the end of the Cold War affecting the international policy agenda in positive ways: the triumph of democracy and market economies as universal values bringing with it, inevitably, a new era of peace and prosperity. On the other hand, pessimists emphasize conflicts of an ethnic or religious nature, the so-called "Clash of Civilizations"; or, commercial disputes as substitutes for ideological confrontation; or, the incapacity of the United Nations, despite its success in the Persian Gulf War, to cope with a new type of localized conflict.

A more accurate assessment will be found at some intermediate point, between these two extremes. From the point of view of governments, though, the most relevant question seems to be how to consolidate and propagate the positive effects brought on by the end of the Cold War, and how to make them more prevalent than the negative.

The positive effects begin with the thawing of international relations since the Cold War, which was marked by a fragile peace maintained by a balance of terror, by

Adapted from Fernando Henrique Cardoso, "A Utopia Viável," in *A Utopia Viável. Trajetória intelectual de Fernando Henrique Cardoso* (Brasília: Secretaria de Documentação Histórica, Gabinete Pessoal do Presidente da República, 1995), 85–94. Originally a lecture at the University of Porto, Portugal, July 22, 1995.

the exacerbation of regional conflicts through ideological confrontation, and by the paralysis of international organizations. Another positive effect that must be noted is the international convergence of values, which has occurred to a reasonable degree. Democracy predominates, if not always as a reality, then at least as an objective to be reached. The respect for human rights has been established as a common norm of civilized conduct, international environmental protection mechanisms are being strengthened, and the notion of economic liberty as the basis for growth is seen as complemented by political liberty.

If we were to take as a basis for measure the United Nations' global conferences on population, women, human rights, social development, and the environment, it could be said that the conditions, the quality, and the potential of human life are at the center of international debates. The recognition that these "new or renewed" issues are also "global" themes, in the sense that the interests of humanity must supersede those of different social and political systems, is an important advance made possible by the end of the ideological divide. As Marx believed the proletariat a universal class, and class struggle a phenomenon that knew no borders, the global issues of today remind us that there is something universal that transcends traditional ideologies.

Nevertheless, we are still in a stage of "conceptual gains." To move to the next stage, to transform this convergence of values into concrete action, is the task that remains before us. And we must move rapidly, for if plans remain "abstract" promises, these common values could quickly lose their basis of legitimacy at the moment when pressure is increasing in the populace for democracy, in the broadest sense of the word, and for material progress.

If democracy and the defense of human rights are perceived as universal values, how may we expand their supremacy? If the international community agrees that environmental protection is a priority, do mechanisms for international cooperation provide a sufficient response to these problems? If the concern for social justice is no longer the monopoly of any single ideological current, how may we combat hunger and poverty in an effective manner? If economic globalization is beneficial, how may we avoid the social exclusion of those parts of the population that are unable to integrate themselves into the economy in light of new standards of competitiveness? If the bipolar world has ceased to exist, why are we unable to make use of the existing mechanisms of collective security, or to reform them so that they may be made more effective? These questions demonstrate a convergence between international and national agendas. The greatest challenge is harmonizing and combining national actions and international cooperation not only as values, but also through the initiation of concrete projects.

Against the backdrops of the worldwide multipolarity of the post–Cold War era, and alongside discussions of economic globalization and the great issues of human survival, the discussion of the ethics of progress will once again be of increasing importance in the coming years. In other words: on the eve of the new millennium, a "new humanism" is emerging on the horizon. The acceleration and the amplitude of scientific and technological development forces contemporary society to confront the issues that, while they may be similar to those faced by the men of the Renaissance, require a different perspective: it is not about man, an individual subject, as the measure of all things, but of humanity, a collective subject, as measured by the survival of all its civilizations and cultures.

For a technological civilization impregnated with a rational and disenchanted culture, to what degree will this notion of humanity bring us back to notions of social justice, of the search for equality, and of a new utopia, not only within every country, but also on the larger scale of international relations? The answer to this question is unclear, because concrete policy options are implicated.

After the collapse of socialism, I do not believe, as many others seem to, that the world will be condemned to choose between triumphant "neoliberalism" and some emaciated social democracy struggling to survive as a viable modern ideology. I believe that faith in the spontaneous regulation of prices and salaries by the "market," both ideologically motivated and genuine, will increasingly cede its place to the recognition of a need to implement compensatory measures that correct the distortions created by this market. And, for this reason, I also believe that social democracy has a new opportunity to become an attractive path, if we were to add to it a new utopian dimension that strengthens spaces for public participation, that institutionalizes participatory democracy, and that reconciles rights and individual motivations with the reality that citizens live in common, collective situations.

This viable utopia, as contradictory a term as it be, begins with the assumption that social justice continues as an objective and value to be pursued. And an assumption of equal order is that the promotion of social justice is viable, because the development of a technological capitalist society creates possibilities, through the accumulation of wealth and knowledge, and needs, for the correction of distortions and imbalances, due to the social exclusions that these create.

The search for justice is ever more a question that concerns all countries, rich and poor, that are confronted with, albeit at different levels, similar problems of social provision for aging populations and employment for youth entering the labor market; of universal access to basic health, education, and housing; and of social marginalization, drugs, and delinquency.

In the international context this viable utopia, in the intermediate term, does not mean the creation of a "new international economic order," an illusory dream developing countries hoped to realize in the 1960s and 1970s through North-South negotiations. It does mean internal reforms, "homework," and "good governance" in all developing and developed countries. But it also requires that the issue of development be reintroduced in the international agenda as a "global issue" of general scope, as it in truth includes all the other "new or renewed" issues. The South will only emerge from its isolation, will only be integrated into the global economy if its issues regain a central place in the efforts at international cooperation.

It is clear that this globalization of development cannot be conducted in blocs, as if the South were a singular entity. We have already committed this error. The "new humanism" will mean, for some countries of the South, access to markets and technology; for others, humanitarian assistance and food aid. In neither of these cases are there reasons for fruitless confrontations. All these efforts obey the same logic of a new utopia, more modest, but accordingly more feasible.

In sum, politics is less "the art of the possible" and more the "art of making possible that which is necessary."

⇥ 25 ⇤

Radicalizing Democracy

Democracy is a fundamental theme in political science. And it is a theme that is as provocative as it is inexhaustible, because it is basically linked to the permanent problem of defining what makes a good society, to the problem of the ability of men and women to create institutions that will ensure liberty and justice. In our times, however, concern over the manner in which democratic regimes are able to face the major contemporary issues is particularly relevant. As Anthony Giddens teaches us, from a somewhat different angle, some of the factors that favor the expansion of liberal democratic institutions contribute themselves to the creation of new challenges that appear to bring into question the ability of those institutions to act.

Some elements that were identified with the functioning of modern democracy, such as political parties, the use of the State as a mechanism for the promotion of social well-being and, at a more basic level, the idea that the State must be in full control of the processes that affect its people, have weakened. I shall mention just some aspects of the problem:

1. First, in relation to institutions, the mechanisms for the aggregation of interests, particularly political parties, find it difficult to keep up with the demands of representation made in the context of the thematic fragmentation that characterizes contemporary political life, which reflects the fragmentation of constituencies along the lines of specific sectional interests, which go far beyond the mere position occupied by the individual in the production system. Political parties share the arena with the NGOs, which offer a different perspective, a nonencompassing and deliberately segmented perspective.

Adapted from the untitled lecture at the London School of Economics, December 3, 1997.

2. Second, due to the fiscal restrictions faced by the State in a situation where international involvement is inevitable and increasingly competitive, new limitations tend to affect the effort towards social inclusion, for the construction of that intelligent combination of formal democracy and substantive democracy that has been the program of European social democracy. In the developed countries, this has led to the rethinking of the structures of social welfare. In the developing countries, this issue becomes even more complex because we are starting from the situation of an "ill-fare state" if I may say so and the challenge is even greater, because advances in communications and transport techniques, as well as in the process of urbanization itself, have brought within everyone's reach, not prosperity itself, but the image of the prosperity of others in their own country and in countries abroad.

3. Third, the process of globalization makes it more difficult for national projects to be carried out even when they have popular support. Several issues that affect people's daily lives involve transnational factors outside the control of governments. International financial flows are an obvious example of this, as they show the extent to which the structures of governance existing at the global level fall short of what would be required for this type of phenomenon to be dealt with within the framework of the democratic process.

4. Finally, in Latin American countries there is often the perception that the reestablishment of democracy in the 1980s did not bring about solutions to social problems, and this sometimes gives way to a certain nostalgia for authoritarian rule. Although not calling for its return, such nostalgia leads to impatience with the negotiating process that is an integral part of democracy and to entertaining the notion that the executive branch of government could hold powers similar to those of an autocratic regime. Having thus outlined the elements of the problem, we may now ask what solutions are available for democracy today. I believe that the answer lies not in less but rather in more democracy. I maintain that it is necessary to radicalize democracy, to go to the roots of the processes that permit a sovereign people to control its destiny in the new context created by contemporary mass society. We should view democracy not only as a point of arrival, but also as a point of departure.

We are going through a unique historical opportunity with reasonably stable international conditions; at the same time, we do not have a clear road map to help us chart the problems. For example, a complete economic theory accounting for the effects of globalization does not yet exist. As regards social relations, it is difficult to know how to carry out a process of change in contemporary society in the absence of all-embracing ideologies and in a situation where society often moves ahead faster than those who are trying to lead it. It is also difficult to know which can be the historical forces behind transformation processes when the state is becoming weaker and when so many new forms of social identity are superimposed on traditional class divisions.

Too often have those who discuss these themes resorted to old concepts in an attempt to understand new situations. However, the fact that the issues are complex does not mean that we cannot have ideals or a sense of direction. Ideals include striking a balance in the process of listening to numerous fragmented demands. The key to this balance that is central to the idea of the radicalization of democracy is the idea that the State must serve all citizens effectively. How is that possible?

1. First of all, it is necessary to work with a broad concept of citizenship, which while retaining the old bases (essentially the notion of participation in politics), goes further and incorporates local and individual demands. The citizen is no longer simply a voter. He or she acts also as a member of a class, an ethnic group, a sexual minority, as an unemployed, a landless peasant, etc., and this multiplicity of points of view must be reflected in the functioning of the political system. The State must be prepared to enter into a dialogue with the diverse groups that reflect the plurality of identities of the individual in contemporary society.

2. How can the citizen have any control in an economy in which the market is central and privatization a necessary course? One must overcome the simplistic notion that what is in the best interest of the citizenry has to originate necessarily in the State. The mechanisms for regulating "privatized public" activities (communications, electricity, transport, etc.) must be guided by the needs of the people and, to that end, the direct participation by representatives of civil society in the bodies concerned is fundamental. The State must be porous and permeable to the needs of its citizens. The identification of the State with national interest cannot be assumed, but it is a political construction work that requires major efforts to reach consensus.

3. Democracy entails the need to ensure universal access to essential public services, as one of the main conditions for bringing about an effectively participating citizenship. And naturally, the first such services are education and health. More than ever, education is a decisive factor in the building of citizenship, particularly in a country like Brazil where so much remains to be done in this respect. Health is an equally indispensable element in the dignity of the citizen. Under present conditions, the solution to social problems calls for a creative partnership between state and society. There is an arena for new forms of dialogue and combined action that could make a fundamental contribution to bringing about what has already been termed "substantive democracy."

4. We face the task of renewing the political dimension, the task of giving a voice to all, under conditions of effective liberty. The public sphere should be really public and, under the conditions of contemporary democracy, this requires a sphere of debate and dialogue, a sphere of tolerance and respect for others. Radicalizing democracy means ensuring the right conditions for effective liberty, so that all citizens, even those who are not formally organized, are able to have a say in the process. There is an important role here for the State in ensuring freedom of expression and in seeking to contribute to the building of the public arena.

5. Finally, it will be necessary to find answers to the challenges posed by the globalization process to democracy. This issue must be examined outside the traditional framework of autarkic schemes. We shall not return to an international system on the Westphalian mold. Interdependence between States, today, is a fact of life and ignorance of this fact would condemn our efforts to the realm of fantasy. However, we can examine the question of what can and what must be regulated in the international field in order that the will of citizens may be exercised democratically. It is necessary, for example, to consider the role of the Bretton Woods institutions and the composition and the procedures of the United Nations Security Council.

The consideration of these challenges to democracy could appear to suggest a task of such enormous complexity as to place an excessive burden on political systems that are already responding with difficulty to the daily needs of government and which are seen to be even less effective when it comes to carrying out major reforms. However, not everything depends on the political system, the parties or the State. In our times society often anticipates transformation and experiences processes of changes that arise straight from social movements at the grass-root level.

This has been the case in Brazil. In the transition from authoritarian rule to democracy, a veritable democratic revolution took place within Brazilian society, with the emergence of new players (organizations and social groups) and the defining of a new pattern of relations between society and the State, characterized by the demand for transparency, openness and access to the decision-making process.

More recently, this substratum of social democracy was what enabled the Brazilian people to exercise a clear and conscious option in favor of the economic stability achieved with the implementation of the Real Plan. As a matter of fact, for the Brazilian people, the success of economic stability has had a very important political significance. Quite obviously, controlling inflation has not been the magical solution to all Brazil's problems. However, the Real Plan or rather, economic stability, has united Brazilians and created a consensus on a national objective that has been defined and brought about through democratic means.

These brief observations on recent Brazilian history illustrate, in my view, the fact that the goal of radicalizing democracy cannot be achieved from top to bottom, by government decree, but it involves the mobilization of society itself. It is largely a matter of removing obstacles to the strengthening of democracy and to its unimpeded exercise. Some of these obstacles are to be found within the state apparatus itself hence the decisive importance of proposals aimed at reforming the State.

We are multiplying and consolidating collective channels of expression, further decentralizing discussion and decision-making processes, making them more open to participation, bringing public authority closer to the people and the people closer to public authority. In essence, we are going to the Latin root of the word power, by conveying to the citizens the certainty that they can voice their opinions and it is worth the effort, that they can contribute to change and that, again, it is worth the effort. This spells out the full meaning to the term "citizenship." Although under different circumstances, I find the same perspective in the concept of a "stakeholder society," so ably elaborated by Prime Minister Tony Blair. When I am asked if this radically pluralist democracy, this increasingly democratic democracy, will resolve the problem of exclusion, my answer is a clear yes, all the more so because there is no alternative.

In addition, if society is many-sided in its essence, the solutions cannot but reflect this fact. The plight of the poor who are marginalized from the development process is not the only form of exclusion. Important as it is, it is only one form. In fact, there are several forms of exclusion: that of women, children, the elderly, the uneducated, the unemployed, the disabled, victims of violence, the landless, and those affected by pollution and environmental damage. It is not enough, therefore, to politicize just one line of exclusion, following the model of class struggle.

All forms of exclusion must be politicized and in all these areas mobilization must be encouraged, organizations must be formed and the channels between such organizations and the State must be expanded. Maintaining that the simplistic dichotomies between left and right, workers and capitalists, should be replaced by an acknowledgement of the complexity of our societies does not mean being conservative, as some "fundamentalists" would have us believe (in the sense in which Professor Giddens uses the term).

On the contrary, it means accepting change and seeking even greater change; it means being prepared to participate in the building of something really new.

It is in the spirit of this intellectual challenge that I sincerely wish the young students of the London School of Economics and Political Science, that they may have the good fortune to contribute to the building of a world that is more democratic, more prosperous and more inclined towards solidarity—a radically better world.

⤳ 26 ⤳

Agenda for the New Century

"If humanity wants to have a recognizable future, it cannot be through the prolongation of the past or the present. If we try to construct the third millennium on these bases, we will fail. And the price of this failure, that is, the alternative for a changed society, is darkness."[1] With these words, Eric Hobsbawm closed his book *The Age of Extremes*, a sober and brilliant reflection on the twentieth century, and led us to a worrisome question. Change is necessary given the evident problems that humanity confronts, but we are lacking a model to guide our changes.

The problems we face are easy to identify. First, absolute poverty is still the principal challenge for most of humanity and we are a long way from establishing the social bases necessary for everyone to have the minimum conditions of a decent existence. For the huge majority of the world's population, education, health, and secure shelter are distant dreams. Developed societies confront the reality of structural unemployment. More than simply an economic given, this represents a dramatic social condition insofar as it affects confidence in the future for many people, especially the youth.

The rich and the poor worlds interact through migration, but in place of solidarity this has led to isolationism, exclusion, and xenophobia. Rapid population growth, linked to an absence of sustainable development projects, threatens the global environment, and once again it is poor populations who suffer the most. In the long term, if we are unable to propose and introduce effective change, our own prospects for life on Earth will be endangered. The drug problem is expanding and becoming more than a problem of policing; we may be faced with a social disease with profound roots.

Adapted from Fernando Henrique Cardoso, "Agenda para o Século XXI," in Presidência da República, *A Utopia Viável. Trajetória intelectual de Fernando Henrique Cardoso* (Brasília: Secretaria de Documentação Histórica, Gabinete Pessoal do Presidente da República, 1995), 95–106. Originally prepared for publication in "Architects of the Upswing: Agenda for the 21st Century" in *Frankfurter Allgemeine Zeitung*.

The international economic system reveals onerous instabilities for all nations, and many problems, such as the volatility of international capital flows, do not have simple solutions. In the political sphere, even though the end of the Cold War has cleared the horizon, we still have not arrived at a broad consensus that will permit efficient and lasting solutions for many crises and regional conflicts.

If identifying problems is easy, as in this list of examples, the difficulty begins when one looks for alternative ways to overcome them and to distance oneself from the "darkness." Can we be optimistic? Are there real possibilities of truly global solutions to the problems I have mentioned? Moreover, if we know that many of these problems are dramatic, some in the short term (such as poverty) and others in the long term (such as the environment), why do they appear to lack those mobilizing elements that induce new attitudes and "force" societies to find effective solutions?

In Brazil, the problems of a developed society are added to the problems of a society that is poor and unjust. We must simultaneously push to modernize our productive sector, maintaining competitiveness and generating employment, and put in place systems that ensure universal access to education, health, and social services. To be sure, coping with marked inequalities is disconcerting; it requires creativity, generosity, and a sense of justice.

Marx said that by analyzing nineteenth-century England, which at the time represented the most advanced example of capitalism, he would be able to shed light on the tendencies of societal evolution. Similarly, as Brazil is still a divided society with obvious contrasts, perhaps we have our own original perspective for understanding what is happening in the world and what is necessary to transform it. In fact, in my list of problems, the theme of inequality always recurs, be it in the form of social contrast, ethnic conflict, or contrasting perspectives in the face of international processes.

I want to say up front that I am not a pessimist. I have affirmed that our age can be transformed into a "New Renaissance." And to structure my reflections, I come back to an important legacy of the twentieth century: the conflict between socialists and liberals. If, like Hobsbawm, we do not wish to simply repeat the past, it is best to understand it well. Here, I do not wish to take up again a comparison between the two systems, but rather call attention to an aspect that, in my mind, is crucial in orienting the change that we strive for: values.

Marx's contributions to the understanding of capitalism were numerous. However, his most profound theoretical contribution has been to link the process of social transformation to an ethical proposition of profoundly egalitarian character. Various aspects of reality—economics, politics, and the world of values—are interconnected and form an intelligible whole, with laws of movement that point in a certain direction in the future. The recognition that the social whole is contradictory, dialectic, and overdetermined by relations to the modes of production will not draw us away from understanding the sense of change, which would necessarily bring greater equality.

When socialism is converted, however, into an ideological form in political regimes, this dialectical understanding of reality is lost. We know that the defect of socialism, and the cause of its downfall, was the incapacity of regimes both to grow in a sustainable manner and to be responsive to the ideals of equality. Economic growth stalled because socialist regimes did not realize that freedom, the uncontrolled circulation of ideas and information, is a necessary ingredient for development. The values and ethical objectives failed because ideas ossified and lost vitality. This cracked the legitimacy of regimes, both because they were creating new modalities of inequality (within socialist states and between them) and because individual liberty was underestimated as a value that is necessary and essential in its own right for the affirmation of citizens.

Liberal ideological solutions, on the other hand, that did not have the coherence that socialism had as its starting point, became more consistent over the long term. The combination of the market, individual liberties, and democracy resulted from a historical construction. From whence come the varieties of formulas for "real capitalism," which includes everything from the individualist forms, of the Anglo-Saxon world, to the state-society linkages of the Japanese model, which are affirmed in Asia. The market economy became ever more malleable. Its dynamism, foreseen by Marx, was notable, above all because it encountered political conditions of progress, provided essentially by democratic regimes. It is important to recall that, contrary to socialism, market economies admit different social solutions to ethical issues. More clearly, the market has political requirements, such as individual liberty, but does not automatically generate uniform models of social coexistence. This accounts for the distance between the social-democratic and neoliberal models under the same rubric of "market economy." The latitude for choice in structuring social solutions is broad. When we speak of this choice, we are speaking of values, or of an ethical orientation.

This contrast between the failure of real socialism and the varieties of real capitalism is still very alive, and I believe that we have yet to learn its lessons on how to orient our behavior as we face the challenges of the twenty-first century.

Insofar as solutions dictated by the logic of the market are seen as triumphant and ideologically hegemonic, we run the risk of attributing to the market something that it is not capable of offering: the capacity to generate models of social coexistence and political orientation. In other words, in wanting to attribute to the market virtues that it does not possess, we can commit the error of uprooting the economy from the social realm, and (this is most grave) of reducing politics to the art of "preserving" the potential of the market.

However, the experience of real socialism revealed that the implementation of an egalitarian ideal, while necessary, is an insufficient criterion of good governance. Ideals that cannot be effectively realized lose their legitimacy. They disorient and become an inverted mirror, in the classic form of ideological expression, showing not what society can reach, but what the structures of domination "pretend" to offer. One of the advantages of democracy is precisely that it has increasingly effective mechanisms to evaluate the direction and efficiency of government. In a certain way, politics today has the possibility of being anchored in reality, and this is an undeniable gain of our times. Ideology, in the Marxist conception, can be replaced with a real dispute about ideas and ideals.

Thus, combining efficiency and equity is a worthy objective. The difficulty is pre-cisely in identifying those parameters that assure that, after starting with an impulse toward efficiency, equity may also be obtained. I would even say that there is a meas-ure of consensus when we speak of broad objectives of transformation, but that this is lost when we come to discuss methods of realizing them, as localized interests then begin to be affected by the change.

With regard to the distance between consensus about objectives and the dispute about methods, recent examples of Brazilian reality may be illustrative. The critiques made of the program of national stabilization, the Real Plan (*Plano real*), above all by economists on the left, were that while the plan may be efficient, it would never be equitable. These critics do not identify, in their ideological repertoire, economic sta-bility as a value of interest to the majority of the population. Moreover, in consider-ing the process of stabilization, they focus not so much on stability, but on the risks of recession. But what happened was just the opposite: the biggest beneficiaries of stability were the poorest of the Brazilian population. Another example is social se-curity, which is a universal problem today, given the financial crisis of the states. Mea-sures that may appear "unjust, albeit efficient" for many, especially when they think exclusively of the short term, can mean more balanced benefits in the long term.

The need to account for both efficiency and equity, in the long and short terms, is not simple, and cannot be satisfied through preconceived formulas. It rather consti-tutes a path and a set of values. It is necessary, therefore, to transform these values into effective parameters for social change. These would be, in my view, some of the essential lessons of the period that we lived, in which my generation was formed for intellectual and political life.

Why do I now speak of a "New Renaissance"? The Renaissance had numerous philosophical and historical implications. One of the most fundamental was to give to individuals the notion that they could control their own fate. The Renaissance Man came to feel, on the one hand, abandoned, since he was missing the certainty of hierarchies created by religion; on the other hand, he came to feel stronger despite this, because in the end he was the master of his own destiny. Nothing expresses this better than the transformations in the modes of scientific investigation, which be-came free and limitless, the liberation of politics from religious constraints, courtesy of Machiavelli, and above all changes in the visual arts. The truly dramatic shift from static iconography toward movement and perspective was a clear signal of a new "worldview."

The Renaissance also coincided with a new consciousness of the "dimensions of the world" brought about by a sequence of discoveries. The Renaissance thus foretold the Enlightenment that would in turn create a certain tranquil confidence in the progress of humanity through the advance of reason.

Today, certainly, artistic expressions also suggest a new epoch. Not through the "discovery" of techniques of representation (like new pictorial perspectives), as in the Renaissance. In a certain manner, the vanguards of the twentieth century already demonstrated the infinite capacity of artistic invention of contemporary man, to such a point that today we can say there exists an "aesthetic exhaustion" resulting from the excess of experimentalism. The novelty in the arts is rather along the lines of what was foreseen by Benjamin. New technologies support ever more perfect and infinite forms, multiplying artistic possibilities. To give an example that caught my attention, I received a few days ago a perfect reproduction of a painting by a great Brazilian painter done by copying the original with a scanner. Such technological possibilities will certainly have some impact on the very progress of artistic creation, and it will also hugely democratize our access to cultural goods. The arts are sending us an important signal. It is as if there is a tacit announcement, in harmony with that of the Renaissance, of how much we can do. There is, however, a fundamental difference in relation to the Renaissance: the sentiment of liberty is not built upon ideal models of a past civilization, like the Greco-Roman era for the Italians of the fifteenth and sixteenth centuries, but it has value in itself. It is a challenge that recalls a feeling of abandonment for many, because the liberty of creation today no longer corresponds to an aesthetic model that serves as a pattern and reference.

It is appropriate that, in mentioning these arts, I have accentuated what they have offered to science and to technology. In fact, everyone recognizes that the core of the contemporary process of transformation lies in scientific and technological diffusion, coupled with the infinite expansion of forms of communication. We are confronted with an era of discovery and advances that create powerful forces of social and economic transformation. The speed and the novelty of technological offerings create a sort of wonderment with the powers not only of technology, but also of the market. We can do so much. Perhaps the stock of scientific and technological knowledge is now sufficient to alleviate some of the chronic problems of our time, such as hunger and absolute poverty. But what can we do to ensure that this knowledge serves humanity, and that it not exacerbates inequalities?

One of the risks we run is precisely that of transferring to the impersonal market the "responsibility" of creating and adapting oneself to the new times. We know, as I pointed out, about the advantages of the market as a generator of wealth and creativity. We also know that the market is based on certain values, like liberties, but that they are insufficient to set an agenda of social coexistence. If the market reigned supreme, there would be, as perhaps in the domain of aesthetics, a sentiment of profound abandonment. And the idea of alienation, in the Marxist sense of the word, would return, as we would be confronted with forces of our own creation that we do not know how to control.

The absence of a more dialectical debate on the objectives of the market and liberty could cause them to lose the mobilizing virtues they have had and rather lead to a crisis of values. In fact, what are missing now are no longer religious certainties, but ideological certainties that, for better or worse, gave us the ethical impulse for change. The existence of an alternative model of society, in turn, put the market economy on the defensive and generated movements for transformation and betterment. It is not by chance that Hobsbawm affirms, in the most dialectic spirit that "Capitalism only survived to show its superior capacity because of socialism."

In sum, man lives with possibilities of "rebirth," a new liberty to reinvent models of social coexistence. The models are still in the process of being defined, and in the present stage point more to limits to what should not be done than to positive patterns.

Another contemporary phenomenon engendered by technological progress that reinforces the thesis of the "New Renaissance" is that of globalization, which is producing a new consciousness of the dimensions of the world. Events everywhere affect nearly all the various aspects of our lives. The Renaissance established the individual as subject, and with the retreat of religious interference in politics, left the terrain open for the definition of a new model of social organization, the sovereign state. Now, the advance of globalization designates "humanity as the new subject," and in a certain way, that very same state is obliged to adapt itself to new circumstances. This powerful notion of a "global community" is altering our worldview and, as a consequence, that of leaders in government, which can no longer see problems simply through a national lens. Solidarity is becoming an exigency that does not result only from the ethical conscience of peoples. The UN Global Conferences, in coping with themes such as the environment, human rights, population, women, urban problems, and social development, reveal clearly that the world of politics is one of conflicts and contradictions, and is no longer contained by national boundaries.

However, the result of this process is not straightforward. If the new agenda is universal in theme, it will not be so—as, for example, during the Cold War—by virtue of any organizing theme. When we think of possibilities for effective transformation, we are obliged to weave arguments that are universal, but that can have different patterns. There does not exist, as Marx proposed, a conflict that is central, unifying, and of transnational character. The processes will necessarily be complex. We do have, however, an advantage over the globalization of the Renaissance. This is the difference in cultural hierarchizations, or the ideology of the civilizational superiority of the West. Today, after anthropology has debunked this myth of superiority, globalization makes clear that problems effectively belong to everyone. "National" responsibilities for solutions can still differ, but the consciousness that problems belong to humanity, and that they ask for the participation of all, is an indisputable gain. A clear institutional expression of this tendency is the exhaustion of the national state as a provider of solutions for economic and social questions. The importance of the so-called new actors—be they NGOs or multilateral organizations—can be summed up in the recognition by the state that innovative institutional solutions are necessary for the challenges of the present. Regional integration is the principal example of the configuration of a new structure of relations between states.

Thus, it is not only the feeling of abandonment that marks the entrance into the twenty-first century. The analogy with the Renaissance is useful because we are faced with unique opportunities for positive changes for humanity that deliver us from "darkness." The capacity to create wealth that the technological advance provides us is incredible, almost limitless. An eloquent example is that of agriculture: in the United States, a relatively small percentage of the active population generates a great percentage of the global food output.

We know today, with clarity, that progress and economic growth are insufficient and empty if they are not oriented by values like respect for human rights, ecology, and a better distribution of wealth. Conceptually, I would say that we are prepared to make a qualitative leap, in terms of one of the central problems of humanity, which is that of social justice. What is lacking, then, is the control of the political arts needed to establish equitable forms of growth.

Would we have to reformulate Marx and inquire if the progress of social justice will be hampered by outdated modalities of the appropriation of wealth? From the point of view of government action, how can we reconcile an economic model that is essentially concentrated in rents (given that forms of production are ever more capital intensive) with social policies with compensatory effects? How can we cope with the problem of structural unemployment, which results from the change of the technological cycle?

With the experience of real socialism past, we know that it will not be through the radical transformation of the system of property rights that we will gain efficiency and equity (partly because private property was democratized through the ever greater presence of private pension funds as investors). We also know there will not be an exclusive route for radical and definitive transformations, as classical Marxism would want. The project of revolutionary transformation, we can say without fear, is void.

We are thus faced with two challenges. The first is in the realm of ideas and values: What societies do we want and what are the possibilities for approximating equality between social groups and nations? The second is in the concrete plans for change: How can we channel the potential of the new technological cycle for creating wealth into creating more social justice?

In a certain manner, the ideals of change are being defined negatively, or rather as a counterpoint to the visible problems that the modern world has engendered. We want growth compatible with an increase in employment and equity; we want our concerns with human rights and the environment to be respected; we want a more stable international system, and better decision-making processes; we want greater predictability in the future; we want minorities to be included; and so on. To illustrate this repertoire of ideals, I recall that, in every final document of the large UN conferences, there are consensual solutions on what humanity wants. And it is symptomatic of the new times to turn to "negotiated" documents to expose objectives common to our societies. We know, however, that the central problem is succeeding in mobilizing these ideas, so that they do not serve merely as distant ethical or rhetorical references.

It is exactly because these ideas are not incorporated immediately into a "universal" class struggle, as in the Marxist model, that its weight as a mobilizing asset is tenuous. Thus, in the same way that a fragmentation of objectives exists, there also exists a fragmentation of modes of action. This is a fundamental parameter for the governments that assume the ethical commitment to bring to their people a more just third millennium.

In closing this reflection, I would like to pass from these generic notes, which are necessarily abstract, to a more concrete point on my agenda. I would like to touch on the dynamic of transformation. In many cases, as with human rights and ecology, the social actors that drive the struggle for values are articulated. However, in my view, one of the central objectives of the process of transformation is changing the state. It is fundamental that the state change, so that it may become an agent of change. Many types of states exist, and their capacities for action are different. But I think that, despite the forces of globalization and despite the partly correct hypotheses about the weakening —or better yet, insufficiency—of the nation-state, the fact is that they yet must be studied as the decisive instrument in the project of transformations.

In this sense, one must first take care to avoid attributing to the state conditions that it has lost through historical change. It is impossible to resurrect the developmentalist state of 1960s Latin America. The state in the twenty-first century will not have the central role in investment. The majority of capital resources are now disseminated in an impersonal financial system through transnational corporations. However, there will not be investment if the state does not know how to complete is tasks of macroeconomic "vigilance," if it is not a stable reference point for private economic agents, and if it is not capable of efficaciously exercising its regulatory and strategic planning functions.

The freedom to invest, and the fact that private enterprises are now providing traditional public services, demands extraordinary caution to prevent abusive forms of oligopoly and disrespect of the consumer. A second objective is to strengthen the democratic sense of political action that, in reality, is a condition for positive-action as much in the economic realm—democracy must perfect its mechanisms for defending the consumer—as in the social. The decision process will be both more effective and more legitimate the more it is permeated by social demands that, as we have seen, fragment within national societies. The processes of classic representation must be complemented by something that political theory has not yet defined with clarity, which is representation by direct participation. I do not wish to return, as the men of the Renaissance did, to Greek models. Such models do not serve for complex societies like ours. I know that one of the greatest challenges of our time, as it was in the Renaissance, is to reinvent politics, but in a way contrary to that of Machiavelli. That is, by using participation to reinstall the world of values and ethics in the corridors of power.

I reaffirm my conviction of optimism with regard to the future. It is within our reach to utilize the extraordinary potential of contemporary science and technology to see structural changes in our societies through to completion, in such a way as to stimulate solidarity between peoples and nations and to fix the foundations of a more just and prosperous world. With the courage and the vision that guided the men of the Renaissance, we will be able to succeed in the consolidation of a better world, one more just than that which we were given.

NOTE

1. Eric Hobsbawm, *The Age of Extremes* (London: Michael Joseph, 1994).

The (In)complete Bibliography of Fernando Henrique Cardoso

The published work of Cardoso is extensive and varied, and is both an expression and reflection of Cardoso's strong presence in the intellectual and political fields. His work is comprised of books, essays, articles, reports, and accounts of academic conferences, as well as political speeches and countless articles in daily papers and weekly journals.

The bibliography that follows brings together the majority of works Cardoso has published to date. It does not include pieces in the daily press but includes long interviews, as well as edited debates in smaller publications. It similarly does not include all of his political speeches; his interventions in Senate plenary sessions and in the National Constituent Assembly are available in the annals of the National Congress. Thus, this is not a complete bibliography, nor could it be, since Cardoso continues publishing. Nor is this an exhaustive list, since it is probable that there are also partial translations or publications of certain texts that have not come to the attention of the author. Indeed, certain works get done almost by chance. This is one of them.

The fact that I have assisted Cardoso throughout the last twenty-two years, intermittently and in diverse ways, is basically due to the fortunate compatibility of our styles of working together. Cardoso has a great sense of humor and cultivates civility. He never gives peremptory orders, and rather barely suggests that perhaps such and such a thing might be important, when he says anything at all. As for me, I worked independently, without resisting guidance, and observed with great pleasure the admirable interpretive agility of this man who was more "mentor" than boss.

Our professional relationship began at the CEBRAP. Apart from my duties as administrative director of that institution, I was working on his curriculum vitae, particularly the list of publications, which even then, was already quite impressive. I came in the middle of the process, with Cardoso having already done a great deal. Without the time for an academic reading, I archived his files, filling drawers, and bookshelves. Soon, I moved to typing texts, deciphering Cardoso's terrible handwriting, reviewing footnotes, and doing small translations. I ended up helping him edit books and even prepared the French version of the book *Ideas and their Place* (*As Idéias e seu lugar*). It is thus in this context of multiple and fragmented tasks, and of my return to academia, that that bibliography was completed.

When Cardoso was elected president of Brazil, the documents that formerly constituted nothing more than a notable personal and family collection suddenly took on historic value, and a large part of his collection is now of public interest. His curriculum vitae has become the center of attention in the press and in the public at large, particularly as regards his bibliography, which I have tried to complete in the best way possible.

Always interested in the rapid circulation of his papers among different "publics," so that his ideas would travel and be discussed, Cardoso did not worry himself much with their compilation. In fact, he was not always aware of the new editions and translations that were being done around the world, particularly in the case of articles published in smaller journals. It also took me a long time to verify that certain articles, while they carried similar titles, were completely distinct, or that different titles, on the other hand, could contain the same content. I incorporated various publications, without possessing them myself— still today the Cardoso archive does not possess a copy of all of them—through citations in books by other authors, relying on their trustworthiness.

In this bibliography, the reader will find a chronological list of works, categorized as follows:

- Articles, Books, and Reports
- Debates
- Interviews
- Speeches

They are always referred to in the language of first publication, with all versions and editions following immediately thereafter. In the case of collections in which Cardoso compiled his most important articles, the reader will find in a "highlighted" box a list of the articles it contains, and the chapters as they are cited in the chronological sequence. This presentation allows an immediate view of the repercussion of his works.

Simply reading the titles of Cardoso's works alone reveals the path of a reflection tirelessly centered on the dynamic of social change in Brazil. The evolution of his reflection (brought about by new forms of economic organization in Brazil and other Latin American countries, and their effects on political regimes) can be seen clearly. Starting in the mid-1950s, with the beginnings of industrialization, two distinct and complementary concerns consistently reappear. The first revolves around the political and economic problems linked to the structural-historical contexts of these countries; the second regards methodological questions. Underlying these is the question: How can one describe and explain the result of the combination of political and economic processes?

Little by little, we see the shape of a more explicitly political investigation: What are the conditions necessary to democratize society and institutionalize democracy in political life? From this question comes a passion for politics, and its constant challenges. This is tempered by the knowledge of a sociologist who conceives the social dynamic as the result of social movements that express the possibilities of action that the global social structure presents to the social classes. What are the social conditions that allow for the expansion of possibilities, or "virtualities," of economic action? With what political power? With what conditions of survival?

One can also see a fruitful dialogue between Cardoso and not only Brazilian colleagues, but also with Latin American, European, and American authors. This reading of titles even allows us to note that the very style of the author is changing, motivated by his production in the press and by political and party action. Today, in leading the country, it is no longer a question of interpreting, but of transforming. Even so, the titles of his most important speeches show a continuing concern with making our world more intelligible.

The works of Cardoso are an inspiration to all social scientists interested in the interpretation of social movements. It shows us that, in trying to understand a new reality, it is necessary to establish and identify the distinctions that highlight the novelty of such configurations, so that it becomes possible to intervene in favor of constructive social change. The interpretation of the new requires a change in our own observation. Faced with social diversity, our responsibility as researchers lies in discerning the qualities of differences, and attempting to understand them.

I believe that that was what I have learned throughout this professional partnership and in the compilation of this bibliography. I hope that my appreciation for order, and the clarity taught in the classes of the French *lycée*, can help Brazilianists and other researchers better know Cardoso's written work, and to familiarize themselves not only with the interpretive style of a renowned sociologist, but also with the ideas and ideals of a political leader dedicated to the construction of Brazilian democracy.

Danielle Ardaillon

I. ARTICLES, BOOKS, AND BOOK REVIEWS
(Publications, Reprints, and Translations)

1952 "Um falso retrato do Brasil." *Fundamentos* (April): 26–28. (Book review: Limeira Tejo. *Retrato sincero do Brasil.* Porto Alegre: Globo)

1955 "As elites de cor." *Anhembi*, 5 (19) (55, Jun): 121–124. (Book review: Thales de Azevedo. *As Elites de cor, um estudo de ascensão social.* São Paulo: Cia. Editora Nacional [Coleção Brasiliense, 282], 1955)

1955 "Antropologia econômica." *Anhembi*, 5 (17) (51, Feb): 570–573. (Book review: M. J. Herskovits. *Antropología Económica, estudio de economía comparada.* Mexico City: Fondo de Cultura Económica, 1954)

1957 AND MOREIRA, R., and IANNI, O. "O estudo sociológico das relações entre negros e brancos no Brasil meridional." In *Anais da II Reunião Brasileira de Antropologia.* Bahia: n.p., 88–98.

1957 "De comunidade à metrópole." *Anhembi*, 7 (26) (77, Apr): 351–353. (Book review: Richard. M. Morse. *De comunidade à Metrópole-Biografia de São Paulo.* São Paulo: Serviço de Comemorações Culturais, 1954)

1957 "Higiene mental e relações humanas na indústria." *Anhembi*, 7 (26) (77, Apr): 372–374. (Book review: T. M. Ling and A. C. Pacheco e Silva [ed.]. *Higiene mental e relações humanas na indústria.* São Paulo: Edigraf, s.d.)

1957 "Desenvolvimento econômico e nacionalismo." *Revista Brasiliense*, 12 (Jul–Aug): 88–99.

1958 "O café e a industrialização." *Jornal do Comércio*, Rio de Janeiro, 19 January, 5.

1958 "Educação e desenvolvimento econômico." *Revista Brasiliense*, 17 (May–Jun): 70–81.

1958 "Ensaios de sociologia eleitoral." *Anhembi*, 3 (31) (93, Aug): 572–575. (Book review: Orlando M. Carvalho—*Ensaios de sociologia eleitoral.* Belo Horizonte: Ed. da Revista Brasileira de Estudos Políticos da Universidade de Minas Gerais [Coleção Estudos Sociais e Políticos, vol. 1] 1958)

1958 "Estudos de Sociologia e História." *Revista Brasileira de Estudos Políticos*, 2 (4, Jul): 196–198. (Book review: Maria Isaura Pereira de Queiroz et al. *Estudos de Sociologia e História.* São Paulo: Ed. Anhembi, 1957)

1958 "O Negro e a expansão portuguesa no Brasil Meridional." *Anhembi*, 8 (32) (94, Sep): 16–21. (1960) chapter 1 CARDOSO, F. H., and IANNI, O. *Cor e mobilidade social em Florianópolis: aspectos das relações entre negros e brancos numa comunidade do Brasil meridional.* São Paulo: Companhia Editora Nacional (Coleção Brasiliana, vol. 307), 3–10.

1958 "Polarização dos interesses de patrões e operários numa indústria." *Ciência e Cultura*, 10 (4, Dec): 213–214.

1959 "A estrutura da indústria de São Paulo." *Diário de São Paulo*, 30 April (Edição comemorativa sobre aspectos da civilização paulista). (1960) "A estrutura da indústria de São Paulo (a partir de 1930)." *Educação e Ciências Sociais*, 5 (7) (13, Feb): 29–42. (1965) "The Structure and Evolution of Industry in São Paulo: 1930/1960." *Studies in Comparative International Development*, 43–47.

1959 AND IANNI, O. "Condiciones y efectos de la industrialización en São Paulo (Proyecto de estudios)." *Ciencias Políticas y Sociales*, Mexico City, 5 (18, Oct–Dec): 577–584.

1959 AND IANNI, O. "As exigências educacionais do processo de industrialização." *Revista Brasiliense*, 26 (Nov–Dec): 141–178.

1959 "Estabilidade no emprego." *Revista Brasiliense*, 23 (May–Jun): 162–169. (1959) *Arquivos do Instituto de Direito Social*, 13 (2, Dec): 23–28.

1960 "Proletariado e mudança social em São Paulo." *Sociologia*, 22 (1, Mar): 3–12. (1960) "Atitudes e expectativas desfavoráveis à mudança social." *Boletim do Centro Latino-Americano de Pesquisas em Ciências Sociais*, 3 (3): 15–22, ago.

1960 "Condições sociais da industrialização de São Paulo." *Revista Brasiliense*, 28 (Mar–Apr): 31–46. (1960) *Ciencias Políticas y Sociales*, UNAM, Mexico City. (1969) In Fernando Henrique Cardoso, *Mudanças Sociais na América Latina.* São Paulo: Difusão Européia do Livro, chapter 8, 186–199.

1960   "Educação para o desenvolvimento." *Anhembi*, 10 (39) (115, Jun): 35–43.

(1960) In Roque S. M. de Barros (org.), *Diretrizes e Bases da Educação Nacional*. São Paulo: Pioneira, 166–176.

(1960) *Revista Brasileira de Estudos Pedagógicos*, 34 (79, Jul–Sep): 209–216.

1960   "Atitudes e expectativas desfavoráveis à mudança social." *Boletim do Centro Latino-Americano de Pesquisas em Ciências Sociais*, 3 (3, Aug): 15–22.

1960   "Os brancos e a ascensão social dos negros em Porto Alegre." *Anhembi*, 10 (39) (117, Aug): 583–596.

1960   AND BARROS, R.S.M. de. "Roteiro para a defesa da escola pública (O projeto é antidemocrático)." In Roque S. M. de Barros (org.), *Diretrizes e Bases da Educação Nacional*. São Paulo: Pioneira, 436–455.

1960   AND IANNI, O. *Cor e mobilidade social em Florianópolis: aspectos das relações entre negros e brancos numa comunidade do Brasil meridional*. São Paulo: Companhia Editora Nacional (Coleção Brasiliana, vol. 307).

1961   "Condições e fatores sociais da industrialização de São Paulo." *Revista Brasileira de Estudos Políticos*, 11 (Jun): 148–163.

1961   "Le prolétariat brésilien: situation et comportement social." *Sociologie du Travail*, 3 (4): 60–65.

(1962) "Proletariado no Brasil: situação e comportamento social." *Revista Brasiliense*, 41 (May-Jun): 98–122.

1961   "Tensões sociais no campo e reforma agrária." *Revista Brasileira de Estudos Políticos*, número especial sobre a Reforma Agrária, 12 (Oct): 7–26.

1961   AND IANNI, O. (orgs.). *Homem e Sociedade: Leituras Básicas de Sociologia Geral*. São Paulo: Companhia Editora Nacional.

(1965) 2nd ed., revised.

(1968) 4th ed.

(1975) 9th ed.

(1976) 10th ed.

(1977) 11th ed.

(1980) 12th ed.

(1982) 13th ed.

(1984) 14th ed.

1962   "O método dialético na análise sociológica." *Revista Brasileira de Ciências Sociais*, 2 (1, Mar): 85–106.

(1962) "El método dialectico en el analisis sociológico." Mexico City: *ABIIS/UNAM*.

1962   "Educação e mudança social." *Pesquisa e Planejamento*, CRPESP/São Paulo, 5 (Jun): 55–65.

1962   "Desenvolvimento econômico e nacionalismo." *Revista Brasiliense*, 12 (Jul-Aug): 88–98.

1962   Pronunciamento de educadores sobre o projeto da criação da Universidade de Brasília." *Universidade de Brasília*, MEC, 63–66.

1962   *Capitalismo e escravidão no Brasil meridional: o negro na sociedade escravocrata do Rio Grande do Sul*. São Paulo: Difusão Européia do Livro (Ph.D. thesis).

(1977) 2nd ed. Rio de Janeiro: Paz e Terra.

1963   *El empresario industrial en América Latina: Brasil*. Mar del Plata, Consejo Económico y Social, CEPAL, E/CN 12/642 (Feb).

1963   "Dispersão e unidade: Rio Grande do Sul e Santa Catarina." In Sérgio Buarque de Hollanda (dir.), *O Brasil monárquico*. Vol. 2, *História Geral da Civilização Brasileira*. São Paulo: Difusão Européia do Livro, 473–509.

1963   "Das hautfarbevorurteil in Brasilien." São Paulo, Instituto Hans Staden, *Staden-Jahrbuch*, Band, 11/12:9–17.

(1965) "Le préjugé de couleur au Brésil." *Présence Africaine. Revue culturelle du monde noir*, 53:120–128.

1964   "Industrialização e sociedades de massa." *Sociologia*, 26 (2, Jun): 159–169.

(1968) "Industrialización y sociedades de massa." In Fernando Henrique Cardoso, *Cuestiones de sociologia del desarrollo*. Santiago: Editorial Universitaria, chapter 4, 106–120.

(1969) "Subdesenvolvimento e sociedade de massas." In Fernando Henrique Cardoso, *Mudanças Sociais na América Latina*. São Paulo: Difusão Européia do Livro, chapter 6, 140–153.

1964   *Empresário industrial e desenvolvimento econômico no Brasil*. São Paulo: Difusão Européia do Livro (Coleção Corpo e Alma do Brasil, 13) (thesis of *livre-docência*).

(Development of the previous work: [1963] *El empresario industrial en América Latina: Brasil.*) (1965) Part of chapter 2: "Análisis sociológicos del desarrollo económico." *Revista Latinoamericana de Sociología,* 1 (2, July): 178–98.

(1965) Chapter 4: "Tradition et innovation: la mentalité des entrepreneurs de São Paulo." *Sociologie du Travail,* 7: 209–224.

(1972) 2nd ed. São Paulo: Difusão Européia do Livro.

1965 *El proceso de desarrollo en América Latina: Hipotesis para una interpretación sociológica.* Santiago: *ILPES* report, Nov.

1965 Report on the Conference on: *Children and Youth in National Development in Latin America* (org.). Santiago: UNICEF, Nov.–Dec.

1965 "Las elites empresariales en Latinoamerica." Santiago: *ILPES* report, Nov.

(1965) "Las elites empresariales en Latinoamerica." *Revista Paraguaya de Sociologia,* 2 (4, Sep–Dec): 49–68.

(1967) "The Industrial Elite." In Seymour Martin Lipset and Aldo Solari, *Elites in Latin America.* New York: Oxford University Press, 94–114.

(1967) *America Latina,* 10 (4, Oct–Dec): 22–47.

(1968) In *Pensamiento Crítico.* La Habana: n.p.

(1968) "Las elites económicas." In Fernando Henrique Cardoso, *Cuestiones de sociologia del desarrollo.* Santiago: Editorial Universitaria, chapter 6, 156–180.

(1969) "Os setores industriais no processo de desenvolvimento." In Fernando Henrique Cardoso, *Mudanças Sociais na América Latina.* São Paulo: Difusão Européia do Livro, chapter 4, 83–153.

(1971) *Las elites: los empresarios de América Latina.* Buenos Aires: Nova Visión.

1966 "Directrices para un programa de trabajo entre economistas y sociólogos." *Economía y Administración,* 2 (5): 33–37.

1966 AND REYNA, J. L. "Industrialización, estructura ocupacional y estratificación social en América Latina." Santiago, *ILPES/CEPAL,* Aug. 23.

(1967) "Industrialização, estrutura ocupacional e estratificação social na América Latina." *Dados,* 2/3:4–31.

(1968) "Industrialization, Occupational Structure and Social Stratification in Latin America." In Cole Blasier, *Constructive Change in Latin America.* Pittsburgh: University of Pittsburgh Press.

(1968) In Fernando Henrique Cardoso, *Cuestiones de sociologia del desarrollo.* Santiago: Editorial Universitaria, chapter 3, 68–105.

(1969) "Industrialização, estrutura ocupacional e estratificação social na América Latina." In Fernando Henrique Cardoso, *Mudanças Sociais na América Latina.* São Paulo: Difusão Européia do Livro, chapter 5, 104–139.

1967 "Los agentes sociales de cambio y conservación en América Latina." Santiago, *ILPES* report, Aug.

(1969) "Les agents sociaux de changement et de conservation en Amérique latine." In *L'Amérique Latine par elle même.* Paris: Christianisme Social, 25–53.

(1968) "Los agentes sociales de cambio y observación en América latina (un programa de estudio)." In Fernando Henrique Cardoso, *Cuestiones de sociologia del desarrollo.* Santiago: Editorial Universitaria, chapter 2, 38–67.

(1969) "Os agentes sociais de mudança e conservação na América Latina." In Fernando Henrique Cardoso, *Mudanças Sociais na América Latina.* São Paulo: Difusão Européia do Livro, chapter 2, 23–50.

1967 "Las elites empresariales en América Latina." Santiago, *Relatório ILPES/CEPAL,* Mar.

(Although with the same title, it is different from the previous work: [1965] "Las elites empresariales en Latinoamerica." Santiago: *ILPES* report, Nov.)

(1966) "The Entrepreneurial Elite in Latin America." *Studies in Comparative International Development,* 2 (10): 148–159.

(1967) "Des élites: les entrepreneurs d'Amérique Latine." *Sociologie du Travail,* 9 (3): 255–280, jul.–set. (special volume: *Classes sociales et pouvoir politique em Amérique Latine*).

(1967) "The Entrepreneurial Elite in Latin America." *America Latina,* 10 (4): 22–47, out.–dez. (presented at the Sixth World Sociological Congress, Évian, September 4–11, 1966).

(1968) "Las elites empresariales." In Fernando Henrique Cardoso, *Cuestiones de sociologia del desarrollo.* Santiago: Editorial Universitaria, chapter 5, 121–155.

(1969) "As elites empresariais latinoamericanas." In Fernando Henrique Cardoso, *Mudanças Sociais na América Latina*. São Paulo: Difusão Européia do Livro, chapter 3, 51–82.

(1973) "Las elites empresariales en América Latina." In Antonio Murga Frassinetti and Guillermo Boils. *America Latina: dependencia y subdesarrollo*. San José: Editorial Universitária Centroamericana, 409–449.

1967   "Hégémonie bourgeoise et indépendance économique." *Les Temps Modernes*, 23 (257, Oct): 650–680.

(1968) "Empresarios industriales y desarrollo nacional en Brasil." *Desarrollo Económico*, 8 (29, Apr–Jun): 31–60.

(1968) "Hegemonia burguesa e independencia economica: raices estructurales de la crisis politica brasileña." In *Brasil Hoy*. Mexico City: Siglo XXI, 85–122.

(1968) In Celso Furtado (coord.), *Brasil tempos modernos*. Rio de Janeiro: Paz e Terra, 77–109.

(1968) *Revista Civilização Brasileira*, 4 (17, Jan–Feb): 67–95.

(1969) In Fernando Henrique Cardoso, *Mudanças Sociais na América Latina*. São Paulo: Difusão Européia do Livro, chapter 7, 154–185.

(1971) "Burgerliche hegemonie und wirtschaftliche unabhangigkeit. Strukturelle wurzeln der politischen krise Brasiliens." In Celso Furtado (org.), *Brasilien Heute*. Frankfurt: Athenaum Verlag, 58–83.

(1993) "Hegemonia burguesa e independência econômica: raízes estruturais da crise do populismo e do nacionalismo." In Fernando Henrique Cardoso, *A Construção da democracia—Estudos sobre Política*. São Paulo: Siciliano, chapter 2, 51–78.

1968   *Cuestiones de sociologia del desarrollo*. Santiago: Editorial Universitaria.

	(1968) *Cuestiones de sociologia del desarrollo*
Chapter 1	Parte 1 do cap. 2 de: (1964) *Empresário industrial e desenvolvimento econômico no Brasil*. São Paulo: Difusão Européia do Livro (Coleção Corpo e Alma do Brasil, 13) (Tese de livre-docência).
Chapter 2	(1967) "Los agentes sociales de cambio y conservación en América Latina"
Chapter 3	(1966) AND REYNA, J. L. "Industrialización, estructura ocupacional y estratificación social en América Latina"
Chapter 4	(1964) "Industrialização e sociedades de massa"
Chapter 5	(1967) "Las elites empresariales en América Latina"
Chapter 6	(1965) "Las elites empresariales en Latinoamerica"

(1969) *Sociologie du développement en Amérique Latine*. Paris: Anthropos.

1969   *Mudanças Sociais na América Latina*. São Paulo: Difusão Européia do Livro.

	(1969) *Mudanças sociais na América Latina*
Chapter 1	Part of Introduction of: (1970) AND WEFFORT, F. (eds.). *América Latina: ensayos de interpretación sociológico-política*. Santiago: Editorial Universitaria.
Chapter 2	(1967) "Los agentes sociales de cambio y conservación en América Latina"
Chapter 3	(1967) "Las elites empresariales en América Latina"
Chapter 4	(1965) "Las elites empresariales en Latinoamerica"
Chapter 5	(1966) AND REYNA, J. L. "Industrialización, estructura ocupacional y estratificación social en América Latina"
Chapter 6	(1964) "Industrialização e sociedades de massa"
Chapter 7	(1967) "Hégémonie bourgeoise et indépendance économique"
Chapter 8	(1960) "Condições sociais da industrialização de São Paulo"

1969   "La contribution de Marx à la théorie du changement social." In *Marx et la Pensée Scientifique Contemporaine*. The Hague, Paris, La Haye: Mouton, 253–265.

1969   AND FALETTO, E. *Dependencia y desarrollo en América Latina.* Mexico City: Siglo XXI. (1970) 2nd ed. Siglo XXI.

(1970) *Dependência e desenvolvimento na América Latina.* Rio de Janeiro: Zahar.

(1971) *Dipendenza e Sviluppo in America Latina.* Milano: Feltrinelli.

(1973) 2nd ed. (Tr. 1970). Rio de Janeiro: Zahar.

(1973) 7th ed. Mexico City: Siglo XXI.

(1976) *Abhangigkeit und entwicklung in Lateinamerika.* Frankfurt: Suhrkamp (841).

(1976) 11th ed. Mexico City: Siglo XXI.

(1977) 13th ed. Mexico City: Siglo XXI.

(1978) 14th ed., revised and enlarged. Mexico City: Siglo XXI.

(1978) *Dépendance et développement en Amérique Latine.* Paris: PUF (Série Politiques).

(1979) 16th ed. Mexico City: Siglo XXI.

(1979) *Dependency and Development in Latin America.* Los Angeles: University of California Press.

(1979) 5th ed. (Tr. 1970). Rio de Janeiro: Zahar.

(1980) 2nd ed. (Tr. 1979). Los Angeles: University of California Press.

(1981) 17th ed. Mexico City: Siglo XXI.

(1981) 6th ed. (Tr. 1970). Rio de Janeiro: Zahar.

(1981) 3rd ed. (Tr. 1978). Los Angeles: University of California Press.

(1981) 4th ed. (Tr. 1978). Los Angeles: University of California Press.

(1982) 5th ed. (Tr. 1978). Los Angeles: University of California Press.

(1983) 18th ed. Mexico City: Siglo XXI.

(1984) 19th ed. (Tr. 1970), 7th ed. Rio de Janeiro: Zahar.

(1985) Translation of the Preface of (1979). "Repensando 'Dependência e desenvolvimento na América Latina.'" In Fernando Henrique Cardoso, Mauricio Font, and Bernardo Sorj (org.), *Economia e Movimentos Sociais na América Latina.* São Paulo: Brasiliense, 13–31.

(1986) 20th ed. Mexico City: Siglo XXI.

(1986) Translation of parts of (1978). In P. Klaren and T. J. Bossert, *Promise of Development: Theories of Change in Latin America.* Boulder, Colo.: Westview Press, 149–166.

(1987) 21st ed. Mexico City: Siglo XXI.

(1990) 24th ed. Mexico City: Siglo XXI.

(1998) chapter 2: "Dependencia y desarrollo en América Latina." In *Cincuenta Años de pensamiento en la CEPAL—Textos seleccionados.* Vol. 2. Santiago: Fondo de Cultura Económica, CEPAL, 475–499.

1970   "Aspectos políticos do planejamento." In Betty Mindlin Lafer, *Planejamento no Brasil.* São Paulo: Perspectiva, 161–184.

(1970) "Aspectos políticos de la planificación." *Revista Latinoamericana de Ciência Política,* 1 (1, Apr): 120–136.

(1972) "Aspectos políticos do planejamento no Brasil." In Fernando Henrique Cardoso, *O modelo político brasileiro e outros ensaios.* São Paulo: Difusão Européia do Livro, chapter 4, 83–103.

(1993) Parts of it in: "Planejamento e política: os anéis burocráticos." In Fernando Henrique Cardoso, *A Construção da democracia—Estudos sobre Política.* São Paulo: Siciliano, chapter 5, 143–154.

1970   "Industrialización, dependencia y poder en América Latina." *Revista Paraguaya de Sociología,* 7 (19): 104–116.

(1970) "Industrializzazione, dipendenza e potere in America Latina." *Annali della Fondazione Luigi Einaudi,* 4 (4): 243–259.

(1972) "Industrialização, dependência e poder na América Latina." In Fernando Henrique Cardoso, *O modelo político brasileiro e outros ensaios.* São Paulo: Difusão Européia do Livro, chapter 2.

(1972) "Industrialization, Dependency, and Power in Latin America." *Berkeley Journal of Sociology,* 17:79–95.

(1979) "Industrialización, dependencia y poder en América Latina." *La política y el poder.* San Salvador, El Salvador: UCA Editores.

1970   "Les obstacles structurels et institutionnels au développement." *Sociologie et Sociétés,* 2 (2, Nov): 297–315. (Mimeo: "Structural and Institutional Impediments to Development." Stockholm: ONU, Background Paper 6, 1969).

(1970) "Impedimentos estructurales e institucionales para el desarrollo." *Revista Mexicana de Sociología*, 3 (6, Nov–Dec): 1461–1482.

1970   AND WEFFORT, F. (eds.). *América Latina: ensayos de interpretación sociológico-política*. Santiago: Editorial Universitaria.

Part of the Introduction is the chapter 1 of: CARDOSO, Fernando Henrique (1969), *Mudanças Sociais na América Latina*. São Paulo: Difusão Européia do Livro.

1970   "Participación social y desarrollo: la clase obrera y los grupos marginales." *Boletin Elas*, 4 (6, Dec): 50–61.

(1972) "Participação e marginalidade: notas para uma discussão teórica." In Fernando Henrique Cardoso, *O modelo político brasileiro e outros ensaios*. São Paulo: Difusão Européia do Livro, chapter 8, 166–185.

1970   "Dependência, desenvolvimento e ideologia." *Revista de Administração de Empresas*, 10 (4, Dec): 43–71.

(1971) chapter 5 and conclusions of: *Política e desenvolvimento em sociedades dependentes: ideologias do empresariado industrial argentino e brasileiro*. Rio de Janeiro: Zahar, 173–200.

1970   "Teoría de la dependencia: análises concreto de situaciones de dependencia." *ABIIS*, Mexico City, DT1.

(1970/71) "Teoria da dependência ou análises concretas de situações de dependência?" *Debates Econômicos*, Porto Alegre, 11:19–34.

(1971) "Teoria da dependência ou análises concretas de situações de dependência?" *Estudos CEBRAP*, 1:25–45.

(1972) "Teoria da dependência ou análises concretas de situações de dependência?" In Fernando Henrique Cardoso, *O modelo político brasileiro e outros ensaios*. São Paulo: Difusão Européia do Livro, chapter 6, 123–139.

(1972) "Teoria de la dependencia o analisis concreto de situaciones de dependencia." *Comercio Exterior*, 22 (4, Apr): 360–365.

(1974) " 'Théorie de la dépendance' ou analyses concrètes de situations de dépendance?" *L'Homme et la Société*, 33/34 (Jul–Sep/Oct–Dec): 111–123.

1971   *Política e desenvolvimento em sociedades dependentes: ideologias do empresariado industrial argentino e brasileiro*. Rio de Janeiro: Zahar.

(1971) *Politique et développement dans les sociétés dépendantes*. Paris: Anthropos.

(1971) *Ideologías de la burguesia industrial en sociedades dependientes*. Mexico City: Siglo XXI.

(1972) 2nd ed. Mexico City: Siglo XXI.

(1974) 3rd ed. Mexico City: Siglo XXI.

(1976) 5th ed. (Tr. 1971). Paris: Anthropos.

(1976) 5th ed. (Tr. 1971). Siglo XXI.

1971   "Comentário sobre os conceitos de superpopulação relativa e marginalidade." *Estudos CEBRAP*, 1:99–130.

(1971) "Comentario sobre los conceptos de sobrepoblación relativa y marginalidad." *Revista Latinoamericana de Ciencias Sociales* (Jun–Dec.):57–76.

(1972) "Comentários sobre os conceitos de superpopulação relativa e marginalidade." In Fernando Henrique Cardoso, *O modelo político brasileiro e outros ensaios*. São Paulo: Difusão Européia do Livro, chapter 7, 140–185.

1971   "Political Systems and Social Pressures in Latin America in the 1970 Decade." *Conference on the Western Hemisphere: Issues for the 1970's*. New York: The Center for Inter-American Relations, April–May, 29–53.

(1972) "Alternativas políticas na América Latina." In Fernando Henrique Cardoso, *O modelo político brasileiro e outros ensaios*. São Paulo: Difusão Européia do Livro, chapter 1, 5–33.

1971   AND CAMARGO, C.P.F. de, and KOWARICK, L. "Consideraciones sobre el desarrollo de São Paulo: cultura y participación." *Eure*, 1 (3, Oct): 43–68.

(1973) "Cultura y participación." In Paul Singer (org.), *Urbanización y recursos humanos: el caso de San Pablo*. Buenos Aires: SIAP, 15–60.

(1973) In C.P.F. de Camargo and L. Kowarick, *Considerações sobre o desenvolvimento de São Paulo: cultura e participação*. São Paulo: CEBRAP (Série Cadernos CEBRAP, vol. 14).

1972 *O modelo político brasileiro e outros ensaios.* São Paulo: Difusão Européia do Livro (Coleção Corpo e Alma do Brasil, vol. 35).

	(1972) *O Modelo político brasileiro e outros ensaios*
Chapter 1	(1971) "Political Systems and Social Pressures in Latin America in the 1970 Decade"
Chapter 2	(1970) "Industrialización, dependencia y poder en América Latina"
Chapter 3	(1972) "El régimen político brasileño"
Chapter 4	(1970) "Aspectos políticos do planejamento"
Chapter 5	(1972) "Althusserianismo ou marxismo? A propósito do conceito de classes em Poulantzas"
Chapter 6	(1970) "Teoría de la dependencia: análises concreto de situaciones de dependencia"
Chapter 7	(1971) "Comentário sobre os conceitos de superpopulação relativa e marginalidade"
Chapter 8	(1970) "Participación social y desarrollo: la clase obrera y los grupos marginales"
Chapter 9	(1972) "Imperialismo e dependência na América Latina"

(1972) *Estado y Sociedad en America Latina.* Buenos Aires: Nueva Visión.
(1973) 2nd ed. São Paulo: Difusão Européia do Livro.
(1979) 4th ed. São Paulo: Difusão Européia do Livro.
(1993) 5th ed. São Paulo: Difusão Européia do Livro.

1972 "Notes sur l'état actuel des études sur la dépendance." Dakar: Institut Africain de Développement Économique et de Planification, août.

(1972) "Notas sobre el estado actual de los estudios sobre dependencia." *Revista Latinoamericana de Ciencias Sociales* (FLACSO), 4 (Dec): 3–31.

(1973) "Notas sobre o estado atual dos estudos sobre dependência." In *Notas sobre estado e dependência.* São Paulo: CEBRAP (Série Cadernos CEBRAP, vol. 11), 23–47.

(1973) "Dependency Revisited." Austin: ILAS, Hackett Memorial Lecture, University of Texas.

(1974) "Notas sobre el estado actual de los estudios sobre dependencia." In José Serra (org.), *Desarrollo latinoamericano: ensayos críticos.* Mexico City: Fondo de Cultura Económica (Lecturas, vol. 6), 325–356.

(1976) "Notas sobre o estado atual dos estudos sobre dependência." In José Serra (coord.), *América Latina: Ensaios de interpretação econômica.* Rio de Janeiro: Paz e Terra (Coleção Estudos latinoamericanos, vol. 5), 364–393.

(1979) "Notas sobre el estado actual de los estudios sobre dependencia." In *Problemas del subdesarrollo en Latinoamérica.* Mexico City: Editorial Nuestro tiempo.

(1980) "A dependência revisitada." In Fernando Henrique Cardoso, *As idéias e seu lugar: ensaios sobre as teorias do desenvolvimento.* Petrópolis: Vozes (Série Cadernos CEBRAP, vol. 33), chapter 2, 81–123.

1972 "Althusserianismo o marxismo? A propósito del concepto de clases de Poulantzas." *Sociedad y Desarrollo*, Santiago, 2 (Apr–Jun): 77–89.

(1972) "Althussérisme ou marxisme? À propos du concept de classe chez Poulantzas." *L'Homme et la Société*, 24–25 (Apr–Sep): 57–71.

(1972) "Althusserianismo ou marxismo? A propósito do conceito de classes em Poulantzas." In Fernando Henrique Cardoso, *O modelo político brasileiro e outros ensaios.* São Paulo: Difusão Européia do Livro, chapter 5, 57–87.

(1973) "Althusserianismo o marxismo? A propósito del concepto de clases en Poulantzas." In R. B. Zenteno (coord.), *Las clases sociales en America Latina.* Mexico City: Siglo XXI, 137–153.

(1973) "Althusserianismo ou marxismo? A propósito do conceito de classes em Poulantzas." *Estudos CEBRAP*, 3 (Jan): 65–85.

1972 "Imperialismo e dependência na América Latina." In Fernando Henrique Cardoso, *O modelo político brasileiro e outros ensaios.* São Paulo: Difusão Européia do Livro, chapter 9, 186–209.

(1972) "Dependent Capitalist Development in Latin America." *New Left Review*, 74 (Jul–Aug).
(1972) "Beroende och utveckling i Latinamerika." *Zenit*, 4 (30): 36–46.
(1973) "Impérialisme et dépendance en Amérique Latine." *L'Homme et la Société*, 27 (5): 64–80.
(1973) "Imperialismo y dependencia en América Latina." *Economia y Ciencias Sociales*, 15 (1–4): 152–171.
(1973) In Frank Bonilla and R. Girling (eds.), *Structures and Dependency.* Stanford: Institute for Political Studies, 7–33.
(1974) "Abhangigkeit und entwicklung in Lateinamerika." In D. Senghaas (ed.), *Peripherer Kapitalismus.* Frankfurt: Suhrkamp (652), 201–220.
(1979) "Imperialismo y dependencia en América Latina." In R. Villareal (sel.), *Economia internacional.: teorias del imperialismo, la dependencia y su evidencia histórica.* Mexico City: Fundo de Cultura (Lecturas, vol. 30), 298–315.
(1982) "Dependency and Development in Latin America." In Hamza Alavi and Theodor Shanin (eds.), *Sociology of "Developing Societies."* London: Macmillan Press Ltd., 112–127.

1972   "El régimen político brasileño." *Aportes*, 25 (Jul): 6–30.
(1972) "El modelo politico brasileño." *Revista Desarrollo Económico*, Buenos Aires, 11 (42–44, Jul., 71–Mar): 217–247.
(1972) "O regime político brasileiro." *Estudos CEBRAP*, 2 (Oct): 83–118.
(1972) "O modelo político brasileiro." In Fernando Henrique Cardoso, *O modelo político brasileiro e outros ensaios.* São Paulo: Difusão Européia do Livro, chapter 3, 50–82.
(1973) "Associated-Dependent Development: Theoretical and Practical Implications." In Alfred Stepan (ed.), *Authoritarian Brazil: Origins, Policies, and Future.* New Haven, Conn.: Yale University Press, 142–176.
(1993) "O modelo político brasileiro." In Fernando Henrique Cardoso, *A Construção da democracia—Estudos sobre Política.* São Paulo: Siciliano, chapter 3, 79–109.
(1995) "Associated-Dependent Development: Theoretical and Practical Implications." In S. Haggard (ed.), *The International Political Economy and the Developing Countries.* Hants, UK: Edward Elgar Publishing Ltd. (The Library of International Political Economy, vol. 1), 218–253.

1972   "A Cidade e a política." In Paul Singer and Fernando Henrique Cardoso, *A cidade e o campo.* São Paulo: CEBRAP (Série Cadernos CEBRAP, vol. 7).
(1973) "La ciudad e la política." *Revista Estudios Sociales Centro-Americanos*, 2 (4, Jan–Apr): 7–34.
(1975) "A cidade e a política: do compromisso ao inconformismo." In Fernando Henrique Cardoso, *Autoritarismo e democratização.* Rio de Janeiro: Paz e Terra (Coleção Estudos Brasileiros, vol. 3), chapter 4, 157–164.

1973   AND WEFFORT, F. "Ciencia y consciencia social." In Antonio Murga Frassinetti and Guillermo Boils Morales, *América Latina: dependencia y subdesarrollo.* San José: Editorial Universitária Centroamericana, 14–33.
(1973) In Antonio Murga Frassinetti and Guillermo Boils Morales, *America Latina: dependencia y subdesarrollo.* San José: Editorial Universitária Centroamericana, 77–104.
(1979) In Antonio Murga Frassinetti and Guillermo Boils Morales, *Las ciencias sociales en America Latina.* Mexico City: UNAM, 55–76.

1973   "Cuba: Lesson or Symbol?" In D. Barkin and N. Manitzas (eds.), *Cuba, the Logic of the Revolution.* Andover: Warner Modular Publications, 267(1)–267(9).

1973   "Industrial Prosperity and Social Chaos." *The Financial Times*, 19 April.

1973   "Las contradicciones del desarrollo asociado." *Cuadernos de la Sociedad Venezuelana de Planificación*, jun.–ago.
(1973) In *Taller de Estudios Políticos.* Lima: Programa Académico de CCSS, Universidad Católica del Perú.
(1974) *Revista Paraguaya de Sociología*, 11 (29, Jan–Apr) 227–252.
(1974) "As contradições do desenvolvimento associado." *Estudos CEBRAP*, 8:41–75.
(1974) *Desarrollo Económico*, Buenos Aires, 14 (53, Apr–Jun): 3–32.
(1974) "Brasilien: Die widersprüche der assozierten entwicklung." In Heinz R. Sonntag (org.), *Lateinamerika: Faschismus oder Revolution.* Berlin: Rotbuch Verlag, 32–62.

(1975) "As novas teses equivocadas." In *Fernando Henrique Cardoso, Autoritarismo e democratização*. Rio de Janeiro: Paz e Terra (Coleção Estudos Brasileiros, vol. 3), chapter 1, 11–62.

(1976) "Current Theses on Latin America Development and Dependency: A Critique." New York University, *Occasional Papers* 20.

(1977) "Current Theses on Latin America Development and Dependency: A Critique." *Boletin de Estudios Latinoamericanos y del Caribe*, 22:53–64.

(1981) "Critica alle tesi sulla dipendenza in America Latina." *Politica Internazionale*, 10:57–66.

(1993) "As contradições do desenvolvimento-associado." In *Fernando Henrique Cardoso, A Construção da democracia—Estudos sobre Política*. São Paulo: Siciliano, chapter 4, 110–142.

1973   "Das 'Brasilianishe entwicklungsmodell': daten und perspektiven." *Problemes des Klassenkampfs*, 6 (Mar): 75–97.

(1973) "O 'modelo brasileiro' de desenvolvimento." *Debate and Crítica*, 1 (1, Jul–Dec): 18–47.

(1974) "O modelo brasileiro de desenvolvimento: dados e perspectivas." In *Modelos de desarrollo en America Latina*. Berlin: Fundación Alemana para el Desarrollo Internacional.

(1975) "O 'modelo brasileiro' de desenvolvimento: dados e perspectivas." In *Fernando Henrique Cardoso, Autoritarismo e democratização*. Rio de Janeiro: Paz e Terra (Coleção Estudos Brasileiros, vol. 3), chapter 2, 63–97.

1973   *Notas sobre Estado e dependência*. São Paulo: CEBRAP (Cadernos CEBRAP, vol. 11).

1973   "Estado e sociedade no Brasil (notas preliminares)." In *Notas sobre Estado e dependência*. São Paulo: CEBRAP (Cadernos CEBRAP, vol. 11), 7–20.

(1975) "Estado e sociedade (notas preliminares)." In Candido Mendes (org.), *Crise e mudança social*. Rio de Janeiro: Livraria Eldorado Tijuca (Coleção América Latina), 111–129.

(1975) "Estado e sociedade no Brasil." In *Fernando Henrique Cardoso, Autoritarismo e democratização*. Rio de Janeiro: Paz e Terra (Coleção Estudos Brasileiros, vol. 3), chapter 5, 165–186.

1973   "Chile: um caminho possível?" *Argumento*, 1 (1, Oct): 95–103.

1973   "Social Policy Offers Little to the Poor." *The Financial Times*, Brazil, *Financial Times* Survey, 13 November, 21.

1973   "Um cientista do ar." (Book review: Robert A. Packenham. *Liberal America and the Third World: Political Development Ideas and Foreign Aid and Social Science*. Princeton, N.J.: Princeton University Press)

1973   "Capitalismo dependente." (Book review: Florestan Fernandes. *Capitalismo dependente e classes sociais na América Latina*. Rio de Janeiro: Zahar)

1974   "O inimigo de papel (The Paper Enemy)." *Latin American Perspectives*, 1 (1, Spring): 66–74.

1974   "A questão do estado no Brasil." *Dados* (Apr).

(1974–1977) "La cuestión del Estado en Brasil." In *Taller de Estudios Políticos*. Lima: Programa Académico de CCSS, Universidad Católica del Perú.

(1975) "La cuesión del estado en Brasil." *Revista Mexicana de Sociología*, 37 (3, Jul–Sep): 603–630.

(1975) "A questão do estado no Brasil." In *Fernando Henrique Cardoso, Autoritarismo e democratização*. Rio de Janeiro: Paz e Terra (Coleção Estudos Brasileiros, vol. 3), chapter 6, 187–221.

(1975) "Die frage des staates in Brasilien" (ed. mimeo).

(1976) "Il quadro politico: le diverse vie all'autoritarismo." *Politica Internazionale*, 3 (Mar): 31–44.

(1978) "La question de l'état au Brésil." *Le Progrès en question*. Paris: Anthropos.

(1993) "A formação do Estado autoritário." In *Fernando Henrique Cardoso, A Construção da democracia—Estudos sobre Política*. São Paulo: Siciliano, chapter 6, 155–184.

1974   "Um Nixon acima de qualquer suspeita." In *Opinião, As gravações secretas de Nixon*. Rio de Janeiro: Inúbia, Jun.

1974   "A questão da democracia." *Debate and Crítica*, 3 (Jul): 1–15.

(1975) In *Fernando Henrique Cardoso, Autoritarismo e democratização*. Rio de Janeiro: Paz e Terra (Coleção Estudos Brasileiros, vol. 3), chapter 7, 223–240.

(1982) In Paulo J. Krischke (org.), *Brasil: do "Milagre" à "Abertura"*. São Paulo: Cortez, 103–119.

1975   *Autoritarismo e democratização*. Rio de Janeiro: Paz e Terra (Coleção Estudos Brasileiros, vol. 3).

(1976) 3rd ed. Rio de Janeiro: Paz e Terra.

1975   "O autoritarismo e a democratização necessária." *Cadernos de Opinião*, 2:3–8 (it is the introduction of: *Autoritarismo e democratização* [Rio de Janeiro: Paz e Terra (Coleção Estudos Brasileiros, vol. 3)]).

1975   "Dos governos militares a Prudente-Campos Sales." In B. Fausto (dir.), *O Brasil republicano*. Vol. 3, da *História geral da civilização brasileira*. São Paulo: Difusão Européia do Livro, 15–50.

(1993) "Implantação do sistema oligárquico (dos governos militares a Prudente-Campos Sales)." In Fernando Henrique Cardoso, *A Construção da democracia—Estudos sobre Política*. São Paulo: Siciliano, chapter 1, 11–50.

1975   AND et al. *São Paulo 1975: crescimento e pobreza*. São Paulo: Loyola.

(1978) *São Paulo Growth and Poverty*. London: The Bowerdean Press.

(1978) 2nd ed. São Paulo: Loyola.

1975   AND LAMOUNIER, B., et. al. *Os partidos e as eleições no Brasil*. Rio de Janeiro: Paz e Terra.

1975   "Partidos e deputados em São Paulo: o voto e a representação política." In Fernando Henrique Cardoso and Bolivar Lamounier (orgs.), *Os partidos e as eleições no Brasil*. Rio de Janeiro: Paz e Terra, 45–75.

1976   "Estatização e autoritarismo esclarecido: tendências e limites." *Estudos CEBRAP*, 15 (Jan–Mar): 5–24.

1976   "Les États Unis et la théorie de la dépendance." *Revue Tiers Monde*, 17 (68, Oct–Dec): 805–825.

(1977) "The Consumption of Dependency Theory in the United States." *Latin American Research Review*, 12 (3): 7–24.

(1977) "El consumo de la teoría sobre dependencia en los Estados Unidos." *El Trimestre Económico*, 44 (173, Jan–Mar): 33–52.

(1977) "O consumo da teoria da dependência nos EUA." *Ensaios de Opinião*, 4:6–16.

(1978) "Los Estados Unidos y la teoria de dependencia." *América Latina, cinquenta años de industrizlización*. Mexico City: Premia Editora.

(1980) "O consumo da teoria da dependência nos Estados Unidos." In Fernando Henrique Cardoso, *As idéias e seu lugar: ensaios sobre as teorias do desenvolvimento*. Petrópolis: Vozes (Série Cadernos CEBRAP, vol. 33), chapter 3, 89–107.

1976   AND FALETTO, E. "Post scriptum a Dependencia y desarrollo en América Latina." Buenos Aires, Centro de Estudios de Estado y Sociedad—CEDES/GE. CLACSO, 6 (Dec).

(1977) "Estado y proceso político en América Latina." *Revista Mexicana de Sociología*, 39 (2, Apr–Jun): 357–387.

(1977) *Desarrollo Económico*, Buenos Aires, 17 (66, Jul–Sep): 273–299.

(1977) The second part only: "Desenvolvimento capitalista e estado: bases e alternativas." In Carlos Estevam Martins (org.), *Estado e capitalismo no Brasil*. São Paulo: HUCITEC– CEBRAP, 205–220.

(1978) The second part only: "Capitalist Development and the State: Bases and Alternatives." *Ibero Americana*, VII(2)/VIII(1): 7–19.

(1979) In Daniel Camacho (org.), *Debates sobre la teoria de la dependencia y la sociologia latinoamericana*. San José, Costa Rica: Editorial Universitária Centroamericana, 95–135.

(1985) "Repensando 'Dependência e desenvolvimento na América Latina.'" In Fernando Henrique Cardoso, Bernardo Sorj, and Maurício Font (orgs.), *Economia e movimentos sociais na América Latina.* São Paulo: Brasiliense, 13–30.

1977 AND REIS, F. W. "As eleições e o problema institucional: notas sobre Estado e sociedade." *Dados,* 14:201–210.

1977 "The Originality of the Copy: ECLA and the Idea of Development." University of Cambridge: Center of Latin American Studies, *Working Papers* 27 (Jun).

(1977) "La originalidad de la copia: la CEPAL y la idea de desarrollo." *Revista de la CEPAL,* 4:7–40, 2nd sem.

(1979) In the Rothko Chapel Colloquium (org.), *Toward a New Strategy for Development.* New York: Pergamon Press.

(1980) "A originalidade da Cópia: a CEPAL e a idéia de desenvolvimento." In Fernando Henrique Cardoso, *As idéias e seu lugar: ensaios sobre as teorias do desenvolvimento.* Petrópolis: Vozes (Série Cadernos CEBRAP, vol. 33), chapter 1, 17–56.

1977 AND MULLER, G. *Amazônia: expansão do capitalismo.* São Paulo: CEBRAP–Brasiliense.

1977 "População e crescimento econômico: notas sobre a estrutura sócio-econômica de São José dos Campos." São Paulo: CEBRAP, *Estudos de População, 1: São José dos Campos.*

1977 "Towards Another Development." In Marc Nerfin (ed.), *Another Development: Approaches and Strategies.* Uppsala: Dag Hammarskjold Foundation, 21–39.

(1978) "*Hacia otro desarrollo.*" In Marc Nerfin (ed.), *Hacia otro desarrollo: enfoques y estrategias.* Mexico City: Siglo XXI, 29–48.

(1980) "Por um outro desenvolvimento." In Fernando Henrique Cardoso, *As idéias e seu lugar: ensaios sobre as teorias do desenvolvimento.* Petrópolis: Vozes (Série Cadernos CEBRAP, vol. 33), chapter 4, 109–128.

(1982) In R. Falk, S. S. Kim, and S. Mendlovitz (eds.), *Toward a Just World Order.* Boulder, Colo.: Westview Press (Studies on a Just World Order, vol. 1), 343–358.

1977 "Expansão estatal e democracia." *Ensaios de Opinião,* 5:17–20.

(1981) "Expansion étatique et démocratie." *Revue de L'Institut de Sociologie,* 1/2:231–238.

1977 "A questão da democracia contemporânea." *Ensaios de Opinião,* 5:21–24.

1977 "Quels styles de développement?" *Études,* 346 (Jan–Jul): 7–22.

(1977) "Latin America: Styles of Development and Their Limits." Center for Latin American and Caribbean Studies, New York University.

(1978) "Latin America: Styles of Development and Their Limits." *Journal of Social Studies,* 1:97–115.

1977 "Las clases sociales y la crisis de Latinoamerica." In Aldo Solari et al., *Poder y desarrollo en América latina: estudios sociológicos en homenaje a José Medina Echavarría.* Mexico City: Fondo de Cultura Económica, 48–76.

(1977) "A formação do capitalismo e as classes sociais na América Latina: Problemas e algumas questões de método." In J. A. Guilhon de Albuquerque, *Classes médias e política no Brasil.* Rio de Janeiro: Paz e Terra, 53–82.

1977 "Estado capitalista e marxismo." *Estudos CEBRAP,* 21 (Jul–Sep): 5–31.

1977 "A polêmica revisitada." *Gazeta Mercantil,* São Paulo, 16 December. (Book review: Caio Prado Jr. *A revolução brasileira.* 5th ed. São Paulo: Brasiliense)

1978 "On the Characterization of Authoritarian Regimes in Latin America." University of Cambridge: *Working Paper Series,* 30.

(1979) In David Collier (org.), *The New Authoritarianism in Latin America.* Princeton, N.J.: Princeton University Press, 33–57.

(1982) "Da caracterização dos regimes autoritários na América Latina." In David Collier (org.), *O Novo autoritarismo na América Latina.* Rio de Janeiro: Paz e Terra (Coleção Estudos Latino-Americanos, vol. 18), 41–62.

(1984) "Per una caratterizzazione dei regimi autoritari in America Latina." In F. P. Cerase (org.), *Sviluppo capitalístico dipendente e regimi burocratico-autoritari.* Roma: Carucci ed., 223–260.

1978   *Democracia para mudar.* 30 horas de entrevistas. São Paulo: Paz e Terra (Coleção Documentos da Democracia Brasileira, vol. 4).

1978   "A Europa Ocidental e o Pacto Atlântico após a crise do petróleo." In Henrique Rattner (org.), *A crise da ordem mundial.* São Paulo: Símbolo, 159–182.

1978   AND LAMOUNIER, B. "A bibliografia de ciência política sobre o Brasil (1949–1974)." *Dados*, 18:3–32.
        (1978) "Bibliography of Political Science on Brazil—1949–1974." *Dados*, 18:3–32.

1978   AND SERRA, J. "Las desventuras de la dialéctica de la dependencia." *Revista Mexicana de Sociología*, 40 (40): 9–55.
        (1979) *Revista Mexicana de Sociologia*, Número extraordinário, 40:9–55.
        (1979) "As desventuras da dialética da dependência." *Estudos CEBRAP*, 23:33–80
        (1980) "Les mésaventures de la dialectique de la dépendance." *Amérique Latine*, CETRAL, 1 (Jan–Mar): 25–44.

1978   "A questão dos partidos." *Contexto*, 5 (Mar): 1–20.

1978   "Brasil: as raízes e o futuro." In *Livros indispensáveis à compreensão do presente, Senhor Vogue*, São Paulo, 1:140. (Book review: Sérgio Buarque de Holanda. *Raízes do Brasil, 1936.* 3rd.ed. Rio de Janeiro: Livraria José Olympio, 1956)

1978   "À espera de Grande indústria e favela." In *Livros indispensáveis à compreensão do presente, Senhor Vogue*, São Paulo, 2:115–116. (Book review: Gilberto Freyre. *Casa grande e senzala.* Rio de Janeiro: Livraria José Olympio, 1933)

1978   "Os bandeirantes do ar." In *Livros indispensáveis à compreensão do presente, Senhor Vogue*, São Paulo, 3:118. (Book review: Roberto Simonsen. *A História econômica do Brasil [1500–1820].* 7th ed. São Paulo: Cia. Editora Nacional, 1977)

1978   "Canudos: o outro Brasil." In *Livros indispensáveis à compreensão do presente, Senhor Vogue*, São Paulo, 4:108–109. (Book review: Euclydes da Cunha. *Os sertões.* Rio de Janeiro: Livraria Francisco Alves, 1957)

1978   "O Descobrimento da Economia." In *Livros indispensáveis à compreensão do presente, Senhor Vogue*, São Paulo, 5 (Aug): 107. (Book review: Celso Furtado. *Formação econômica do Brasil.* 12th ed. São Paulo: Cia. Editora Nacional, 1974)

1978   "A história e seu sentido." In *Livros indispensáveis à compreensão do presente, Senhor Vogue*, São Paulo, 6:125. (Book review: Caio Prado Jr. *Formação do Brasil contemporâneo.* 2nd ed. São Paulo: Brasiliense, 1945)

1978   "Fotógrafo amador." In *Livros indispensáveis à compreensão do presente, Senhor Vogue*, São Paulo, 7 (Oct):129. (Book review: Paulo Prado. *Retrato do Brasil.* 5th ed. São Paulo: Brasiliense, 1944)

1979   "A fome e a crença (Sobre *Os parceiros do Rio Bonito*)." In *Esboço de figura: homenagem a Antonio Candido.* São Paulo: Livraria Duas Cidades, 89–100. (Book review: Antonio Candido. *Os parceiros do Rio Bonito, estudo sobre o caipira paulista e a transformação de seus meios de vida.* Rio de Janeiro: José Olympio Editores, 1964)

1979   AND MARTINS, C. E. (orgs.). *Política e sociedade.* São Paulo: Nacional. 2 vols. (Série Ciências Sociais, vols. 53 and 54).
        (1982) 2nd ed. São Paulo: Nacional.

1979   "A fronda conservadora—O Brasil depois de Geisel." *Folha de S.Paulo*, 21 January, 5–6.
        (1980) "Después de Geisel. La fronda conservadora." *Cuadernos de Marcha*, Segunda época, 2 (8, Jul–Aug): 21–27.
        (1993) "A Fronda conservadora—O Brasil depois de Geisel." In Fernando Henrique Cardoso, *A Construção da democracia—Estudos sobre Política.* São Paulo: Siciliano, chapter 7, 185–197.

1979   "El desarrollo en el banquillo." *Caderno do ILET*, Mexico City, DEE/Dí24/e, ago.
        (1979) "Development under Fire." Buenos Aires: Centro de Economia Transnacional, Instituto para América Latina.
        (1980) "O Desenvolvimento na berlinda." In Fernando Henrique Cardoso, *As idéias e seu lugar: ensaios sobre as teorias do desenvolvimento.* Petrópolis: Vozes (Série Cadernos CEBRAP, vol. 33), chapter 5, 129–163.
        (1980) "El desarrollo en capilla." *Estudios Sociales Centroamericanos*, 9 (26, May–Aug): 195–228.

(1981) "Die entwicklung auf der anklagebank." *Peripherie*, 5/6:6–31, sommer.

(1981) "Contributo alla critica del concetto di sviluppo." *Laboratorio di Scienze dell'Uomo*, 1 (1, Mar): 25–42, mar. (parte prima) e (2, Jun): 123–136 (parte seconda).

(1982) "Development under Fire." In Harry Makler, Aldo Martinelli, and Neil J. Smelser (eds.), *The New International Economy*. London and Beverly Hills: Sage Studies in International Sociology, 26:141–165.

(1982) "El desarrollo en capilla." In José Molero (sel.), *El análisis estructural en economía: ensayos de América Latina y España*. Mexico City: El Trimestre Económico (Lecturas, 40), 25–62.

(1982) "El desarrollo en capilla." In *Planificación social en América Latina y el Caribe*. Santiago: UNICEF/ILPES, 25–55.

1979 "Les impasses du régime autoritaire: le cas brésilien." *Problèmes d'Amérique Latine*, LIV, Notes et études documentaires, 4545–4546 (Dec): 89–107.

(1980) "Os impasses do regime autoritário: o caso brasileiro." *Estudos CEBRAP*, 26:169–194.

(1980) "El atolladero de los regímenes autoritarios: el caso de Brasil." *Revista Mexicana de Sociología*, XLII, 42 (3, Jul–Sep): 1145–1165.

(1980) "La cuadratura del círculo." *Nexus*, III (30): 11–22.

(1981) "The Authoritarian Regime at the Crossroads: The Brazilian Case." Washington: The Wilson Center, *Working Papers*, 93.

(1993) "Os impasses do regime autoritário: início da distensão." In Fernando Henrique Cardoso, *A Construção da democracia—Estudos sobre Política*. São Paulo: Siciliano, chapter 9, 212–233.

1979 "Os rumos da oposição." *Ensaios de Opinião*, 13 (Aug–Sep): 86–90.

1980 "The Surprises of Development in Latin America." *IFDA Dossier*, 16 (Mar–Apr): 31–37.

(1980) "Le sorprese dello sviluppo in America Latina." *IDOC Internazionale*, 3/4:7–12.

(1983) "As surpresas do desenvolvimento." In *Eurípides Simões de Paula. In Memoriam*. São Paulo: FFLCH/USP, 31–85.

1980 *As idéias e seu lugar: ensaios sobre as teorias do desenvolvimento*. Petrópolis: Vozes (Série Cadernos CEBRAP, vol. 33).

	(1980) *As idéias e seu lugar: ensaios sobre as teorias do desenvolvimento*
Chapter 1	(1977) "The Originality of the Copy: ECLA and the Idea of Development"
Chapter 2	(1972) "Notes sur l'état actuel des études sur la dépendance"
Chapter 3	(1976) "Les États Unis et la théorie de la dépendance"
Chapter 4	(1977) "Towards another Development"
Chapter 5	(1979) "El desarrollo en el banquillo"

(1984) *Les idées à leur place*. Paris: A. M. Métaillé/Maison des Sciences de l'Homme.

(1993) new revised edition (presentation and post-script). Petrópolis: Vozes.

1980 "Perspectiva de desarrollo y medio ambiente: el caso de Brasil." *Revista de la CEPAL*, 12 (Dec): 115–132.

(1980) "Development and the Environment: The Brazilian Case." *Cepal Review*, 12 (Dec): 21–35.

(1981) Perspectivas de desenvolvimento e meio ambiente: o caso do Brasil." *Travaux et Mémoires de L'Institut des Hautes Études de L'Amérique Latine*. Paris: I.H.E.A.L./CREDAL, 34:209–238.

1980 "General Introductory Statement on Interdependence and Development." *Inter-regional Cooperation in the Social Sciences for Development*, Paris, (OECD, 5:25–32, New Series.

(1980) "Interdependência e desenvolvimento." *Cadernos de Opinião*, 15:34–39.

1980 "Partidos políticos." In Paul Singer and Vinicius Caldeira Brant (orgs.), *São Paulo: o Povo em Movimento*. Petrópolis: Vozes–CEBRAP, 177–205.

(1981) "Os Partidos políticos e a participação popular." In David V. Fleischer (org.), *Os Partidos Políticos no Brasil*. 2 vols. Brasília: Ed. Universidade de Brasília, 47–66.

1981 "Regime político e mudança social: algumas reflexões a propósito do caso brasileiro." *Revista de Cultura e Política*, 3 (Jan): 7–25.

(1981) "Political Regime and Social Change: Some Reflections Concerning the Brazilian Case." *Boletin de Estudios Latinoamericanos y del Caribe,* Amsterdam, 30 (Jun): 3–20.

(1981) "Régimen Político y Cambio Social (Algunas Reflexiones a propósito del Caso Brasileño)." In Norberto Lechner (ed.), *Estado y política en América Latina.* Mexico City: Siglo XXI, 272–299.

(1981) "Political Regime and Social Change: Some Reflections Concerning the Brazilian Case." *Occasional Papers in Latin American Studies,* Berkeley: University of California, 3 (Aug–Oct).

(1984) "Regimen politico y cambio social (Algunas reflexiones a propósito del caso brasileño)." *Revista Centroamericana de Administración Pública,* 2 (5, Jul–Dec): 7–31.

(1993) "Regime político e mudança social: a transição para a democracia." In Fernando Henrique Cardoso, *A Construção da democracia—Estudos sobre Política.* São Paulo: Siciliano, chapter 11, 267–272.

1981   "Notes sur la structure de classes dans les sociétés capitalistes d'aujourd'hui." *Amérique Latine,* CETRAL, 6:3–15, été.

(1982) "As classes nas sociedades capitalistas contemporâneas (Notas preliminares)." *Revista de Economia Política,* 2/1 (5, Jan–Mar): 5–28.

(1982) "Las clases en las sociedades capitalistas contemporáneas. Notas preliminares." *Comércio Exterior,* 32 (2, Feb): 107–118.

1981   "Transición política en América Latina?" *Socialismo y Participación,* 14 (Jun): 19–28.

(1985) "Transizione política in America Latina." In R. Scartezzini et al., *I Limiti della democrazia.* Napoli: Lignore Editore, 333–346.

1981   "La democracia en las sociedades contemporáneas." *Nueva Sociedad,* 55:25–3.

(1982) *Crítica and Utopía,* 6 (Mar): 25–38.

(1983) "La democrazia nella società contemporanea." *Política Internazionale,* 6 (Jun): 46–52.

(1988) In J. C. Rubinstein (comp.), *El estado periférico latinoamericano.* Buenos Aires: Ed. Universitária de Buenos Aires, 161–169.

1981   "Social and Cultural Consequences of Urban and Rural Change." In *Growth and Entrepreneurship: Opportunities and Challenges in a Changing World.* Paris: ICC, 26–39, Oct.

1981   "Os anos Figueiredo." *Novos Estudos* (CEBRAP), 1 (1): 4–11.

(1982) "La apertura politica en el gobierno Figueiredo." In Jorge Wilheim (comp.), *"Planificación y Desarrollo en Brasil, Comentarios."* *Revista Interamericana de Planificación,* 16 (63–64, Sep–Dec): 195–204.

(1993) "Os anos Figueiredo." In Fernando Henrique Cardoso, *A Construção da democracia—Estudos sobre Política.* São Paulo: Siciliano, chapter 8, 198–211.

1981   "A crisma de São Bernardo." In Fernando Henrique Cardoso et al., *Álbum memória de São Bernardo.* São Bernardo do Campo: Prefeitura Municipal, Secretaria de Educação, Cultura e Esportes, 27–93.

1981   "Social Development: A Latin American View." In C.A.O. Van Nieuwenhuijee (ed.), *The Quest of "Another Development": A Social Approach?* The Hague: Institute of Social Studies, proceedings of a Seminar on Social Development, May, 83–95.

1982   AND TRINDADE, H. (orgs.). *O novo socialismo francês e a América Latina.* Rio de Janeiro: Paz e Terra, 188.

1982   "A América Latina e o socialismo na década de 80." In Fernando Henrique Cardoso and Helgio Trindade (orgs.), *O novo socialismo francês e a América Latina.* Rio de Janeiro: Paz e Terra (Coleção O mundo hoje, vol. 37), 13–29.

1982   "Socialismo e liberdade." *Senhor Vogue,* (São Paulo, Apr) (notes on: Rubens César Fernandes, *Os dilemas do socialismo* [São Paulo: Paz e Terra, 1982]; Celso Lafer, *Ensaios sobre a liberdade* [São Paulo: Perspectiva, 1980]; and Fernando C. Prestes Motta, *Burocracia e auto-gestão* [São Paulo: Brasiliense, 1981])

1982   "La persistencia democrática (Resúmen de la conferencia sobre el tema de la democracía en la obra de Jose Medina Echavarría)." In *Medina Echavarría y la sociologia latinoamericana.* Madrid: Ediciones Cultura Hispanica, Instituto de Cooperación Iberoamericana, 113–125.

1982   "Poulantzas e os partidos do Brasil." *Novos Estudos* (CEBRAP), 1 (2, Apr): 3–7.

1982   "As eleições e o resto." *Novos Estudos* (CEBRAP), 1 (4, Nov): 1.

1982 "Reflexiones sobre la estructura social y política de los paises más industrializados de América Latina." In R. Green (coord.), *En Torno al Estado y el Desarrollo.* Mexico City: Centro de Estudios Económicos y Sociais del Tercer Mundo—EESTEM/Ed. Nueva Imagen, 133–228.

1983 "Un desafio a los sociólogos" (Tenth World Congress of Sociology, Mexico City, August, 82). *IFDA Dossier,* 36 (Jul–Aug): 57–65.

1983 "O papel dos empresários no processo de transição: o caso brasileiro." *Dados,* 26 (1): 9–27.
(1986) In Guillermo O'Donnell, Philippe Schmitter, and Laurence Whitehead (eds.), *Transitions from Authoritarian Rules: Prospects for Democracy.* Baltimore: Johns Hopkins University Press (2nd paperback volume: *Comparative Perspectives*).
(1988) In Guillermo O'Donnell, Philippe Schmitter, and Laurence Whitehead (eds.), *Transições do regime autoritário.* Vol. 4, *Comparações e Perspectivas.* São Paulo: Ed. Revista dos Tribunais/Vértice.
(1993) "O papel dos empresários no processo de transição." In Fernando Henrique Cardoso, *A Construção da democracia—Estudos sobre Política.* São Paulo: Siciliano, chapter 10, 234–256.

1983 "Partidos, hoje." In Eurico de Lima Figueiredo, Gisálio Cerqueira Filho, and Leandro Konder (org.), *Por que Marx?* Rio de Janeiro: Graal (Coleção Biblioteca de Ciências Sociais, vol. 24), 97–109.

1983 "Las políticas sociales en la década de los anos ochenta: nuevas opciones?" *El Trimestre Económico,* Ll (197, Jan–Mar): 169–188.
(1983) "Social Policies in Latin America in the Eighties: New Options?" *Alternatives, A Journal of World Policy,* New Delhi, 8 (4): 553–571, Spring.
(1984) "Las politicas sociales en crisis, nuevas opciones?" In *Desarrollo social en los años 80.* Santiago: CEPAL/ILPES/UNICEF.

1983 *Perspectivas—Idéias e Atuação Política.* Rio de Janeiro: Paz e Terra, (Coleção Estudos Brasileiros, vol. 70).

1983 "Universidade e desenvolvimento." *Educação Brasileira,* Brasília, 5 (11): 11–19, 2nd sem.

1983 "As quatro crises." *Novos Estudos* (CEBRAP), 2 (3, Nov): 1.

1984 "La sociedad y el estado." *Pensamiento Iberoamericano,* 5 (Jan–Jun): 25–36.

1984 "O Poder Legislativo moderno no estado: declínio ou valorização." *Revista de Informação legislativa,* 21 (81).

1984 "A democracia na América Latina." *Novos Estudos* (CEBRAP), 10 (Oct): 45–56.
(1986) "Democracy in Latin America." *Politics and Society,* 15 (1): 23–41.
(1989) La democracia en America Latina." *Punto de vista,* Buenos Aires: 1–8.

1985 AND SORJ, B., and FONT, M. (org.). *Economia e movimentos sociais na América Latina.* São Paulo: Brasiliense.

1985 *A Democracia necessária.* Campinas (SP): Papirus.

1985 "Diversitá sociale e democrazia." In *Ordine internazionale, società e política in America Latina.* Casale Monferrato: Ed. Marietti (Convegno Internazionale di Bologna), 371–383.

1986 "Cambios sociales en el espacio politico." *Dossier II, Encuentro Internacional de Sociologia,* Generalitat Valenciana, Valencia (Jan): 1–10.

1986 "Problemas de mudança social, outra vez?" (Eleventh World Congress of Sociology, New Delhi, August, 86), *Novos Estudos* (CEBRAP), 16 (Dec): 54–61.
(1987) "Problems of Social Change, Again?" *International Sociology,* 2 (2, Jun): 177–187.
(1987) "Los retos teóricos del cambio social." *Revista Mexicana de Ciencias Políticas y Sociales,* 33 (127, Jan–Mar): 111–123.

1986 "Foreword." *International Sociology,* 1 (1, Mar): 1–2.

1987 "A paixão pelo saber." In Maria Ângela D'Incao (org.), *O Saber militante. Ensaios sobre Florestan Fernandes.* São Paulo: Paz e Terra/UNESP, 23–30.

1987 "Les rapports entre villet et campagne dans les théories du développement." In Centro di Ricerca e Documentazione Febbraio (CERFE) '74 (org.), *Urban-rural Relationships in the Framework of Development Processes.* Roma: CERFE Febbraio '74, 543–550.

1987 "Mudanças na sociedade brasileira." In Anna Carboncini (org.), *A virada do século.* Rio de Janeiro/São Paulo: Paz e Terra/UNESP/Secretaria de Estado de Cultura/SP, 19–30.

1988 "Memórias da Maria Antônia." In Maria Cecília Loschiano dos Santos (org.), *Maria Antônia: uma rua na contramão.* São Paulo: Nobel, 27–34.

1988   "Dependência e democracia." In David Fleischer (org.), *Da distensão à Abertura: as eleições de 1982.* Brasília: Ed. Universidade de Brasília, 37–59.

(1988) "Desenvolvimento associado-dependente e teoria democrática." In Alfred Stepan (org.), *Democratizando o Brasil.* Rio de Janeiro: Paz e Terra, 443–482.

(1989) "Associated-Dependent Development and Democratic Theory." In Alfred Stepan (ed.), *Democratizing Brazil: Problems of Transition and Consolidation.* New York: Oxford University Press, 299–326.

1990   "Congresso, desenvolvimento e democracia: perspectivas e ação imediata." In João Paulo dos Reis Velloso (coord.), *As perspectivas do Brasil e o novo governo.* São Paulo: Nobel, 41–52.

1990   *Estratégias para el desarrollo de la democracia en America Latina.* Lima: Instituto de Estudios Peruanos (Documento de Trabajo, vol. 38).

1990   "Desafios da social-democracia na América Latina." *Novos Estudos* (CEBRAP), 28 (Oct): 29–49.

(1990) "Perspectivas da socialdemocracia na América Latina vistas do ângulo do Brasil." In Maurício Dias David (org.), *Socialdemocracia hoje.* Rio de Janeiro: Fundação Teotônio Vilela, *Cadernos da socialdemocracia,* 1:7–32.

(1992) "Desafios de la socialdemocracia en América Latina." *Leviatán—Revista de Hechos e Ideas,* 48:63–82, 2ª época.

(1993) "The Challenges of Social Democracy in Latin America." In Menno Vellinga (ed.), *Social Democracy in Latin America.* Boulder, Colo.: Westview Press, 273–296.

(1993) "Desafios de la socialdemocracia en América Latina." In Menno Vellinga (coor.), *Democracia y política en América Latina.* Mexico City: Siglo XXI editores, 383–414.

1990–   "Falsa democratização." *Revista USP,* 8 (Dec–Jan–Feb): 39–42.
1991

1990   "La construcción de la democracia: desafios y dificultades." In Julio Cotler (ed.), *Estrategias para el desarrollo de la democracia: en Perú y América Latina.* Lima: Instituto de Estudios Peruanos/ Fundación Friedrich Naumann, 195–210.

1990   "As relações Norte-Sul no contexto atual, uma nova dependência?" In *Três discursos sobre a nova ordem mundial.* Brasília: Senado Federal.

(1991) "Nord-Syd-relationerna i dagsläget—Ett nytt beroende?" In *Efter Muren—Nya Järnridaer.* Smaland Peace Forum of the Swedish Labour Movement.

(1991) "I rapporti Nord-Sud nel constesto attuale: una nuova dipendenza?" *Il Socialismo del Futuro,* Roma, 2 (3, Jan–Jun): 135–140.

(1991) "Las relaciones Norte-Sur nel contexto actual, una nueva dependencia." *El socialismo del Futuro,* 3:135–140.

(1993) "North-South Relations in the Present Context: A New Dependency?" In Martin Carnoy, Manoel Castells, Stephen S. Cohen, and Fernando Henrique Cardoso, *The New Global Economy in the Information Age: Reflections on Our Changing World.* University Park: Pennsylvania State University Press, 149–159.

1991   "The Crisis of Development in Latin America." In *Eight Essays on the Crisis of Development in Latin America.* Amsterdam: Centrum voor Studie en Documentatie van Latinjs Amerika (CEDLA), 132–142.

1991   "A implantação do parlamentarismo." *Revista do Instituto de Estudos Brasileiros,* São Paulo, 32:19–27.

1991   "A esquerda não registrou as mudanças." *O Socialismo do Futuro,* São Paulo (May): 8–12.

1991   "Democracia e desigualdades sociais." *Revista Crítica de Ciências Sociais,* 32 (Jun): 23–27.

1991   "Caminhos para o Novo Milênio." In *Portugal no limiar do século XXI.* Cadernos Sedes. Lisboa: Sedes, 25–46.

(1991) In Maurírio Dias David (org.), *Economia e política da crise brasileira: a perspectiva social democrata.* Rio de Janeiro: Rio Fundo, 217–228.

1991   AND ALENCAR, Gisela S. "Desenvolvimento sustentável: variações sobre o mesmo tema." *Ciência e Ambiente,* 2 (3, Jul–Dec): 7–14.

1991   "Produção com liberdade." In Elza M. Ajzenberg (org.), *Comunicações e artes em tempo de mudança—Brasil, 1966–1991.* São Paulo: ECA–USP/SESC, 151–154.

1992 "Inesperado processo de formação política." In *Brasileiro: Cidadão?* São Paulo: Cultura Editores Associados, 151–184.
1992 "Reflexões sobre o Brasil e o Fórum hoje." In João Paulo dos Reis Velloso (org.), *Visões do Brasil.* São Paulo: Nobel, 45–50.
1992 "Parlamentarismo x Presidencialismo—Uma visão comparativa." *Cadernos do CEDESEN,* Brasília, 2 (4): 176–186.
1992 "Um ex-aluno." In Maria Ângela D'Incao and Eloísa Faria Scarabôtolo (orgs.), *Dentro do texto, dentro da vida. Ensaios sobre Antonio Candido.* São Paulo: Companhia das Letras/Instituto Moreira Salles, 37–40.
1992 "Passages à la démocratie: leçons de l'Est et du Sud." *Le Courrier de l'UNESCO* (Nov).
      (1992) "Freedom for the Have-nots." *UNESCO Courier* (Nov): 21–24.
      (1992) "Libertad y penuria." *El Correo de la UNESCO,* Ano 45 (Nov): 21–24.
      (1992) "Freiheit für habenichtse." *UNESCO Kurier,* 11:19–22.
      (1992) "Liberdad e penuria." *Correo da UNESCO* (Dec): 21–24.
      (1992) "Vapautta vähäosaisille." *UNESCO Kuriiri,* 12:21–25.
      (1993) "Vrijheid in Armoede." *Koerier,* 233 (Jan): 17–20.
      (1993) "Liberdade e penúria." *Correio da UNESCO,* 11 (1, Jan): 9–22.
      (1993) "Libertá e povertá." *Corriere dell'UNESCO* (1, Jan): 21–24.
      (1993) Edition in Russian and other languages.
1993 "Communication for a New World." In José Marques de Melo (ed.), *Communication for a New World: Brazilian Perspectives.* São Paulo: ECA/USP, 9–19.
      (1993) "Comunicação para um novo mundo." *Vozes Cultura,* 87 (3, May–Jun): 7–13.
1993 "Alternativas econômicas para a América Latina." In *As Idéias e seu lugar.* 2nd ed. Aumentada, Petrópolis: Vozes, 227–244.
1993 *A Construção da democracia—Estudos sobre Política.* São Paulo: Siciliano.

1993 AND CARNOY, M., CASTELLS, M., and COHEN, S. S. *The New Global Economy in the Information Age: Reflections on Our Changing World.* University Park: Pennsylvania State University Press.
1993 "Livros que inventaram o Brasil." *Novos Estudos* (CEBRAP), 37 (Nov): 21–35.
1994 "Postface." *Revue Tiers Monde,* 35 (138, Apr–Jun): 443–446.
1994 *Mãos à obra, Brasil. Proposta de governo.* Brasília: n.p.
1995 "Agenda para o século XXI." In Presidência da República, *A Utopia viável. Trajetória intelectual de Fernando Henrique Cardoso.* Brasília: Secretaria de Documentação Histórica, Gabinete Pessoal do Presidente da República, 95–106.
      (1996) "Agenda para el Siglo XXI." *Política Internacional.* Revista Venezolana de Asuntos Mundiales y Política Exterior, 42 (Apr–Jun): 1–4.
      (1996) "Brasilien: Unser Programm für das 21 Jahrhundert." In Günther Würtele (org.), *Agenda für das 21 Jahrhundert. Politik und Wirtschaft auf dem Weg in eine neue Zeit.* Frankfurt am Main: Frankfurter Allgemeine, 39–58.

1998   "Notas sobre a reforma do Estado." *Novos Estudos* (CEBRAP), 50 (Mar): 5–12.

1998   "L'utopie et le politique: du professeur au président." In Solange Passaris and Krystyna Vinaver (eds.), *Pour aborder le XXIème siècle avec le développement durable.* Paris: Centre International de Recherche sur l'Environnement et le Développement (*Économies et sociétés, Cahiers de l'ISMEA*, 32 [1]: 29–35 [Série "Développement, croissance et progrès," F, (36)]).

1998   *Avança Brasil. Mais quatro anos de desenvolvimento para todos. Proposta de governo.* Brasília: n.p.

II. DEBATES
(Publications, Reprints, and Translations)

1983   "A cidade e a cultura," in Abertura Oficial do Centro Cultural de São Paulo. *Primeiro Fórum de Debates "A cidade e a cultura."* Vol. 1. São Paulo: Prefeitura Municipal de São Paulo, 13.

1987   "A negociação da dívida externa e a transição política interna." Reitoria da Universidade de São Paulo. *A Transição política: necessidade e limites da negociação.* Usp, 328–369.

1987   "Constituinte, Estado e Sociedade." *Arquivos do Ministério da Justiça*, edição especial, 40 (169, Jul–Sep): 51–91.

1989   "O Brasil no mundo: participação, reformas e modernização." *Revista Brasileira de Comércio Exterior*, 5 (25, Sep–Oct): 26–42.

1989   "A construção da democracia no Brasil." In *Documentos Cedec.* Vol. 1, *Visões da transição.* São Paulo: Cedec, 3–74.

1992   *Primeira sessão de debates.* In Amaury de Souza and Bolivar Lamounier (orgs.), *As elites brasileiras e a modernização do setor público, um debate.* São Paulo: Sumaré, Série Seminários e Debates, Idesp, 31–41.

2000   *Debate entre os Chefes de Estado e de Governo na Reunião de Florença.* In Lúcio Alcântara, Vilmar Faria, and Carlos H. Cardim (orgs.), *Globalização e governo progressista—Novos caminhos, Reunião de Florença 1999.* Brasília: Quick Printer Ltda./Instituto Teotônio Vilela, 100–104, 141–144, 165–169, 180–182.

2000   Progressive Governance for the Twenty-first Century. Conference Proceedings. Florence, 20–21 November, 31–34, 43–45, 67–70, 80–82.

III. INTERVIEWS (Press interviews are not included)
(Publications, Reprints, and Translations)

1976   "Populismo: uma crise no Estado." *Cadernos de Debate*, 1:35–39.

1978   "Democracia hoje." *Plural*, 1 (2, Oct–Dec): 7–18.

1983   "Le prospettive del Brasile dopo le elezioni." *Politica Internazionale*, 1 (Jan): 35–39 (by Giancarlo Pasquini).

1983   "Deve-se discutir com os militares as funções que lhes cabem e os seus limites." (August 7, 1983). In *Entrevistas a Lourenço Dantas Mota.* Brasília: n.p.

1985   "Primeiro limpar o entulho." (January 27, 1985). In *Entrevistas a Lourenço Dantas Mota.* Brasília: n.p.

       (1985) "Primeiro limpar o entulho autoritário." In Lourenço Dantas Mota, *A Nova República: o nome e a coisa.* São Paulo: Brasiliense, 54–76

1989   Originally published in Russian. Revista *América Latina*, Moscou, 5:71–90.

1990   In Claudiney Ferreira and Jorge Vasconcellos (orgs.), *Certas palavras.* São Paulo: Estação Liberdade, 101–118.

1995   "Pour un Brésil plus juste." Entrevista concedida por Fernando Henrique Cardoso a Stéphane Montclaire. *Politique Internationale*, 67:9–25.

1995   "Fulfilling Brazil's Promise: A Conversation with President Cardoso." *Foreign Affairs*, 74:62–75, printemps, by James F. J. Hoge.

1996   "Entrevista." *Sintesis Revista de Ciencias sociales Iberoamericanas*, 25 (Jan–Jun): 17–23.

1997   "Entrevista com Fernando Henrique Cardoso." *Lua Nova*, 39:11–33, Brasílio Sallum Jr.

1997   "Fernando Henrique Cardoso: La sociedad cercó al Estado." In Diego Achard and Manuel Flores, *Gobernabilidad: un reportaje de América Latina*. Mexico City: PNUD/Fondo de Cultura Económica, 80–90

1998   *O Presidente segundo o sociólogo*. Entrevista a Roberto Pompeu de Toledo. São Paulo: Companhia das Letras.

1998   "Entrevista com Fernando Henrique Cardoso." *Política Comparada*. Revista Brasiliense de Políticas comparadas, ano 2, 2 (1, Jan–Jun): 7–12.

1998   AND SOARES, Mário. *O mundo em português*. *Um diálogo*. São Paulo: Paz e Terra.

1999   "Brésil: um nouveau miracle?" Entrevista concedida por Fernando Henrique Cardoso a Stéphane Montclaire. *Politique Internationale*, Paris, 84:197–219, été.

2000   "The Cardoso Agenda." *Outlook—The Journal of Ideas that Create the Future*, 12 (1): 7–13.

IV. SPEECHES
(Publications, Reprints, and Translations)

1979   "Diagnose social: causas da marginalização social de menores." In *A criança, prioridade um da cidade de São Paulo*. São Paulo: Câmara Municipal de São Paulo, 55–77.

1983   "Considerações sobre a situação do País." Brasília: Senado Federal.

1983   "As razões da oposição." Brasília: Senado Federal.

1984   "A nova maioria." Brasília: Senado Federal.

1984   Sessão solene em homenagem à Sua Excelência o Senhor Miguel de la Madrid Hurtado, Presidente dos Estados Unidos Mexicanos. Brasília: Senado Federal, March 30.

1986   "O PMDB depois do Pacote." Brasília: Senado Federal (Convenção Nacional do PMDB, April 6).

1986   "Social Change and the Role of Social Sciences." Eighth Conference, International Federation of Social Science Organizations, New Delhi, December 2. *IFSSO News Letter*, 17:18–22, Occasional Paper 5.

1987   "Constituinte, o início da caminhada." Brasília: Senado Federal.

1987   "A síntese política." *O Rio discute a dívida*. Secretaria de Governo, Rio de Janeiro, 84–88.

1988   "A crise e as opções nacionais." Brasília: Senado Federal.

1990   "Três discursos sobre a nova ordem mundial." Brasília: Senado Federal.

1991   "Discursos sobre a Ordem Mundial." Brasília: Senado Federal.

1991   "A crise brasileira." Brasília: Senado Federal.

1992   "Sobre a Reforma fiscal." (November 6–7, 1991). In *Fórum nacional sobre Reforma Fiscal*. Brasília: UNAFISCO NACIONAL/Congresso Nacional.

1993   "El mundo y la ciencias sociales: ayer y hoy." (Doutorado *Honoris Causa*, Universidade de Chile, March 25, 1993). *Boletín* (Associación Chilena de Ciencia Política), 1 (2, Jan–Jun): 16–18.

1993   "Aula Magna no Instituto Rio Branco." (March 8, 1993). *Cadernos do IPRI*, Edição Especial, Fundação Alexandre de Gusmão, Brasília (Jun).

1993   "Desarrollo e integración: respuestas al nuevo contexto internacional." (Pronunciado em March 24, 1993). *Diplomacia*, Academia Diplomática de Chile, 61 (Jun): 6–14.

1993   Discurso no encerramento da XI Conferência Interparlamentar Comunidade Européia-América Latina, 6 de maio. *Papers*, Fundação Konrad-Adenauer-Stiftung, 7:9–15.

1993   "Estado, mercado, democracia: existe uma perspectiva latino-americana?" In Lourdes Sola (org.), *Estado, mercado e democracia*. *Política e Economia comparadas*. São Paulo: Paz e Terra, 19–34.

1993   Pronunciamento, Reunião da Diretoria da Confederação Nacional do Comércio. Brasília: CNC, 7–18.

1994   "O Real e o sonho." S.l. (Memorial JK, Jul. 28)

1994   *Política Externa em Tempos de Mudança. A gestão do Ministro Fernando Henrique Cardoso no Itamaraty (discursos, artigos na imprensa e entrevistas)*. Brasília: Fundação Alexandre Gusmão, Ministério das Relações Exteriores.

1995   *Discurso de despedida do Senado Federal—*"Filosofia e diretrizes de governo." (December 14, 1994). Brasília: Presidência da República, Secretaria de Comunicação Social.

1995   *Discurso de Posse*. (January 1, 1995). Brasília: Presidência da República, Secretaria de Comunicação Social.

1995   *Política Externa, Pronunciamentos.* Vol. 1, *De janeiro a junho 1995.* Brasília: Presidência da República, Secretaria de Comunicação Social.

1995   "Ciência e Política." In Presidência da República, *A Utopia viável. Trajetória intelectual de Fernando Henrique Cardoso.* Brasília: Secretaria de Documentação Histórica, Gabinete Pessoal do Presidente da República (Professor Emérito, USP, May 15, 1992), 19–23.

1995   "A Nova Agenda Sociológica da América Latina." In Presidência da República, *A Utopia viável. Trajetória intelectual de Fernando Henrique Cardoso.* Brasília: Secretaria de Documentação Histórica, Gabinete Pessoal do Presidente da República (Doutorado *Honoris Causa*, Universidade Central da Venezuela, July 6, 1995), 31–44.

1995   "A Nova Esquerda." In Presidência da República, *A Utopia viável. Trajetória intelectual de Fernando Henrique Cardoso.* Brasília: Secretaria de Documentação Histórica, Gabinete Pessoal do Presidente da República (Doutorado *Honoris Causa*, Universidade de Coimbra, July 21, 1995), 59–76.

1995   "A Utopia Viável." In Presidência da República, *A Utopia viável. Trajetória intelectual de Fernando Henrique Cardoso.* Brasília: Secretaria de Documentação Histórica, Gabinete Pessoal do Presidente da República (Doutorado *Honoris Causa*, Universidade do Porto, July 22, 1995), 85–94.

1995   "Democracy and Development." *Cepal Review,* 56 (Aug): 7–12 (Cepal, Santiago, March 2).

1995   "Discurso sobre os Direitos Humanos." (September 7, 1995). In *Direitos Humanos: novo nome da liberdade e da democracia.* Brasília: Presidência da República, Secretaria de Comunicação Social.

1995   "The Ethics of Conviction." *Hemisfile,* Institute of the Americas, 6 (6, Nov–Dec): 4–5 (Appeal of Conscience Foundation's World Statesman Award, October 21).

1995   "Desenvolvimento: o mais político dos temas econômicos." *Revista de Economia Política,* 15 (4) (60, Oct–Dec): 148–155 (originally delivered as a lecture at the Center of International and Strategic Studies, Washington, D.C., April 24, 1995).

       (1997) "El desarrollo: el más político de los temas económicos." *Diplomacia,* Academia Diplomática de Chile, 72 (May–Jun): 3–9.

1996   "La globalización y el nuevo orden mundial." *Boletín editorial de El Colegio de México,* 68 (Jul–Aug): 3–12 (El Colegio de Mexico, February 20, 1996).

       (1997) "O impacto da globalização nos países em desenvolvimento, riscos e oportunidades." In *Globalização e outros temas contemporâneos.* Brasília: Presidência da República, Secretaria de Comunicação Social.

       (1997) "O impacto da globalização nos países em desenvolvimento, riscos e oportunidades." In *Idéias e Debate.* Brasília: Instituto Teotônio Vilela, 15–28.

1996   *Por um Brasil mais justo, ação social do governo.* Brasília: Presidência da República, Secretaria de Comunicação Social (Palácio do Planalto, May 6, 1996).

1996   *Política Externa, Pronunciamentos.* De julho a dezembro de 1995. Brasília: Presidência da República, Secretaria de Comunicação Social.

1996   "Brasil em ação." (August 9, 1996). In *Brasil em ação—Investimentos para o desenvolvimento.* Brasília: Presidência da República, Secretaria de Comunicação Social (XI Reunião do Conselho de Governo, Palácio do Planalto, August 9).

1996   "Discurso sobre Política de Defesa." (November 7, 1996). *Parcerias Estratégicas,* Centro de Estudos Estratégicos, Brasília, 1 (2, Dec): 16–18.

1996   "Consecuencias sociales de la globalización." *Politica,* Santiago de Chile, vol. 34, Otoño (Indian International Centre, New Delhi, India, January 27).

       (1997) "Consequências sociais da globalização." In *Globalização e outros temas contemporâneos.* Brasília: Presidência da República, Secretaria de Comunicação Social.

       (1997) "Consequências sociais da globalização." In *Idéias e Debate.* Brasília: Instituto Teotônio Vilela, 6–14.

       (1998) "Die sozialen Folgen der Globalisierung—Marginalisierung oder Besserstellung?" *Kas/Auslands-Informationen,* Konrad Adenauer Stiftung, 5 (1): 4–16.

1997   "Estado, comunidad y sociedad en el desarrollo social." (April 6, 1997). *Revista de la Cepal,* 62:7–13, ago (Primera Conferencia Regional de Seguimiento de Cumbre Mundial sobre Desarrollo social, São Paulo, abril).

1997   "A revitalização da arte da política (sobre a democracia representativa)." In *Globalização e outros temas contemporâneos.* Brasília: Presidência da República, Secretaria de Comunicação Social (Robert Wesson Lecture, Joaquim Nabuco Chair of Brazilian Studies, University of California, Stanford, March 11, 1996).

1997   "Conferência sobre alguns aspectos contemporâneos da questão social." In *Globalização e outros temas contemporâneos.* Brasília: Presidência da República, Secretaria de Comunicação Social (Doutorado honoris causa, Universidade Lumière-Lyon 2, May 30, 1996).

1997   "Conferência sobre temas de política internacional." In *Globalização e outros temas contemporâneos.* Brasília: Presidência da República, Secretaria de Comunicação Social (Universidade de Witwaterstand. Joanesburgo, November 27, 1996). "Globalização e Política Internacional." *Política Comparada,* Ano 1, 1 (1): 67–80, jan.–abr.

1997   *Trechos de pronunciamentos do presidente da República, 1996.* Selecionados pela Coordenação-Geral de Apoio ao Conselho de Defesa Nacional da Secretaria de Assuntos Estratégicos. Brasília: Presidência da República.

1998   *Trechos de pronunciamentos do presidente da República, 1997.* Selecionados pela Coordenação-Geral de Apoio ao Conselho de Defesa Nacional da Secretaria de Assuntos Estratégicos. Brasília: Presidência da República.

1998   Discurso pronunciado na XII Reunião Geral do Conselho da Cooperação Econômica do Pacífico—PECC XII, Santiago do Chile, October 1–3, 1997. In Pilar Alamos, Luz O'shea, and Manfred Wilhelmy (ed.), *America Latina y Asia-Pacífico: oportunidades ante la crisis.* Santiago de Chile: IES, 41–51.

1999   "Reforma política: prioridades e perspectivas para a nação brasileira." *Parcerias estratégicas,* 6:5–20, março (Solenidade de abertura do Seminário Nacional "Projeto Brasil 2020—Visões estratégicas para um cenário desejável," Brasília).

2000   "Discurso na ocasião do Sesquicentenário do nascimento de Joaquim Nabuco." In Joaquim Nabuco, *Balmaceda.* Santiago de Chile: Editorial Universitaria S.A., 13–17.

2000   In Instituto Teotônio Vilela, *Realizações e desafios de um programa social-democrata.* Rio de Janeiro: 15–32. (Solenidade de abertura do seminário "Realizações e desafios de um programa socialdemocrata no Brasil," Rio de Janeiro, November 29, 1999)

2000   "Las tareas de la diplomacia brasileña contemporánea." *Revista Mexicana de Politica Exterior,* 60:244–249, Jun.

2000   In *Synthesis,* OPCW, Autumn/Nov.:22-23. (Special Session of the Executive Council of the Organisation for the Prohibition of Chemical Weapons, The Hague, October 9)

Index

abertura democrática (democratic opening), 114

abolitionism, 229

abolition of slavery, 38, 41, 186

academia, relationship of, to politics, 181–85, 257

accountability, of politicians, 195

accumulation of capital, 65, 67, 76, 119n8; control of, 90, 126, 135; process of, 99, 102, 110; in socialist state, 103; values and, 168, 265

agrarian-based economy. *See* economy, agrarian-based

agrarian reform, 24

agrarian sector, 99, 102

agriculture, capitalization of, 143, 268

Aguilar, Alonso, 75, 77

Ahumada, Jorge, 75, 173

Alba, Bernarda, 156

ALCSA (Latin American Free Trade Association), 216

Allende, Salvador, 175

Allende government, 62, 123, 127

Alliance for Progress, 58

Almond, Gabriel A., 32n71, 116

Althusser, Louis, 76, 164

Amaral, Azevedo, 149

American economic policy, 55–59

American Sociological Association, 29n32

Andean Pact, 59

"anti-statist" struggle, 65

Ardaillon, Danielle, 26n1, 298

ARENA, 153, 154, 157, 201

Arida, Pérsio, 33n79

Aron, Raymond, 154, 164, 252

Arriagada, Genaro, 31n57

Asian tigers, 19, 20, 90, 253, 254

associated-dependent development, 9, 11, 30n45, 83, 84, 96n12, 97–101, 105–6, 116, 140–42, 152, 158, 276; and centralization of power, 142–47. *See also* associate-dependent capitalism; associate-dependent industrialism

associate-dependent capitalism, 58, 67

associate-dependent industrialism, 86n12

Atomic Agreement, 60

authentically national development, 102, 105. *See also* nationalist development model

authoritarian-democratic continuum, 147–51

authoritarianism, 68, 70, 89, 92, 93, 94, 127, 147–51, 176–78; beneficiaries of, 134–37; in Brazil, 6–7, 9, 10, 12, 17, 30n38, 30n41, 66, 98, 111, 116, 121n31, 192, 214, 229; civil, 129, 131, 134, 137; and democracy, 116–19, 191–92; resurgence of, 122–23; structural bases of in Latin America,

321

About . . .

THE AUTHOR

Fernando Henrique Cardoso is President of Brazil, beginning his first term January 1, 1995, and winning reelection by an absolute majority in October 1998. A sociologist trained at the University of São Paulo, he has been (since the late 1960s) one of the world's most influential figures in the analysis of large-scale social change, international development, dependency, globalization, democracy, and state reform. Building on this successful intellectual and academic career, Cardoso became deeply involved in Brazil's struggle for democracy to overcome the authoritarian military regime (1964–1985). Elected senator in 1982, he was a founding member of the Brazilian Social Democratic Party (PSDB). He served as Minister of Foreign Relations from 1992–1993 and Minister of Finance from 1993–1994. Professor Emeritus at the University of São Paulo, Cardoso has been awarded honorary degrees from several universities in Europe, Latin America, and the United States. His previously translated books include *Dependency and Development in Latin America, São Paulo: Growth and Poverty,* and *The New World Economy in the Information Age.*

THE EDITOR

Mauricio A. Font is Director of the Bildner Center for Western Hemisphere Studies and professor of Sociology at The Graduate Center and Queens College, City University of New York. His previous publications on Brazil include *Coffee, Contention, and Change* and several articles. He is currently working on *Transforming Brazil* (Rowman & Littlefield, forthcoming), a book about Brazil's reforms since the early 1990s.

333

THE BIBLIOGRAPHER

Danielle Ardaillon, a social scientist with a Ph.D. from the University of São Paulo, is Director of the Department of Historical Documentation, Office of the President, Presidency of the Republic, in Brasília.